Information Systems: A Digital World

Information Systems: A Digital World

Edited by Brian Jackson

CLANRYE
INTERNATIONAL
www.clanryeinternational.com

Clanrye International,
750 Third Avenue, 9ᵗʰ Floor,
New York, NY 10017, USA

ISBN: 978-1-63240-582-1

Cataloging-in-publication Data

Information systems : a digital world / edited by Brian Jackson.
     p. cm.
Includes bibliographical references and index.
ISBN 978-1-63240-582-1
1. Information technology. 2. Management information systems. 3. Information resources management.
4. Information retrieval. 5. Information science. I. Jackson, Brian.
T58.62 .I54 2017
658.403 801 1--dc23

For information on all Clanrye International publications
visit our website at www.clanryeinternational.com

Printed in the United States of America.

Contents

Permissions

List of Contributors

Index

Preface

This book outlines the processes and applications of information systems in detail. It presents researches and studies performed by experts across the globe. Information systems refer to an organized system, which is used to store, organize, filter, collect, create, process, distribute and communicate information. It is an essential part of management, operations and decision-making. The different types of information systems are expert, search, geographic, etc. This text attempts to understand the multiple branches that fall under the discipline of information systems and how such concepts have practical applications. It will prove to be immensely beneficial to students and researchers in this field. As this field is emerging at a rapid pace, the concepts of this book will help the readers understand the innovative and emerging trends of the subject.

This book is the end result of constructive efforts and intensive research done by experts in this field. The aim of this book is to enlighten the readers with recent information in this area of research. The information provided in this profound book would serve as a valuable reference to students and researchers in this field.

At the end, I would like to thank all the authors for devoting their precious time and providing their valuable contributions to this book. I would also like to express my gratitude to my fellow colleagues who encouraged me throughout the process.

Editor

Citation of Court Cases with Shift-Or Pattern Matching

Omisore O. M.[*], Samuel O. W

Department of Computer Science, Federal University of Technology, Akure, Nigeria
*Corresponding author: ootsorewilly@gmail.com

Abstract Parties often appear in law courts with cases that have festered for long periods of time at great expense. This makes judges to face the challenge of overcoming impasses that frequently occur during adjudication. In developing countries, reports on previous judgments are kept piece meal in file cabinets and thereby giving edge to manual citation of court cases. This citation form had posed a great deal of problem such as, lengthened period between the time a case is opened and when accurate judgment is delivered, in the administration of Law and Justice. The advent of digital computers has made the routine use of pattern-matching possible in various applications and has also stimulated the development of many algorithms. In this study, a model that adopts Shift-Or Pattern Matching technique is proposed for citing authorities during legal jurisdiction. The model is implemented on Windows Vista Home Premium and WAMP APACHE as the web server. Record of court cases decided upon in the Ondo State High Court (OSHC), Akure between 2000 and 2012 was used to evaluate the performance of the system.

Keywords: court cases, case citation, crimes, information retrieval, Approximate String Matching

1. Introduction

In most countries, crimes are defined by statutory rules and regulations enacted by the law and are resolved by judiciary gathering in a courtroom [1]. Different types of punishment including: fines, imprisonment, disqualification from offices, and death; are ascribed with diverse crimes.

Courts are the central means of dispute resolution with a general notion *"all individuals have the right to bring their claims before a court"* [2]. Judicial settlement conferences present novel challenges to judges in assisting parties to settle their dispute rather than continue to litigate. Parties often appear in law courts with cases that have festered for long periods of time at great expense [3]. In many instances, the judge faces a particular challenge of overcoming impasses that frequently occur during the negotiations [4]. A successful settlement judge must employ creative approaches to bring about a resolution, particularly, when the negotiations appear at a dead end. The judge should be able to help the parties break through impasses with a process suggestion, additional information, or a settlement recommendation. Judges should therefore have a number of useful impasse-breaking techniques at their disposal [3].

Court facilities range from simple facilities in rural communities to sophisticated technology in cities, recent changes in courtroom technology of everyday life is affecting case dispositions increasingly quickly [5].

Anecdotal evidence suggests that electronically presented trials save from one-fourth to one-third of the time normally taken to try a similar case in a traditional fashion. Most of our appellate systems require verbatim records when serious cases are appealed and judges have interest in the court records such that the records are accessible in a timely and accurate fashion. This aids them in clarifying factual and legal matters during trial processes [5]. However, conscientious and competent judges are best supported by accurate trial records [6]. Hence, the more accurate the record, the less likely a case will be reversed.

In legal reasoning, judges follow rules defined by written law but also include legal precedents in their decision process. Often, the interpretation of law varies to a large extent among judges and it is difficult to find a common ground [7]. A court decision is usually published in one or more reporters. These are series of published bounded volumes which are publicly or privately available to legal practitioners [8]. Legal profession is not immune to the wind of change as legal research is very dynamic. In recent times, there had been some pragmatic and progressive developments in legal research however citation of court cases in a fast, accurate and accessible manner is still lagging.

The use of Expert Systems (ESs) can be espoused to leverage the existing limitations in citation of court cases. Expert System (ES) is an intelligent interactive computer based decision tool that uses facts and rules to solve difficult real life problems. The development of ES is based on knowledge acquired from human experts in a particular field, it features user friendly interfaces which make them highly interactive in nature, and provide accurate and timely solutions to difficult real life problems [9,10,11].

Over the years, pattern-matching has been routinely used in various computer applications such as: text editors, information retrieval, imaging analysis and searching nucleotide sequence patterns in genome and protein sequence databases [12]. This research therefore proposes a model that can cite court cases. The proposed model adopts Shift-Or Pattern Matching, an Approximate String Matching (ASM) technique that compares the characters of strings based on their distance. The model is driven by web based system for the purpose of citing court cases in an online and real-time manner.

The rest of this paper is organized such that: section 2 covers an overview of background study and related works; section 3 describes the proposed model and explains how the matching techniques can be adopted in the citation of court cases; section 4 presents an experimental study and evaluation of the model using the records obtained from OSHC, Akure, Nigeria. Lastly, section 5 presents the conclusion and future works.

2. Background Study and Related Works

This section presents an overview related studies on the application of Information Technology (IT) in citation of court cases.

Delay in legal proceedings due to manual searching of law reports causes longer time before cases' judgments are delivered [13]. Lawyers and judges often spend longer time to get matching authorities during litigation processes so as to backup their points. With computerization of law reports, a single storage media such as hard disk can house thousands of law reports [14]. In order to provide a means of reducing the volume of books that legal practitioners have to convey from their chamber to the law court at any point in time, a computer based law information system for storing and retrieval of legal materials was developed in [13]. The system provides a mechanism for quick references and citation of court cases by lawyers and judges. The application software did not provide means for direct searching of specific cases rather user will have to scroll through thousands of cases before he/she can access an case of interest.

During court sessions, litigants are represented by lawyer(s) who are versatile in the case(s) to be handled, and that of previous related cases [15]. Due to this, lawyers are expected to have anytime access to Law Reports for proper search. Direct search and search through law indexes remain the standard approaches to locate an authority in law reports [1,16]. In the former, access to law reports can be based on chronological and alphabetical indices. These techniques involve moving through different volumes of law reports and checking the index of authorities as contained at the back page of the publication [16]. Searching ends when a desired authority is located or such point cannot be defended. These steps, thereby, make the search methods cumbersome and time consuming [1]. As a result, search methods contribute to the lengthened time expended on legal matters.

Law Index is a publication that combined different volumes of Law Reports. This publication does not report authorities but points to the volume and pages of the reports for proper usages [16]. Since law index combined several volumes of law report, it makes searching for authorities more convenient. The complete index to Federation Weekly Law Report (FWLR) published

annually in Nigeria contains 52 volumes. A legal practitioner who wishes to cite an authority picks a volume of the complete index to an FWLR and search for the headings of the law he wishes to cite. This will direct him to the law report and pages of the report where such case is cited [14].

Law index had brought about a great relief to legal practitioner who would not have to pick several volumes of law report before getting an index to a desired authority; yet it has its limitation. A single volume of law index contains limited volumes of law report hence as years roll by, several volumes of law reports are available [15]. As law index grows with years passing, it is not wondrous having a situation that will be as bad as that of direct searching. Also, to locate an authority using law index, the legal practitioner searches through several legal headings/categories arranged in alphabetical order.

Information retrieval is the activity of retrieving stored data that provides information to support user's anomalous state of knowledge [17]. Professionals who are subject specialists in their task domain are distinguished from clerks based on document handling [18]. Lawyers are professionals who have refined their tools and work routines for many years [19]. They are also classified as experts in legal matters. Legal text retrieval has held a central position in information retrieval; it is concerned with legal norms which are subject to continuous interpretation and argumentation by lawyers. Reference [18] developed a prototype Information Retrieval System (IRS) with the aim of investigating how to provide lawyers with relevant recorded knowledge. The research demonstrated a facility for the use of terms in Thesaurus as keywords with visible references to documents of special interest using *Reversed Indexing*. Reversed indexing offers a direct way of retrieving relevant documents but it is time consuming [20].

Some of the legal practitioners in developing countries are intemperate with their scorn, one account notes that "many law librarians were appalled to learn that computer-assisted legal research would operate free of their dearly beloved, elaborate structure of indexes and digests" [21]. Technology came to courthouses long ago; today jurisdictions throughout Australia, Canada and the United State are using Case Management Systems and experimenting with Electronic Filing Systems [5]. High level of computer illiteracy has being an impacting factor that slows down the operation of cyber court as most parties, judges and court administrators are still trying to grasp the technologies on individual basis [22]. In the non-developed parts of the world, human attitudes toward invention of IT are very poor [14]. Reference [13] highlighted the need to develop a computer based law information system for storing and retrieving legal materials. This was to provide a mechanism for quick reference and citation of court cases during court sessions.

The influence of Computer-Assisted Legal Research (CALR) on legal issues and court citations had become an issue of debate among legal practitioners. Some law professionals are of the opinion that CARL is not effective as the conventional methods hence it should not be adopted in legal issues. In 2005, [9] clarified that CALR does not affect courts in the same way it is affecting other parts of the legal profession. Hence, commentators who asserted that CALR is reshaping the law are of weak position. CALR does not change the results of legal research rather it improves litigation processes with better speed and accuracy [9].

Previously, the monitoring and citation of court cases have been carried out manually. This takes great amount of time and other resources which raised eyes brows towards the need for the development of an indigenous database package for the effective and efficient administration of justice in Nigeria [15]. A software package christened 'CaseLaw' was developed in a two-tier architecture using Microsoft Access Database Management System and Microsoft Visual Basic 6.0. The model composed of three major files capable of keeping data of lawyers, sets of cases handled by the lawyers, and the details of each case as found in law reports. The model was tested in a Local Area Network environment.

ESs are designed to solve complex problems by reasoning about knowledge in human's nature rather than following the procedure of a developer as in the case of conventional programming [11]. Neural Network (NN) and Fuzzy Logic (FL) appear to be the major techniques adopted for developing ESs [23]. Computer models can be developed in line of human thinking concepts such that they are used in recognition, categorization, and analogy making. The major part of legal reasoning is formally interpreted as analogy making process using methods that incorporate the ability to specify likelihood with known court decisions. As a result, modeling expert systems that can attend to real life issues in Law and Justice is necessary [9]. Model for analogy and decision making in citing court cases was proposed in [9]. The model adopted NN and FL as its brain builder.

The basic purpose of legal citation is to allow legal practitioner locate cited sources accurately and efficiently. Case citations follow a standard convention in widely accepted format. However, variations in citation styles of portfolio data and metadata extracted from the text of a decision shows that the program logic would need to be highly flexible. There is need to develop repositories for storing decision text and metadata before they are linked. FL has been used to resolve court citation issues by creating links to previous court decisions [9].

High technology courtrooms have been public initiatives that are aimed at assessing the value of technology so as to improve the overall efficiency of courts and advance the sophisticated administration of court issues. The emergence of these technologies has assisted in processing, reviewing, distributing and storing large amount of court data on Internet [24]. Jurisdiction can also be exercised via the World Wide Web as the case of Caitlin, in New York City [22].

String matching algorithms are an important class of algorithms that checks the occurrence of string subsets, called patterns, in larger string called text [25]. A variety of algorithms for searching patterns have been proposed. Reference [24] describes a pattern-matching algorithm which finds all occurrences of a pattern of length m within a text of length n in $O(m + n)$ units of time. The algorithm does not without back up the input text hence, it only requires $O(m)$ locations of internal memory if the text is read from an external file, only $O(\log m)$ units of time will elapse between consecutive single-character inputs. All of the constants of proportionality implied by these "O" formulas are independent of the alphabet size [25].

The advent of digital computers has made the routine use of pattern-matching possible in various applications [12]. This has also stimulated the development of many algorithms. Large number of algorithms is known to exist to solve string matching problem [25]. Based on the number of patterns searched for, the algorithms can be classified as single pattern and multiple pattern algorithms. The algorithms scan text with the aid of a window whose size is equal to the pattern's length. The present day pattern-matching algorithms match the pattern exactly or approximately within the text [12]. An exact pattern-matching is to find all the occurrences of a pattern ($x = x_1, x_2, \ldots , x_m$) of m-characters in a text ($y = y_1, y_2, \ldots , y_m$) of n-characters which are built over a finite set of characters of an alphabet set denoted by $\sum$ and the size of this set is equal to σ. This approach is commonly known as a brute-force method.

Approximate string matching consists of finding all approximate occurrences of pattern **x** in text **y** with of length **m** and **n** respectively [27]. Approximate occurrences of x are segments of y that are close to x according to a specific distance which must be not greater than a given integer **k**. Hamming and Levenshtein distance are commonly considered [28]. The former is known as approximate string matching with k mismatches while the later is known as approximate string matching with k differences.

The understanding regarding citation of legal authorities during jurisdiction has been identified as information processing [18]. Numerous studies have been carried out in the field of information processing yet it has not being properly applied for citing court cases. Hence, in this study experiments how shift-or pattern matching can be adopted for citation purpose in courtrooms and other public or private law chambers.

3. Citation of Court Case Using Shift-Or Pattern Matching

This section presents the architecture of Citation of Court Cases using shift-or pattern matching.

3.1. Court Case Citation Architecture

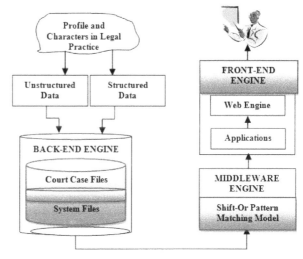

Figure 1. Architecture for Citing Court Cases using Shift-Or Pattern Matching

The architecture contains of three main components as shown in Figure 1. These are the: front-end engine, the back-end engine, and middleware engine.

Front-end engine is composed of the application modules and web engine with which the users of the system can interact with it. The modules coordinate users' access to the data stored in the system's database while the web engine aids creation and management of system data in an online and real-time mode. The data required by the citation architecture are captured and encoded in text formats which are kept in the back-end engine. Example of captured data includes details of cases that had been decided in some law courts, and the profile and characters of agents involved in legal practice.

The shift-or matching does the actual processes for a chosen transaction in order to cite relevant case and this is performed by the middleware engine.

3.2. Shift-Or Pattern Matching Algorithm

The Shift-Or pattern matching algorithm which was proposed by [29] is widely employed in text comparisons, database search, and pattern matching. The algorithm is very fast in practice and very easy to implement [27]. It overhauls both **Hamming** and **Levenshtein** distance of ASM. *Shift-Or* Pattern-Matching is thereby adopted by this research for the purpose of citing relevant authorities during legal jurisdictions. The explanation of the algorithm given in this paper is exact string-matching problem, however, a detailed explanation on how it can handle the cases of k mismatches and of k differences (insertions, deletions, or substitutions) is given in [27].

Given a pattern x and text stream y built by concatenating m and n characters of the finite alphabets Σ with size σ. All distinctive characters in Σ are generated as:

$$\Sigma = \bigcup_{x}^{y} \tag{1}$$

For each character of Σ, a state bit S_c is derived as:

$$S_c[i] = \begin{cases} 0 \; if \; x[i] = c \\ 1 \; otherwise \end{cases} \tag{2}$$

Where $S_c[i]$ is the bit array for character c of the Σ as related to its position in x. Each bit array has a size which is the same size as that of the pattern to be searched for. After building the state bits, a matching table T with dimension *mxn* is that holds information of all matches between the characters of x and y is generated. This is done by comparing the characters $x[i]$ and $y[i]$ using the bitwise-logical operators known as Shift-Or. The operation is done as:

$$T_{j+1} = T_j \gg 1 \; OR \; S_y[j+1] \tag{3}$$

Where $i = (0,1,...,m)$, and $j = (0,1,...,n)$. At $j = 0$, an initial value T_0 is set as the table value, this denotes an empty matching table. Then for each character $x[i]$ in the pattern, starting from $x[0]$, a comparison is made with character $y[i]$ in the text, if a match is reported the initial value is shifted one bit downward and stored as T_j, the next character $x[i + 1]$ in the pattern is taken against the next character $y[i + 1]$ in the text. If the comparison

process returns a no-match, the initial value T_0 is stored as the new value T_j, and another comparison process is observed between the characters $x[0]$ and $y[i + 1]$.

A success check is performed each time the matching reports success that is when $x[i] = y[j+1]$, the bit at $T_j[m-1]$ is checked. Once $T_j[m-1] = 0$, the process is completed and an exact match of x is reported to be found in y. Otherwise the matching processes continue till the characters of string y are exhausted. If a match is found, the matching start-position P_0 and end-position P_1 are calculated using:

$$P_0 = (j-m)+1 \tag{4}$$

$$P_1 = (P_0 + m)-1 \tag{5}$$

Where m is the length of x. The whole matching process is diagrammatically conceptualized as Figure 2.

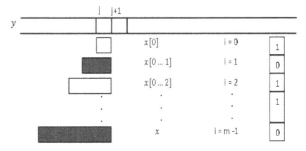

Figure 2. Conceptual Diagram of Matching Processes between Pattern x and text stream y

For instance, to search for a pattern $P = GATAA$ from text $T = CAGATAAGAGAA$

$$m = 5; n = 12; \Sigma = \{A,C,G,T\}$$

The state bits of each character in the pattern are generated using Eq (1) as shown in Table 1, while the matching information for searching the pattern P in the text stream T is shown in Table 2. It is clear that from Table 2, the bit at $T_{j=6}[m-1] = 0$. Hence, at $T_6[4]$, an occurrence of x has been found. The values of P_0 and P_1 are computed using equation 4 and 5 respectively as:

$$P_0 => (j-m)+1 => (6-5)+1 = 2.$$

$$P_1 = (P_0+m)-1 => (2+5)-1 = 6.$$

Therefore the pattern P which occurs in text T is a substring found between positions 2 to 6.

Table 1. State Bits Generated for character of Σ

S_A	S_C	S_G	S_T
1	1	0	1
0	1	1	1
1	1	1	0
0	1	1	1
0	1	1	1

3.3. Adopting Shift-Or in Court Case Citation

Court cases are cited by matching the search-key(s) found in a system generated query against appropriate relations of court case files. If a match is found, tuples of the case record(s) whose ID matches the search-key(s) are then displayed for the user's consumption. The search-key and court case files are taken to be respectively synonymous to the pattern and text stream explained above. Therefore, the matching process described in section 3.2 is established between the pattern and text stream whenever there is call for citation of court cases.

The Shift-Or matching technique is adopted in this study to perform multiple pattern check. Hence, a system query can be generated from one or more pattern(s). The patterns from which cases can be cited are shown diagrammatically in Figure 3.

Table 2. Matching Table for Searching Occurrence of P in T

	j	0	1	2	3	4	5	6	7	8	9	10	11
i		C	A	G	A	T	A	A	G	A	G	A	A
0	G	1	1	0	1	1	1	1	0	1	0	1	1
1	A	1	1	1	0	1	1	1	1	0	1	0	1
2	T	1	1	1	1	0	1	1	1	1	1	1	1
3	A	1	1	1	1	1	0	1	1	1	1	1	1
4	A	1	1	1	1	1	1	0	1	1	1	1	1

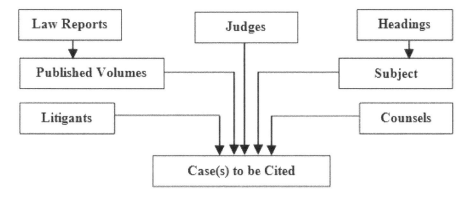

Figure 3. Pattern Location during Case Citation

4. Experimental Study and Evaluation

This section presents the features of the environment on which the study was carried out. The description of data which was used to evaluate the efficiency of the proposed model is as well given in this section.

4.1. Experimental Settings

The proposed model is implemented as a web based system with three-tier architecture. The web system consists of three main components which are the web browser agent, the web server application, and the database server which are well installed and configured independently.

The front-tier is the end through which the user communicates with the application. It requires the installation of a web browser at the client system. Fortunately, a web browser accompanies almost all operating systems in use today. Hence, the user is only required to launch the browser and specify the address of the web application: http://127.0.0.1/Case Citation System/index.php in the address bar of the browser. The front-end is designed with HTML tags that give the structure of a page while Java Scripts determine the behaviour of the page.

HTML documents are simple to learn and developers, irrespective of the level, can code classy web systems with minimal efforts [30]. Also, there are several free editors that support HTML tags. With JavaScript, small snippets of program code can help to fulfill complex tasks. Its interpreter is built into every scriptable browser [31]. Hence, there is no need of acquiring any additional tool so as to utilize the proposed system.

The middle-tier is the end through which users' requests are processed. It requires the presence of web application server that can listen to connection requests from client computers and direct the requests to the corresponding web application module for service. The middle-tier also requires a network connection to the database server at the back end. The middle-tier is implemented using Hypertext Preprocessor formally known as Personal Home Page (PHP).

PHP has its Object Oriented features combing those of Java and C# languages. PHP runs 5 to 20 times faster than Java. It is extremely easy to use in developing complex web applications, in a considerable period of time. PHP is the real gem of all scripting languages with a huge number of users worldwide [32].

The back-end hosts the data used by the web application and it is managed by the System Administrator. In this research, the back-end is hosted using MySQL DBMS, an open source application. The System Administrator performs administrative tasks such as the creation and backing up of database, recovery in case of database failure, data and system tuning.

MySQL DBMS is a fast Relational DBMS with the functionalities of varying leading database applications; it does not carry a hefty price tag as it is an open source application which can be easily downloaded [33]

The design of the web based system was developed to run in either a Localhost characterized by WAMP Server or in an Internet environment with a view to ensuring online and real time access to previously decided court cases. The Localhost environment characterized by **W**indows **A**pache **M**ySQL **P**HP (WAMP) Server is adopted in this project, however other platforms like Linux has LAMP providing the same services in Linux based machines. WAMP is an open source application that allows users to run web based applications on their local machine just the same way the applications behave in an Internet environment.

4.2. Data Description

For the purpose of evaluation of the model proposed in this study, the list of cases administered at the OSHC,

Akure between January, 2000 and August, 2012 were collected and analyzed. Visitations were made to the Court for the purpose of interviewing some legal staff of the court. After a series of interview, only criminal cases decided in the period of study was extracted for this study. A total of 442 cases that were extracted are summarized in Table 3. The details of each case are entered in their raw description in text files and stored in the database component of the architecture shown in Figure 1. In each file, cases are cited by taken any of the characters in Figure 3 as pattern and the case files as text stream.

The representation of the case types are: (a) Forgery and Stealing; (b) Man Slaughter; (c) Armed Robbery; (d) Rape and Kidnap; (e) Conspiracy; and (f) Murder.

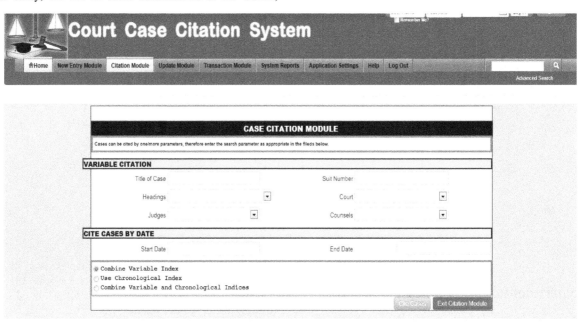

Figure 4. Web Form for Citing Court Case

Session Id: 01	Total Number of Cases Cited: 36	Number of Relevant Cases: 5
	First Page || Previous Page || 1 - 10 of 36 || First Page || Last Page	

S/No.	Suit No.	File No.	Subject Matter	Date	Case Litigants	Legal Adviser Position	Decision
1	CA/C/223/168	OD/102/90	Murder	2001-01-20	Olumiluide Christopher Vs. The State)	Whether the conviction on accused for the offence is confirmed	Initiate a settlement proceedings out of court
2	CA/OD/258/2001	OD/006/01	Murder and Conspiracy	2002-03-21	Adesina Kayode Vs. The State	The evidence of prosecution was cogent enough and met the standard of proof beyond reasonable doubt to sustain teh conviction for murder	No Scintilla of provocative attack found/proved by the deceased. The accused is therefore convisted and sentenced to death by hanging
3	CA/OD/24M/90	OD/001/2002	Murder and Conspiracy	2003-03-04	Stephen Okafor Vs. The State	The death of the deceased was caused by the fist blow inflicted on him by the accused person	The death of the deceased was not caused by the fist blow as shown by medical evidence, but by laceration of the liver. Accused accordingly discharged and acquited
4	SC.12/200	OD/002/04	Murder and Conspiracy	2004-01-12	Adesina Olumide Vs. Aderinde Oluwafemi	Litigate the case to a logical conclusion	Accused person not guilty. Acussed discharged and acquited. Sum of N450,000:00 be paid to the Accused
5	OD./28/99	OD/007/03	Murder and Conspiracy	2004-08-10	Alguokhliou Chidimmeka Vs. The State	Litigate the case to conclusion	Accused person guilty of murder. Acused to be executed by hanging
6	CA/09?/2005	OD/02?/15	murder and	2006-05-05	Akeem Atidanah	that the peculiar circumstance is	he accused is convicted and

Figure 5. Details of Cases Cited for Session-05

Table 3. Criminal Cases reported at Ondo State High Court, Akure between January, 2000 and August, 2012

Type	2000	2001	2002	2003	2004	2005	2006	2007	2008	2009	2010	2011	2012	Total	%
a	2	1	3	0	4	3	5	6	3	1	5	2	3	41	9.10
b	0	2	0	0	6	14	1	2	1	0	5	0	4	36	8.00
c	0	0	5	0	26	34	25	15	4	0	36	21	24	192	42.67
d	0	0	0	0	3	3	0	2	0	0	0	1	3	12	2.67
e	2	0	1	0	3	0	2	7	3	1	16	7	44	87	19.33
f	4	0	0	0	10	15	7	6	1	0	12	6	20	81	18.22
Total	8	3	9	0	52	69	40	38	12	2	74	37	98	442	100

4.3. Experimental Results and Evaluation

Cases can be cited with the aid of the web form displayed in Figure 4. The form is designed to cite cases using both alphabetic and chronological approaches; hence it demonstrates a degree of flexibility for users.

To evaluate the performance of the proposed system, the legal practitioners that works at both chambers of O. J. Jejelola and Michael Owolabi were given access the web based system for citing cases during their jurisdictions. This was observed between May to August, 2013.

A sample report generated by the system when used during a session is displayed as Figure 5. The report gives the number of cases that are related to the users' quest. For the purpose of evaluation, the user is made to go through the cases cited by the proposed system so as to confirm the cases that are both relevantly and irrelevantly cited. This is used to determine the Degree of Confidence (DoC) of the citations made by the model. The responses of the legal practitioners after 10 sessions with the proposed system are, as presented in Table 4, extracted and used to evaluate the performance of the proposed system.

In information retrieval context, standard measures, like precision, recall and receiver operating characteristic have been used to determine the performance of several systems [34]. In this study, DoC is taken as a measure to establish the confidentiality of the system. This is done by performing relational join operation on the result of the proposed system and the comments of legal practitioners. The DoC of a citation is determined as follows:

$$DoC_i = \frac{\text{Relevant Cases Cited}}{\text{Total Cases Cited}} * 100 \quad (6)$$

Where relevant cases are is number of cases cited by the model and one/more legal practitioner(s) confirm to be truly related to a case upon which the system is used, the total cases cited by the system can include irrelevant cases that is, the cases cited by the system but none of the legal practitioner confirms the relevancy of the case. The DoC of citations made during session 01 is computed as follows:

$$DoC_{S-01} = \frac{36}{41} * 100 = 87.8\%$$

The same procedure was observed to compute the DoC of citations made in other sessions too. To determine the Mean Accuracy (MA) and the Efficiency of the system, the error in citations made in each session was derived as:

$$Error_i = \frac{100 - DoC_i}{100} \quad (7)$$

Table 4. Response from Legal Practitioners

Session Id	Relevant Cases Cited by System	Irrelevant Cases Cited by System	DoC (%)	Error_i	1-Error_i
01	36	5	87.8	0.122	0.878
02	14	0	100.0	0.000	1.000
03	54	6	90.0	0.100	0.900
04	21	1	95.5	0.045	0.955
05	39	4	90.7	0.093	0.907
06	18	2	90.0	0.100	0.900
07	44	4	91.7	0.083	0.917
08	56	5	91.8	0.082	0.918
09	27	3	90.0	0.100	0.900
10	30	3	90.9	0.091	0.909

Therefore, the MA is calculated as:

$$MA = \frac{\sum_{i=1}^{n}(1 - Error_i)}{n} \quad (8)$$

$$MA = \frac{9.184}{10} = 0.9184$$

$$Efficiency = MA * 100 \quad (9)$$

$$Efficiency = 0.9184 * 100 => 91.84\%$$

Therefore, it can be inferred from the statistical analysis shows that the proposed system is 91.84% efficient in providing relevant citation using the Shift-Or Pattern matching technique.

5. Conclusions

In this paper, we have proposed a system that can aid legal practitioners such as judges and lawyers during their jurisdiction. In particular, a comprehensive model for citing relevant cases during court sessions is focused. This model is not meant to replace the orthodox method rather as an augmentation to it. The objective of the experimental study is to demonstrate the functional capability of the system with a view to gaining confidence of legal practitioners and the administrators of Law and Justice who hand round as the end-users of the system.

The paper also described Shift-Or, a pattern matching technique, as an active platform that can be adopted for processing court data. We also describe web services as a suitable medium used for intelligent Information Retrieval, the citation of court cases in an online and real-time approach and, as well as for consistent presentation and management of data. The experiments conducted showed that the web based court citation system as here proposed has been proved to be both workable and effective with an acceptable level of accuracy in citing relevant cases hence, existing courtrooms in the developing part of the world should be encouraged to adopt this system during their court sessions.

It is clearly shown that the deployment of IT facilities in legal practices had drastically reduced the stress passed through while adjudging a matter and had brought a better result therefore, soft computing tools such as Genetic Algorithm, Fuzzy Logic, and Neural Networks can be applied to court cases citation.

Acknowledgement

We wish to acknowledge the staff of Ondo State High Court, Akure, Ondo State, Nigeria, for their assistance in the area of data collection and analysis, and the chambers of O. J. Jejelola, and Michael Owolabi for their contributions.

References

[1]   Omisore M. Olatunji and Samuel O. Williams, *Design of Internet Model for Court Case Citation*, Journal of Communication and Computer, "In Press".

[2]   Walker David, *The Oxford Companion to Law*, Oxford University Press, Pg. 301, 1980.

[3]   Morton Denlow *Breaking Impasses in Judicial Settlement Conferences: Seven (More) Techniques for Resolution*, Court Review - The Journal of the American Judges Association, Vol 46, Issue 4, Pg 130-4, 2009.

[4]   Morton Denlow, Breaking Impasses In Settlement Conferences: Five Techniques for Resolution, JUDGES' J., Fall 2000.

[5]   Fredric I. Lederer, *Courtroom Technology from the Judge's Perspective*, Journal of the American Judges Association, American Judges Association Vol. 35, No. 1, Pg. 20-24, 1998.

[6]   James A. Maher, *National Center for State Courts, Do Video Transcripts Affect the Scope of Appellate Review?* An Evaluation in the Kentucky Court of Appeals, 1990.

[7]   Jurgen Hollatz, *Analogy Making in Legal Reasoning with Neural Networks and Fuzzy Logic*, Artificial Intelligence and Law, Kluwer Academic Publishers, Netherlands, Vol. 7, Pg. 289-301, 1999.

[8]   Jack Rugh and Julia Lennen, *Using Fuzzy Logic to Create Links: Resolving References to Court Decisions*, Idea Alliance, Senior Publishing Specialist, Media and Publications Division, pg 1-14, 2003.

[9]   Hellyer Paul, *Assessing the Influence of Computer-Assisted Legal Research*, Law Library Journal, San Jose University, Vol. 97, No 2, Pg. 285-298, 2005.

[10] Savory, S. E.,*Artificial Intelligence and Expert Systems*, Ellis Horword Series in Artificial Intelligence, Halsted Press, a division of Wiley, Chichester, England, pp. 28-29, August, 2006.

[11] Samuel, O. W., Omisore, M. O., and Ojokoh, B. A., *A Web Based Decision Support System Driven By Fuzzy Logic for the Diagnosis of Typhoid Fever*, Expert Systems with Applications 40 (2013) 4164-4171.

[12] Sheik, S., Aggarwal S., Poddar A., Balakrishnan N., and Sekar K., *A FAST Pattern Matching Algorithm*, J. Chem. Inf. Comput. Sci., Vol. 44, pp. 1251-1256, 2004.

[13] Oladipupo B., *Law Information System: Searching and Retrieval of Legal Materials*, Computer Based Law Database on Compact Disc, Private Communications, 2001.

[14] Irene Baghoomians and Frederick Schauer (2009), *Thinking Like a Lawyer: A New Introduction to Legal Reasoning*, Harvard University Press, Cambridge (Ma), pp239.

[15] Akinyokun O. Charles, *Computer Aided System for Monitoring and Citation of Court Cases*, Law and Practice Journal; Nigerian Law School, Abuja, Nigeria, 2006.

[16] Adegoke M. A. (2004), *Development and Implementation of a Computer-Aided System for Monitoring and Citation of Court Cases*, Master Thesis, Federal University of Technology, Akure.

[17] Belkin N. J., Oddy R. N., and Brooks H. M. (1982), *ASK for Information Retrieval: Background and Theory*, Journal of Documentation, vol. 3 issue 8, Pg. 61-71.

[18] Morten Hertzum, Henrik Soes, and Erik Frokaer, *Information Retrieval Systems for Professionals: A Case Study of Computer Supported Legal Research*, European Journal of Information Systems, vol. 2, No. 4, pp. 296-303, 1993.

[19] Tenopir C, Full-Text Databases, *Annual Review of Information Science and Technology vol .*19, 215-246, 1984.

[20] Foskett D J, *Thesaurus. In Subject and Information Analysis* (DYM E D, Ed.), pp. 270-316. Marcel Dekker, New York, 1985.

[21] Harrington, *supra* note 1, at 546.

[22] Lucille M. Ponle, *Michigan Cyber Court - Bold Experiment in the Development of the First Public Virtual Courthouse*, North Carolina Journal of Law and Technology, University of Michigan, Vol. 4, Issue:1, Pg: 51-60, 2002.

[23] Samuel, O. W. and Omisore M. O., *Hybrid Intelligent System for the Diagnosis of Typhoid Fever*, Journal of Computer Engineering and Information Technology, Journal of Computer Engineering and Information Technology, Vol. 2, issue 2, 2013.

[24] Gwenn M. K., *From the Internet to Court: Exercising Jurisdiction over World Wide Web Communications*, Fordham Law Review, Vol. 65, No. 5, Article 8, Pg. 4-25, 1997.

[25] Vidya SaiKrishna1, Akhtar Rasool, and Nilay Khare, *String Matching and its Applications in Diversified Fields*, International Journal of Computer Science Issues, Vol. 9, Issue 1, No 1, 1694-0814, 2012.

[26] Knuth Donald, Morris James, and Pratt Vaughan, *Fast Pattern Matching in Strings*, SIAM J. COMPUT., Vol. 6, No. 2, 1977.

[27] Maxime Crochemore and Thierry Lecroq, *Pattern Matching and Text Compression Algorithms*, Technical Report, Institut Gaspard Monge, Universite´ de Marne la Valle´e, 2 rue de la Butte Verte, F-93166 Noisy-le-Grand, Cedex, France.

[28] Wu, S. and Manber, U., *Fast Text Searching Allowing Errors*, Communication of ACM, vol 35, Issue 10, pp. 83-91, 1992.

[29] Baeza-Yates, R. A., Gonnet, G. H., *A New Approach to Text Searching.* Communication of ACM vol. 35, no. 10, pp. 74-82, 1992.

[30] Robert G. Fuller and Laurie Ann Ulrich (2004), *HTML in 10 Simple Steps or Less*, Wiley Publishing, Inc, Indianapolis.

[31] Danny Goodman, *JavaScript Bible,* 4th Edition, Hungry Minds Publishing Inc, Indianapolis (United States), 2001, pp. 3-4.

[32] Greenspan Jay and Brad Bulger (2001), *MySQL-PHP Database Applications*, M&T Books Worldwide, Inc. New York, pp. 71-94

[33] Maslakowski Mark and Butcher Tony (2000), *Teach Yourself MySQL in 21 Days*, Sams Publishing, New Jersey, United States.

[34] Herlocker, J. L., J. A. Konstan, A. Borchers, and J. Riedl, *An Algorithmic Framework for Performing Collaborative Filtering*, In Proceedings of the 22nd Annual International ACM SIGIR Conference on Research and Development in Information Retrieval (SIGIR'99).

2

Adapt Clustering Methods for Arabic Documents

Boumedyen Shannaq[*]

Computer science and Information Technology Department, Mazoon College, "University College", Muscat, Sultanate of Oman
*Corresponding author: aboumedyen@gmail.com

Abstract This research paper develops new clustering method (FWC) and further proposes a new approach to filtering data collected from internet resources. The focus of this research paper is clustering groups' data instances into subsets in such a manner that similar instances are grouped together, while different instances belong to different groups. The instances are thereby organized into an efficient representation that characterizes the population being sampled thereby reducing the gigantic size of retrieved data. This has been done by removing dissimilar text files, and grouping similar documents into homogeneous clusters. Arabic text files of 974 MB has been collected, processed, analyzed and filtered by using common clustering methods. This new clustering methods are presented, divided into: hierarchical, partitioning, density-based, model-based and soft-computing methods. Following the methods, the challenges of performing clustering in large data sets are discussed and tested by the proposed new clustering method. Two experiments were conducted to establish the effectiveness of FWC methods and the obtained results show that the new FCW method suggested in this paper produced better results and outperformed existing clustering methods.

Keywords: *clustering, knowledge management, information retrieval system*

1. Introduction

Nowadays Search and Navigation activities become one of the common and needed services on the Internet Technology. How to be fast and smart in your search? Is now a top priority for most individuals and Organization? The internet technology has flooded the world with online information [1,2]. Organizing the abundant information available on the internet has become a major challenge to the researchers [3]. In today's world, children, students, schools, universities, colleges, companies, government etc… used internet as a main source for collecting their essential information. The dependence on the internet increases the traffic on the net, accordingly there is a challenge faces by search engines to find new helpful techniques to deal with enormous volume of information available on the internet. Furthermore serving the great number of internet users [4,5]. Since we live in an information age, it is thus necessary to design or make a search engine which can successfully index or classify the web pages in a manner that help its users to derive the exact information required by them. However despite of companies claiming their success in producing a search engine which will satisfy the internet users, still the user complain of the lack of accuracy and relevance of retrieved information [6] particularly the Arabic user. The attitudinal change in the user behavior, has forced many IT companies to seriously think and develop advance search technologies that may enable the user to retrieve the desired information. Google, Yahoo, Microsoft etc.

companies are well aware of this fact [7]. This work put into practice a strategy for filtering webpage's retrieved from search engines, as a result reduced the gigantic size of retrieved text collection, as well as improved the presentation and performance of knowledge base.

2. Literature Review

A growing amount of research has studied the organization of web data. [8] discuss standards and evaluations in test collections Using different clustering models and various text transformation approaches were proposed, to arranged text collection for searching and building knowledge based systems. Most of these techniques were concerned with text operation i.e. lexical analysis, elimination of stop words, stemming etc…, moreover such text operation are useful for selection of index terms and building thesauri. However, there is no evidence that such text operations improved or removed unnecessary text from text collection [7]. Other researchers used the operation of compressing text aims at reducing space and communication cost, there is no doubt such compressing operations requires less storage space and takes less time, to be good compression ratio, fast coding, fast decoding, and this basically not easy task. [3] includes an analysis of the inverted index, inverted lists, suffix arrays, Pat arrays and Huffman coding, however such techniques are dealing with text retrieval to implement query operation, but not for removing unnecessary text files from text collection. [9] Explained three classic models in Web Information Retrieval: the

Boolean, the vector and Probabilistic models, those models were used as a ranking algorithms. [9] Presented new clustering techniques to discover when two documents are similar. The proposed techniques aimed to resolve the difficulties of articles repetition; the new clustering technique was based on LIPNS, SAMA1, Text Normalization, DNSA and, NADST techniques respectively. [10] Describes the process of analyzing text considers various measurement to evaluate corpus and collections by zip's and Mandelbrot distribution law [11]. [12] works on analyzing corpus data in order to generate useful text analysis and categorization over different file formats, such application may help and support researchers in selecting the best text collection for example, building a knowledge base; an ontology; Thesaurus, and glossary [13]. Currently numerous questions are raised on how the internet provides the electronic document? How to structure this electronic document? Which document to be retrieved? Can we trust this information retrieved by search engines? The challenge is how to describe what document is about? One of the common approaches is to select terms to represent what the document is about. Today, the current trends looking to find a group of activities to facilitate the access to a specific information and knowledge which often can be seen implicitly, and most of discussion methods above have not clearly introduced a helpful techniques for answering the raised questions above.

3. Experiments

3.1. Text Collection

For the implementation of this work, data text was collected and downloaded from wekipedia http://wikipedia.org/wiki/Text_corpus, size of 974 MB (1,021,566,976 bytes), text collection was in Arabic, XML format, and stored in one file only. The text collection has been partitioned to group of files and transformed to. Txt format using Python software. The splitting process consumed 2hrs 8 min. There after statistical information from the new text collection was obtained, and the processed data was 1.10 GB (1,187,983,360 bytes) containing 228,308 Files and 65,704 Folders. HTML tags, Stop words like

" لن له من   هو   هي قوة كما لها منذ وقد ولا لمكل
هناك وقال وكان وقالت وكانت   فيه كلم لكن وفي وقف
ولم ومن وهو وهي يوم فيها منها "

, numbers, punctuations and spaces between adjacent words have been removed, Super Arabic morphological analyzer (SAMA1) [14] has been used for stemming purposes, the stemming process was done for handling many issues raised from Plurals, gerund forms and past tenses. Simple stemming algorithm can be described as follow: If word starts in "ال" "then replace with " ",

"الأنترنت" ⟶ " انترنت "

C# program has been developed to remove the Arabic stop words.

3.2. Experiment # 1

The text collection were transformed to document/Term matrix, first column represents Documents, first row

represents terms in text collection, and elements(values) represent the frequencies of terms in a specific document. Figure 1 shows fragments of document/Term matrix, we provide this fragment as an example to illustrate our contribution to the existing methods.

A	B	C	D	E	F	G
	T1	T2	T3	T4	T5	T6
D1	3	1	3	2	6	7
D2	3	22	0	33	7	5
D3	0	0	1	1	9	21
D4	1	8	0	1	2	0
D5	0	8	2	4	0	37
D6	0	3	0	2	3	5
D7	1	5	4	3	0	3
D8	9	6	0	1	4	0
D9	22	3	3	0	3	2
D10	14	0	9	3	0	0
D11	0	5	2	4	4	1
D12	2	0	0	2	9	2
D13	1	1	0	3	0	0
D14	0	0	0	0	1	3
D15	1	5	0	0	0	6
D16	5	7	0	9	3	0
D17	2	6	0	1	1	1

Figure 1. Fragments of document/Term matrix

Different cluster methods like, 'groups linkage', 'centroid' and 'ward's' method respectively have been used and tested, in addition to available alternatives like 'euclidean distance' and 'cosine', after many iterative operations, 'Ward's' method and Euclidean distance measure have been selected, for the reason that they provide best clustering results against others methods. Figure 2 shows the proximity matrix of Document/Document (distance matrix D)after applying 'Ward's' method and 'Euclidean distance' measure. The next illustrate the implemented formulas used to obtained Distance matrix D. all formulas were obtained from [15,16].

'Centroid method'

$$\frac{\overline{x}_1 n_1 + \overline{x}_2 n_2}{n_1 + n_2}$$

'Ward's method'

The total deviance (T) of the p variables, corresponding to n times the trace of the variance–covariance matrix, can be divided in two parts: the deviance.

Within the groups (W) and the deviance between the groups (B), so T = W + B.

The total deviance (T) can be denoted by:

$$T = \sum_{s=1}^{p} \sum_{i=1}^{n} \left(x_{is} - \overline{x}_s \right)^2$$

Groups (W) are given by the sum of the deviances of each group and can be denoted by:

$$W = \sum_{k=1}^{g} W_k$$

W_k represents the deviance of the p variables in the k_{ith} group and can be denoted by:

$$W_k = \sum_{s=1}^{p} \sum_{i=1}^{n_k} \left(x_{is} - \overline{x}_{sk} \right)^2$$

The deviance between the groups, (B) is given by the calculated sum on all the variables and can be denoted by:

$$B = \sum_{s=1}^{p} \sum_{k=1}^{g} n_k \left(\overline{x}_{sk} - \overline{x}_s \right)^2$$

'Cosine measure'

$$sim\left(d_j, q\right) = \frac{\overline{dj} \bullet \overline{q}}{\left|\overline{dj}\right| \times \left|\overline{q}\right|}$$

$$= \frac{\sum_{i-1}^{t} w_{i,j} \times w_{i,q}}{\sqrt{\sum_{i-1}^{t} w_{i,j}^2} \times \sqrt{\sum_{j-1}^{t} w_{i,q}^2}}$$

'Euclidean distances'

$$d_{ij} = \left(\sum_{K=1}^{N} \left(x_{ik} - x_{jk} \right)^2 \right)^{\frac{1}{2}}$$

The introduced methods above amid to put the similar documents in different groups by calculating the similarities between the documents. Let us consider the following input matrix obtained from matrix, assumed all the way that the input data are in the form of a matrix, illustrated in Figure 1, the obtained Proximity matrix from matrix shown in Figure 1 is described in Figure 2.

	D1	D2	D3	D4	D5	D6	D7
D1	0	37.62978	14.8324	11.31371	31.60696	5.91608	8.602325
D2	37.62978	0	42.16634	35.69314	46.07602	36.7015	35.52464
D3	14.8324	42.16634	0	23.57965	20.27313	17.4069	21.07131
D4	11.31371	35.69314	23.57965	0	37.24245	7.28011	6.480741
D5	31.60696	46.07602	20.27313	37.24245	0	32.64966	34.21988
D6	5.91608	36.7015	17.4069	7.28011	32.64966	0	5.91608
D7	8.602325	35.52464	21.07131	6.480741	34.21988	5.91608	0
D8	11.13553	36.74235	24.16609	8.485281	38.50974	10.81665	10.48809
D9	20.07486	42.95346	29.91655	21.93171	41.95235	22.49444	21.56386
D10	15.6205	40.7431	28.03569	17.94436	40.9756	17.91647	15.09967
D11	8.3666	34.17601	21.44761	5.291503	36.34556	5.385165	5.09902
D12	6.708204	38.19686	19.15724	10.90871	37.17526	7.615773	11.18034
D13	9.949874	37.66962	23	7.549834	37.73592	6.324555	6.403124
D14	8	40.27406	19.74842	8.717798	35.22783	4.582576	7.211103
D15	8.3666	37.84178	18.27567	7.071068	31.48015	4.358899	5.830952
D16	12.49	29.08608	24.81935	9.055385	37.85499	10.72381	9.486833
D17	9.848858	36.51027	22.47221	2.645751	36.30427	5.830952	5.196152

Figure 2. fragment of obtained Proximity matrix

To extend the procedure of clustering described in [15], we perform the following:

Consider every row vector as a point and rearrange the row vectors according to their similarity, in Figure 2 the row vectors ordersare d1d2d3d4d5d6d7d8d9d10d11d12 d13d14d15d16d17, next if we rearrange the row vectors orders to d4d17d7d11d6d15d13d14d1d12d8d16d9d10d3d5.

Table 1 illustrates the steps of creating clusters from Figure 2.

Table 1. The steps of creating clusters

Number of Cluster	Clusters
1	4,7
2	7,11
3	6,15
4	13,14
5	1,12
6	8,16
7	9,10
8	3,5
9	4,17,7,11
10	6,15,13,14
11	3,5,2
12	4,17,7,11,6,15,13,14,1,12,8,16
13	4,17,7,11,6,15,13,14,1,12,8,16,9,10
14	4,17,7,11,6,15,13,14,1,12,8,16,9,10,3,5,2

3.3. Experiment # 2

The proposed idea illustrates that, to cluster the collected text into groups of similar documents based on the idea of analyzing and extracting the first word only from each document then group all documents which have the same first word together.

The next procedure illustrates the proposed approach:
1-Read First Document Di from Corpus
2-Extract only first keyword (fk) (eliminate any stop words or signs)
3-Find the frequency (fr) of extracted first keyword over the document Di
4-Add Address of the document, first keyword (fk) and frequency (fr)
5-Repeat all steps for all documents in the corpus
Table 2 shows a sample of the output after performing the above procedure:

Table 2. Extracted sample from the corpus

Document number(Di)	Keyword (fk)	Frequency(fr)
Document 1	معالج	23
Document 2	انترنت	13
Document 3	بحث	17
Document 4	انترنت	17
Document 5	شبكة	9
Document 6	بحث	7
Document 7	انترنت	5

Reorganize the table horizontally until formulating groups of similar documents based on matching first keywords. (Table 3 shows this operation after reorganization the rows in the above table).

Table 3. Reorganized rows

Document number(Di)	Keyword (fk)	Frequency(fr)
Document 2 (Collection # 1)	انترنت	13
Document 4 (Collection # 1)	انترنت	17
Document 7 (Collection # 1)	انترنت	5
Document 3 (Collection #2)	بحث	17
Document 6 (Collection #2)	بحث	7
Document 1	معالج	23
Document 5	شبكة	9

4. Evaluation and Results

Evaluating the results of the obtained grouping means verifying that the groups are consistent with the primary objective of the cluster analysis, to satisfy the conditions of internal cohesion and external separation. Choosing the right number of groups is fundamentally important. Here we evaluate the results obtained from experiment one and experiment two, considering the factor of how many new words appear each time versus new extracted words from new documents. It was hard to compare all the obtained clusters from experiment one and Two, furthermore we select only the largest clusters considering size factor(number of documents).

Figure 3 shows the results derived from largest clusters obtained from experiment.

One using basic clustering methods.

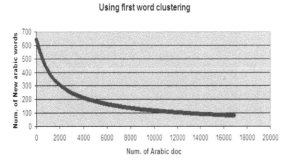

Figure 3. Number of new words against number of documents

Figure 3 illustrate that out of 200 to 170 new words continue to appear in this cluster. This means that there are some files which is not related to the cluster, and this in general will affect the final results of any research experiment oriented to a specific domain.

Figure 4 shows the obtained results from experiments two.

Figure 4. Using first word clustering

Figure 4 illustrate that out of 100 to 75 new words continue to appear in this cluster. This means that there are some files which are not related to the cluster, but the later is better than the former. Our consideration is, as the numbers of extracting new words each time reduces as we keep on testing other documents. This factor can be considered as a fact that the cluster contains similar and related documents, which are used to describe a specific domain. Regarding the obtained results from both experiments, the proposed approach was able to remove/filter about 100 dissimilar documents from the text collection.

Table 4 shows the finding and comparison between the basic clustering methods and the new developed method.

Table 4. Finding and results

Method	Number of total words	Number of new words
Basic method	>20000	200 to 170
First word method	>20000	100 to 75

5. Discussion

Most of the experimenters and researchers depend on concrete dataset, to test their hypothesis and algorithms. However finding and collection the related data set become a challenge, when the question is how to obtain the related data set for a specific topic i.e. data set must describes a specific domain and contains only the related terms of this domain [17]. Organizing the data considering as the hottest topic today in research and development area. Aims to build ontology of a specific domain. The advantage of building such ontology is to unified ideas and create standards over the web, more ever to enable self communication between machines. As a matter of fact, to build the ontology, first you need to prepare a glossary for your ontology, the glossary must contains all terms, their synonyms and other attributes [18]. Such terms must be used only to describe a specific domain. Extracting those terms manually is time and efforts consuming, thus automation this process is highly appreciated, however you must be sure that your text collection contains only related terms of your interested topic. How to choose which method to apply, In practice there is not a method that can give the most qualified result with every type of data. Experiment with the different alternatives and compare them in terms of the chosen criteria. This work proposes a novel approach to filter the text collection from dissimilar documents, by developing new clustering method. The developed clustering method, depends on the factor of considering the first word only from documents, the developed technique was tested, and the obtained result outperform the other existing clustering methods. We believe this developed techniques will be as a new development for the available clustering methods, there were some limitation of documents processing, such as selecting stop words and stemming issues, but we believe that these errors and limitation was not affect the obtained results since they are applied to the both experiments. This work can be applied to English and other languages to test the performance of the proposed approach. Other text collection can be used also to test the developed clustering method.

6. Conclusion

This work introduces one of the most interesting fields in computer-oriented data analysis. Developing new clustering technique FCW, aims to cluster the collected text into groups of similar documents, it is based on the idea of analyzing and extracting the first word only from each documents then grouping documents which have the same first word together. We were able to solve the problem of cluster analysis, and to group similar documents into homogeneous clusters. It is still too early to reach a consensus on the advantages of using this developed technique for the web, but we believe that this work and obtained results will prove to be effective in web application. Therefore this developed strategy will have wide application in the domain of E-Learning, Knowledge management and web management.

References

[1] Allen J., Aslam J., Belkin N., Buckley C., CallanJ.,"Challenges in information retrieval and language modeling", *Special Interest Group on Information Retrieval(SIGIR)*, Vol 37,No. 1, pp. 31-47, 2003.

[2] Shannaq B., Aleksandrov V.," Clustering the Arabic Documents(CAD) ", *Universal Journal of Applied computer Science and Technology (UNIASCIT)*, Vol. 1 No. 3, pp. 90-94, 2011.

[3] Araujo M.,Navarro G., Zivani N.," Large text searching allowing errors", *4th South American Workshop on String Processing (WSP '97)*, pp. 2-24, 1997.

[4] Allan J.,Carterette B., LewisJ., "When will information retrieval be "good enough?", *Proceedings of the ACM SIGIR Conference on Research and Development in Information Retrieval*, pp. 443-440, 2005.

[5] Shannaq B., " Using Russian and English Ontology In Expanding The Arabic Query", *Universal Journal of Applied computer Science and Technology (UNIASCIT)*, Vol. 1 No. 3,pp. 95-100, 2011.

[6] Shannaq B., Aleksandrov V.,"Using Product Similarity for Adding BusinessValue and Returning Customers ", *Global Journal of Computer Science and Technology*, Vol. 10, No. 12. pp. 2-8, 2010.

[7] MorleyD., Parker C., " *Understanding Computers Today and Tomorrow Comprehensive* " 13th edition, 2010.

[8] Shaw W., Burgin R., Howell P., " Performance standards and evaluations in IR test collections: Cluster-based retrieval models". *Information Processing and Management*, Vol. 33, No. 1, pp. 1-14, 1997.

[9] Baeza R., Ribeiro B., "*Modren Information Retrieval* ", ACM Press, New York, 1999.

[10] Mason, Oliver, Berglund, Ylva, "Low-level parameters reflecting the naturalness of texts". *Proceedings of JADT2002, 6th International Conference on Textual Data Statistical Analysis*, Saint Malo, March 13-15. Vol.2, pp. 507-516, 2002.

[11] Giinther R., Levitin L., Chapiro B., Wagner P.," Zipf's law and the act of ranking on probability distributions", International Journal of Theoretical Physics, Vol. 35, pp. 395-417, 1996.

[12] Shannaq, Boumedyen. "Investigating the Distribution of Arabic and English Keywords and Their Progress Over Different Text File Formats." American Journal of Computing Research Repository 1.1 (2013): 1-5.

[13] Kokorin P.,Shannaq B., "Algorithm of Normalization and Ontological Clusters Texts", Information-measuring and operating systems *Journal*, Vol. 7, No. 8,pp 60-64, 2010.

[14] Shannaq B., Aleksandrov V., " Super Arabic Morphological Analyzer (SAMA1)", *information-measuring and operating systems Journal*, Vol.11, No. 7,pp. 60-63, 2009.

[15] Witten H., Frank E., " *Data Mining & Practical Machine Learning Tools and Techniques*",Elsevier,2005.

[16] Giudici P., "*Applied Data Mining, Staistical Methods for Business and Industry* ", Wiley,England, 2003.

[17] Boumedyen Shannaq," Methods and Algorithms for Searching Arabic Name Entity", *International Journal of Computer Applications*, Vol.82 - Number 8, 2013.

[18] Boumedyen Shannaq, Kaneez Fatima, " Hierarchy Concept Analysis in Accounting Ontology ", *Asian Journal Of Computer Science And Information Technology*, Vol.2: 2, 2012 13-20.

3

Second Life: An Emerging Technology for 3D Websites

Fabeha Waqar Shmasi, Ahmad Waqas*

Department of Computer Science, Sukkur Institute of Business Administration, Sukkur, Pakistan
*Corresponding author: ahmad.waqas@iba-suk.edu.pk

Abstract Second Life is virtual reality based technology for designing 3D websites. This paper demonstrates the detailed process of creating a 3D website from scratch using Second Life. The steps required to make a 3D website are divided into sections to make things clear and understandable. The sections will be introducing the basic things that will need to be understood in order to make a website.

Keywords: Second Life, avatar, Linden Scripting Language (LSL), animation, texture, script, Linden Dollar

1. Introduction

As time changes everything change. Similarly, the era of flat web is being replaced by three-dimensional websites. There are many questions which a person can ask these days, such as, are you bored of dealing with the flat web and its problems? How great it would be if you don't have to wait for the replies of the solutions of your problems? What if there lies a technology which along with making browsing interesting for you by helping you to enhance your experience in a very friendly way, also provides you with a real-time conversation facility which requires no waiting to get a suitable response of the questions? This paper demonstrates one such technology that is based on virtual reality which let the users explore their imaginations and bring them to a shape named Second Life, commonly known as SL.

There lies various other technologies besides Second Life which supports virtual reality named Active World [1] and Cyber Town [2], whereas Second Life is very popular among them. Second Life (SL) is the leading 3D virtual world, launched in 2003 [3] as a technology platform which enables millions of clients, represented in world as avatars, to imagine and build immersive environments that are easy and economical to create. SL, along with being one of the oldest virtual reality and virtual world platforms, it is also the largest platform with millions of active users residing in more than 160 countries globally [4].

SL has always been used by a wide variety of businesses, individuals, governments, educators and non-profit organizations as an environment for education, entertainment, research, social interaction, shopping, and more. Over the last few years, many famous multinational companies and government institutions have realized that Second Life is also a powerful collaboration tool for meetings, training sessions, and simulations and prototypes [5].

A client program named SLViewer(Second Life Viewer)enables SL residents to communicate through avatars [4]. Residents are the users who use Avatars to represent themselves in the virtual world of Second Life. Avatars are customizable and can resemble to a user's Real Life (RL) appearance or be somebody else. It depends on a user's imagination that how they want themselves to be represented. SLViewer enables Residents to interact virtually with each other around the globe. There are other client side applications too beside SLViewer, for example, Phoenix viewer, dolphin, and Snowglobe viewer. These viewers also provide same functionality as SLViewer but they have different interfaces [4].

Second Life allows its users to make their own objects using prims. Prims are the building blocks of SL, they are stretchable, rotatable, and movable, they can be scaled according to the needs[6]. In short, prims can be used to make anything a user can imagine. Second Life has its own scripting language known as Linden Scripting Language (LSL) [7]. It allows users to make their animations and textures which can be applied on objects to make them look better and more real. Users can import textures and animations from other software for use. SL facilitates with business activities, so it has its own currency called Linden Dollars (L$). Second Life users can sell objects, lands and homes.

1.1. Advantage of SL

There are several key advantages of using SL technology over the traditional static web technologies. For example, Second Life is now stretched over the globe and has users from the entire world [10]. In this way, SL promotes socialization. The SLViewer facilitates with avatars to communicate among each other. This is a major source of learning new things, generating new ideas, collaboration of users to work on projects together and remain intact with technologies and know multi-cultural values. Secondly, Avatars can earn money using Second Life. They can either have their own business or can do job somewhere. Stanford University and University of Texas have their campuses in Second Life [8,9] and they conduct classes there. Dell has a 3D outlet in Second Life [10]. Snow Books has their outlet in Second Life, who allows avatars to read the books in 3D. Furthermore, Second Life's flexibility as a platform is supreme instead of having a virtual space dedicated to one use. In Second Life, you can place a team meeting space next to an event arena that is adjacent to a training simulation. It is easy to do because you have complete control over what is placed in your Second Life work environment. In other words, it saves a lot of server space as compared to other similar technologies.

1.2. Limitations of SL

Despite of advantages, there are also few disadvantages of this technology. The Second Life is still evolving so nothing is concrete. The versions of SLViewer keeps on updating in a very short span of time that causes inventory loss sometimes. The functions used in the Linden Scripting Language also keeps on changing. The scripts do not function properly specially the ones written long time back. Another important limitation of Second Life includes the high computation resources requirement for executing SLViewer fluently.

2. Building Blocks of SL

2.1. Prims: The Building Blocks

Prims are the building blocks in Second Life [6]. All the objects created in SL are built using different prims. For example, if a user has intended to make a table. They will have to rezz 5 prims (4 for legs and 1 for table Stop), together they will make an object which will be a table. An object has the capability to be shaped in any form. Residents can apply functions on objects and make them look however they have pictured it. Figure 1 depicts the prims in SL.

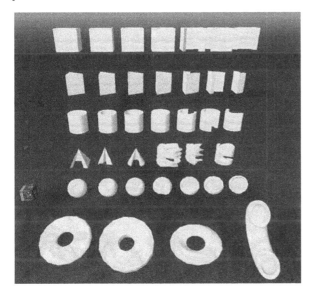

Figure 1. Prims

2.2. Inventory

All the objects you create are stored in inventory. Inventory in Second Life can be referred to as a storage box. It stores everything owned by an Avatar. All the objects either created by avatars themselves or bought from market places are all stored in the inventory. All avatars have their own private inventory which is visible to them only. No one else can see it except the particular avatar.

2.3. Linden Scripting Language

Second Life has its own language called Linden Scripting Language, commonly known as LSL [7]. It is an event- driven language, which has its own events and functions. All the functions and events are present on the official wiki website of Second Life [5]. For example, few functions regarding Avatar are *llAttachToAvatar* to attach objects to the avatar. Similarly, there is another function called *llDetachFromAvatar* to detach objects from avatar. There are many numerous functions available to be used to interact with the environment. Scripts are written to bring objects to life. For example, to convert a simple glass into a money bank, we need to write a script using the appropriate events and functions. Scripts can directly be written inside SLViewer in an editor, this is convenient because it makes let the user see the effect of the script on the particular object then and there. It also makes it easy to catch the errors in the run time.

Figure 2. LSL Code Environment

2.4. Animation

Animation enables an avatar to perform some sequence of actions. For Example, An avatar has gone to a library and wants to sit on a table and read some book. As soon as Avatar will sit on the table, sitting Animation will get triggered and Avatar will get into the posture of reading a book. There is lots of software to create the animations like Qavimator, Mixamo.com, Poser, but we prefer to use *Qavimator* [11] because it gives the user friendly environment. Figure 3 depicts the environment of Qavimator. It is also called bvh animation editor, because the extension for animations accepted by Second Life is .bvh. Qavimator is widely used software because it is easily adaptable by letting the users to change each and every position of the body, from head to feet with respect to x, y, and z axis. Many types of animation can be created through this and can be imported to the SLViewer for applying to the objects.

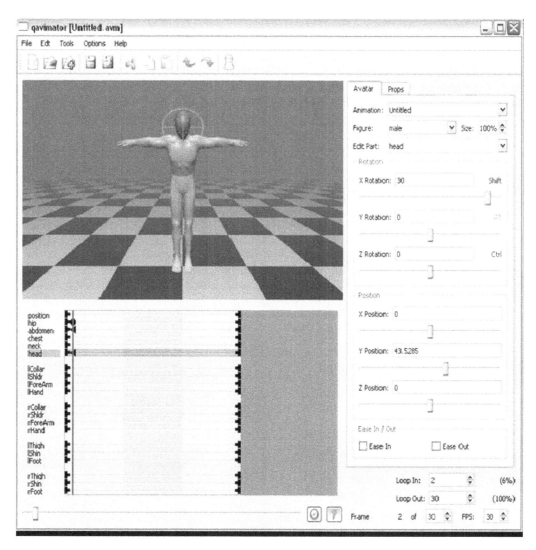

Figure 3. Snapshot of Qavimator

2.5. Textures

A texture is used to give a real face to the objects. They are like covers which are wrapped on the object to make them look real. For example, if an Avatar has created a beach chair, then they would like to give it a light colored stripped-fabric texture. The software used to make textures are GIMP - The GNU Image Manipulation Program [12], Photoshop, ArtRage2, Genetica, Texture Maker and more, but we have preferred GIMP.

2.6. Currency

Second Life has its own currency called Linden Dollars. Linden Dollars can be bought in exchange of US Dollars. Nowadays, *USD 1 = L$ 250* [13]. Residents of Second Life can create, buy and sell items in the virtual world. They can attend classes to learn about building in SL, attend concerts, party all the time and they can go to market place and do shopping. Marketplace has all type of stuff. They can be bought in exchange of Linden Dollars or for free. Business can also be conducted in Second Life, people can sell the objects created by them, and can give tuitions, sell land, rent land, teach in some school, and can do much more.

3. Implementation Using SL

We have mentioned in previous section that Second Life is an emerging technology so it keeps on changing very often. Because of its changing factor, all of its content is scattered over the internet which ends up making its users, especially the beginners confuse. Millions of residents, who are using SL since a very long time have invented their own way of explanations which they do by blogging it either on SL blogs or they have created their own forums. This makes it cumbersome and burdensome to find an exact thing. Here is an easy way to learn SL.

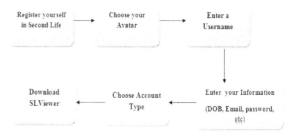

Figure 4. User's View

Figure 4 describes the introductory steps a user has to follow while stepping into the world of Second Life. The first thing a user should do is to register themselves to Second Life forum by logging in to their official website www.secondlife.com. The users are required to give their personal information including first and last name, email address and gender. Users will be asked to choose an avatar, which will represent them in the virtual world of SL. User can change the avatar later or they can create one themselves.

There are two types of accounts for a user to register as: Free and Premium. To be a Premium member a user has to pay registration fee in dollars. This type of account lets a user to buy a land where they can build their buildings and conduct the activities. Whereas free account is a limited account and the objects created by free users will not be permanent. Once user becomes a SL member, now they will require buying a land where they will be allowed to conduct any activity they like. The last step is to download the SLViewer. For users having free account is not required buy land but they can start directly. The major disadvantage of being a free member is that a user does not have their own land to work for. They have to be teleported to sandboxes, which are public places that allow residents to create objects. This is similar to the real world that no one would allow some other person to build a house or conduct any other activity within their premises. People have to buy their own properties even in Second Life.

| 1. Register, familiarize, get a land or a sandbox | 2. Learn to make Prims and Objects | 3. Learn to make Textures & add them in objects |
| 4. Learn to make animations & add them in objects | 5. Learn Scripting Language | 6. Get a SLURL |

Figure 5. Developer's View

Figure 5 shows the steps which a developer has to go through in order to be able to make something in Second Life. The first step is to get registered and also get familiarize with the environment by meeting with the people and conducting different activities. Developers also can work on both types of accounts i.e. free and premium. If they are working on a free account they will have to build objects in a Sandbox and take those objects back to their inventory to save their work. Sandboxes do not keep the stuff for longer. The premium members have the advantage of keeping the objects in their own premises as longer as they want.

The root which has to be learned is making objects from prims as prims are the building blocks of Second Life they contain the property of being stretched, moved from one place to another, rotation. Textures can be applied to them to make an object look more real. Second Life provides built-in textures though residents can make textures of their own and even buy them from marketplace. To make textures of choice an external software is used called GNU Image Manipulation Program (GIMP). The texture made has to be saved with the extension of .png in order to import image in SL. It also requires having L$10 to upload the image into the resident's inventory. Same

case is with the animation, L$ 10 are required to upload the animations in to the inventory. Once the texture and animations are uploaded into the inventory they can be reused on unlimited objects.

The last step is to have SLURL of the location. SLURL is similar to URL, they lead to the location in the virtual world of Second Life. Users can publish their SLURL for marketing their SL virtual world.

4. Literature Review

Websites are the collection of related web pages which contains content like text, images, videos, and audio. The websites are to be hosted on a web server which should be accessible by an internet connection. Hosting a site means user want to get it access globally. The collection of all website makes World Wide Web (WWW). Webpage is a simple document written in plain text with some formatting of a special language called Hyper-Text Markup Language (HTML).

Websites can be of many types. There can be a gaming website, web-based email website, academic journal website, file-sharing website, websites providing real time stock market data, social networking websites and many other websites providing millions of services.

Generally there are static and dynamic websites. A website is said to be static when the web pages are stored on a server and are brought to the client as it is when a client request for them. In other words, static webpage are once-for-all; they do not have the capability to be modified after being brought on the client machine. Static websites display same type of information to all users. Mostly informative websites are static because they do not require a user to interact with them rather they only intend to discriminate the information. Whereas, the first part, also called Dynamic Code, is constructed using an active programming language. It particularly refers to the construction of web pages. A dynamic web page is further divide into small block of codes, routines or procedures. Database has to be active in this case, because dynamically generated web pages calls and recalls information bits from it and place them together as per the format of the page and deliver the matter to the viewer.

The second part of the dynamic websites is where the dynamic content displayed in simple plain view. A website having dynamic content points out to how the messages, text, images and other information contained in it are displayed on the web page, and majorly focuses on how the change in content happens at any given time. Second Life falls in dynamic website.

The world of entertainment started from black and white television; trend slowly shifted towards colored televisions but now, we have 3D televisions. China has recently launched a 3D channel. Similarly, web sites took their start with static websites, and then shifted to dynamic; they also started supporting transactions through websites like Amazon.com. Anticipating the advancement in technology, it can be assumed that the coming era of the websites would shift to 3D websites from flat websites.

Second Life is a technology that promotes 3D websites along with virtual reality with 3D effects. It allows a user to have their own SLURL (URL which directs to the land owned by the user) and use it as a hyperlink to the location.

References

[1] "Active World." [Online]. Available: https://www.activeworlds.com/index.html. [Accessed: 15-Nov-2013].

[2] "Cyber Town," Cyber Town. [Online]. Available: http://en.wikipedia.org/wiki/CyberTown. [Accessed: 15-Nov-2013].

[3] A. Serrano, "Second Life," IS Research Paper, 2010. [Online]. Available: http://misclassblog.com/is-research-paper/research-paper-second-life-by-alan-serrano/.

[4] P. R. Michael Rymaszewski, Wagner James Au, Mark Wallace, Catherine Winters, Cory Ondrejka, Benjamin Batstone-Cunningham, Second Life: The Official Guide. John Wiley & Sons, Inc., 2006.

[5] "Second Life." [Online]. Available: http://en.wikipedia.org/wiki/Second_Life. [Accessed: 13-Nov-2013].

[6] P. R. Michael Rymaszewski, Wagner James Au, Mark Wallace, Catherine Winters, Cory Ondrejka, Benjamin Batstone-Cunningham, "Prims," in in Second Life: The Official Guide, John Wiley & Sons, Inc., 2006, p. 132.

[7] P. R. Michael Rymaszewski, Wagner James Au, Mark Wallace, Catherine Winters, Cory Ondrejka, Benjamin Batstone-Cunningham, "Linden Scripting Language," in in Second Life: The Official Guide, John Wiley & Sons, Inc., 2006, p. 212.

[8] "Standford University." [Online]. Available: http://secondlife.com/destination/600. [Accessed: 15-Nov-2013].

[9] "University of Texas." [Online]. Available: http://secondlife.com/destination/university-of-texas. [Accessed: 15-Nov-2013].

[10] "Dell Second Life." [Online]. Available: ww.dell.com/secondlife. [Accessed: 08-Jan-2013].

[11] "QAvimator." [Online]. Available: http://qavimator.org/. [Accessed: 15-Nov-2013].

[12] "GIMP." [Online]. Available: http://www.gimp.org/. [Accessed: 15-Nov-2013].

[13] "Economy of Second Life." [Online]. Available: http://en.wikipedia.org/wiki/Economy_of_Second_Life. [Accessed: 15-Nov-2013].

4

Sindhi Academic Informatic Portal

Zeeshan Bhatti[*], Dil Nawaz Hakro, Aamir Ali Jarwar

Institute of Information and communication Technology, University of Sindh, Jamshoro
*Corresponding author: zeeshan.bhatti@usindh.edu.pk

Abstract The Information and Communication Technology has been an integral part of development of any country. Sindhi Academic Informatics Portal plays a very important vital role in this context for Sindhi Speaking community. Our country is in the phase of economic development process; therefore it badly needs to build software market for the Sindhi users. The development of software products, which fulfill the Sindhi people requirements in the form of community while sharing ideas, pictures, knowledge, creative content, etc. are extremely essential and high in demand. The idea of developing this type of software can be building block of Sindhi Language revolution and it leads towards the Sindhi peoples. This academic web portal system is based on three tier architecture and follows the principle design features of Content Management System for the server side. This software is developed in PHP, JavaScript, Adobe Flash CS3, HTML, Ajax and MySQL, compatible with all operating system. The main object of this system is to provide a generalized academic and management based knowledge sharing of department to Sindhi students on the internet.

Keywords: *Sindhi, Informatics, web portal, academic portal*

1. Introduction

Portals are source of obtaining various types of information at one place. Portals provide a single interface to access the different categories of webs resources [1]. A university portal is a web based system that is responsible to facilitate and provide all-in-one mode of information access to a variety of backend resources [2,3]. Unfortunately, all the portals are rich with *English* language and in other languages and no such a system exists in *Sindhi* language. Information Portal for Sindhi students is an online web resource through which it can provide easiness of obtaining the academic information and resources quickly and easily. As most of the students live in remote area of the province, it becomes very difficult for them to come to the University for obtaining their academic information like, results, notices, course schedules, transcripts etc. Therefore this system is developed to provide a complete platform for Students of Sindh based on the knowledge sharing under one roof. The development of portals, which fulfill the people's requirements in the form of seeking online result information, course Schedule, transcript and mark sheets etc. can be effective for time of space trade off. The idea of developing this type of portal can provide Sindhi students with computing resources on the internet with rich faculties and rich information in Sindhi Language, and then our nation can be included in the list of developed nation.

The Sindhi Academic Informatics Portal is a special type of web resource designed for Sindhi community. This software is developed in PHP, AJAX, JavaScript, HTML, CSS, Adobe Flash CS 3 and MySQL for any operating system like as Windows/2000/XP/NT or Latest or Linux, UNIX. The main object of this software is to provide a platform, available on regular web browser and secure online portal facilities on the web. A secure database management system is also designed for collective resources to provide management of knowledge sharing. The resources would be connected securely to database and database would be connected to the Internet. Hence the services would be available worldwide. The Sindhi communities, Sindhi users can access their accounts on the web and wireless device without any fear of cybercrime, because strong security features are implemented in the whole system. The Sindhi community users can also view any other information depending on the Sindhi Academic Informatics Portal rules and regulations to expose the services and information for them. The major goal to develop this web resource is to remove the complex problem of Sindhi peoples, and Sindhi students etc., and facilitate them to process their knowledge sharing, and discussions so on at the palm of their hands. The designed system will provide rapid solutions, so the peoples process all kinds of knowledge sharing.

Online Portal is an extremely popular area of research and development. Yasser in his paper discusses using cellular automata for developing web portal system for Egyptian University with adaptive link-structures [4]. Moreover Shu Liu recommends a conceptual model for library portal [5], whereas Steve et al. discusses a usability study for a customized library portal [6]. Contrary to this Lin et al. introduces "playfulness in Expectation

Confirmation Theory (ECT)" in context to the use of web portals [7]. Similarly Gant investigates "the role of web portals in state-government service delivery", where findings conclude that every web portal system are still in their early stage of development [8].

2. The Database ERD

The Web Portal IICT maintains the records of examinations, course schemes, result announcements, positions, library books, teacher names etc. It completely real solution of existing problem, following ERD shows the strong relationship between tables. We used relational database management system rules and regulation. Figure 1 (a- f) shows various schematics of the ERD model of database used in this system.

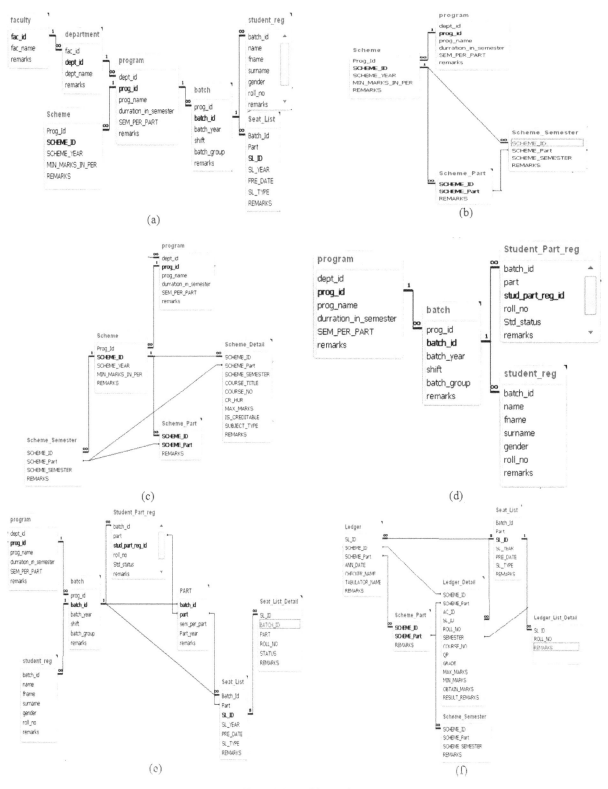

Figure 1. ERD of the Database

3. System Overview

The designed system has been generalized and is applicable for any examination wing in any university. It is totally dynamic system with strong database connectivity and relationships provided, the designed system is fully network based. A student can access the system through the local LAN network of the campus, as the system is based on SQL Server 2000; the built-in network protocol support is available in SQL server, so that LAN clients can frequently use this system without any hesitation. We used the most powerful technology (dot)Net Framework to develop this application, it is a dynamic programming language with .Net runtime environment required to run the application.The designed system is portable and can be deployed anywhere having .Net runtime environment.Up to now Microsoft provided .Net runtime environment for two platforms (Personal PC's) Windows and Linux Operating System.

Sindhi Academic InformaticsPortal has a life cycle, just like any other commercial product or portals. The process of the software development that we have used is developed by the three amigos of the UML, known as Rational Unified Process [9]. Each product passes through these stages although the duration, sequence, number of iterations and exact effect of each stage may vary. An Incremental and Iterative development process was used in Sindhi Academic informatics portal as the project will be updated and released in incremental pieces. The construction phase of Sindhi academic informatics portal consists of multiple iterations and within each stage; the quality of software is increased with testing and integration of various academic modules that satisfies a subset of the requirements for the undertaken project. Each phase of development containsthe usual life cycle phases of analysis, design, implementation, and testing [10].

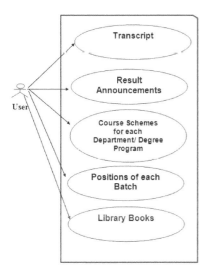

Figure 2. Simple use case diagram of the system

We established an academic foundation for the project and decided on the scope. This is where we get the commitment to go further. In elaboration, we collected more detailed requirements, done high-level analysis and design to establish baseline architecture, and created the plan for construction.

In this iterative process of software life cycle, the implementation of various modules has been left till the end for the transition phase.These modules include the testing, performance evaluation and user training. Generally as the project initially analyzed is huge in implementation and thus has been divided into numerous modules that are implemented at various phases.We tried to keep the modules to a minimum level.We have used the iterations in the initial construction of modules. Figure 2 shows the basic use case diagram of the system.

4. Implementation and Results

Although the Implementation is the fruition of chain of the efforts starting with analysis, it is most demanding stage in the Sindhi Academic Informatics Portal life cycle. In fact, if detailed design has been done properly, thought and creativity are less needed than persistence, accuracy, and attention to detail.

During the implementation stage of the system, we converted the detailed design into code in a programming language using PHP and SQL database. The major product of the implementation stage, the source code, is the ultimate goal of the entire software development process. There is real sense of accomplishment when software reaches its deliverable form. Executable code seems much more immediate, real and exciting than specifications or designs. Nevertheless, implementation is not the culmination of developers' efforts. Developers must still test the source code to determine that it meets the specifications, and that it satisfies the needs of the user.In this portal system we developed three tier architecture and Content Management System for the server side and for the online access Web Browser is used as.One of the most import point is above all systems are based on Client/server architecture; Most of the coding has been done byusing PHP & AJAX.

Figure 3(a) shows the main screen of our academic informatics portal system, built for Institute of Information and Communication Technology, University of Sindh. In this system various academic resources have been integrated for the ease of Sindhi Students.

Figure 3(b) shows the announcement module where the student can view various academic related announcements make by the administration.

Figure 3(c) shows the results section of the portal where the user can easily browse and select the class in which he belongs. The Figure 3(d) will then shows the details results sheet of the entire class with final detail results.

Once the user is in Result sheet, then he can click his roll no, to view further breakdown of his results and an online academic transcript is also displayed to him as shown in Figure 3(e).

Other modules of the portal consists of displaying the course scheme of each discipline or program course offered as shown in Figure 3(f) with details displayed in Figure 3(g), Figure 3(h).

As discussed earlier there are multiple modules and section of this portal and not all have been discussed here but are fully functional.

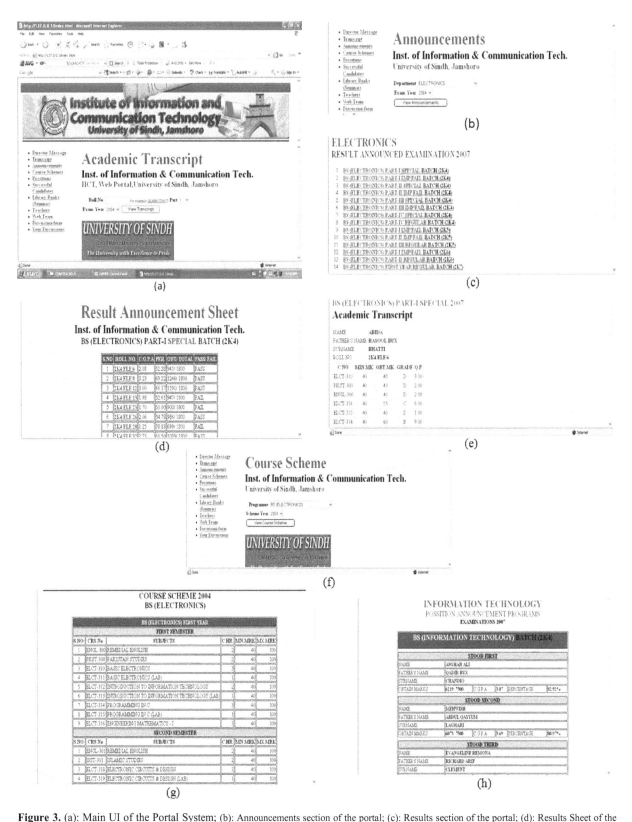

Figure 3. (a): Main UI of the Portal System; (b): Announcements section of the portal; (c): Results section of the portal; (d): Results Sheet of the Portal(e): Online Academic transcript; (f): UI of the Portal System; (g): UI of the Portal System; (h): UI of the Portal System

4.1. Testing

Testing is the last stage of software development, before a developer releases the product to the customer. During testing of Sindhi Academic Informatics Portal, we tried to make sure that the product does exactly what it is supposed to do.The testing stage goes beyond a simple effort of running the academic webportal with some input to see whether it works properly. A major activity of testing is the disclosure and correction of errors in the specification, design and code. Three different kinds of tests were performed, Unit test, Integration Test and System acceptance test. Initially Unit test was performed, which investigates the correctness of individual modules and checks for the structural weaknesses within the system if any. Secondly Integration tests, where the interactions of modules and the functionality of integrated subsystems are examined. Finally, System and acceptance tests were performed, which determine whether the final product complies with the user's original specifications or not.

5. Conclusion and Future Work

In this paper we presented a academic web portal with a new framework for providing more knowledge and information to Sindhi students,teachers and Sindhi Community. The above portal is designed and developed by using the modern programming languages.It is concluded that the Software "Sindhi Academic Informatics Portal" is efficient, reliable, portable and user-friendly. It is effectively and accurately applicable for heterogeneous network environment where internet facility exists.It is also concluded that Sindhi academic informatics portal is designed in such a manner that it costs less and provides a lot of benefits and is easily expandable due to incremental framework of various modules.

In future we will implement and increase the functionality of the system with dynamic user intervention, increasing the modules to incorporate various other academic resources such as admission information, pass certificates, marks sheet correction, verification requests and updates, etc. and adding the digital signatures for the security purpose.

References

[1] Wikipedia, "Web Portal" retrieved on ; December, 2012, URL: http://en.wikipedia.org/wiki/Web_portal.

[2] Luca, V., Epicoco, I., Lezzi, D., and Aloisio, G., *A web API framework for developing grid portals*, procedia computer science 4, pp. 392-401, 2011.

[3] Bringula, R., *Influence of faculty- and web portal design- related factors on web portal usability: A hierarchical regression analysis*, computer & education 68, pp. 187-198, 2013.

[4] Hassan, Y. F. (2013) *"Cellular Automata For Adaptive Web Portal Structure In Egyptian Universities"*.International Journal of Engineering Sciences & Emerging Technologies, Volume 6, Issue 2, pp: 133-141.

[5] Liu, S. (2008). *Engaging users: the future of academic library web sites*.College & Research Libraries, 69(1), 6-27.

[6] Brantley, S., Armstrong, A., & Lewis, K. M. (2006). *Usability testing of a customizable library web portal*. College & Research Libraries, 67(2), 146-163.

[7] Lin, C. S., Wu, S., & Tsai, R. J. (2005). *Integrating perceived playfulness into expectation-confirmation model for web portal context*. Information & Management, 42(5), 683-693.

[8] Gant, J. P., & Gant, D. B. (2002, January). *Web portal functionality and State government E-service*. In System Sciences, 2002. HICSS. Proceedings of the 35th Annual Hawaii International Conference on (pp. 1627-1636). IEEE.

[9] Wikipedia, "Unified Modeling Language" retrieved on December, 2012, URL: http://en.wikipedia.org/wiki/Unified_Modeling_Language.

[10] Wikipedia, "Iterative and incremental development", retrieved on; December, 2012, URL: http://en.wikipedia.org/wiki/Iterative_and_incremental_development.

5

In-Depth Analysis of the Arabic Version of the Felder-Silverman Index of Learning Styles

Nahla Aljojo[1,*], Carl Adams[2], Abeer Alkhouli[3], Huda Saifuddin[4], Iqbal Alsaleh[5]

[1]Faculty of Computing and Information Technology, Information Systems Department, King AbdulAziz University, Jeddah, KSA
[2]School of Computing, University of Portsmouth, Portsmouth, UK, Buckingham Building, Lion Terrace, Portsmouth PO1 3HE
[3]Faculty of Sciences, Department of Statistics, King AbdulAziz University, Jeddah, KSA
[4]Arts and Humanities College, Cognitive Psychology Department, King AbdulAziz University, Makkah, KSA
[5]Faculty of Economics and Administration, Information Systems Department, King AbdulAziz University, Jeddah, KSA
*Corresponding author: naljojo@kau.edu.sa

Abstract The aim of this paper is to compare learning style characteristics from two very different linguistic and cultural groups to see how homogeneous they are.. The paper analyses the learning styles of a large sample of Arabic learners using the first validated Arabic version of the Felder-Silverman learning style model (FSLSM), and compares these with samples from English learners in previous studies, notably a study from Graf et al. The analysis takes the form of linear discriminant analysis, cross validated by frequencies and correlation analysis to identify representative characteristics of each learning style dimension and to determine how representative these characteristics are within the different samples. To ensure robust methodological support, the paper applies the methods used by Graf et al., therefore providing a direct comparison between the English and Arabic groups of learners from the two studies. Our results show differences between representative characteristics for the different learning cohorts, which could indicate that culture and learning environment have an influence on learning style preferences.

Keywords: *learning styles, Felder-Silverman learning style model, discriminant analysis, Arabic cohort*

1. Introduction

As Reigeluth (1996) [1] has observed, in the context of education, "one size does not fit all". Research indicates that the characteristics of learners differ [2] and intimates that these variations manifest themselves with regard to learning, processing information, representation of knowledge and the forms of educational resources that are preferred. As Rasmussen (1998) [3] has noted, a student's learning style may be diagnosed, and certain learners progress better utilising modes of instruction tailored to their individual needs. These needs may be met via employment of instruction enriched with technology; flexible and organic systems of education have the potential to generate an environment in which individual needs are satisfied. However, these adaptive learning supports are dominated by English-language examples based on English versions of psychometric learning style instruments.

The most appropriate psychometric instrument found to support adaptive learning systems is the Felder-Silverman learning style model (FSLSM) [4,5], as it has been success-fully implemented in previous works when individually adapting the electronic learning material [6,7,8,9]. From a system design perspective, it is also practical, enabling a number of learning dimensions to be represented and implemented; and the corresponding results are easy to interpret [8]. Bajraktarevic et al., (2003) [10], for example, confirmed the benefits of providing adaptivity in a study showing that students taking an online course that matched their preferred learning style (sequential or global) achieved significantly better results than those who took a course that did not match their preferred learning style.

Notwithstanding, it did not appear that any robust Arabic variant existed, though a literal translation example was acquired by contacting Professor Felder. The literal translation proved to be inadequate in accurately capturing the psychometric attributes within the instrument. In the following stage, a more accurate Arabic version was produced, which involved obtaining permission and advice from the authors of the FSLSM with regard to carrying out a thorough verification of the instrument in Arabic [11]. This verification consisted of an iterative process involving blind forward and backward translation and the participation of a bilingual psychologist and education and linguistics experts. The validated Arabic FSLSM instrument was then applied to a sample of 1,024 female students in the faculties of Arts and Humanities and Economics and Administration at King Abdul-Aziz University in Saudi Arabia [12] as part of the process of developing an Arabic adaptive learning system (in this case to support the teaching of statistics to undergraduate students).

The development of adaptive systems often draws upon learning style models; however, the majority of adaptive systems incorporate only some aspects of these traditional learning style models rather than all proposed characteristics of the model. This is motivated by the restriction of most adaptive systems to specific functions and a specific course structure [13], but also for practical reasons (e.g. some learning style char-acteristics may not have sensible alternative presentations for the learning material). When conducting investigations into learning styles, it is therefore important to consider which characteristics of the learning style model are supported by the system. The development of an efficient adaptive learning system is likely to be aided by understanding the dominant learning characteristics and preferences of the target cohort of learners [14].

There is clearly a question about the level of homogeneity among learning style characteristics across different cultures and learning environments. There may be subtle differences embedded in the different language constructs, all of which may influence the representative characteristics and preferences of different learning cohorts, and consequently the design of efficient adaptive learning support. What is needed is a robust comparison of learning style characteristics between different groups of learners from different educational, cultural and linguistic environments. For this research, we compared the work of Graf et al. (2007) [14], which was based on English-speaking samples (from New Zealand and Austria) and a learning environment using an English version of the FSLSM, with the results of our own sample from within an Arabic learning environment. In order to ensure that the comparison was robust, we followed the same methods adopted by Graf et al. (2007) [14], thereby making direct comparison possible.

The primary approach of the method developed by Graf et al. is to develop a graded characterisation within the four dimensions of the FSLSM and to use tools such as linear discriminant analysis to examine the representativeness within these dimensions of each characteristic of the sample responses. The results of the study will then be used to guide the design of an improved adaptation process.

The structure of this paper roughly follows that of Graf et al.'s research (2007) [14], as follows: first there will be a discussion of the Felder-Silverman learning style theory. The paper then discusses the development of the Arabic adapted learning system, which raised questions about the homogeneousness of learning style characteristics and provided stimulus for the research. Next, the paper discusses the methods and the different stages of the process, including methods used to identify the semantic grouping and classification of characteristics within the instrument. The paper then discusses the results of applying these classifications to the responses, including applying linear discriminant analysis, and the cross-validation methods used. Next, the paper compares these results with those of Graf et al. before providing further discussion about the implications of the results, limitations of the work and areas for further study.

1.1. Felder-Silverman Learning Style Theory

There are a number of theories regarding individual learning styles, including those of Pask (1976) [15], Honey and Mumford (1986) [2], Kolb (1984)[16] and Felder and Silverman (1988) [17]. Most descriptions of individual learning styles categorise people into only a limited number of groups. However, the FSLSM goes further: this system differentiates preferences on four dimensional levels, thus allowing adaptive education systems to create learning systems that are more tailored towards learners' preferences. Felder notes that students with pronounced preferences in their learning styles may encounter hardships in perceiving information delivered via methods not congruent with these preferences [17,18].

The FSLSM [17] identifies four dimensions in which to categorise the learning styles of individuals; these can be observed independently and illustrate the ways in which individuals prefer to process (active/reflective), perceive (sensing/intuitive), receive (verbal/visual), and understand (sequential/global) information. The first table describes, in brief, the contextual preferences of typical learners from each of the four dimensions of the Felder-Silverman model.

Table 1. Felder's learning dimensions [6]

Description	Dimension		Description
Learn by working in groups and handling things.	Active	Reflective	Learn better when they can think and reflect about the information presented to them. Work better alone or with one other person at most.
Prefer to deal with facts, raw data and experiments; patient with details, but don't like complications.	Sensing	Intuitive	Prefer to deal with principles and theories, are easily bored when presented with details and tend to accept complications.
Easily remember what they see: images, diagrams, timetables, films, etc.	Visual	Verbal	Remember what they've heard, read or said.
Follow a linear reasoning process when solving problems and can work with a specific material once they've understood it partially or superficially.	Sequential	Global	Take large intuitive leaps with the information; may have difficulty when explaining how they got to a certain result; require an integral vision.

1.2. Development of an Arabic Adaptive Learning System Based on the FSLSI

Several educational systems have been developed that adapt to learning styles, including the system of Carver et al. (1999a) [6], the Arthur system [19], MASPLANG [20], INSPIRE [21], TANGOW [8], and the AHA! system created by Cristea and de Bra (2006). Many researchers currently agree on the importance of modelling and using learning styles. However, there is little agreement on

which aspects of learning styles are worth modelling and what can be done differently for users with different styles [22].

The first such adaptive system produced in Arabic was the Teacher Assisting and Subject Adaptive Material (TASAM) system [4,12]. The TASAM system used Felder and Silverman's learning style theory to determine an individual's preferred learning style and then presented learners with material based on their learning style preferences within the four dimensions of sensing-intuitive, visual-verbal, active-reflective and sequential-global [17,23].

The TASAM system used an adaptive teaching taxonomy that integrated learning styles with teaching strategies to select learning materials to be presented to individual learners via electronic media. This taxonomy was constructed based on an evaluation of the Soloman-Felder learning style theory and builds on previous work, such as that of Franzoni et al. (2008) [24], which employed an expert panel using the Delphi method. The TASAM system was initially applied to a statistics course aimed at first-level undergraduates across two faculties at the King Abdul-Aziz University in Saudi Arabia [4,12].

The subject of statistics was chosen for several reasons. Firstly, expert-refined and validated learning materials were available, which were kindly provided by evaluation of a teacher. Secondly, it was a relatively straightforward task to redesign statistics-related materials for a computer-based environment. Thirdly, statistics was considered to be a timely and desirable learning objective for potential participants. Finally, statistics is an abstract topic, which presented opportunities to develop different representations for the same concept by employing different representational forms within electronic media. The statistics course using the TASAM system ran between 2010 and 2011.

The adaptation model in TASAM specified the way in which the presentation of content should be adapted based on learning styles. It was implemented as a set of classically structured 'if condition, then action' style rules. These rules form the connection between the domain model and the learner model in order to update the learner model and provide appropriate learning materials. Following Kinshuk and Lin (2003) [25], moderate and strong preferences were grouped together to enable 16 combinations of learning style dimensions from which representational templates were generated (see Table 2). While working on the development of the Arabic adaptive learning system based on learning style instruments developed for English-based learning environments, questions emerged about the homogeneousness of learning style characteristics across language, environment and culture. This provided the stimulus for the current research.

Table 2. 16 combinations of learning style dimensions

Combinations of learning style dimensions
active/sensing/visual/sequential
active/sensing/visual/global
active/sensing/verbal/sequential
active/sensing/verbal/global
active/intuitive/visual/sequential
active/intuitive/visual/global
active/intuitive/verbal/sequential
active/intuitive/verbal/global
reflective/sensing/visual/sequential
reflective/sensing/visual/global
reflective/sensing/verbal/sequential
reflective/sensing/verbal/global
reflective/intuitive/visual/sequential
reflective/intuitive/visual/global
reflective/intuitive/verbal/sequential
reflective/intuitive/verbal/global

2. Methodology

The method consisted of following the approach used by Graf et al. (2007) [14], which involved the selection of a relevant sample to test the learning style instrument, followed by the use of a variety of tools to ascertain and analyse the learning style characteristics and representativeness of the sample responses.

2.1. Participants

The Arabic version of the ILS questionnaire was applied to a selection of 1,024 female bachelor's degree students from two faculties at the King Abdul-Aziz University in Saudi Arabia: namely, the Arts and Humanities faculty (consisting of two different departments: Arabic Psychology and Mass Communication) and the Economics and Administration faculty (consisting of five departments: Public Administration, Accounting, Economics, Political Science, Law and Business Administration).

Table 3. Semantic Groups Associated with the Arabic Index of Learning Styles (ILS) Questions, Grouped Manually

Style	Semantic group	Arabic ILS questions	Style	Semantic group	Arabic ILS questions
		(Answer a)			(Answer b)
Active	Trying something out	1, 17, 25, 29	**Reflective**	Think about material	1, 5, 17, 25, 29
	Socially oriented	5, 9, 13, 21, 33, 37, 41		Impersonally oriented	9, 13, 21, 33, 41, 37
Sensing	Existing ways	2, 26, 30, 34	**Intuitive**	Innovative or creative	2, 14, 22, 26, 30, 34
	Concrete material	6, 10, 14, 18, 38		Abstract material	10, 38
	Careful with details	22, 42		Not careful with details	42
				Dealing with theory	6, 18
Visual	Pictures	3, 7, 11, 15, 19, 23, 27, 31, 35, 39, 43	**Verbal**	Spoken words	3, 15, 19, 27, 35
				Written words	7, 11, 23, 31, 39
				Difficulty with visual style	43
Sequential	Detail oriented	4, 28, 40, 44	**Global**	Overall picture	4, 8, 20, 16, 28, 40
	Sequential progress	12, 20, 24, 32		Non-sequential progress	24, 32
	From parts to the whole	8, 16		Relations	36
	Focusing on subjects	36		Thinking about results	12, 44

2.2. Manual Grouping of Questions

Continuing with the method used by Graf et al. (2007) [14], there then followed a manual grouping of questions within the ILS according to the similarity of semantics. Table 3 shows the semantic groups identified for each learning style as well as the questions belonging to each of these groups. A question may appear twice in Table 3 if the answer to this question points to two different semantic groups. The original work of Graf et al. (2007) [14] in the previous version have been identified the semantic groups according to English ILS question . in our study we identified the semantic groups according to the Arabic ILS questions.

The semantic groups of Table 3 have been identified manually by three experts psychologists from department of Psychology at the King Abdul-Aziz University in Saudi Arabia as following:

1-   Identified the Arabic ILS questions in the same category for each learning style , such as the questions (1, 17, 25, 29) Identified in the same learning style so these questions are posted in the semantic group (Trying something out).

2.3. Classification of Learner Preferences

Learners' preferences were classified by analysing the distribution of preferences for each dimension within the Arabic Index of Learning Styles (ILS) questionnaire, resulting in Table 4, which categorises learners' preferences as strong/moderate (values from 5 to 11) or balanced (values from +3 to -3).

Table 4. Strength of Preferences (distinguishing between strong/moderate and balanced preferences) in the Data from the Arabic Index of Learning Styles Questionnaire

Str./mod.ACT	Balanced	Str./mod. Ref	Str./ mod. Sen	Balanced	Str./mod. Int	Str./mod. Vis	Balanced	Str./mod.Ver	Str./mod.Seq	Balanced	Str./mod.Glo
26%	64%	10%	20%	62%	18%	60%	37%	3%	24%	66%	10%

2.4. Semantic Grouping by Linear Discriminant Analysis

The next stage in Graf et al.'s (2007) [14] method was to use the classifications provided in Table 3 to determine the most representative groups for each learning style and to find the most representative semantic groups for each dimension. This activity was based on linear discriminant analysis.

Fisher's linear discriminant analysis, a common multivariate technique used for linear dimension reduction, was performed to identify the most characteristic semantic groups within each dimension (Duda et al., 2000) [26]. The following details of applying the linear discriminant analysis are drawn from the work of Graf et al. (2007) [14].

Let A be the 1024 x 88 matrix containing in rows individuals and in columns the a_i, i=1,...,88. The matrix A has rank at most 44 by construction, since two columns are constrained to sum up to 1 in rows [14].

The answers provided to the Arabic ILS questionnaire were then subjected to Fisher's linear discriminant analysis (LDA) in terms of matrix A.

This technique is a commonly employed multivariate method of reducing dimensions and can be used to identify the optimal linear direction of separation. This is calculated using a typically one-dimensional vector of coefficient w that highlights the separation between groups. Using this vector, the highest absolute values of coefficients are indicative of the most significant discrimination variables. Thus, this study used LDA to identify significant discriminating variables within each FSLSM dimension of the ILS system based on the responses given by participants. In effect, X being an m-by-n matrix, let $w`m_i^{(1)}$ and $w`m_i^{(2)}$, $i=1,...,n$ be the d-dimensional sample means of the projected points according to the classes of individuals, and ($1/m$) ($s_1^2 + s_2^2$) an estimate of the whole variance of the pooled data, where

$$SC^2 = \sum_{x \in C_i} w`x_i - w`m_i^{(c)} \qquad (1)$$

and c $\in$ C = { 1,...,k } indicates the class; LDA aimed at finding a vector w that maximises the criterion function

$$J(w) = \frac{\left| w`m_i^{(1)} - w`m_i^{(2)} \right|^2}{s1^2 + s2^2} \qquad (2)$$

As a means of determining the significance of each semantic class within each dimension, the coefficients of w in terms of each possible answer were analysed according to a mock index that listed the importance of each group based on dimension; this was determined by identifying the average of absolute coefficient values as listed in Table 3. The findings are listed in Table 5.

2.5. Cross-Validation

The next step was to cross-validate the results. To this end, both Pearson's correlation and frequency analysis were used. Let Q be the 1024 x 44 matrix containing in rows individuals and in columns the answer to each of the Arabic Index of Learning Styles (ILS) questions. For each question q_i, Q = 44, two numerical variables, namely the two answers to each question, $a1$ = 1 if q_i = 1 (otherwise 0) and $a2$ = 1 if q_i = -1 (otherwise 0) were obtained (Graf et al., 2007). Table 6 summarises the results of the frequency analysis.

3. Results

3.1. Classification of Learner Preferences

Firstly, the distribution of preferences for each dimension was examined. The results showed that 61% of the students had an 'active' learning preference, 56% had a 'sensing' preference, 88% had a 'visual' preference, and 62% displayed a 'sequential' preference.

Table 4 contains a more in-depth breakdown, categorising learners' preferences as strong/moderate (values from 5 to 11 in the data from the Arabic Index of Learning Styles questionnaire) or balanced (values from +3 to -3 in the data from the Arabic Index of Learning Styles questionnaire).

3.2. Linear Discriminant Analysis

The linear discriminant analysis identified four clusters. The attributes of each of these clusters are presented in Table 5.

Significant elements in the clusters are represented by the figures in bold.

Table 5. Relevance of Semantic Groups in Learning Style Dimensions in the Data from the Arabic Index of Learning Styles Questionnaire (values > 0.5 are highlighted)

ILS	Semantic Groups	Cluster 4	Cluster 3	Cluster 2	Cluster 1
		ACT/REF	SENS/INT	VIS/VERB	SEQ/GLO
Active	Try something out	**0.523**	0.402	**0.541**	0.346
	Socially oriented	**0.694**	**0.502**	**0.659**	**0.58**
Reflective	Think about material	0.444	**0.541**	0.435	**0.609**
	Impersonally oriented	0.305	**0.53**	0.342	0.419
Sensing	Existing ways	**0.79**	**0.811**	**0.561**	0.379
	Concrete material	0.32	**0.513**	**0.752**	0.27
	Careful with details	**0.527**	**0.521**	0.4	0.215
Intuitive	Innovative or creative	0.34	0.308	**0.514**	**0.729**
	Abstract material	**0.799**	**0.583**	0.246	**0.748**
	Not careful with details	0.362	0.469	0.339	**0.539**
	Dealing with theory	**0.725**	0.463	0.223	**0.729**
Visual	Pictures	**0.79**	**0.544**	**0.817**	**0.68**
Verbal	Spoken words	0.186	0.343	0.153	0.268
	Written words	0.251	**0.607**	0.227	0.394
	Difficulty with visual style	0.122	0.271	0.117	0.214
Sequential	Detail oriented	0.428	0.485	0.407	0.302
	Sequential progress	**0.74**	**0.673**	**0.713**	**0.52**
	From parts to the whole	**0.714**	**0.594**	**0.652**	**0.547**
	Focusing on the subjects	**0.611**	**0.671**	0.476	0.338
Global	Overall picture	0.474	0.474	**0.53**	**0.595**
	Non-sequential progress	0.304	0.419	0.331	**0.588**
	Relations/connections	0.389	0.33	**0.524**	**0.662**
	Thinking about results	0.225	0.25	0.187	0.434

The clusters show interesting profiles for different groups of learners. For instance, since a high value indicates a strong impact of the semantic group for the respective learning style, it can be seen that for an active learning style the preference for social orientation (e.g., for discussing and explaining learning materials to others or for working in groups) has more impact than the preference for trying something out (e.g., "Let's try it out and see how it works").

Active learners tend to like group work, and as a further impact relating to preferences tend to be patient with details and good at memorising facts, more comfortable with abstractions, better at remembering what they see (pictures, diagrams), and tend to gain understanding in linear steps, with each step following logically from the previous one. Further study is required, as the FSLSM does not describe these relationships.

Each group in the sensing/intuitive dimension shows a predilection for the 'sensing' learning characteristics, notably in terms of fondness for existing ways (e.g., enjoying courses that have connections to the real world and disliking innovation). A fondness for abstract material

(e.g., for finding interpretations or theories that link facts) is most common among intuitive learners.

Additional study is required, as the FSLSM does not account for these connections – for instance, there is an extra influence in the observations pertaining to the sensing/intuitive dimension in terms of a preference for learning by working in groups and handling things; periodically reviewing what has been read and thinking of possible questions and applications; remembering what has been seen, such as pictures and diagrams; getting the most out of written and spoken explanations; and gaining understanding in linear, logical steps.

Only a picture preference (e.g., remembering what is seen, such as pictures and diagrams) semantic group exists within the visual learning style – also very common – but in the verbal learning style, no common semantic can be identified.

In terms of the sequential/global dimension, highly pertinent factors for these learning styles include relations/connections, overall pictures, and non-sequential progress (e.g., skimming through an entire chapter to get an overview before starting to study specific information and relating the subject to information already known in order to see the bigger picture). For 'global' individuals, the most relevant preference is that for relations and connections to other areas; for sequential learners, the ability to infer the whole solution from parts and make sequential progress (e.g., outlining course lecture material in a logical order) are the most relevant.

3.3. Cross-Validation

3.3.1. Empirical Frequency Analysis

The empirical frequency analysis aspect of the cross-validation process examined how participants favouring a particular learning style responded to specific questions. In terms of the active/reflective dimension, for example, a question was deemed representative if an 'active' student responded to it with more clarity more frequently than a 'reflective' participant. Therefore, to validate the representative nature of queries in the active/reflective dimension, a comparison was made between the number of 'active' participants who responded with active

preferences and the number of 'reflective' participants who responded with active preferences.

The representative nature of a question for the active/reflective dimension is signalled by the discrepancies in these percentages. Similar calculations were therefore carried out for the other dimensions. A divergence of 30%+ was noted in 7 questions in the active/reflective dimension, 6 in the sensing/intuitive, 11 in the visual/verbal and 8 in the sequential/global. Table 6 shows the 5 questions with the greatest representativeness (in order of rank).

To interpret the table, in relation to the active/reflective dimension, for instance, evidently the primary and tertiary questions in terms of relevance concern preferences among learners for trying things out and thinking about the learned material, whereas the secondary, fourth and fifth most relevant questions concern social orientation, inquiring as to whether learners are extroverted and social within their class groups and enjoy team exercises. The Index of Learning Styles Questionnaire (available at www.engr.ncsu.edu/learningstyles/ilsweb.html) was used.

Table 6. The Five Most Representative Questions for Each Dimension of the Arabic Index of Learning Styles (ILS) Questionnaire According to Frequency Analysis

	Rank	Question No	Question
Active/Reflective	1	17	When I start a homework problem, I am more likely to (a) start working on the solution immediately (b) try to fully understand the problem first.
	2	37	I am more likely to be considered (a) outgoing (b) reserved.
	3	29	I more easily remember (a) something I have done (b) something I have thought a lot about.
	4	9	In a study group working on difficult material, I am more likely to (a) jump in and contribute ideas (b) sit back and listen.
	5	5	When I am learning something new, it helps me to (a) talk about it (b) think about it.
Sensing/Intuitive	1	26	When I am reading for enjoyment, I like writers to (a) clearly say what they mean (b) say things in creative, interesting ways.
	2	34	I consider it higher praise to call someone (a) sensible (b) imaginative.
	3	2	I would rather be considered (a) realistic (b) innovative.
	4	10	I find it easier (a) to learn facts (b) to learn concepts.
	5	6	If I were a teacher, I would rather teach a course (a) that deals with facts and real life situations (b) that deals with ideas and theories.
Visual/Verbal	1	15	I like teachers (a) who put a lot of diagrams on the board (b) who spend a lot of time explaining.
	2	43	I tend to picture places I have been (a) easily and fairly accurately (b) with difficulty and without much detail.
	3	19	I remember best (a) what I see (b) what I hear.
	4	39	For entertainment, I would rather (a) watch television (b) read a book.
	5	35	When I meet people at a party, I am more likely to remember (a) what they looked like (b) what they said about themselves.
Sequential/Global	1	12	When I solve math problems (a) I usually work my way to the solutions one step at a time (b) I often just see the solutions but then have to struggle to figure out the steps to get to them
	2	28	When considering a body of information, I am more likely to (a) focus on details and miss the big picture (b) try to understand the big picture before getting into the details.
	3	16	When I'm analysing a story or a novel (a) I think of the incidents and try to put them together to figure out the themes (b) I just know what the themes are when I finish reading and then I have to go back and find the incidents that demonstrate them.
	4	20	It is more important to me that an instructor (a) lays out the material in clear sequential steps (b) gives me an overall picture and relates the material to other subjects.
	5	44	When solving problems in a group, I would be more likely to (a) think of the steps in the solution process (b) think of possible consequences or applications of the solution in a wide range of areas.

3.3.2. Correlation Analysis

Correlations were calculated spanning the total positive responses to each of the 88 responses generated by the ILS questionnaire (with 2 possibilities for each question), and the information was converted from a binary scale into a numerical equivalent in order to apply Pearson's correlation coefficient.

Numerous augmented (higher than 0.7) values were observed, and the p values related to these values were minimal ($p < 0.05$), which is important. Significance was noted for questions belonging to the range of semantic groups linked with the active/reflective, sensing/ intuitive and sequential/global dimensions and questions that were cross-correlative among those groups, as well as for questions pertaining to the semantic groups related to the visual/verbal dimension (pictures/spoken and written words).

4. Further Comparison Between the Two Studies: Preferences in Saudi Arabian Sample and Preferences in New Zealand and Austrian Samples

The study conducted by Graf et al. (2007) [14] is based on a 207-member sample group from Massey University in New Zealand and the University of Technology in Vienna. The members of this sample group had achieved varying levels of education and were drawn from the departments of Web Engineering, Information Management and Information Systems. The sample groups consequently display significant differences, which allows for comparison in order to explore the homogeneity of learning style characteristics.

4.1. Classification of Learner Preferences

Looking at the overview of similar studies provided by Felder and Spurlin in 2005, the results of the present study are largely coherent; there are a number of minute divergences in the sensing/intuitive dimension because a fractionally greater number of intuitive subjects participated in this study. As well, in comparison with the overview of similar studies provided by Graf et al. in 2007, some differences can be seen in the sequential/global dimension where more sequential learners have participated in the Manual Grouping of Questions.

The comparison between the semantic groups associated with the Arabic Index of Learning Styles (ILS) questions and the English Index of Learning Styles (ILS) questions as follows:

- results concerning the active/reflective, sensing, and visual/verbal dimensions are generally the same as the results generated by Graf et al. (2007) [14].
- results concerning the intuitive, sequential/global and verbal dimensions show some differences when compared to the results generated by Graf et al. (2007) [14].

4.2. Analysis of Semantic Groups of the Learning Style Dimensions Using Linear Discriminant Analysis

Most participants in Saudi Arabia expressed a preference for socially inclined within the active dimension, which was the least represented attribute in the reflective dimension. However, in New Zealand and Austria, the majority of participants expressed a preference for trying something out in the active dimension and impersonal orientation within the reflective dimension. Existing ways was the most representative element of the sensing/intuitive dimension in Saudi Arabia, whereas in the other two countries, it was concrete material in the sensing dimension, while abstract materials was most prominent in the intuitive dimension in the case of all three nations. In the visual/verbal dimension, the majority of Saudi Arabian students preferred pictures only, whereas for the other two nations, the preference was for written and spoken words as well as pictures; however, in the sequential/global dimension, students in all three countries expressed a preference for from parts to the whole and relations/connections (see Table 7).

Table 7. Comparison of Preferences and Semantic Groups Between Saudi Arabia and New Zealand/Austria

Dimension	Most representative preferences and semantic groups in Saudi Arabia (this study)	Most representative preferences and semantic groups in New Zealand and Austria (Graf *et al.* study)
Active	Socially oriented	Trying something out
Reflective	Non-most representative preferences	Impersonally oriented
Sensing	Existing ways	Concrete material
Verbal	Non-most representative preferences	Written and spoken words

Different representative characteristics were found in the English-speaking and Arabic-speaking samples, with the primary differences based in the active, reflective, sensing, and verbal dimensions. Thus, the representative characteristics of learning style preferences do not seem to be homogeneous across the English-speaking and Arabic-speaking learner sample groups.

5. Discussion

In the classification of learner preferences, the results of this study generally correlate with the overview provided by Felder and Spurlin in 2005 of similar studies; there are a number of minute divergences in the sens-ing/intuitive dimension because there were a fractionally greater number of intuitive subjects in this sample group. Also, in comparison with the results generated by Graf et al. (2007) [14], variations were detected in the sequential/global

dimension, as more learners of this style formed part of the sample group. In addition, based on the preference data, the results generated by our study are largely complementary to those found by Graf et al. (2007) [14]. This information can be seen in Table 4.

Following analysis of the clusters, the most common aspects of learning styles were identified using discriminant analysis. Table 3 outlines these results. According to these findings, most participants from the Saudi Arabian sample expressed a preference for socially oriented within the active dimension, which was the least represented attribute in the reflective dimension. In comparison, in New Zealand and Austria, most participants showed a preference for trying something out within the active dimension and impersonal orientation within the reflective dimension. Existing ways was the most representative element of the sensing/intuitive dimension in Saudi Arabia, whereas in the other two countries, it was concrete material in the sensing dimension, while abstract materials was most prominent in the intuitive dimension in the case of all three nations. In the visual/verbal dimension, the majority of Saudi Arabian students preferred pictures only, whereas in the other two nations, the preference was for written and spoken words as well as pictures; however, in the sequential/global dimension, students in all three countries showed a preference for from parts to the whole and relations/connections (see Table 5).

Given that many adaptive learning systems are centred on only a limited number of learning style elements as opposed to the entirety of suggested characteristics, it is important to identify which features of learning styles should be supported by such a system. LDA appears to be a suitable means of identifying representative characteristics, and it also appears that it may be used to produce indications of greater accuracy pertaining to the significance of each characteristic. The LDA tool may be used to determine which learning style characteristics should be used in an adaptive learning system for a particular cohort of learners.

Key findings from this study seem to indicate that representative characteristics of learning style preferences are not homogeneous across English-speaking and Arabic-speaking learner sample groups. There is a clear requirement for further research exploring representative characteristics of learning style preferences for other groups of learners, including how much these characteristics vary between groups and how adaptive learning systems should be designed to address the needs of specific groups.

The results of this study will be used to further develop learning environment to guide the design of an improved adaptation algorithm, as follows:

1- Reduce the 16 combinations of learning style dimensions to 4 combinations of learning styles, as the most representative preferences and semantic groups in Saudi Arabia were in the dimensions of active, sensing/intuitive, visual and sequential/global. We were able to reduce the combinations of learning styles from 16 to 4 (A/S/V/S, A/S/V/G, A/I/V/S, and A/I/V/G).

2- In creating adaptations of our system, utilise questions based on the preference for socially oriented in the active dimension, such as questions 5, 9, 13, 21, 33, 37 and 41, thus reducing the questions concerning the active dimension from 11 to 7.

3- In the sensing/intuitive dimension, utilise questions based on the preference for discussion of existing ways (such as questions 2, 30 and 34) for the sensing dimension or questions based on abstract material for the intuitive dimension (such as questions 10 and 38), thus reducing 'sensing' questions from 11 to 3 and 'intuitive' questions from 11 to 2.

4- Only the visual employ questions grounded in visual preference, such as questions regarding discussion of pictures (i.e. questions 3, 7, 11, 15, 19, 23, 27, 31, 35, 39, and 43).

5- For the sequential dimension, utilise questions based on the preference for from parts to the whole (8, 16) and questions based on the relations/connections preference (36) for the global dimension, thus reducing 'sequential' questions from 11 to 2 and 'global' questions from 11 to 1.

6- We adapted our system to be based on 26 of the FSILS questions of instead of all 44, thus making the

enrolment and learning style capture process easier for users and making the corresponding adaptation more efficient.

6. Study Limitations and Areas for Future Research

There are clearly limitations to this study. Firstly, the sample used, though relatively large (1,024), was biased as all participants were drawn from one university in Saudi Arabia and all were female undergraduates. Similarly, the samples from Graf el al.'s study (2007) used for comparison had their own biases. However, the samples used for comparison could be classified as distinct groups based on language, learning environment and culture, and thus provide a valid base for exploring the homogeneousness of learning style characteristics. Further studies involving learners from different cultural groups with a more balanced mix of gender, language, and culture would clearly add to this area of research and help map the variations of learning style characteristics. Such work would contribute to the development of a comprehensive overview of the attributes of learning style preferences that could inform the development of adaptive learning support systems.

There may also be biases within the learning styles instrument and the analysis tools used. For instance, using a different learning styles model may produce different results; the same applies to the analysis tools used as well as the overall method. There is clearly an opportunity for further research in exploring relevant learning style characteristics using other learning style instruments or other tools of analysis.

We have identified possible cultural, linguistic and educational environment influences on learning style preferences. There may also be other influences on learning styles, such as performance, student characteristics or cognitive traits. It is obvious that further research is required to investigate these differences. In addition, the formulation of learning style characteristics can be used to quickly identify the learning styles of individuals who are studying online, i.e. by reducing the number of FSILS questions from 44 to 26 to identify learning style preferences. However, though this reduction may have benefits in terms of efficiency and ease of use, it may actually miss some subtle attributes of learning style preferences.

There are further avenues for research in applying the Arabic version of the Felder-Soloman ILS instrument, as well as other learning style instruments, to different groups in Arabic-speaking learning environments, and more generally for investigating the homogeneity of learning styles among different groups of people around the world.

7. Conclusion

This paper has added to the debate about the homogeneity of learning styles among groups of people around the world with differences in language, learning environment and culture. Our study identifies different learning style characteristics than those identified by a previous study, namely that of Graf et al. (2007), which used a significantly different cohort of learners. This paper followed as closely as possible the method suggested by

Graf et al. to ensure the most robust possible comparison. The method involved using a range of statistical tools, such as linear discriminant analysis and various methods of frequency analysis and correlation analysis, to cross-validate the data and identify significant clusters of learning style characteristics represented in the sample. This paper has consequently provided support for a more in-depth evaluation of learning styles, such as the method suggested by Graf et al., which could provide a better understanding of learning styles and aid the development of appropriate adaptive learning systems.

This paper has shown how identifying learning style characteristics for a cohort of learners (with their own specific linguistic, educational and cultural attributes) may be used to inform the development and application of adaptive learning systems. Furthermore, this analysis may be used to identify the learning style attributes that would be most beneficial in informing the development of adaptive systems by identifying which learning style attributes are most relevant for a particular cohort of learners.

The results show differences in representative characteristics between different learning cohorts, which indicate possible cultural and learning environment influences on learning style preferences. Semantic groups in Saudi Arabia are generally similar to semantic groups in New Zealand and Austria in terms of the intuitive, visual, sequential and global dimensions. However, differences between semantic groups can be seen in the sensing, active/reflective and verbal dimensions. The representative characteristics of learning style preferences do not seem to be homogeneous between English-speaking and Arabic-speaking samples of learners.

These results offer a more accurate representation of learning styles among different groups of learners, which increases the potential to create learning environments that can be adapted to the individual needs of students. As well, the detailed examination of the characteristics of learning styles could enhance teaching methods, therefore creating a learning environment that is more efficacious and tailored.

Acknowledgement

We would like to thank Professor Kinshuk from Athabasca University, who works as the professor and director of the School of Computing and Information Systems.

References

[1]   Reigeluth, C.M., (1996). A new paradigm of ISD?. Educational Technology and Society, 36 (3), 13-20.

[2]   Honey, P., & Mumford, A., (1986). Using your Learning Styles. Peter Honey, Maidenhead.

[3]   Rasmussen, K.L., (1998). Hypermedia and learning styles: can performance be influenced? Journal of Multimedia and Hypermedia, 7(4).

[4]   Aljojo, N. & Adams, C. (2010b), The Teacher Assisting and Subject Adaptive Material (TASAM) System: An Arabic Adaptive learning Environment. In J. Sanchez & K. Zhang (Eds.), Proceedings of World Conference on E-Learning in Corporate, Government, Healthcare, and Higher Education 2010 b (pp. 1541-1550), Chesapeake, VA: AACE, Orlando, Florida, USA

[5]   Aljojo N., Adams C., Alkhouli A.F., Fitch T. & Saifuddin H. (2009) A Study of the Reliability and Validating the Felder-Soloman Index of Learning Styles in Arabic. 8th European Conference on e-Learning (ECEL), University of Bari, Italy, 29-30 October.

[6]   Carver, C. A., Howard, R. A., & Lane, W. D. (1999). Enhancing Student Learning Through Hypermedia Courseware and Incorporation of Student Learning Styles, IEEE Transactions on Education, 42(2), 33-38.

[7]   Hong, H., & Kinshuk (2004). Adaptation to Student Learning Styles in Web Based Educational Systems. Proceedings of EDMEDIA2004, Chesapeake, VA: AACE, (pp.21-26).

[8]   Paredes, P. & Rodriguez, P.(2004) A Mixed Approach to Modelling Styles in Adaptive Educational Hypermedia, Advanced Technology for Learning, 1(4), 210-215.

[9]   Felder, R.M. & Spurlin, J. (2005). Reliability and Validity of the Index of Learning Styles: a Meta-analysis. International Journal of Engineering Education. 21(1), 103-112.

[10]   Bajraktarevic N., Hall W., & Fullick P. (2003). ILASH: Incorporating learning strategies in hypermedia. Paper presented at the Fourteenth Conference on Hypertext and Hypermedia, August 26-30, Nottingham, UK.

[11]   Aljojo, N. & Adams, C., Saifuddin, H. & Abdulghaffar. N.A. (2011a), Diagnostic Techniques and Procedures for Cross-Cultural Adaptation of Arabic Version Instrument. In J. Sanchez & K. Zhang (Eds.), Proceedings of World Conference on E-Learning in Corporate, Government, Healthcare, and Higher Education, Honolulu, Hawaii, October 17-21, 2011a.

[12]   Aljojo, N., Adams, C., Saifuddin, H., & Alsehaimi, Z. (2011b). Evaluating the Impact of an Arabic version of an adaptive learning system based on the Felder-Silverman's learning style instrument, The 10th European Conference on e-Learning, University of Brighton, UK, 10-11 November 2011, Academic Publishing International.

[13]   Brusilovsky, P. (2004). Knowledge Tree: A distributed architecture for adaptive e-learning. In S. I. Feldman, M. Uretsky, M. Najork, & C. E. Wills (Eds.), Proceedings of the International Conference on World Wide Web (pp. 104-113). New York: ACM Press.

[14]   Graf, S., Viola, S., Leo & T., Kinshuk (2007). In Depth Analysis of the Felder-Silverman Learning Style Dimensions. Journal of Research on Technology in Education, 40(1).

[15]   Pask, G. (1976). Styles and strategies of learning. British Journal of Educational Psychology, 46, 128-148.

[16]   Kolb, D. A. (1984). Experiential learning: experience as the source of learning and development. Englewood Cliffs, New Jersey: Prentice-Hall.

[17]   Felder, R. M. & Silverman, L. K. (1988). Learning Styles and Teaching Styles in Engineering Education, Engr. Education, 78(7), 674-681.

[18]   Felder, R. M., & Soloman, B. A. (1997). Index of Learning Styles Questionnaire. Retrieved 30 November, 2007, from http://www.engr.ncsu.edu/learningstyles/ilsweb.html.

[19]   Gilbert, J. E. & Han, C. Y. (1999). Adapting Instruction in Search of a Significant Difference. Journal of Network and Computing Applications, 22(3).

[20]   Peña, C.,I. (2004). Intelligent Agents to Improve Adaptivity in a Web-Based Learning Environment. University of Girona.

[21]   Papanikolaou, K., M. Grigoriadou, H. Kornilakis, and G. D. Magoulas. 2003. Personalising the interaction in a Web-based educational hypermedia system: the case of INSPIRE. User Modeling and User-Adapted Interaction, 13(3), 213-267.

[22]   Brusilovsky, P. (2001). Adaptive hypermedia. User Modeling and User Adapted Interaction, Ten Year Anniversary Issue (Alfred Kobsa, ed.) 11 (1/2), 87-110

[23]   Felder, R. M. (1993). Reaching the Second Tier: Learning and Teaching Styles in Faculty Science Education, J. Coll. Sci. Teaching, 23(5), 286-290.

[24]   Franzoni, A., Assar, S., Defude, B., & Rojas, J. (2008). Student Learning Styles Adaptation Method Based on Teaching Strategies and Electronic Media. The 8th IEEE International Conference on Advanced Learning Technologies, Los Alamitos, CA: IEEE.

[25]   Kinshuk. And T. Lin. 2003. Application of Learning Styles Adaptivity in Mobile Learning Environments. ASEE Annual Conference and Exposition, Nashville, Tennessee.

[26]   Duda, R. O., Hart, P. E., & Stork, D. G. (2000). Pattern classification (2nd ed.). New York: Wiley.

6

Application of IS-Balanced Scorecard in Performance Measurement of e-Government Services in Kenya

Grace Leah AKINYI[*], Christopher A. MOTURI

School of Computing and Informatics, University of Nairobi, Nairobi, Kenya
*Corresponding author: ograceleah@gmail.com

Abstract This research applied the Balanced Scorecard concept to audit performance of e-Government services at Kenya Revenue Authority. An analysis was made on how KRA developed performance measurement data. A systematic study of the existing performance tools was carried out in establishing the basis for conceptualizing the Information Systems Balanced Scorecard. Various dimensions of e-Government services were measured and a tool was proposed that would assess the quality dimensions of the e-Government services from a management perspective. The proposed tool was validated using i-Tax service of KRA. We list the indicators and metrics to be used to measure the performance of e-Government services. This research suggests an adoption of an IS-BSC which measures and evaluates e-Government services from four perspectives: business value, user orientation, internal process and future readiness. The research concludes with recommendations to help governments develop a performance measurement mechanism to assess the impact of investing in e-Government. Considering that performance measurement is a prerequisite to e-Government efforts to audit services and assure citizen of government's accountability, the findings will be beneficial to ministries adopting e-Government initiatives as they will gain an understanding about the mixed method of using metrics in IT governance balanced scorecard.

Keywords: *performance measurement, e-Government, e-Government Services, IS-Balanced Scorecard, IS Strategic Management*

1. Introduction

1.1. Background

Measurement is a prerequisite to management. Performance measurement is important to assess e-Government efforts. A government needs to track what is working and what is not and assure citizens that the government's time and funds are being spent well. E-Government is increasingly being emphasized as a way for governments to strengthen good governance. If implemented strategically, it can not only improve efficiency, accountability and transparency of government processes, but it can also be a tool to empower citizens by enabling them to participate in the decision-making processes of governments.

The Balanced Scorecard (BSC) was developed as a performance measurement framework that added strategic non-financial performance measures to the traditional financial metrics to give managers and executives a more balanced view of organizational performance [1]. The aim of the BSC is to direct, help manage and change in support of the long-term strategy in order to manage performance. The scorecard reflects what the company and the strategies are all about. It acts as a catalyst for bringing in the 'change' element within the organization. It has evolved from its early use to a full strategic planning and management system. It provides a framework that helps strategic planners identify what should be done, measured and executed

The Government of Kenya has committed itself towards achieving an effective and operational e-Government to facilitate better and efficient delivery of information and services to the citizens, promote productivity among public servants, encourage participation of citizens in Government and empower all Kenyans [2]. This achievement has enabled realization of national development goals and objectives for Wealth and Employment Creation [3]. Since its establishment in 2004, the e-Government initiativeis viewed as a tool that can transform the way interactions take place, methods of public education and services are delivered, knowledge is acquired and utilized, policy is developed and implemented, citizens participate in governance, and public administration on reform and good governance goals are met. Its primary vision is to transform a government's value to its citizens, by digitizing government operations so that they are accessible and interactive, thus translating into real-time service delivery. e-Government can be segmented into primary delivery models; the relationship between government and citizens (G2C), electronic interactions between government corporations and private businesses (G2B), relationship between governmental organizations (G2G), and the relationship between government and its employees (G2E) [4].

Kenya Revenue Authority (KRA) was established by an Act of Parliament in 1995 and is charged with the responsibility of collecting revenue on behalf of the Government of Kenya.KRA is the largest revenue earning setup of the Government of Kenya. Its functions are qualification of tax liability and collection of tax [5]. Commercial Tax Information System has been implemented by the Directorate to augment revenue and minimize evasion of tax. It covers functional areas of registration of dealers, monitoring the payments by dealers which trade in high volumes, monitoring imports, along with other utility reports. The objectives of e-Government application were to ensure transparency in the system; to get data, dealer-wise, commodity-wise, office-wise, transporter-wise for efficient functioning; to reduce evasion of tax in the state; to create a central data model, which could feed all check-posts in the state; to ensure checks and validations, which assumed critical status as goods. Performance measurement in the public sector is topical both for practitioners and academics. There have been several efforts to build a theory of performance measurement in the public sector based on actual practice [6,7,8,9].

1.2. Problem Statement

In sub-Saharan Africa, e-Government is reduced to the extent to which public service processes are conducted online. Actual usage levels or the impact of electronic services are hardly measured. Organizational changes relevant to e-Government are only illustrated using randomly selected best practice cases. Estimating the extent of e-Government implementation is difficult, as only a few benchmarks exist and exclusively focused on internet services. Considering the present level of development of e-Government in developing economies, the question as to which frameworks influence the spread and implementation of e-Government becomes more relevant [10,11]. The Government of Kenya has been making significant attempts to automate services to its citizen. Lack of an evaluation culture and appropriate methodologies has prevented government units and their constituents from integrating website projects with e-Government service delivery performance. Strategic implementation remains challenging due to the non-existence of strategic e-Government models. Excessive reliance on financial accounting has made performance measurements inadequate and misleading. Strategic performance measures must be developed to provide accountability for e-Government efforts [12].

1.3. Objectives of the Study

The objectives of the study were:
1. To investigate the level applied by KRA in measuring and evaluating e-Government services.
2. To establish the objectives of performance measurement of e-Government services at KRA.
3. To establish the tools and methodologies used to evaluate e-Government services in Kenya
4. To analyze the challenges in the evaluation of the e-Government services in Kenya
5. To elaborate a model based on the IS-BSC concept towards performance measurement of e-Government services in Kenya

2. Literature Review

E-Government (Figure 1) should be addressed from technological, social, political, and cultural perspectives [13]. The key stakeholders are show in Figure 2.

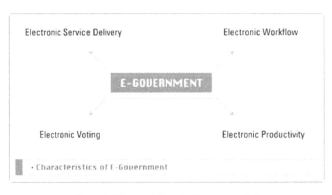

Figure 1. Characteristics of e-Government [14]

Figure 2. Stakeholders of e-Government [14]

Key focus areas of IT Governance can be summarized as delivering value to the business driven by strategic alignment, mitigating risks driven by embedding accountability into the enterprise. Strategic Alignment enables bringing ICT investments in harmony with the strategic business objectives. Value Delivery enables bringing ICT investments in harmony with the strategic business objectives. Risk Management concerns ascertaining that there is transparency about the significant risks to the organization and clarifying the risk-taking or risk-avoidance policies of the enterprise. Performance Measurement shows how the organization is performing to meet the goals of governance in the organization. Use of tools can be adopted, such as BSC, to ascertain how business goals are achieved. Use of an IT balanced scorecard is an effective means to help the board and management achieve IT and business alignment [4].

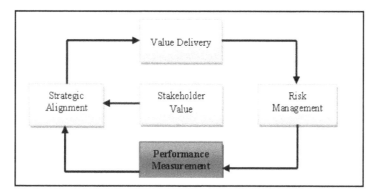

Figure 3. Four Focus Areas of E-Government

2.1. Objectives of Performance Measurement of e-Government Services

A private university in Indonesia applied the IT Balanced Scorecard framework into the performance of the higher education information system [17]. The framework consisted of four perspectives: Corporate Contribution, User Orientation, Operational Excellence, and Future Orientation. The findings affirmed the positive effects of BSC into the performance of higher education. Performance evaluation of e-Government services using BSC, emphasized on a balance between quantitative and qualitative measures in evaluating the success in IT project investments [18]. The development of ICTs had enabled e-Government to continue playing important role in administration and public service in China [19]. Developing e-Government had become the important means to enhance government management, service competence and civil satisfaction. The findings prove that BSC could not only reflect the output and outcome, but also influenced policy making, hence a better future of e-Government.

The Balanced Scorecard was used to manage the current situation and future improvement for IT governance and controls in Thailand [20]. A global IT governance perspective was drawn and a performance analysis applied to the metrics of IT governance balanced scorecard with collected survey data from IT executives. The resultant was a method for applying IT governance balanced scorecard metrics and importance-performance analysis to contribute IT governance strategy.

To understand the impact of business cases on IT investment decisions, municipal e-Government projects indicated that more initial costs were identified in technological investments, hence informed investment decisions would aid in conserving resources for the organization [21].Evaluating the impact of e-Government entailed a complex process of performance assessment which took into account the perspective of citizens [22].

2.2. Tools and Methodologies Used to Evaluate e-Government Services

DeLone and McLean Information Systems Success Model had one operationalization, the SERVQUAL instrument, limited to service quality, which had been shown to be a functional tool for measuring service quality in IS [23]. The ISO/IEC 38500 standard depicted that IT governance frameworks contributed to implementation of the key principles of the good corporate governance, particularly, in the public sector, especially the transparency and accountability goals for IT assets [24].

The effectiveness and efficiency of e-Government services are critical issues which have to be stimulated by successful practices in the areas of service quality, capability-based theories, and IT related capability management. A framework was examined from dimensions of content service capability, service delivery capability, and on-demand capability, using data derived from local governments. A structural analysis illustrated that the practical management applications of the framework could facilitate the improvement of e-Government services [25]. Critical success factors would increase the contribution of IT towards achieving organization objectives; hence, the use of IT in public sector had become necessary for sustaining and extending public service delivery [26].

2.3. Challenges to Evaluation of the e-Government Services

Success and failure of e-Government depend on the size of gap that exists between actual outcomes and the initial targets set for any e-Government project. Jordan was developing strategies in order to bridge this gap in order to enhance the services of e-Government by investigating the application of quality approaches on the impact e-Government. The study explored e-services programme embraced by public sector organizations. The aim was to serve several customer sectors; citizens, businesses, and the government. The investigation evaluated quality of e-service standards including the acceptance criteria of Websites' usability as a factor for customer satisfaction. This study identified areas of customer satisfaction levels that could be enhanced for improving quality e-services delivery [27]. A BSC approach was developed to measuring a set of criteria from four different points of view [28,29].

3. Research Methodology

3.1. Research Design

The study used an organizational case study design. The research was meant to uncover the possible performance measurement levels and objectives being experienced on e-Government services at KRA. The research explored the tools used and challenges experienced in measuring performance of e-Government services, and explored if an IS Balanced scorecard would be the foundation for a strategic management of e-Government services in KRA. The study also tested e-Government effectiveness using IS Balanced Scorecard technique by incorporating qualitative measures within a quantitative research methodology with data collected by means of a questionnaire.

3.2. Data Source & Collection

The study gathered primary and secondary data which were quantitative and qualitative in nature. Primary data was collected from respondents using questionnaires. The questionnaire sampled stakeholders including executive and technical employees of e-Government, within the ICT department of KRA.

The first category of the respondents was the Deputy Commissioner of ICT Services at KRA, being the top officer dealing directly with e-Governance infrastructure and architecture. Other respondents of this study were drawn from the ICT department executive, officers and technical staff. The data collected gave the inside of G2G and G2E communication. Secondary data was gathered from records existing in the archives of the ICT department of KRA: Revenue Administration Reforms in Kenya -Experience and Lessons; the Corporate Strategic Plan 2012 – 2015; and the KRA i-Tax portal. Data collection took place in October 2014.

3.3. Sampling Technique

Judgment sampling method proved to be effective because only limited number of people served as primary data sources. Advantages of this technique included low cost and less time needed to select perspective sampling group members compared to many other alternative methods. The sampling approach adopted for this study was aligned with purposeful sampling, based on the fact that literature reviewing had been done. Respondents were chosen based on their direct involvement in e-Government initiatives at KRA. The respondents of the study were randomly sampled from the target population of study by judgmental sampling method due to the nature of the study which was descriptive in nature. The targeted sample was 50 respondents and the response rate was 96%. A sample of 30% of the population from the ICT

department was selected, where a representative sample is 10% to 30% of the population [30]. The following formula was used to determine the minimum sample size:

$$n = \frac{Z\alpha^2 p(1-p)}{d^2} \ [31]$$

Where, $Z\alpha$ is the standard normal deviate at the required confidence level; n, the sample size; d, the level of statistical significance set; p, the proportion in the target population estimated to have characteristics being measured. $Z\alpha$ represents that value, such that the probability of a standard normal variable exceeding it is $(1- \alpha)/2$. This value for a chosen α level can be obtained from the table, hence giving Z value for the standard normal distribution.

Using a confidence level of 95%, $Z\alpha$ is 1.96. Since, there is no estimate available of the proportion in the target population; the 30% was used [30]. Since larger sample sizes give more reliable results, the researcher targeted to have 50 valid responses, thereby a sample size of 100 was picked. The sample was drawn from officers in charge of the ICT division who were purposively selected. The positions held within the ICT section were diverse therefore the properties of emergent concepts could be established [32]. The selected population was issued with questionnaires whose findings were mapped to the IS-BSC towards measuring the performance of e-Government services at KRA.

3.4. Data Analysis

Data from the study was analyzed using both qualitative and quantitative techniques. Primary data collected was coded and analyzed using SPSS version 20 to determine descriptive statistics as percentages and frequencies. Data was analyzed to test e-Government effectiveness from IS-Balanced Scorecard's four dimensions: User Orientation, Business Value, Internal Process and Future Readiness. The findings were presented using tables and charts. A global IT governance perspective was drawn from the literature review and a performance analysis applied to the metrics of IT governance BSC with collected data from IT executives and staff. Data obtained was statistically analyzed to test for reliability and validity. The data collected was analyzed by use of content analysis due to the fact that the data was qualitative in nature.

4. Results and Discussion

This section presents the findings of the study and their interpretation. Participants were instructed to agree or disagree with each of these statements based on a five-point Likert-scale) where 1 = Strongly disagree, 2 = Disagree, 3 = Neutral, 4 = Agree and 5 = Strongly agree).

4.1. Reliability

Reliability is an assessment of the degree of consistency between multiple measurements of a variable. A measure is said to be reliable if a person's score on the same test given twice is similar. Reliability Analysis on the questionnaires using data collected from the study was performed using Chronbach's alpha. The results are presented in Table 1. The reliability analysis gave an alpha coefficient of 0.871, which exceeds 0.7, which is the lower limit of the acceptable reliability coefficient, thereby demonstrating reliability.

Table 1. Chronbach's alpha on data collected

Reliability Statistics		
Cronbac's Alpha	Cronbach's Alpha Based on Standardized Items	N of Items
.826	.871	11

4.2. Factor Analysis

Factor analysis is a statistical approach used to analyze the interrelationships among a large number of variables and to explain these variables in terms of their common underlying dimensions. Principal Components Analysis (PCA) method provides a unique solution so that the original data can be reconstructed from the results. The Kaiser Meyer-Olkin (KMO) is a measure of sampling adequacy and varies between 0 and 1.

The four perspectives of the IS-BSC were subjected to PCA with verimax rotation. An inspection of the correlation matrix revealed the presence of many coefficients of 0.3 and above. KMO value was 0.767, which is good. These values indicated that Factor Analysis could be used to validate the test items under the respective constructs.

Table 2. KMO Test on data collected

Component Transformation Matrix			
Component	1	2	3
1	.593	.593	.544
2	-.762	.631	.143
3	-.258	-.499	.827

Extraction Method: Principal Component Analysis
Rotation Method: Varimax with Kaiser Normalization

The screen plot (Figure 4) was used to assist to refine the test items. The number of components was determined from the shape of the screen plot. An inspection of the screen plot revealed a clear break after the third component; hence it was decided to retain three components for further investigation.

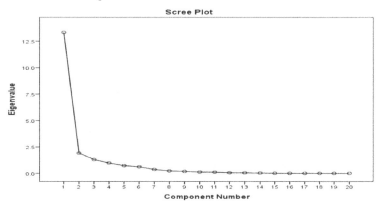

Figure 4. Screen Plot for Determining the Number of Factors

Table 3. Rotated Component Matrix

Rotated Component Matrix[a]			
	Component		
	1	2	3
Good image and reputation by end users	.871		
Exploit IT opportunities	.865		.332
IS projects provide business value	.795	.454	
Satisfy end user requirements	.744	.483	
Influence requests from end users	.718		.561
Control IS costs	.685	.432	.493
Manage IS related problems that arise		.891	
Cost effective training		.825	.435
Anticipate IS related problems that could arise	.405	.794	.345
Upgrade IS skills through training & develop	.474	.749	
Good relationship with end users	.484	.743	
Sell IS products to third party		.664	.634
Acquiring & testing new hardware &software	.315	.572	
Upgrade IT applications portfolio	.540	.572	.525
Cost-effective research		.442	.825
Good image and reputation with management	.375		.724
Operating and maintaining IT applications	.487	.311	.716
Planning and developing IT applications	.616		.700
Upgrade hardware and software	.494	.492	.614
Perceived as preferred supplier		.362	.566

Extraction Method: Principal Component Analysis
Rotation Method: Varimax with Kaiser Normalization. Rotation converged in 16 iterations

Verimax rotation was performed to aid in interpretation of the components. The rotated solution presented in Table 3 revealed all showing a number of strong loadings, and all variables loading significantly on one component. Most of the variables under the same constructs loaded on a common component indicating that the test items had a high correlation which was important for variables under a common construct.

Descriptive analysis was done on staff designation, specialization areas, roles of personnel involved in implementing performance measures at KRA and duration of employment. The findings were relevant in determining the relevance of achieving the study's objectives.

4.3. Levels of Measuring and Evaluating e-Government Services

KRA as a National Revenue collection body in Kenya had seen different levels for evaluation of its e-Government services. At Corporate level, KRA had defined a common approach to track progress of all components in the e-Government strategy. This monitoring and evaluation framework, applicable at all stages of strategy implementation, was envisaged to create an institutional mechanism for organization, formulation, activation, monitoring, reporting, controlling and disseminating results from monitoring and evaluation for all e-Government related projects.

At Departmental level, the evaluation of e-Government services would be done with respect to expected outcomes. KRA's e-Government strategy would have the outcomes derived from translating the departmental e-Government vision into measurable targets. It would be observed that there would be a need to measure the progress of e-Government at the departmental level. The e-Government strategy would begin with a vision statement with its elements translating into different customer-centric outcomes. For achieving these outcomes, there would need to be specific measurable targets/goals identified for each of the outcomes. To measure progress against these targets/goals, key indicators would need to be identified along with their measurement mechanisms. Monitoring and evaluation mechanism which operated at the project level of abstraction would be addressed by designing and incorporating project-specific indicators during evaluation.

4.4. Objectives of Performance Measurement of e-Government Services

A large majority of respondents to the questionnaires reported that e-Government goals and targets had been included in the KRA e-Government strategy and that some type of indicators had been developed to measure these objectives. This data could reflect the high priority placed on monitoring and evaluation activities in in this organization. However, the frameworks allowing actual implementation of measurement and evaluation e-Government services, presented a somewhat less clear picture. Only 25% respondents required monitoring and evaluation of e-Government projects. This indicated relatively less emphasis attributed to performance measurements initiatives at the organizational/ departmental level. Disseminating the results of performance measurements could be of great value to e-Government decision makers, helping them plan, manage and improve e-Government performance. Only another 25% of respondents indicated that the results of their internal monitoring and evaluation were made available to interested parties.

Table 4. Objectives of performance measurement

At National Level

1. To establish a real political administration
2. To adopt a unified strategic plan common to all ministerial departments
3. To establish organizational structures with the co-operation of all ministerial departments
4. To ensure strategic target compliance
5. To create productive and healthy competition among government departments
6. To align government departments around standards and better practices
7. To ensure transparency and accountability
8. To recognize the best achievers
9. To measure effectiveness and to a certain extent efficiency
10. To evaluate the contribution of e-Government to achieving public sector reform objectives
11. To monitor overall compliance of initiatives with national strategy
12. To allow for realignment of initiatives with overarching plan if necessary
13. To ensure a whole-of-government approach to e-Government by strengthening the co-ordination of initiatives at the national level

At Corporate Level

1. To reform the public sector
2. To simplify administrative procedures
3. To ensure compliance with strategy
4. To monitor overall progress against targets
5. To ensure transparency, accountability and awareness
6. To take corrective actions

At Department/Project Level

1. To ensure project status tracking
2. To ensure project deliverables
3. To ensure project timelines compliance
4. To assess and monitor costs, benefits, and risks of project implementation
5. To measure efficiency and effectiveness of implemented projects
6. To identify good practices and promote knowledge sharing among institutions
7. To provide data/information to decision makers
8. To justify investments and determine resource allocation for new projects

At the National level, the Kenyan e-Government services needed to implement a unified and centralized agency level performance measurement system. At the Corporate level, KRA needed a progress monitoring system and adopt its own measurement systems internally. The measurements should be conducted periodically depending on the indicator (e.g. monthly, quarterly, annually, etc.). The measurement results should be made available to e-Government stakeholders and related staff. At the Departmental /Project level, the project-level measurement needed to be decentralized across various departments. The project-level results, as measured weekly or bi-weekly, needed to be made available to all the staff involved in e-Government services, including the Director.

4.5. Tools and Methodologies Used to Evaluate e-Government Services

Evaluation methods must be selected to match the resources available for evaluation, the magnitude of an initiative, and individual departmental circumstances. The study found that a range of evaluation methods and tools for e-Government were available to KRA (Figure 5 and Figure 6). However, e-Government stakeholders had not developed significant strategies to use these methods especially more sophisticated user-engaging tools.

The results showed that KRA had adopted Cost-Benefit Analysis as the most common tool for evaluation at 80%. This indicated that traditional methods were still in use which could not evaluate e-Government services comprehensively. Ad-hoc surveys and official statistics were the least common tools for e-Government evaluation at 20% and 30% respectively. These would be used for evaluating infrastructure capacities and the use of the Internet by target populations. Service level agreements were in place to ensure high quality standards for services to citizens and businesses.

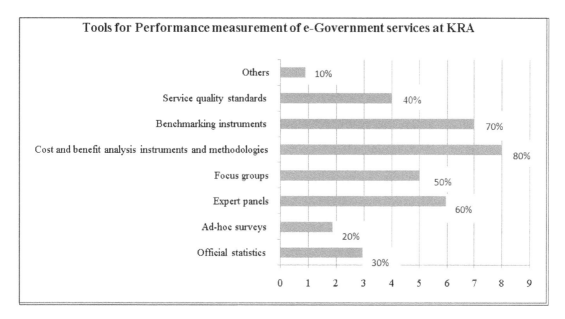

Figure 5. Results for Tools applied on performance measurement of e-Government services at KRA

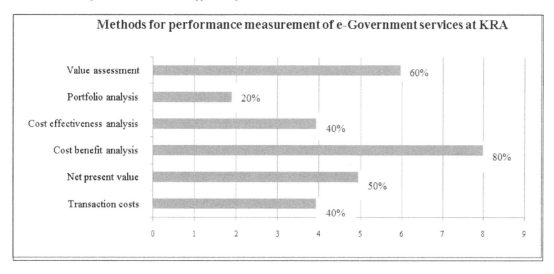

Figure 6. Results of Applied Methods of e-G government services measurement at KRA

4.6. Challenges to Evaluation of the e-Government Services

The study found that monitoring and evaluation of government programmes was generally difficult, given the frequent lack of clarity of objectives owing to the different and often competing views held by different stakeholders (Figure 7). In addition, overlapping initiatives, policies and continuous fine-tuning of initiatives complicated the monitoring and evaluation efforts.

The fact that e-Government was relatively new and that there were few advanced services meant fewer models and actual outcome experiences that could be used for benchmarking. These problems were magnified when attempting to monitor and evaluate e-Government programmes. ICT projects were hard to evaluate because

of the pervasive nature of ICTs, the integration of ICT goals with policy goals and the organizational changes that necessarily accompanied e-Government initiatives. Effective evaluation required good metrics, regular monitoring and reporting, disciplined and professional use of robust evaluation frameworks and the use of long-term evaluation practices. These qualities depended on an organization's overall evaluation culture.

A general lack of evaluation culture in government and disinclination to measure e-Government services seemed to pose a serious challenge to the diffusion of e-Government evaluation practice and represented the single most important obstacles to e-Government evaluation at 80% of respondents provided a valid answer while, the relatively least importance was assigned to non-clarity of who should perform evaluation at 10% and non-clarity on the clients of evaluation at 20%. E-Government initiatives were designed and implemented by individual e-Government programme units with very loose institutional links with other ministries. This could prevent

development of a common culture and experience of implementation and evaluation across government.

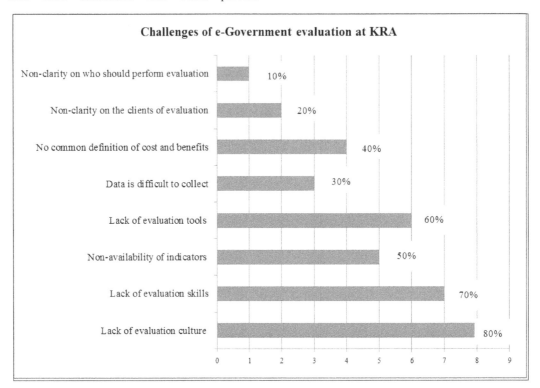

Figure 7. Challenges to evaluation of e-Government services

4.7. The IS - Balanced Scorecard (IS-BSC)

The Balanced Scorecard was used to align business activities to the vision and strategy of the organization, improve internal and external communication and monitor organizational performance against strategic goals. It is a performance measurement tool that considers not only financial measures but also customer satisfaction, business process and learning measures [33]. Effective performance was measured not merely by delivery of results in one area but by delivering satisfactory performance across all measures. An essential aspect of the BSC was the articulation of linkage between performance measures and strategy objectives. Once linkage was understood, strategic objectives were further translated into actionable measures to help organizations improve performance [34,35].

The BSC framework tries to bring a balance and linkage between the Financial and the Non-Financial indicators, Tangible and the Intangible measures, Internal and the External aspects and Leading and the Lagging indicators [36]. The four perspectives are highly interlinked. There is a logical connection between them: If an organization focuses on the learning and the growth aspect, it is definitely going to lead to better business processes. This in turn would be followed by increased customer value by producing better products which ultimately gives rise to improved financial performance [37].

4.7.1. IS - BSC framework for Performance Measurement

The Information Systems-Balanced Scorecard (IS-BSC) methodology (Figure 8) was selected because it ensures

the appropriate logical model that translates the strategy into operational terms. It also provides the appropriate interface for different types of users: from the highest strategic level to the very operational level in every single administration included in the process. The successful functioning of e-Government would be possible only through mutual collaboration of administration, citizens and businesses on all stages of its realization, from definition of vision and priorities to conceptualization and implementation of particular services. It is recognized that an IS-BSC-based framework can make the e-Government implementation process transparent and can provide detailed information for efficient participation of citizens and businesses in the e-Government by publishing the key indicators on the web [38].

Business Value Perspective describes the tangible outcomes of the strategy in traditional financial terms, such as return on investment (ROI), shareholder value, profitability, revenue growth, and lower unit costs. User Orientation Perspective defines the drivers of revenue growth. It includes generic customer outcomes, such as satisfaction, acquisition, retention, and growth, as well as the differentiating value proposition the organization intends to offer to generate sales and loyalty from targeted customers. It has four categories of criteria: Performance issues, decision quality, personal impact and organizational impact. Internal Processes Perspective identifies the operating, customer management, innovation, regulatory and social process objectives for creating and delivering the customer value proposition and improving the quality and productivity of operating processes. Future Readiness Perspective identifies the intangible assets that are most important to the strategy. The objectives in this perspective identify jobs (the human capital), systems (the information capital), and what kind of climate (the organization capital) are required to support the value creating internal processes.

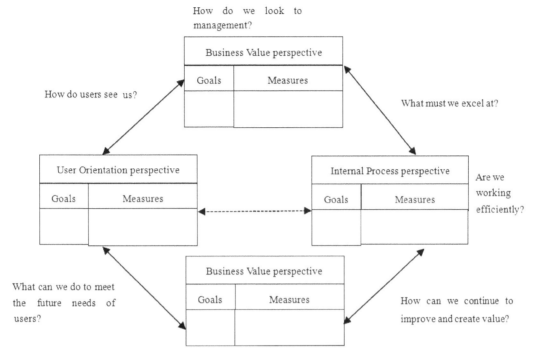

How do we look to management?

Business Value perspective

Goals	Measures

How do users see us?

User Orientation perspective

Goals	Measures

What must we excel at?

Internal Process perspective

Goals	Measures

Are we working efficiently?

What can we do to meet the future needs of users?

Business Value perspective

Goals	Measures

How can we continue to improve and create value?

What methodologies and business opportunities/challenges are emerging?

Figure 8. Relationships between the four perspectives in IS-BSC [35]

4.7.2. BSC Performance Measurement Indicators

A BSC approach was developed for measuring a set of criteria from four different points of view; business value, user orientation, internal process and future readiness. Each perspective contained a set of criteria. Measuring and evaluating IS from multiple perspectives and in assorted ways is helpful to assess its efficiency, effectiveness and transformative potential, both at present and in the future. The IS-BSC includes three additional perspectives [27,28]. 60% of the respondents agreed that the objectives, targets and measures in IS-BSC corresponded with those at KRA. This implied a relationship between what IS-BSC sets out to measure and the actual activities that take place on the ground. 80% of the staff concurred that IS-BSC would meet the objectives of e-Government services.

Business Value Perspective: It is useful to distinguish between two categories of IS performance evaluation: the short-term cost-benefit evaluation that is commonly applied to individual projects, and the longer-term perspective relevant to both IT applications and the IS department as a whole. Many of the business value measures fall into the latter category. Cost control would be evaluated in the short-term, where the traditional financial perspective would encompass the control of the IS budget as well as the benefits arising from the sale of IT-related products and services to third parties. Business value of IT Project is a much broader concept than benefits, and IS projects can generate business value in many ways. The implementation of KRA's i-Tax system, a menu-driven customer database may reduce the amount of IS specialist support needed to execute an ad hoc query,

and generate a modest amount of direct benefits. Salespeople would be expected to integrate the database into their activities, thereby improving the productivity of the sales process, and consequently raising revenue levels or profit margins.

User Orientation Perspective: The end-user of an IS may be an internal customer that is utilizing an inter-organizational system. In contrast to the large potential market for the products and services of most companies, an IS department usually has limited opportunities to attract new customers, which may change in the expanding electronic marketplace. The satisfaction of existing customers will be more important than building up market share or acquiring new customers. It will be critical to monitor existing customer satisfaction on a frequent basis, especially if they can select among alternative suppliers of IS services. User satisfaction would play an important role in the overall evaluation of the IS department or function. The metrics for the user perspective focus on three areas: 1. Being the preferred supplier for applications and operations, 2. Establishing and maintaining relationships with the user community and 3. Satisfy end user needs.

Internal Processes Perspective: Internal operations may be assessed by measuring and evaluating three of the basic processes performed by the IS department: 1. the planning and prioritization of IS projects; 2. the development of new IT applications; and 3. the operation and maintenance of current IT applications. Other processes may also be considered, such as hardware and software supply and support, problem management, user education, the management of IS personnel, and their usage of efficient communication channels.

Future Readiness Perspective: This is concerned with continually improving the skill set of IS specialists in order to prepare them for potential changes and challenges in the future; regularly updating the applications portfolio; and putting effort into researching emerging technologies and their potential value to the organization. The findings, reflected the need to continually enhance the skills of IS specialists. There was a need to periodically upgrade the applications portfolio in order to take advantage of technological advances. There was also a need to gain a thorough understanding of emerging technologies as well as their specific suitability to the company's IS architecture. The ability of IS to deliver quality services

and to lead new technology assimilation efforts in the future will depend on the preparations that are made today and tomorrow. IS managers must assess future trends and anticipate them.

4.8 Cause-and–Effect Relationship of e-Government Services at KRA

If cause-and-effect relationships are not adequately reflected in the BSC, it will not translate and communicate the company's vision and strategy. They can involve all four of the perspectives in the BSC framework as seen in, Table 5.

Table 5. IS-BSC with key Questions and Relationships between the Four Perspectives

The four perspectives in an IS Balanced Scorecard	
User orientation perspective **(end-user's view)**	**Business value perspective** **(management's view)**
Mission: Deliver value-adding services to end-users **Key question**: Are e-Gov. services provided by IT department fulfilling the user's needs? **Objectives**: Exploit IT opportunities Satisfy end-user requirement Establish and maintain a good reputation with end-users	**Mission:** Contribute to the value of the business **Key question:** Is the IT department accomplishing its goals and contributing value to the organization as a whole? **Objectives:** Establish and maintain a good image and reputation with management Ensure the IT projects provide business value Control IT costs
Internal processes perspective **(operations-based view)**	**Future readiness perspective** **(innovation and learning view)**
Mission: Deliver IT services in an effective and efficient manner **Key question**: Does the IT department create, deliver and maintain its services in an efficient manner? **Objectives**: Provide cost-effective training that satisfies end-users Be efficient in planning and developing IT applications Be efficient in operating and maintaining IT applications Effectively manage IT-related problems that arise	**Mission:** Deliver continuous improvement and prepare for future challenges **Key question:** Is the IT department improving its services, and preparing for potential changes and challenges? **Objectives:** Regularly upgrade IT applications portfolio Regularly upgrade hardware and software Continuously upgrade IT skills through training and development Conduct cost-effective research into emerging technologies

The corporate contribution perspective evaluates the performance of the IT from the viewpoint of executive management. The customer orientation perspective evaluates the performance of IT from the viewpoint of internal business users. The operational excellence perspective provides the performance of the IT processes from the viewpoint of IT management. The future perspective shows the readiness for future challenges of IT itself.

Table 6. Metrics for the Four Perspectives of IS-BSC [39]

Perspective	Goals	Metrics
Business Value	Business/ IT alignment Value delivery Risk management Intercompany synergy	Operational budget approval Business unit performance Attainment of expense targets Results of internal audits
User Orientation	Competitive costs Customer satisfaction Operational performance Development performance	Attainment of unit cost target Business unit survey ratings Major project scores Attainment of targeted levels
Internal Processes	Process maturity Development process Operational process	Level of IT processes Function point measures Change management effectiveness
Future Readiness	Employee satisfaction Human Resource Management Knowledge management	Satisfaction survey scores Staff turnover Implementation of learned lessons

The current indicators of competence may be more difficult to measure than either the leading innovation or lagging performance indicators. Figure 9 shows an illustration of how innovation and learning efforts can raise competence levels that in turn will improve business performance in the future.

5. Conclusions

The findings of this study would be beneficial to various ministries adopting the e-Government services (G2G), citizen (G2C) and business functions (G2B).

These stakeholders would gain more understanding about the mixed method of using metrics in IT- governance-BSC in order to identify the current situation of IT governance and controls in their organizations. An IS-BSC can easily become part of the operational-level management system. In KRA, this was due largely to the absence of specific long-term objectives, particularly related to the future readiness perspective. KRA was able to identify a few cause-and-effect relationships and performance drivers during their development of an IS-BSC. In one case, system availability, responsiveness to user requests, and timely delivery of new IT applications were agreed to be performance drivers for user satisfaction.

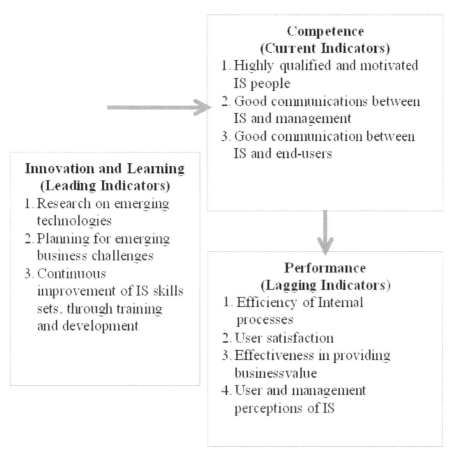

Figure 9. How innovation and learning lead to future performance improvements

It was observed that there was a lack of intra-organizational communication and this hindered sharing of information.

KRA management should initiate a top-bottom approach policy on matters to do with e-Government. Most respondents recommended that KRA's ICT executive management should give full support and commitment to assessment and implementation of e-Government initiatives. Different organizations will have different set of performance indicators and evaluation techniques for their e-Government plan. They will be driven by the goals and targets set in their overall vision. Organizations should not view evaluation as a onetime activity and should regularly assess the e-Government initiatives to ensure the success of the Plan. Evaluation should not be conducted only at the end of the project, because the feedback received from evaluation at that stage becomes very difficult to incorporate or introduces cost and time overruns. Evaluation strategy as well as indicators should be a part of the overall plan of the project.

The application of the IS-BSC concept to business functions, departments and individual projects would allow managers to see the positive and negative impacts of IT applications and IS activities on the factors that are important to the organization as a whole. Its value would rise if used to co-ordinate a wide range of IS management processes, such as individual and team goal-setting, performance appraisal and rewards for IS personnel, resource allocation and feedback-based learning. The management of both IS people and projects are likely to benefit from a systematic framework based on goals and measures that are agreed upon in advance.

Monitoring and Evaluation for e-Government services could be carried out with two distinct dimensions, namely: performance measurement of individual projects; and performance measurement of the overall e-Government plan. This research had considered specific metrics for each of the perspectives. Future research is required to determine whether the proposed perspectives and measures are a necessary and sufficient set. The framework represents a strategic IS management tool that can be used to monitor and guide specific projects as well as general performance improvement efforts. The case study reinforced a belief that while the specifics of an IS-BSC will differ from organization to organization, it is beneficial to build upon a standard framework, rather than starting from scratch. Additional case studies are likely to reveal otherwise.

Acknowledgement

We are grateful to the management of Kenya Revenue Authority for allowing us undertake this research in their organization.

References

[1] Kaplan, R., &Norton, D. P., "The balanced scorecard: measures that drive performance," *Harvard Business Review* 70(1). 71-79. 1992.

[2]   Republic of Kenya, *E-government strategy: The strategic framework, administrative structure, training Requirements and standardization framework*, Nairobi, Government Printer, 2014.

[3]   Vision 2030Kenya - http://www.vision2030.go.ke/. 2014.

[4]   Waema T. M.,"A Conceptual Framework for Assessing the Effects of E-Government on Governance," *Proceedings of The 1st International Conference in Computer Science and IT*, Nairobi, 98-103. 2007.

[5]   http://www.kra.go.ke. 2014.

[6]   Bouckaert, G., Halligan, J.,*Managing Performance: International Comparisons*, Routledge, Abingdon. 2008.

[7]   Halligan, J., & Bouckaert, G. "Performance governance: from ideal type to practice", *paper presented at the Conference of the International Research Society for Public Management*, Dublin, 11-13, April, 2011.

[8]   Van Dooren, W., Bouckaert, G., Halligan, J., *Performance Management in the Public Sector,* Routledge, Abingdon, 2010.

[9]   Rhodes, M., L., Biondi, L., Gomes, R., Melo, A. I., Ohemeng, F., Perez-Lopez, G., Rossi, A., & Sutiyono, W., "Current state of public sector performance management in seven selected countries," *International Journal of Productivity and Performance Management,* 61(3), 235-271. 2012.

[10]   UNDESA, "From E-government to E-inclusion. UN global E-government readiness report,"*New York: United Nations publication,* 2005.

[11]   Schuppan, T., "E-Government in developing countries: Experiences from sub-Saharan Africa," *Government Information Quarterly,* 26, 118-127. 2009.

[12]   Lawson-Body, A., Mukankusi, L., & Miller, G., "An adaptation of the Balanced Scorecard for e-Government service delivery: a content analysis," *Journal of Service Science*, 1(1), 75-82. 2011.

[13]   Al-Hujran, O., Al-dalahmeh, M., &Aloudat, A., "The Role of National Culture on Citizen Adoption of e-Government Services: An Empirical Study," *Electronic Journal of e-Government,* 9(2): 93-106. 2012.

[14]   UNESCO, *E-Government Toolkit for Developing Countries*, 4(2), 2005.

[15]   Scheer, A.W., Abolhassan, F., Jost, W. & Kirchmer, M., *Business Process Excellence* , ARIS in Practice, Berlin : Springer, 2002.

[16]   Seel, C. & Thomas, O., "Process Performance Measurement for E-Government: A Case Scenario from the German Ministerial Administration," *Systemics, Cybernetics and Informatics, 5* (3). 2012.

[17]   Afriliana, N., &Gaol, F. L., "Performance Measurement of Higher Education Information System Using IT Balanced Scorecard. In Intelligent Information and Database Systems," *Springer International Publishing,* 412-421, 2014.

[18]   Alhyari, S., Alazab, M., Venkatraman, S., Alazab, M., &Alazab, A., "Performance evaluation of e-government services using balanced scorecard: An empirical study in Jordan. Benchmarking:," *An International Journal,* 20(4). 512-536.2013.

[19]   Ying, J., "The application of BSC in China's e-government performance evaluation," *In Symposium on Reform and Transition in Public Administration Theory and Practice in Greater China*, Brown University, 1-4. June. 2010.

[20]   Jairak & Praneetpolgrang, 2013.

[21]   Berghout, E., & Tan, C. W., "Understanding the impact of business cases on IT investment decisions: An analysis of municipal e-government projects," *Information & Management*, 50(7), 489-506. 2013.

[22]   Barbosa, A. F., Pozzebon, M., &Diniz, E. H., "Rethinking E-Government Performance Assessment From A Citizen Perspective," *Public Administration*, 91(3), 744-762. 2013.

[23]   Delone, W. H., "The DeLone and McLean model of information systems success: a ten-year update," *Journal of management information systems,* 19(4), 9-30. 2003.

[24]   Juiz, C., Guerrero, C., &Lera, I., "Implementing Good Governance Principles for the Public Sector in Information Technology Governance Frameworks," *Open Journal of Accounting*, 2014.

[25]   Huang, C. D., & Hu, Q., "Integrating web services with competitive strategies: the balanced scorecard approach," *Communications of the AIS*, 13(6), 57-80. 2004.

[26]   Nfuka, N., &Rusu, L., "Critical Success Framework for Implementing Effective IT Governance in Tanzanian Public Sector Organizations," *Journal of Global Information Technology Management*, 16(3), 53-77. 2013.

[27]   Venkatraman, S., &Alazab, M., *Quality Approaches for Performance Measurement in Jordanian E-Government Services. IT in the Public Sphere: Applications in Administration, Government, Politics, and Planning*, 99-119. 2014.

[28]   Martinsons, M., Davison, R., &Tse, D., *The balanced scorecard: a foundation for the strategic management of information systems. Decision support systems,* 25(1), 71-88. 1999.

[29]   Palmius, J., "Criteria for measuring and comparing information systems. In 30th Information Systems Research Seminar in Scandinavia .IRIS (30). 2007.

[30]   Mugenda, O. M., & Mugenda, A. G. *Research methods. Quantitative and qualitative approaches*. Nairobi. Acts Press. 2003.

[31]   Kothari, C. R. *Research methodology. Methods and techniques*. New Delhi. New AgeInternational (P) Limited Publishers. 2004.

[32]   Matavire, R., Chigona, W., Roode, D, Sewchurran, E, Davids, Z, Mukudu, A., &Boamah-Abu, C., "Challenges of eGovernment Project Implementation in a South African Context," *The Electronic Journal Information Systems Evaluation,* 13(2), 153-164. (2010).

[33]   Thompson, K. R., &Mathys, N. J., "It's time to add the employee dimension to the balanced scorecard," *Organizational Dynamics*, 42(2), 135-144. 2013.

[34]   Banker, R. D., Chang, H., Janakiraman, S. N., &Konstans, C., "A balanced scorecard analysis of performance metrics," *European Journal of Operational Research,* 154(2), 423-436. 2004b.

[35]   Banker, R.D., Chang, H., Pizzini, M.J., "The balanced scorecard: judgmental effects of performance measures linked to strategy," *The Accounting Review*, 79(1), 1-23. 2004a.

[36]   Kaplan, R.S., & Norton, D.P., "Using the balanced scorecard as a strategic management system," *Harvard Business Review*, 74(1). 75-85. 1996.

[37]   Sinha, A., "Balanced Scorecard: A Strategic Management Tool," *Vidyasagar University Journal of Commerce*, 11. 2006.

[38]   Gueorguiev, I., "Balanced Scorecard Based Management Information System – A Potential for Public Monitoring and Good Governance Advancement," *The Electronic Journal of e-Government*, 3(1), 29-38. 2005.

[39]   Grembergen, W., Saull, R. &Haes, S. D., "Linking the IT Balanced Scorecard to the Business Obectives at a Major Canadian Financial Group," *Journal of Information Technology Cases and Applications*, 2003.

Appendix 1

Conceptual Framework

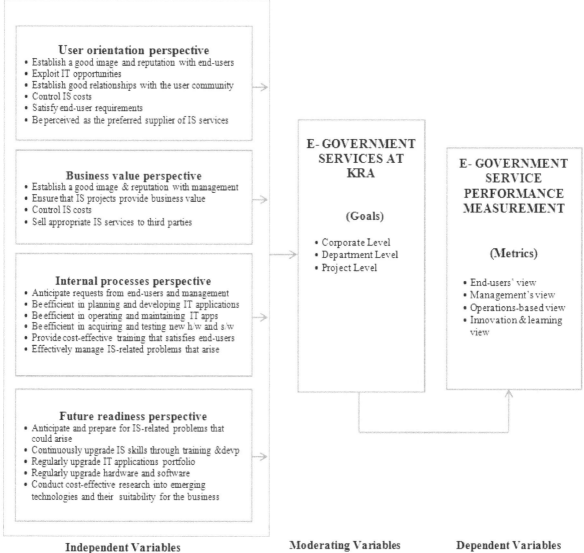

| Independent Variables | Moderating Variables | Dependent Variables |

Appendix 2

A. Step-by-step model for building a company-specific IS-Balanced scorecard

1. Create awareness for the concept of the balanced IS scorecard among top management and IS management.
2. Collect and analyse data on the following items:
   a. Corporate strategy, business strategy, and IS strategy;
   b. Specific objectives and goals related to the corporate, business and IS strategy;
   c. Traditional. metrics already in use for IS performance measurement; and
   d. Potential metrics related to the four balanced IS scorecard perspectives;
3. Clearly define the company-specific objectives and goals of the IS department or functional area from each of the four perspectives;

4. Develop a preliminary IS-BSC based on the defined objectives and goals of the enterprise and the approach outlined in this study;
5. Receive comments and feedback on the IS-BSC from management, and revise it accordingly;
6. Achieve a consensus on the IS-BSC that will be used by the organization; and
7. Communicate both the scorecard and its underlying rationale to all stakeholders.

Steps to effectively implement the IS-BSC framework:
1. Clarify and translate the vision and strategy into specific action programs;
2. Link strategic objectives to team and individual goals;
3. Link strategic objectives to resource allocation;
4. Review performance data on a periodic basis, and
5. Adjust the strategy as appropriate.

B. The principles for developing a balanced scorecard

It is essential to have a common understanding of the corporate-level strategy and the IS strategy, and have well-defined specific goals related to each before developing the IS-BSC. The metrics included in the IS-BSC should meet three criteria: quantifiable, easy to understand, and ones for which data can be collected and analysed in a cost-effective manner.

C. Errors to be avoided while implementing the IS-BSC

1. Failure to include specific long-term objectives;
2. Failure to relate key measures to performance drivers by means of cause-and-effect relationships;
3. Failure to communicate the contents of and rationale for the balanced IS scorecard.

7

Business Intelligence as a Knowledge Management Tool in Providing Financial Consultancy Services

Gul Muhammad, Jamaludin Ibrahim, Zeeshan Bhatti[*], Ahmad Waqas

Kulliyyah of Information and Communication Technology, International Islamic University Malaysia
*Corresponding author: zeeshan.bhatti@live.iium.edu.my

Abstract The main objective of this paper is to elaborate how Business Intelligence (BI) as a knowledge management tool could help consultants in providing professional services to the financial sector. The Business Intelligence (BI) solution could be a competitive advantage for the consultants if they are able to exploit the Business Intelligence (BI) tools and technology such as Data Warehouse, Data Mining, On-Line Analytical Processing (OLAP) and Extraction Transformation Load (ETL). The consultants can use Business Intelligence (BI) solution to analyze the organizational data such as structures and business processes of the Financial Institution. By analyzing the organizational data, the financial institution can imp better rove and streamline functional efficiencies to not only bolster up sales and marketing strategies and better develop customer services program, but also mitigate risk by developing more appropriate risk management actions. In brief, by having this competitive advantage, the consultant will be able to withstand in the market, which is always changing.

Keywords: *Business Intelligence (BI), Knowledge Management (KM), Data Mining, Data Warehouse, Extraction Transformation Load (ETL), On-Line Analytical Processing (OLAP)*

1. Introduction

In 2008, Business Intelligence (BI) was the number one technology priority for the third year in a row (Gartner, 2011). It has become the top presidency of Chief Information Officer (CIOs) since it (BI) can have a direct positive impact on business performance of an enterprise. The capability to complete the task by making brighter decision at every level of the business is another significance that what Business Intelligence (BI) can improve dramatically.

Most leading corporations expect personnel in every role to seek fresh and intelligent ways to improve performance, increase employees' effectiveness, and grow profit and stronger customer relationship. In order to achieve these expectations, Business Intelligence (BI) is the answer. Supporting decision-making at every level, modifying managers, executives and knowledge actors to take the most efficient action in given situations are the reasons why most leading organizations require Business Intelligence (BI) as a essential element.

Business Intelligence (BI) strategy must be aligned with the organization objectives, advance business and improves knowledge management. Business Intelligence strategy (BI) helps organization in creating the best utilize of information with tactical, strategic and operational decision-making.

Generally, the use of Business Intelligence (BI) in financial services has provided values. A survey conducted by Gartner, Inc found that more than 95 percent of banking answerers agreed that Business Intelligence (BI) is a strategically first step driven by senior management. The respondents are from banks, insurers and nonfinancial businesses. Gartner, Inc also found that more than 90 percent agreed they received the value awaited from their Business Intelligence investment.

Nowadays, most financial institution depends on Business Intelligence (BI). Financial services include banking (saving and loans, commercial banks, mortgage banks, credit union), securities and exchange (brokerages, investment banks, investment advisor), and international finance. The financial institution could exploit Business Intelligence (BI) as a competitive advantage.

In this competitive market age, financial sectors must have strategies to survive. Generally, a financial sector has huge amount of data that they process everyday, which is stored in their complex system. The efficient analysis of the data is very important and will determine the success of the financial industry. The way a Financial Institution in analysing the fraud, risk and customer behavior are very critical. Business Intelligence (BI) has been used for a years in order to help a company to solve this kind of problems, because Business Intelligence (BI) can handle huge amount of data for the comprehensive analysis.

2. Literature Review

2.1. Business Intelligence (BI)

(BI) comprises wide variety of applications for analysing, gathering, storing and making data easily accessible to help users to make better business processes. A good Business Intelligence (BI) definition must encompass both business purpose and technical functionality. Business Intelligence (BI) tools that are widely used are Data Warehouse, Data Mining, Extraction Transformation Load (ETL) and On-Line Analytical Processing (OLAP) (See Figure 1).

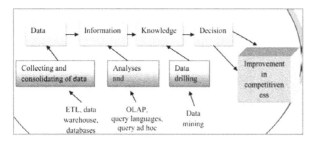

Figure 1. Business Intelligence

2.2. Data Warehouse

Data warehouse is an integrated collection of the summarized and historic data, which is collected by the spider web environment from internal and external data sources. Data warehouse is user friendly especially for business analyst and manager (Radonic, 2007). It collects relevant data to the repository where it is validated and organized to serve the decision-making objectives (Rao & Kumar, 2011).

2.3. Data Mining

Data mining is a process of discovering patterns, correlation and trends by modifying through the large amount of data, which stored in the warehouse. Recognition technologies, statistical and mathematical techniques are normally used in Data Mining technology.

2.4. Extraction Transformation Load (ETL)

Extract, transform and load - is set of actions by which data is extracted from numerous databases, applications and systems, transformed as capture, and loaded into target database - including, but not limited to, data warehouses, data marts, analytical applications, etc.

2.5. On-Line Analytical Processing

(OLAP) technology allows users to explore and analyse a huge amount data, involving complex computation and their relationship. On-Line Analytical Processing (OLAP) tools are a combination of graphical user interface (GUI) and processing procedures, which is produce a visual result in different perspectives to the users.

3. Knowledge Management

Knowledge Management (KM) is the collection of processes that govern the creation, dissemination, and utilization of knowledge. (KM) this is, as the word entails the power to handle "knowledge" and right knowledge

available to the right people. It is about making sure that an organization can learn, and that it will be able to retrieve and use its knowledge assets in current applications as they are needed. In Peter Drucker paper, he defines Knowledge Management (KM) as the coordination and exploitation of organizational knowledge resources, in order to create benefit and competitive advantage.

Knowledge Management (KM) is not always about technology, but also about understanding how the people work, brainstorming, identify groups of people who work together and how they can share and learn from each other and in the end the organization learning about their workers experience and about the leadership the organization (Arora, 2011).

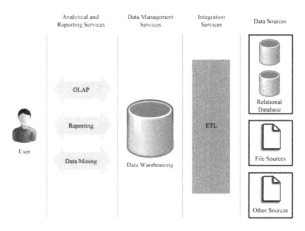

Figure 2. Business Intelligence Architecture

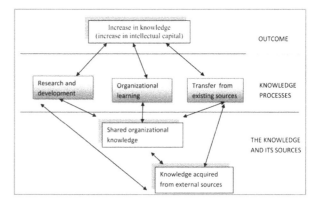

Figure 3. Knowledge Management

In Rao and Kumar paper, they explain that Knowledge Management (KM) is the practice to add actionable value to the information from the tacit to the explicit knowledge using storing, filtering retrieving and disseminating explicit knowledge and also by testing and creating new knowledge. "Knowledge Management (KM) will deliver outstanding collaboration and partnership working. It will ensure the region maximizes the value of its information and knowledge assets and it will help its citizens to use their creativity and skills better, leading to improved effectiveness and greater innovation", West Midlands Regional Observatory, UK.

4. Financial Services

Financial sector has definition as a class of ancestries carrying business firm, which offer financial services to the customer and commercial (investopedia.com). The financial sector includes insurance companies, real estate, investment funds and banks. Moreover, the financial services perform best in low interest rate environments while in large portion, this sector needs generates the revenue from mortgage and loans. Furthermore, when the business is, this sector benefits from the additional investments.

The challenges in the financial services are:
1. developing and changeable regulative surroundings,
2. Continued focus on risk management,
3. Expansion of products and services,
4. disbursement direction and restructuring,
5. Security and privacy risk keep coming,
6. Ensuring data integrity and proper data management,
7. Model risk management,
8. Derivatives reform,
9. Balancing incentive compensation,
10. In closing.

Wall Street, Fleet Street and Main Street: Corporate integrity at a Crossroads, A recent survey of the financial services industry in United Kingdom and United States revealed the wrongdoing in the financial industry. Among the key finding are (Wehinger, 2013):
1. 26% of respondents indicated that they had observed or had first-hand knowledge of wrongdoing in the workplace.
2. 16% of respondent would commit a crime (inside trading) if they could get away with it.
3. 24% of respondents believed that financial service professional need to engage in illegal activity in order to be successful.

5. Implementation of BI as KM Tools

To implement Business Intelligence as Knowledge Management tool to provide financial consultancy, many BI tools are available. Following are some of the example.
1. Enterprise BI tools,
2. Databases or packaged BI tools,
3. Visual Data Discovery tools,
4. Pure reporting tools.

Many organizations, both private and public, are currently evaluating or deploying Open Source BI tools (OS BI) like JasperSoft, Pentaho or SpagoBI. These three leading open source Business Intelligence suites offer a full range of Business Intelligence capabilities, ranging from ETL to ad-hoc analysis and reporting.

6. The Limitation of Business Intelligence (BI) and Knowledge Management (KM)

(Kascelan, 2011) try to elaborate some limitations in Business Intelligence systems especially on small companies, the reason are:
1. The initial price of the system is costly which even can reach one million euros of the big companies.
2. Data mining tools use sophisticated tools and they require the company to give additional training or even hire external consultant which increase the costs of implementation.
3. The time of implementation take a long time (6 months- several years). It gives disadvantages to the company which have limited financial assets.
4. Uncertainty in the success of implementation. The research from Gartner reveals that 2.000 data warehouse projects, only 20% are succeed.
5. A poor quality of source data is responsible for the majority of the time and cost overruns during the implementations. This is because the small companies has obsolesce of standard information system.

Based on (Joo & Lee, 2006), they doing research on the factors which are lead to dissatisfaction to the knowledge management's users, they divided the factors by two categories:
1. Restriction factors of System Quality:
i. Time and Space: time and space limitation in the Knowledge Manamgent (KM) system use and limitation of access methods.
ii. Inconvenience: the degree of discommode of the system which is resulting the slow response and imbalance.
iii. Knowledge search: the limitation of keyword-based search and also limited knowledge categorization.
iv. Knowledge consolidation: the restrictions in integrating of heterogeneous systems as knowledge resources and integration of the existing Knowledge Management system with the Web resources.
2. Limitations factors of Knowledge Quality:
i. Incongruence and rawness of Knowledge: the degre of incongruence or incompleteness of knowledge proffered by the KM system.
ii. Untrustworthiness of Knowledge: the degree of inaccuracy and untrustiness of knowledge proposed by the KM system.

The result of the research are have significant affirmative answers, the limitations factors for system quality such as search and integration, inconvenience and system quality positively affect user dissatisfaction with the Knowledge Management (KM) system. Moreover, the limitations components of knowledge prime such as incongruence/ inexperience and untrustiness and increase the dissatisfaction.

Figure 4. Business Intelligence (BI) and Knowledge Management (KM)

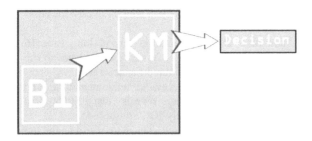

Figure 5. Business Intelligence (BI) and Knowledge Management (KM) in Decision Making

Business Intelligence (BI) makes for as educing worthful information and discover hidden patterns in internal and outside source of data. The main aim is to meliorate knowledge on the information which accords the top manager to create efficient decision to achieve organizational objectives. But, the majority of organizational knowledge is in unstructured form or in the minds of the employess. Furthermore, Knowledge Management (KM) plays to encompasses both tacit and explicit knowledge within the organizations increase the organization carrying into action by providing cooperative tools to create, acquire and contribute the knowledge within organization. (Khan & Quadri, 2012).

Business Intelligence (BI) and Knowledge Management (KM) are the main tools to achieve the organizational tool by providing the environment which users receive, desired and reliable and also timely information or knowledge. The organizations need both BI and Knowledge Management (KM) as an integrated system to get value from explicit and implicit knowledge (Khan & Quadri, 2012).

7. The Similarities and Differences between Business Intelligence and Knowledge Management

Fundamentally, Business Intelligence and Knowledge Management have the same aspires. Attaining the level best degree of empathizing of one's controlling environment and pertinent considerations that can be bring forward or delay advancement toward an aim is one of the purposes of Knowledge Management (KM). No matter how the same principle implements to the idea of Business Intelligence (BI). Supporting strategic decision-making, growing the business and monitoring competitor of organization are the purpose of conducting Business Intelligence (BI). Undoubtedly, there are absolute similarities between Knowledge Management as well as Business Intelligence.

Knowledge Management and Business Intelligence are established on information technology. They depend on the Internet, hardware, software, database storage technology. Besides that, their application in business processes both includes accumulating, collating, dealing and the use of information and knowledge. In addition, both accomplish their function depending on information and knowledge. It undoubtedly trues that Knowledge Management (KM) and Business Intelligence (BI) is interacting and complements each other.

Generally, the focus of Knowledge Management (KM) is cognition. It specifically interested about people have good noesis, cultural behavior. It also stressed the significance of the knowledge innovation and whether it is leveraged effectively. In the same way, Business Intelligence (BI) initially concentrated on technology and data, the applied effect of which in fact is closely related to the skills of user as people normally use quantitative analysis of technical expertise to solve business problem with the assistance of business intelligence system.

There are some fundamental differences, while both Business Intelligence (BI) and Knowledge Management (KM) concepts have similarity high-level objectives. The differences are to be found in the manner in which they are applied toward achieving that goal. While the value of Business Intelligence (BI) and its product, opportunity analysis is found in its usefulness as a decision making tool, the value of Knowledge Management (KM) relies in the ability of the organization to identify, capture and reuse knowledge and in particular best practices in such a manner that can save the organization time, effort and resources.

Another difference between Knowledge Management (KM) and Business Intelligence (BI) is the intension. Business Intelligence (BI) developed gradually through transactional serving systems, like administrative information system, management information systems and decision support system. Knowledge Management (KM) is the management idea and methods in the development of the knowledge economy era. It emphasized that knowledge is most important resource and strategic capital, the corporate competitor advantage relies on knowledge creation, dissemination and utilization.

Beside the connotation, both have difference in the focus. Business Intelligence mostly deals with data resources. As its aim to make information resources orderly and structured, the whole process of Business Intelligence (BI) is relatively closed and independent. Business Intelligence (BI) also focuses to the combining and integration of the external morphology of information. Opposite side, the Knowledge Management (KM) system deals with knowledge resources, knowledge sharing and innovation are the primary goals of it. For organization, while Business Intelligence (BI) manages with objective information in the real world, Knowledge Management system tends to action immanent and personal knowledge.

Lastly, the difference between Business Intelligence (BI) and Knowledge Management (KM) is the core technology. The core technology of Knowledge Management also imply in document management, groupware engineering science, text mining, retrieval technology, enterprise knowledge portals and so on, Business Intelligence (BI) on the other side attach more than meaning to data analysis and its core technologies consist of data warehousing, online analytical processing, data mining and enterprise portals.

8. Business Intelligence (BI) and Knowledge Management in Financial Sector

Business intelligence has gained acceptance in the most financial sector, even though there are many definitions of Business Intelligence (BI), however Knowledge Management (KM) has mixed response. Knowledge Management concept in organization has struggled because they frequently attempted to enforce huge enterprise-wide knowledge management projects failed. The complexity is another reason why the implementation failed.

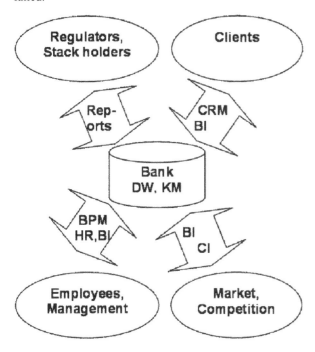

Figure 6. Banking Operation

Figure 6 shows how the strict and rigorous competition and market in bank's operation which are further regulated and restricted by several international and national authorities who demand prompt and constant auditing and reporting to assure the stockholders and supervisors of stability (Radonic, 2007). The figure also shows customer relationship management and business intelligence is needed in relationship to the clients and Human resource, Business Intelligence and business process management to their employee.

The globalizations, mergers, deregulations and acquisitions, competition from non-financial institutions and technological innovations make the company to always to rethink about their business strategy. In this case, financial services have to create new revenue streams, enter new markets, gain market share and reduce operational cost and also must concern about the customer expectations.

The application of Business Intelligence (BI) in banks can be summarized as follows: (Rao & Kumar, 2011)

Bank performance: It is about analysing the historical data of the institution to make decision on the future. The key performance indicators are deposit, credit, profit, income, branches, employees etc.

Marketing: Marketing is the most widely used for data mining in the banking industry. Usually it is been used for analyse the customers, in term of their preferred product or services.

Risk management: With the uncertain and changing market, it's also affected financial situation. Lack of the knowledge may have great risk in the future customer. Especially in banks there are present risk of payment default, fraud, theft and operational risk connected with internal procedures and processes.

Customer segmentation: Most business activities are focusing on the customer. All business activities must understand who their customer is. The segmentation is a method of grouping customer based on their character or patterns which will help the organization to understand whom and where the product target.

Fraud detection: According to Decker, there two approaches to detect the fraud. First, the bank taps the data warehouse of a third party and use the data mining to identify. Second, using bank's own internal information

Budget planning: Try to understand the performance indicators from a specific area and calculated from the existing information from the system.

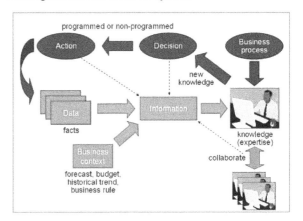

Figure 7. Knowledge Management (KM)

The Figure 7 shows the knowledge management technologies. In a traditional Business Intelligence (BI), the system must provide capabilities such as business process management, collaborative portal, and business planning software, portals and content management systems and be able to support more timely data feeds.

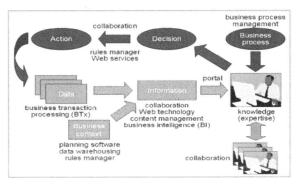

Figure 8. Knowledge Management (KM) with Business Intelligence (BI)

The Figure 8 illustrates the knowledge cycle on how the Knowledge Management (KM) can help the business to improve their processes. The figure shows how the Business Intelligence which contents information becomes the central role in knowledge management. It has data, business context, decision, action and the collaboration of experts.

In order to support all major financial and accounting activities, most financial institutions have implemented software. Customer Relationship Management and Supplier Management software are the most powerful systems that have become trend in managing relationship with customers and suppliers. However, the main purpose of these systems is to record, organize and retrieve information that resides in their specific database. But, these systems are not built as analysis tools.

Although some systems offer limited analytical features, but the features are cover only their own application's database and cannot be used with other systems in the company. Consequently, it is very difficult to get access to summarize as well as detailed information through a single user interface. So, the people who responsible for operating different systems will have a great deal in writing, maintaining and printing their report for management. This is the reason for one of today's great frustration of corporate managers and analysts.

There are some limitations and issues in decision-making based on static reports from different systems:

1. Information overload,
2. Lack of information,
3. No interactivity,
4. Lack of unified cross-database analysis tools.

Implementing a Data Warehouse with modern Business Intelligence (BI) software can be the solution to the problem of a poor analytical environment in a company. The poor analytical environment will have multiple data sources, different report writers and lack of analytical tools.

It is finally becoming feasible for financial institution to implement Data Warehouse that can be updated and maintained with relative case by utilizing modern ETL (Extraction Transformation Load).

A common data repository is resulted, which provides decision makers with endless possibilities for investigating (Data Mining) and analysing variances, trends and exceptions. Because a modern Business Intelligence (BI) solution feeds off a frequently updated Data Warehouse that includes detailed information. This becomes a tool for any person within the organization or related to it who needs easy and fast access to summarized and detailed information from across the database of company and it becomes much more than just a tool for executives.

There are some key features that offered by many Business Intelligence tools. The some key features are:

1. Drill-down,
2. Graphs, charting and trees,
3. Exception highlighting,
4. Pivot rows and columns,
5. Drag and drop dimension into the current view or to the background,
6. Custom calculations,
7. Queries,
8. Comments,
9. Combo views,
10. Dashboards,
11. Business Intelligence (BI) and web portals,
12. Distribution of cubes/reports,
13. Other popular analytical features (ranking, filtering, sorting, etc).

Most financial manager found difficulties in asking new data from one or more of the corporate information systems to the Information System (IS) department. Because, the feedback is rarely what financial manager asked for. Not all people in Information System (IS) department would understand about finance smatters such as the difference between debit and credit, Year To Date (YTD) or periodic balance.

In some leading organizations, they are specializing some of their Information System (IS) staff by hiring Information System (IS) personnel into the accounting department trying to deal with these barriers. This is an expensive solution and does not necessarily solve the problem.

In order to meet the never-ending request for more financial information, the proactive approach for the financial department seems to be to become self-supplied with timely financial information and better quality on the data.

Over last few years, there are many companies have succeeded to create proactive approach by creating Data Warehouse that host data from disparate sources and making them available to end user through Excel, Internet browser and On-Line Analytical Processing (OLAP) or managed query tools.

9. Conclusion

In conclusion, this paper describes how business intelligence plays its role as knowledge management tool to give benefit to the financial sector which always has fast-changing market and vast-amount of data. The business intelligence plays role to extracting the hidden patterns and valuable information from internal and external source of data. Moreover, the knowledge management has roles to cover the tacit and explicit knowledge within the organizations, which has function to enhance its performance. It can be said that business intelligence sustains the knowledge management to maintain and enhance the performance of financial organization.

The leverage of Business Intelligence (BI) as a Knowledge Management (KM) tool could be competitive advantages for the financial consultancy. Because, Business Intelligence (BI) solution helps consultants provide professional services to the financial sector. Business Intelligence (BI) solution might be the collaboration between any Business Intelligence (BI) tools and concepts. So, the consultant must have a competitive advantage to remain in the global market that keeps changing every time.

References

[1] Albescu, F., Pugna, I., & Paraschiv, D. (2008). Business Intelligence & Knowledge Management – Technological Support for Strategic Management in the Knowledge Based Economy. *Revista Informatica Economică*,, 6-12.

[2] Arora, E. (2011). Knowledge Management In Public Sector. *Journal of Arts Science and Commerce*.

[3] *BMO Bank of Montreal Slices Costs Time With Web-Based Reporting.* (n.d.). Retrieved April 15, 2013, from http://www.informationbuilders.com/applications/bank_montr:

[4]   *Business Intelligence Helps SMBC Adapt to Dynamic Market.* (n.d.). Retrieved April 15, 2013, from http://www.informationbuilders.com/solutions/banking.

[5]   *Business Intelligence Solution for Financial Services-microstrategy.com.* (2011). Retrieved April 13, 2013, from http://www.microstrategy.com/bi-applications/solutions/: http://www.microstrategy.com/download/files/solutions/byindustry/Microstrategy-mobile-bi-financial

[6]   Cheng, L., & Cheng, P. (2011). Integration: Knowledge Mangement and Business Intelligence. *Fourth International Conference on Business Intelligence and FInancial Engineering.*

[7]   Gartner. (2011). A step-by-step approach to successful Business Intelligence. *Featuring research from Gartner.*

[8]   Gartner. (2008). Gartner EXP Worldwide Survey of 1,500 CIOs Shows 85 Percent of CIOs Expect "Significant Change" Over Next Three Years. Retrieved from Gartner: http://www.gartner.com/newsroom/id/587309

[9]   Information Builders. (n.d.). *WebFocus Business Intelligence.* Retrieved from Information Builders: http://www.informationbuilders.com/products/webfocus

[10]   Joo, J., & Lee, S. M. (2006). Technical Limitation Factors of Knowledge Management Systems and a New Approach. *Management Review: An International Journal*, 4-16.

[11]   Kascelan, L. (2011). Advantages And Limitations In Implementation of Business Intelligence System In Montenegro: Case Study Telenor Montenegro. *Journal of Economic and Business*, 19-30.

[12]   Khan, R. A., & Quadri, S. K. (2012). Dovetailing of Business Intelligence and Knowledge Management: An Integrative Framework. *Information and Knowledge Management.*

[13]   KBase. (n.d.). *ETL Services.* Retrieved from KBase: http://www.kbase.com/etl.htm

[14]   McCarthy, S. (1999). *Business Intelligence versus Knowledge Management.* Retrieved from Inside Knowledge: http://www.ikmagazine.com/xq/asp/sid.0/articleid.6EEB9883-1D0D-4771-BC94-66F470A0F50E/eTitle.Business_Intelligence_versus_Knowledge_Management/qx/display.htm

[15]   MicroStrategy Incorporated. (2011). Business Intelligence Solution for Financial Services.

[16]   Nadeem, M., & Jaffri, S. A. (n.d.). Application of Business Intelligence in Banks (Pakistan).

[17]   Olszak, C. M., & Ziemba, E. (2007). Approach to Building and Implementing Business Intelligence Systems. *Interdisciplinary Journal of Information, Knwoledge and Management.*

[18]   Pant, P. (2009). Business Intelligence (BI): How to build successful BI strategy. *Business Intelligence (BI): How to build successful BI strategy.*

[19]   Skriletz, R. (2003). *Business Intelligence in the Financial Services Industry.* Retrieved from Information Management: http://www.information-management.com/issues/20030801/7152-1.html

[20]   Radonic, G. (2007). A Review of Business Intelligence Approaches to Key Business Factors in Banking. *Journal of Knowledge Management.*

[21]   Rao, G. K., & Kumar, R. (2011). Framework to Integrate Business Intelligence and Knowledge Management in Bankin Industry. *Review of Business and Technology Research.*

[22]   Ranjan, J. (2009). Business Intelligence: Concepts, Components,Techniques and Benefits. *Journal of Theoretical and Applied Information Technology*, 60-70. *RBC Royal Bank Capitalizes on WebFOCUS for Operational Reporting.* (n.d.). Retrieved April 15, 2013, from http://www.informationbuilders.com/applications/rbccanada:

[23]   Reinschmidt, J., & Francoise, A. (2000). *Business Intelligence Certification Guide.* IBM.

[24]   Wehinger, G. (2013). Banking in a challenging environment: Business models, ethics and approaches towards risks. *OECD Journal: Financial Market Trends.*

8

The Method for Comparative Evaluation of Software Architecture with Accounting of Trade-offs

Alexander Kharchenko[1], Ihor Bodnarchuk[2,*], Vasyl Yatcyshyn[3]

[1]Department of Computer Informational Technologies, National Aviation University, Kyiv, Ukraine
[2]Department of Computer Science, Ternopil Ivan Pul'uj National Technical University, Ternopil, Ukraine
[3]Department of Computer Engineering, Ternopil Ivan Pul'uj National Technical University, Ternopil, Ukraine
*Corresponding author: bodnarchuk.io@gmail.com

Abstract Since growing complexity of software systems it is more difficult to meet demands of quality during the process of their design. To solve this problem with minimal loss this process is transferred onto more early stages of design, particularly onto the design of architecture. The architecture is treated as the set of components that encapsulates the logic of calculations, and connections that ensure the interaction between components and create their configuration. Since the architecture of software system is a high-level abstract model for representation of system structure and key properties, its selection grounds the insurance of quality for software system. In the paper the questions of evaluation of architecture quality on the set of quality attributes with Analytic Hierarchic Process (AHP) with applying of optimization algorithm for estimating of weights of alternatives are discussed. The conflicts between quality indices and trade-offs between them are analyzed.

Keywords: *Software Architecture, Multivalued Optimization, Quality of Software Architecture, Software Architecture Evaluation*

1. Introduction

The quality of architecture decision is evaluated on the totality of criteria, and its selection always is a trade-off, because for the given set of functional requirements and requirements for quality there is no single best solution, and improving of some criteria leads to deterioration of others and vice versa. So why when selecting the architecture decision for software system it is necessary to apply the methods of multicriteria evaluation with accounting of conflicts between indices of quality and to make trade-offs.

There are early and late evaluation of architectures. Early one is based on the experience of designers and logical reasoning because there are not any arte facts that allow to simulate the performance of the software system. Methods that realize early evaluation are based of scenarios. Following methods are belong to this group: SAAM and ATAM [1]. On the base of stakeholder priorities defined quality criteria. A scenario is working out to check the satisfaction for each quality attribute, and assessing the level of satisfaction of the attribute by given architecture alternative is carried out.

ATAM method is similar to SAAM, but here for selected architectures the risks of satisfaction of quality attributes are evaluated on the base of analysis of scenarios. Evaluation of risks the group of experts performs, and this group as well ranges alternatives according to the level of risk and defines so called points of sensitivity on the components or connections of architecture, trade-offs between indices of quality are analyzed too.

For reasonable selection of decision in the method SAAM/ATAM selected architectures are analyzed on the subject of costs and benefits with applying of method CBAM [2]. This method ensures economic analysis of software system, which are based on the selected on previous methods variants of architecture and scenarios of simulation. Experts assign scores for quality indices from 1 to 100 and range architectures according to scores what these architectural deci $Cont_{ij}$ sions ensure for certain attribute. Evaluation of each architecture alternative is calculated according to the following expression:

$$B(A_i) = \sum_{j=1,K} \left(Cont_{i,j} \cdot Q_j \right) \ i = \overline{1,n}. \qquad (1)$$

Here – $Cont_{ij}$ is the weight of ith architecture corresponding to j^{th} attribute;
Q_j – the priority of jth attribute.

This method allows to evaluate cost for realization of each alternative and gives possibility to calculate the index of desirability as relation of benefit to costs. On the base of obtained data the best solution is selected.

Often appears the problem to create software system on the base of existing one via redesign to meet new requirements for quality. To solve problems like this the method SSAR for reengineering of software system architecture on the base of scenarios was created[3], that is the aggregate of four methods of architectures evaluation relatively to quality attributes:

  – evaluation on the base of scenarios;
  – simulation;
  – math simulation;
  – evaluation of the base of practical experience.

When using SSAR the one method among other is selected, but the main is the method on the base of scenarios. This method is similar to that one realized in SAAM.

Detailed analysis of scenario-oriented methods for evaluation of architectures such as ATAM, SAAM, SAEM and others is made in the work [4]. Shown the schemas of scenarios for different methods of evaluation. The conditions when applying of certain method will be most effective aredescribed.

The common disadvantage for all discussed above methods is consequent evaluation of the architecture relatively to one parameter, what require to elaborate new scenario and to carry out expert evaluation of risks each time, so it makes the process of selection laborious and nonformalized. Here as well impossible to obtain comparative estimations for the set of alternatives.

Further researches in this field showed the effectiveness the method on the base of Analytical Hierarchic Process (AHP) for solving of such problems [5,6]. One of the first publications on applying of AHP for evaluation of software system architectures on the totality of quality indices is the work of M. Svahnberg [6]. It contains the step-by-step algorithm of solution for the problem of evaluation of the set of architectures on the totality of quality indices and choosing of the best architecture of software system. The method's utilization is illustrated on the concrete example.

To overcome the disadvantages of AHP connected with inconsistency of the matrix of pair wise comparisons for big quantity on alternatives ($n \geq 7$) it is proposed to correct the elements of the matrix. But it leads to partial use and disfiguration of expert data what decrease the truthfulness of obtained results. In the works [6,8,9] for correct applying of AHP in case of big quantity of alternatives ($n \geq 9$) the modified AHP was used.

In the modified AHP the comparative evaluation of architectures are used relatively to their realization of quality attributes. It allows to find relative weights of alternatives for each quality attribute and to range them. According to assigned by stakeholders priorities of quality attributes their averaged value is calculated and the weights of alternatives are estimated regarding to the totality of quality attributes.

Obtained relative assessments of alternatives can be used for analysis of conflicts between quality attributes and for identifying of compromise decision.

The advantages of modified AHP method are the evaluation of alternatives for all quality attributes, optimization of decisions, and enough high level of formalization, what allows to automate the process.

Offered in this paper approach is grounded on the applying of AHP with optimization algorithm for finding of weights of alternatives. This allows to expand the usage of algorithm on greater quantity of compared alternatives ($n>9$). The sensitivity of solution to the change of priorities for quality criteria is examined, and conflicts and trade-off between criteria are analyzed.

2. The Evaluation of Architectures with Analytical Hierarchic Process

The process of comparative evaluation of architectures with applying of AHP is shown on the Figure 1.

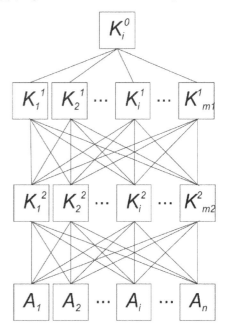

Figure 1. Hierarchic representation of the problem of architecture evaluation

The selection of architecture must be performed so that built on its base software system will meet quality requirements. Hence here we see two levels of interconnected quality attributes:

$K_i^1, i = \overline{1, m1}$ – quality attributes of software system according to the standard ISO/IEC 25010;

$K_i^2, i = \overline{1, m2}$ – quality attributes of architecture;

$A_i, i = \overline{1, n}$ – alternative architectural decisions.

The set of quality criteria of software system $\left\{ K_i^1 \right\}$ and constraints for them are defined on the stage of gathering of requirements to the software system. The set of quality indices for the architecture $\left\{ K_i^2 \right\}$ can be defined with applying of QFD (Quality Function Deployment) method or the method of pair wise comparisons [10].

It is necessary to select among available alternatives $\left\{ A_i \right\}$ such one, that will ensure the quality of software system. In other words it is necessary to solve the optimization problem regarding to the totality of parameters $\left\{ K_i^1 \right\}$ and $\left\{ K_i^2 \right\}$. This is the problem of multicriteria hierarchical optimization and to solve it the AHP will be applied [11].

When AHP is applying for solution of problems like this the relative weights $\{w_i^s\}$ of alternatives are found on each level using of matrices of pairwise comparisons $B^s\{b_{ij}^s\}$. These matrices are filled up by experts and here b_{ij}^s means the supremacy of ith alternative over j^{th} one.

Coefficients of matrices must be consistent, i.e. $b_{ij}^s = w_i^s / w_j^s \quad \forall b_{ij}^s \in B^s$. The weights in this case will be found as components of eigenvector for matrix of pair wise comparisons, which correspond to the maximum characteristic number of the matrix. The calculation of eigenvector is enough complicate procedure. So why the approximate value is used very often [11]:

$$w_i^s = \frac{1}{n}\sum_{j=1}^{n}\frac{b_{ij}^s}{\sum_{j=1}^{n}b_{ij}^s} \qquad (2)$$

But for considerable quantity of alternatives, since influence on experts of different factors, the matrix $B^s\{b_{ij}^s\}$ is inconsistent and its rank will differ from 1, i.e. the matrix will have some different eigenvalues. A. Pavlov in his paper [12] proposed for solution of this problem models and method for calculation of weights for alternatives on the base of minimization of inconsistency of the matrix $B^s\{b_{ij}^s\}$.

And in [6,8,9] this method was applied for the problem of architecture selection with accounting of quality indices. For this problem the measure of inconsistency was used like following.

$$\left|\frac{w_i^s}{w_j^s} - b_{ij}^s\right| \le \delta_t \cdot b_{ij}^s, \quad \delta_t \ge 0, \qquad (3)$$

where δ_t – is given threshold value.

Then, when the condition of independency of error form $\frac{w_i^s}{w_j^s}-1$ in estimation of b_{ij}^s by experts is kept, weights w_i^s, which minimize (3) can be found as solution of linear programing problem [13]:

$$\min_{\{w_i\}}\sum_{i=1}^{n}\sum_{j=1}^{n}\left(y_{ij}^+ - y_{ij}^-\right)$$
$$w_i^s \ge a_i, \quad i=\overline{1,n}, \qquad (4)$$
$$w_i^s - b_{ij}^s w_j^s = y_{ij}^+ - y_{ij}^-; \qquad b_{ij}^s \ge 1;$$
$$-\delta_t \cdot b_{ij}^s \cdot w_j^s \le w_i^s - b_{ij}^s \cdot w_j^s \le \delta_t \cdot b_{ij}^s \cdot w_j^s, \qquad (5)$$
$$y_{ij}^+, y_{ij}^- \ge 0; \quad i,j=\overline{1,n}.$$

Thus, estimation of weights for alternative architectures w_i is reduced to the solution of problem (4), (5). During solving of this task the incompatibility of constraints (5) can appear, so the δ_t must be increased. Application of

this algorithm gives possibility to obtain the weights of alternatives both for realization of each quality criteria and for their totality. In the work [7] the advantages of used modified AHP were illustrated.

But when making decision on selection of architecture on the found estimations of w_i^s for taking into account stakeholders' constraints and priorities it is need to analyze conflicts between quality criteria and to find compromise decisions.

3. Investigation of the Sensitivity when Ranging the Alternatives and Analysis of Trade-offs

After finding according to (4), (5) the solution w_i^s for each criterion the architectures can be ranged according to the values of weights.

Such research were carried out regarding the sensitivity of architectures' ranging to the changes of priorities for quality criteria. For this matter the weights of alternatives were calculated regarding for each following criteria: modifiability, scalability, performance, ease of install, cost, development effort, and portability.

And calculations for the totality of criteria were executed too.

Below most typical results of calculations are represented for four alternatives as most representative for their field of usage:

1. Three-level on the base of Java Enterprise Edition (TJEE) as the base for development uses the platform Java 2 Enterprise Edition (J2EE) what is at same time the industry-accepted standard that enables solutions for developing and deploying of distributed multitier enterprise applications.

2. Three-level on the base of .NET (TNET)is analogical to the TJEE but for its realization the tools and frameworks for applications development from Microsoft ® are used.

3. Two-level (TWOL)provides the realization of all business logic on the client side.

4. Platform with support of distributed agent (DAS).Using of distributed agent (DAS) for building of the application provides higher flexibility. As a technology CORBA, DCOM or SOAP can be used.

Figure 2 shows weights of alternative architectures regarding forthe quality criteria.

To define integral index of architecture quality we need to define the priorities of quality criteria. Since in the process of design of software systems some groups of stakeholders are involved, which have different priorities for each quality attribute, it is necessary firstly to define the priorities for each group via composing by them matrices of pairwise comparisons with applying of modified AHP to these matrices. Then priorities of criteria $\{P_i^s\}$, $i=\overline{1,k2}$ is calculated (s – is the number of group of experts).

Compromise decision can be found as a geometric mean $r_{ij}^+ = \sqrt{r_{ij}^1 \cdot r_{ij}^2 \ldots r_{ij}^n}$ or as mean with accounting of index of competency for each expert group

$$P_{ij}^* = P_{ij}^{\alpha_1} \cdot P_{ij}^{\alpha_2} \cdot \ldots \cdot P_{ij}^{\alpha_n} \quad (\alpha_1, \alpha_2, \ldots, \alpha_n - \text{ are indices of} \quad \text{competency}).$$

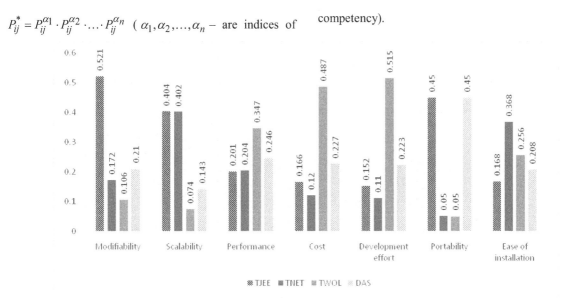

Figure 2. Weights of architectural alternatives regarding to quality criteria

The assessments of priorities for quality criteria from different expert groups obtained by method of pairwise comparisons are shown on the Figure 3.

As we can see from the Figure 3, modifiability is most important attribute with weight 0.28, then follows ease to install. In the final order of ranged alternatives the sample TJEE considerably exceeds all the rest alternatives. DAS and TWOL are very closed with weights 0.237 and 0.248 correspondingly. TNET is the worst variant.

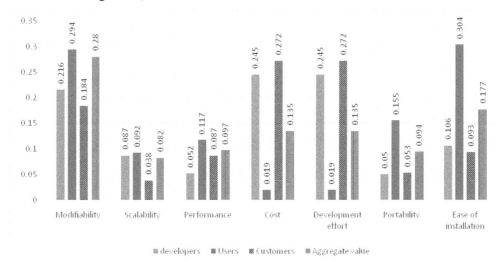

Figure 3. Priorities of quality criteria

It is not convenient to analyze correlations between weights of alternatives when they are represented as numbers. So more acceptable is graphical representation of these results.

Graphical representation is good as well for analyzing of trade-offs between quality attributes of architecture.

3.1. Trade-offs Analysis for Quality Attributes

The diagram of trade-offs between cost and modifiability for examined alternatives is shown of the Figure 4.

Such representation gives possibility to visualize possible trade-offs, their relative values and relations between alternative designs from the point of view of compromises.

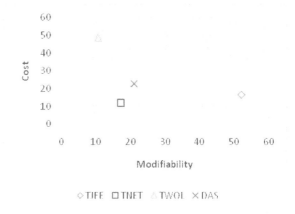

Figure 4. Trade-off between quality attributes

When conflicting attributes have same priority then graphically the trade-off between them will be shown on the diagonal of first quadrant. When architectural decision must be selected with accounting of the priority of one quality attribute so, that Pareto-optimal decision will be selected what is highest relatively to the diagonal of first quadrant when the attribute with priority is on the axis of ordinate. When the attribute with priority is on the x-axis, so the Pareto-optimal decision will be the lowest relatively the diagonal of first quadrant in the rightest position.

For the decision TWOL (left upper cornet on the Figure 4 the architecture is Pareto-optimal regarding to the criterion cost and when this criterion has higher priority than modifiability this architecture will be selected. In same time, the alternative TJEE is Pareto-optimal for the index of modifiability, and this is represented as point that is located under the diagonal in the most right position.

So the size of a trade-off is represented by the location of the point in the left-and-up or right-and-down direction relatively the diagonal of first quadrant. When the alternative is located in the third quadrant it means that both attributes have negative influence on the architecture decision.

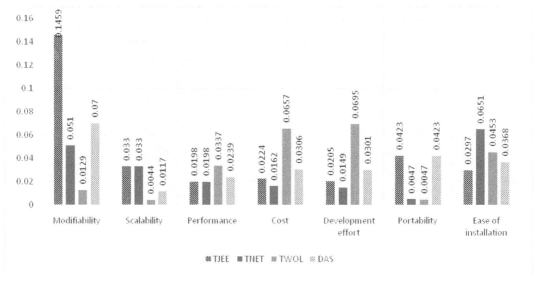

Figure 5. Ranged architectural alternatives with accounting of priorities of quality attributes

When to take into account the weights of attributes for analysis of trade-offs then the results can change. On the Figure 5 the architectural alternatives are shown, ranged according to the weights of attributes. Then the trade-offs diagram from the Figure 4 will be reduced to the diagram on the Figure 6.

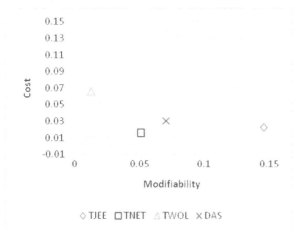

Figure 6. The trade-offs diagram between cost and modifiability (with accounting of weights of quality attributes)

The alternative TJEE has considerable superiority in modifiability regarding to other alternatives. So for the TJEE trade-offs between modifiability and any other quality attributes will strengthen on the diagram of trade-offs. Thus, these diagrams visualize trade-offs and their values, which are not visible when AHP is used.

3.2. Analysis of Sensitivity

Now let us examine the sensitivity of decisions obtained with AHP, to the change of priorities of quality criteria.

Let we have ranged architectural alternatives $\{A_i\}$, obtained with Analytical Hierarchic Process. The formula below is for definition of minimal change of absolute value of weight for quality attribute such, that the order of adjacent architectures A_i and A_j will be flipped on reverse as shown in the Eq. (6) below.

$$D'_{s,i,j} = \frac{|J_i - J_j|}{|w_i^s - w_j^s|} \cdot \frac{100}{P_s} \qquad (6)$$

Here $D'_{s,i,j}\left(s = \overline{1,m2}; i, j = \overline{1,n}, i \neq j\right)$ is minimal change of the value of the priority P_s for the quality criterion K_s, which changes the order of adjacent alternatives A_i and A_j in ranged list on opposite. The minimal value of $D'_{s,i,j}$ shows that the priority P_s for the quality criterion K_s is critical for the changing of assessments in pairwise comparisons. This expression can be used as well for the case of change of requirements to the software system during the design process, what can lead to the change of priorities for quality criteria.

For each quality attribute more than one value of $D'_{s,i,j}$ is possible, which can cause the change in the order of adjacent alternatives.

4. Conclusions

The above analysis of methods for tevaluation of architectures has shown, that the most acceptable is the Saaty's Analytical Hierarchic Process, which allows to get relative assessments of alternative architectures both for one quality criteria and for their totality. To expand the correctness of AHP the optimizational method of calculation (definition) for weights of alternatives is used, what is based on the model of inconsistency minimization for the matrix of pair wise comparisons. Obtained in AHP solutions are convenient for the analysis of the sensitivity of ranged alternatives to the change of priorities of quality criteria, and for definition of trade-offs when making decision. For the fixed example of alternatives and criteria the effectiveness of proposed method is shown.

Further researches are dedicated to creation of adaptive to changes of quality requirements method for evaluation of alternative architectures of software system on the set of quality indices. Such method will allow to make operative corrections in the evaluation of alternatives without repeat solution of the problem. One more direction of researches is the modification AHP with taking to account of degree of alternatives' incomparability and its applying for the problem of architectures selection on the set of quality indices. In fact the standard AHP cannot be applied when supremacy of some alternative over other one is more than 9 [11].

References

[1] Kazman, R. *ATAM: Method for Architecture Evaluation* / Rick Kazman, Mark Klein, Paul Clements. Pittsburgh, PA: Software Engineering Institute, Carnegie Mellon University, August 2000. CMU/SEI-2000-TR-004, ADA377385. 83 p.

[2] Kazman, R. Quantifying the costs and benefits of architectural decision/ Kazman, R., Asundi, J., and Klein // *Proceedings of the 23rd International Conference on Software Engineering (ICSE)*, 2001. pp. 297-306

[3] Bengtsson, Perolof Architecture-level modifiability analysis (ALMA) / Perolof Bengtsson, Nico H. Lassing, Jan Bosch, Hans van Vliet // *Journal of Systems and Software*. 2004. Vol. 69, No. 1-2. pp. 129-147.

[4] L. Dobrica and E. Niemela. A Survey on Software Architecture Analysis Methods. *IEEE Transactions on Software Engineering*, vol. 28, no. 7, pp. 638-653, July 2002.

[5] T. Al-Naeem, I. Gorton, M.A. Babar, F. Rabhi, and B. Benatallah, "A quality driven systematic approach for architecting distributed software applications", *Proceedings of the 27th International Conference on Software Engineering(ICSE)*, St. Louis, USA, 2005. pp. 244-253.

[6] M. Svahnberg, C. Wholin, and L. Lundberg. A Quality-Driven Decision-Support Method for Identifying Software Architecture Candidates. // *Int. Journal of Software Engineering and Knowledge Engineering*, 2003. 13(5): pp. 547-573.

[7] Harchenko Alexandr, Bodnarchuk Ihor, Halay Iryna. Stability of the Solutions of the Optimization Problem of Software Systems Architecture // *Proceeding of VIIth International Scientific and Technical Conference CSIT 2012*. pp. 47-48, Lviv, 2012.

[8] AlexandrHarchenko. The Tool for Design of Software Systems Architecture // AlexandrHarchenko, Ihor Bodnarchuk, Iryna Halay, VasylYatcyshyn // *Proceeding of XIIth International Conference CADSM' 2013*. pp. 47-48, Lviv.

[9] AlexandrHarchenko.DecisionSupportSystemofSoftwareArchitect // AlexandrHarchenko, Ihor Bodnarchuk, IrynaHalay // *Proceeding of the 2013 IEEE 7th International Conference on Intelligent Data Acquisition and Advanced Computing Systems (IDAACS). Volume 1*, pp. 265-269, Berlin.

[10] Kharchenko O.H. Instrumentaljnyj zasib rozrobky ta komunikaciji vymogh jakosti do proghramnykh system / O.G. Kharchenko, V.V. Yatcyshyn, I.E. Rajchev // *Inzhenerija proghramnogho zabezpechennja*. Kyiv, – 2010. # 2. pp. 29-34.

[11] Saaty T. *Decision Making with the Analytic Network Process./* Saaty T. Vargas L.// – N.Y.: Springer, 2006. 278 p.

[12] Pavlov A.A. Matematicheskie modelioptimizaciidljanahozhdenijavesov obyektov v metode parnyh sravnenij. Pavlov A.A, Lishchuk E.I., Kut V.I.// *Sy`stemni doslidzhennya ta informacijni texnologiyi* – Kyiv: IASA (Institute for Applied System Analysis), 2007. #2, pp. 13-21.

[13] Zgurovskij M.Z., Pavlov A.A., Shtankevich A.S. Modificirovannyj metod analiza ierarhij // *Sy`stemni doslidzhennya ta informacijni texnologiyi* – Kyiv.: IASA (Institute for Applied System Analysis),–2010. #1, pp. 7-25.

9

Balanced Scorecard vs Standard Costing

Cheporov Valeriy[*]

Economic Faculty, V.I. Vernadsky Crimean Federal University, Simferopol, Republic Of Crimea
*Corresponding author: cheporov@crimea.edu

Abstract A management control system (MCS) is a system which gathers and uses information to evaluate the performance of different organizational resources like human, physical, financial and also the organization as a whole in light of the organizational strategies pursued. The development of strategy maps and Balanced Scorecards has transformed the foundation of management control systems. Costs of managerial control system can be significantly reduced when found common framework for its various instruments. The aim of paper is to establish communication between the Balanced Scorecard and Standard costing as an instrument of management information systems. It is proposed to use a variance analysis for the changes in the financial position as the metrics for perspectives of Balanced Scorecard. The possibility of using accounting balance equation and double entry for the perspectives of Balanced Scorecard also shown.

Keywords: balanced scorecard, standard costing, strategic variance analysis, changes in financial position

1. Introduction

Accounting is the process of recording, classifying, summarizing, reporting and interpreting information about the economic activities of an organization. As well as an information system is a formal process for collecting data, processing the data into information, and distributing that information to users. The purpose of an Accounting Information System (AIS) is to collect, store, and process financial and accounting data and produce informational reports that managers or other interested parties can use to make business decisions. Although an AIS can be a manual system, today most accounting information systems are computer-based.

Both MIS (Management Information System) and AIS are information systems based on computers that are very helpful for organizations towards keeping their records properly. AIS is a division of MIS and is all about a system of maintaining the entire accounting, sales and purchase records, financial statements, and other transactions. It is very helpful in organizing the account system in an organization. It is true that AIS is very helpful in judging the previous performances and it plays a vital part is deciding the actions the future projects. However the financial information is not enough to maintain the success of any operation. Any management needs information that AIS simply cannot provide.

The design of an effective measurement systems have proven very challenging, particularly in light of the dramatic change of the business and manufacturing environments we have witnessed during the last three decades or so. Traditional, financially based performance measures were, at best, unable to cope with the requirements of the new environment (Shank & Govindarajan, [10]). Kaplan & Johnson [3] argue that these financial measures are "too late and too aggregate to be of use to managers". They further argue that these financial measures were misleading by distracting managers away from real problems.

Any management information system may consist of a set of accounting and management tools, which forms the portfolio or tool kit. The more instruments in the set, the greater the cost of developing and supporting information system. Therefore, the search for the common ground of different tools is a practical interest from the point of view of cost reduction and theoretical interest in terms of identifying the general nature of those or other tools. The success of the accounting information systems is largely due to the format of data storage, based on double-entry accounting. Using a double entry accounting in the management information system can reduce the cost of its development and support.

The aim is to identify the nature of the accounting Balance Scorecard, including the use of balance equation, accounting double entry, standard costing, and Statement of changes in financial position.

2. Literature Review

From the point of view of the objectives of the work we are interested in research in several directions. Firstly it research related to the cost information. Overview of approaches and models are given, for example, in works of A. Haug et al [2] and A. Mutze & D. van Ierland [8]. The second area of research is to review the practice of application management tools (CIMA [6], D. Rigby & B. Bilodeau [9]). The third line of research involves the search for similarities and differences between various managerial and accounting tools: TD ABC vs ABC (R. Kaplan & S. Anderson [5], BSC vs TDB (M. Souissi [12]), ABC vs ABM (G. Cokins & S. Căpușneanu [1]. Target

Costing vs other managerial tools (H. Sharaf-Addin et al [11]) and other works.

Finally, the last line of research related to the profit variance analysis (Shank & Govindarajan, [10]) or strategic variance analysis as a strategic perspective on a common cost management tool.

A Strategic Variance Analysis (SVA) is a management tool used to establish reasons for differences in a firm's operating income between two time periods – reasons that may not always be apparent from the financial statements (Mudde, P. A., & Sopariwala, P. R. [7]). SVA allows management to determine, in the form of performance variances, changes in operating income resulting from changes in sales volume, sales prices, costs per unit of activity, productivity and capacity utilization.

Our approach is similar to the latter approach because the Statement of changes in financial position and Income statement gave got a close connection.

Our research concerns the relationship between The Balanced Scorecard and traditional accounting frameworks.

In 1992, Robert S. Kaplan and David P. Norton introduced the balanced scorecard, a set of measures that allow for a holistic, integrated view of business performance. The scorecard was originally created to supplement "traditional financial measures with criteria that measured performance from three additional perspectives—those of customers, internal business processes, and learning and growth" (Kaplan and Norton 1996, [4, p. 75]).

By 1996, user companies had further developed it as a strategic management system linking long-term strategy to short-term targets. The development of the balanced scorecard method occurred because many business organizations realized that focus on a one-dimensional measure of performance (such as return on investment or increased profit) was inadequate. Too often, bad strategic decisions were made in an effort to increase the bottom line at the expense of other organizational goals. The theory of the balanced scorecard suggested that rather than the focus, financial performance is the natural outcome of balancing other important goals. These other organizational goals interact to support excellent overall organizational performance.

The Kaplan and Norton balanced scorecard looks at a company from four perspectives:
• Financial: How do we look to shareholders?
• Internal business processes: What must we excel at?
• Innovation and learning: Can we continue to improve and create value?
• Customer: How do customers see us?

By viewing the company from all four perspectives, the balanced scorecard provides a more comprehensive understanding of current performance.

Robert S. Kaplan and David P. Norton's concept of balanced scorecard revolutionized conventional thinking about performance metrics. By going beyond traditional measures of financial performance, the concept has given a generation of managers a better understanding of how their companies are really doing.

3. Methodology

Balanced Scorecard (BSC) is one of the performance measuring tools due to performance drivers. Improving the efficiency (performance) means moving the company to a higher level, which is associated with an increase in value of the company by increasing its capital.

The capital increase is measured by the change in the financial condition of a certain period, primarily due to the net profit. The Company may increase its own capital as long as you want, and each year a profit at the same level, if not changed external or internal environment. The change in the financial condition is measured simply by subtracting the initial statement of the final statement (the difference between the two balance statements), and is effected in the Statement of changes in financial position (Cash flows statement or Statement of changes in working capital).

However, the company can wish to change their internal environment, business processes or improve the company's image among its customers.

In this case there is a variance in financial position (Statement of changes in financial position) during comparing the usual changes and the changes that occur as a result of certain performance activities.

In our opinion, it is this variation in changes in financial position, can be measured through the BSC perspectives. BSC should have a close relationship with accounting. The key word in this context is the word "balance." Balance requires a causal phenomena that are associated with the method of accounting double entry. In this sense, the BSC perspectives can be considered as elements of the financial statements.

The causal link between the BSC perspectives through their performance indicators in this context can be considered as accounts.

Therefore, the balanced scorecard is actually used in standard costing.

In our opinion, the balanced scorecard (BSC) proposed by Kaplan and Norton, in fact, is a system that produces the appearance of the desired variance for all types of costs and revenues.

4. Results

Let's consider the basic accounting equation which connects the assets, liabilities and capital:

$$A = L + C$$

This equation is known to arise from the definition of equity as the difference between assets and liabilities, and which is otherwise called as the net assets i.e.

$$NA = C \qquad (1)$$

This equation must be maintained after any financial transaction.

Let's fix the value of capital (net assets at the beginning of a certain period).

At the end of the year as a result of the transaction there is a change in the financial position of the company compared with the beginning of the year. This change in accordance with Accounting Standards describes the Statement of changes in working capital (cash flow statement). When such activity is a regular change in the financial position measured one and the same quantity. If the company does not plan to increase or decrease the volume of its activities, this amount can be withdrawn from the company, such as the payment of dividends. This constant unvarying activity can be called stationary, because after payment of dividends financial position (balance sheet) at the beginning and end of the period will be the same.

The use of the Balanced Scorecard, as well as other systems of strategic planning lead to a breach of a stationary, that, in fact, is the change (variance) in the financial position before and after the introduction of the new strategy. We will use the term " variance".

Further reasonings we will carry out the example of the production operations of the company.

Add and subtract a summand $Cm_o \cdot M_o$ on the left side of the equation (1), which is the product of the unit price of the purchased material in the stationary statement of enterprise (before the implementation of a balanced scorecard).

$$NA + Cm_o \cdot M_o - Cm_o \cdot M_o = C \qquad (2)$$

From the point of view of mathematics at such operation does not change the equation. From the viewpoint of the accounting this transaction is written as shown in Figure 1:

Account	Debit	Credit
Inventory	$Cm_o \cdot M_o$	
Account payable		$Cm_o \cdot M_o$

Figure 1. Usual double entry

Let's suppose that as a result of the implementation of the BSC the company plans to reduce the purchase price to the value Cm_p , that is less than Cm_o . Let's imagine the amount of $Cm_o \cdot M_o$ as:

$$Cm_o \cdot M_o = (Cm_o - Cm_p) \cdot M_o + Cm_p \cdot M_o \qquad (3)$$

In terms of accounting, this means an attempt to reflect the change in inventories, and liabilities in connection with the new purchase price. The last two summand on the left side of equation (2) can be represented with regard to (3). Then on the left side of the equation will be two summands $(Cm_o - Cm_p) \cdot M_o$ with different signs. A summand with a minus sign will be moved to the right side of the equation (2).

In terms of accounting the expression $(Cm_o - Cm_p) \cdot M_o$ on the right-hand side of the equation represents the increase in the value of future financial result (profit), and on the left side - increase in net assets due to the appearance of lesser liabilities to suppliers.

Mathematically, the same can be obtained by adding and subtracting the left- side of the equation of (2) value $Cm_p \cdot M_o$.

Thus, after the implementation of these reforms the equation (2) can be transformed to the following form:

$$NA + (Cm_o - Cm_p) \cdot M_o + Cm_p \cdot M_o - Cm_p \cdot M_o$$
$$= C + (Cm_o - Cm_p) \cdot M_o \qquad (4)$$

From the viewpoint of the accounting transaction can be written as shown in Figure 2:

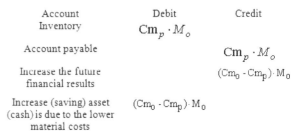

Account	Debit	Credit
Inventory	$Cm_p \cdot M_o$	
Account payable		$Cm_p \cdot M_o$
Increase the future financial results		$(Cm_o - Cm_p) \cdot M_o$
Increase (saving) asset (cash) is due to the lower material costs	$(Cm_o - Cm_p) \cdot M_o$	

Figure 2. BSC oriented double entry

Our aim in this record is a representation of the reasons for the increase of the financial result, in this case, by saving asset. This notation is similar to the transaction record on buying material in the standard costing, which usually looks like:

Account	Debit	Credit
Inventory	$Cm_n \cdot M_n$	
Account payable		$Cm_a \cdot M_n$
Direct material price variance		$(Cm_n - Cm_a) \cdot M_n$

Figure 3. Standard cost oriented double entry

The index n and a represent respectively standard and actual value.

The difference in the above two accounting records that in standard costing materials are recorded in debit on a standard price and the Accounts payable –on a fact price . Therefore, there is a difference, which is reflected in the account «Direct material price variance». If the actual price is lower than the standard price, such a value is called a positive variance, or else - negative. This is a positive or negative variance eventually at the end of the period is usually charged to the income statement.

Unlike standard costing in which the accounts payable is carried at actual cost and there is only one account for variation entry the difference between the amounts recorded in the debit of materials and credit of payments to suppliers, we propose to use two variance accounts with different types of balance, but the same amounts . One of them is traditionally associated with the financial result and the second reflects the future growth of the net assets. It can be called "The increase (maintaining) the asset (cash) due to the decrease in accounts payable." This account in the traditional accounting and standard costing does not exist. However, we propose to introduce it to reflect the link between standard costing and BSC as one of the variances in the BSC due to the financial result (financial perspective), and the second with the asset (customers or perspective business processes perspective).

For the standard costing, eventually, by variance account charged to the financial result, the value of which will coincide with the financial result using the method of actual costs. For the purposes of the BSC, we will "collect" these variances to reflect the effect of achieving the planned indicators.

The BSC approach in determining the perspective price is tentatively scheduled to save the asset, such as money that would be spent for the payment of accounts payable at the usual price of the material

For simplicity, we will use mathematical operations, sometimes commenting their accounting content.

Now add and subtract on the left side of the equation (4) a double summand $\mathrm{Cm}_p \cdot M_p$, which is the product of the perspective price of the purchased material and its planned quantity for the production.

$$NA + (\mathrm{Cm}_o\text{-}\mathrm{Cm}_p) \cdot M_o + (M_o - M_p) \cdot \mathrm{Cm}_p$$
$$+ \mathrm{Cm}_p \cdot M_p - \mathrm{Cm}_p \cdot M_p \qquad (5)$$
$$= C + (\mathrm{Cm}_o\text{-}\mathrm{Cm}_p) \cdot M_o + (M_o - M_p) \cdot \mathrm{Cm}_p$$

The third term on the right is associated with the growth of the future financial performance through more efficient use of the materials, and the corresponding term in the left side due to the economy with the purchase of the asset less quality of materials for the same volume of output.

The final accounting entry with the effect of price and volume of the used material can be written as:

Account	Debit	Credit
Inventory	$\mathrm{Cm}_p \cdot M_p$	
Account payable		$\mathrm{Cm}_p \cdot M_p$
Increase the future financial results		$\mathrm{Cm}_o \cdot M_o -$ $- M_p \cdot \mathrm{Cm}_p$
Increase (saving) asset (cash) due to the smaller amount of purchased material	$(M_o - M_p) \cdot \mathrm{Cm}_p$	
Increase (saving) asset (cash) is due to the lower material price	$(\mathrm{Cm}_o - \mathrm{Cm}_p) \cdot M_o$	

Figure 4. BSC perspectives's oriented double entry

Note that the difference between $\mathrm{Cm}_p \cdot M_p$ and $\mathrm{Cm}_o \cdot M_o$ can be expressed in two ways:

$$\mathrm{Cm}_o \times M_o \text{-} \mathrm{Cm}_p \cdot M_p = (\mathrm{Cm}_o\text{-}\mathrm{Cm}_p) \cdot M_o +$$
$$+ (M_o - M_p) \cdot \mathrm{Cm}_p \qquad (6)$$

or

$$\mathrm{Cm}_o \cdot M_o \text{-} \mathrm{Cm}_p \cdot M_p = (\mathrm{Cm}_o\text{-}\mathrm{Cm}_p) \cdot M_p +$$
$$(M_o - M_p) \cdot \mathrm{Cm}_o \qquad (7)$$

Most textbooks recommend to calculate a price variance of materials through the product of the difference between the standard and the actual price and the actual quantity of the materials used, not the standard one.

If your organization uses this approach, the variance that occurs due to simultaneous changes in price and use of the material, is a variance of the price of the material. This approach is explained by the fact that an employee of the purchasing department is responsible for the performance of all purchased materials, whether justified if these materials are then used by the production departments.

This combined variance associated with activities such as the purchasing department and manufacturing department, i.e. associated with business processes.

In terms of the BSC we are not interested in changes in the financial position at the end date, which is described by equation (5), and the variance on the same date on the stationary financial condition of a perspective one.

Let we have identified a perspective price and quantity of material used. Then after purchase the required amount of raw materials needed in production, we can write the balance equations for stationary and perspective situations.

$$A + \mathrm{Cm}_o \times M_o = L + \mathrm{Cm}_o \times M_o + C$$
$$A + \mathrm{Cm}_p \times M_p = L + \mathrm{Cm}_p \times M_p + C$$

Subtracting the second equation from the first one can be obtained

$$(\mathrm{Cm}_o\text{-}\mathrm{Cm}_p) \times M_o + (M_o - M_p) \times \mathrm{Cm}_p$$
$$= (\mathrm{Cm}_o\text{-}\mathrm{Cm}_p) \times M_o + (M_o - M_p) \times \mathrm{Cm}_p \qquad (8)$$

The left side of equation (8) is a savings asset, due to lower costs for materials related to the price and efficiency of use. Really, sales of finished products and the disposal of an asset (cost of goods sold) due to the lower its cost, bringing the same income. Therefore, the right side of (8) is connected with the financial result and not with liabilities.

Indeed, it can be assumed that the positive summand $\mathrm{Cm}_p \cdot M_p$ in the left-hand side of equation (5) is not raw materials, but the materials that are already in the finished product. This summand can be written as $\mathrm{Cm}_{pq} \cdot Q$ where Cm_{pq} is the share of promising direct material costs in the unit cost of the finished product, Q is the number of units of finished products to be sold. Note that the index Q is absent, as we consider the situation in which usual sales coincides with the perspective.

For a more accurate representation of the fact that the right-hand side of equation (8) shows the variance in financial result, not the liabilities, to replace this expression with the above in mind.

$$(\mathrm{Cm}_o\text{-}\mathrm{Cm}_p) \cdot M_o + (M_o - M_p) \cdot \mathrm{Cm}_p$$
$$= (\mathrm{Cm}_{oq}\text{-}\mathrm{Cm}_{pq}) \cdot Q \qquad (9)$$

The left side of this equation is the variance of the net assets and the right side of the variance in the financial results related to the variance of the direct material costs.

The process of converting raw materials into finished products with the subsequent sale may take a considerable period of time, but the operating cycle is much smaller compared with the terms of achieving strategic objectives in accordance with the BSC.

In the classical standard costing with a more efficient use of materials in progress remain unused materials. In our case, we purchased a quantity of material that needs to go completely the manufacture of products, i.e, there are no stocks of unfinished production.

For the classical standard costing more efficient use of materials results in the unused materials in process. In our case, company purchases a quantity of material that needs to complete the manufacture of products, i. e, there are no stocks of work in process.

In the future, we will use not the absolute characteristics of the financial position condition and the variance in the example of the equation (9). In contrast, changes in financial position, which is actually due to the difference between the financial statement at the end and beginning of the period, a variance in the financial position, we will understand the difference between stationary and future financial position.

We write the analog of equation (9) for direct labor costs

$$(Cw_o\text{-}Cw_p)\cdot T_o + (T_o - T_p)\cdot Cw_p \\ = (Cw_{oq}\text{-}Cw_{pq})\cdot Q \tag{10}$$

Here Cw_o, Cw_p are the usual and perspective tariff rates of direct labor for one hour of work, and T_o, T_p are the usual and perspective times per unit of production, and Cw_{oq}, Cw_{pq} are parts of the usual and perspective direct labor costs in the unit cost of the finished product.

The right side of equation (10) represents the change in the financial result due to direct labor costs, where the first term on the left side - savings / overruns of resources (assets) related to the introduction of a perspective rate of hourly wages, and the second term - to increase / decrease the labor effectiveness (elapsed time).

Add the equation (10) to (9)

$$(Cm_o - Cm_p)\cdot M_o + (M_o - M_p)\cdot Cm_p + (Cw_o - \\ - Cw_p)\cdot T_o + +(T_o - T_p)\cdot Cw_p = (Cq_o - Cq_p)\cdot Q \tag{11}$$

here Q is usual / perspective output, $Cq = (Cqm + Cqw)$ is a production cost per unit that is the sum of direct material and direct labor costs per unit produced and sold products, which are determined by the formula.

$$Cqm = Cm \times \frac{M}{Q}, Cqw = Cw \times \frac{T}{Q}$$

At this stage of production overheads, including depreciation will not be taken into account.

P_o, P_p are respectively usual and prospective sales price per unit of output, $P_p \cdot Q, P_o \cdot Q$ are the corresponding revenue. We add the expression $(P_p - P_o)\cdot Q$ to both sides of the equation (11).

$$(Cm_o - Cm_p)\cdot M_o + (M_o - M_p)\cdot Cm_p + (Cw_o - \\ - Cw_p)\cdot T_o + (T_o - T_p)\cdot Cw_p + (P_p - P_o)\cdot Q = \Delta Pr \tag{12}$$

Here ΔPr is variances in income (excess profit, taking into account the introduction of BSC over usual profit), which is determined by the formula.

$$\Delta Pr = (P_p - P_o) \times Q - (Cq_p - Cq_o) \times Q \tag{13}$$

Let's introduce the following notation in the equation (12)

$$Pc = (Cm_o - Cm_p)\cdot M_o + (P_p - P_o)\cdot Q \\ Pb = (M_o - M_p)\cdot Cm_p + (Cw_o - Cw_p)\cdot T_o \\ Pd = -(T_p - T_o)\cdot Cw_p \\ Pf = \Delta Pr \tag{14}$$

Here Pc, Pb, Pd, Pf are the values that can be associated respectively with the perspectives of customers, business processes, innovation and growth, as well as finance.

Note that we have term Pd with a minus sign, compared with perspectives Pc and Pb because the

perspective of innovation and growth may be associated with an increase in wages and lead to a negative deviation. For example, hiring more skilled workers should lead to a positive variance in the use and price of the material, i.e, a positive value customer and the business processes perspectives.

Equation (12) in terms of prospects BSC can then be written as

$$Pc + Pb = Pd + Pf \tag{15}$$

Thus, by analogy with the accounting equation perspectives of customers and business processes can be considered an analogue of the asset, the financial perspective is precisely the variance of results, ie, It is associated with its own capital.

How valid is the linking of the perspectives of innovation and growth with human capital, leave is beyond this study.

Since the left-hand side of equation (15) is an analog of the assets and the right side - an analogue of liability plus own capital, then operation entries or a balanced relationship between perspectives for the BSC can be carried out similar to the rules of accounting balance and double entry.

Debit	Credit
Increase Pc	Decrease Pc
Increase Pb	Decrease Pb
Decrease Pf	Increase Pf
Decrease Pd	Increase Pd

Figure 5. Double entry for Increase / Decrease BSC perspectives

The main difference between the transaction entries in the accounts and the perspectives accounts is the fact that the first accounts reflected on the absolute amount, but the second – on the variances. All of the concepts related to the accounting entries also apply to perspectives accounts.

Note that the direct operation as:

Increase Pc (Debit) – Increase Pd (Credit)

can have a duration of time as to achieve growth indicators related to customer relationship, you must first carry out an investment in innovation and growth, i.e.,

Decrease Pf (Debit) – Increase Pd (Credit)

And then the following operation must be performed:

Increase Pc (Debit) – Increase Pf (Credit)

Account Pf in this case is a control account which may reflect such a difference in time.

This gap in time reflects the special role of the BSC, which links strategic objectives with tactical tasks. That is, to move the company from one statement to another (defined mission and vision) that are established indicators BSC as either absolute or relative parameters that must be changed in steps over a period, reaching the set value by the end of the period of strategic transition. After that, the company can again operate normally, but on another level.

Therefore, we can say that the relationship between strategy and tactics according to the MTP is shown in this process step by step, clear to all participants

In order to reflect the incremental nature of the relationship between strategy and tactics of the target can be expressed by the words "to reduce the price of raw materials purchased by 5% every year for N years."

Often companies are not willing to publicly display the absolute values of each of the perspectives, so we can talk about relative terms, such as price reduction on the purchase of raw materials by 5%.

Note that each of the prospects of the Balanced Scorecard can only appear when the company planned to move to a new state.

5. Conclusions

Since the standard costing system is a product of the general accounting system, between BSC accounting as there is a connection. Perspectives for the BSC are variances in the elements of financial statements and can be run in accordance with the accounting rules of the recording in the accounts.

In this sense, the BSC is a system of standard costing, focused for a longer time compared to the classical. By analogy with the accounting balance equation, perspective clients and business processes can be considered analogous to the asset. The financial perspective is precisely the variances of results, that is associated with its own capital. The perspective of innovation and growth is associated with human capital. That is to say, the perspective of customers is an increase in net assets as result of relations with suppliers and customers; the perspective of business processes is an increase in net assets due to internal business - processes; development perspective is an increase in human capital; finance perspective is an increase in equity due to profits.

It seems logical to include these four perspectives, as one of them is related to the financial results, the second - with the production process within the company, while the other two - with external parties (customers, suppliers, or government) and employees of the company, ie by the company's operations, while which occurs receivables or payables.

Balance equation in terms of perspectives leads to the possibility of applying the rules of accounting double entry for the perspective indicators of BSC using debit and credit of accounts (indicator of perspectives for BSC). The essential point is that the balance equation is assessed on a gross basis.

The standard costing the cost centers are opposed to each other. For example, if the actual direct material costs were higher usual costs, the reason may be the high price

of raw materials or inefficient use of the materials. Responsible for this is the different responsibility centers (supply department or pant). For example, the purchasing department has decided to buy the raw material of lower quality at a lower cost, which has increased the volume of raw materials used. BSC establishes closer causal relationship between various the cost and the responsibility centers, which soon leads to cooperation rather than confrontation between these centers.

References

[1] Cokins, G., Căpușneanu, S., "Sustaining an Effective ABC/ABM System," *Theoretical and Applied Economics,* XVIII 2 (555). 47-58. 2011.

[2] Haug, A., Zachariassen, F., & van Liempd, D. "The costs of poor data quality," *Journal of industrial engineering and management,* 4(2). 168-193. 2011.

[3] Johnson, H.T and Kaplan, R.S., *Relevance lost: The rise and fall of management accounting.* Harvard Business School Press, Boston, MA, 1987.

[4] Kaplan, R., and Norton, D., "Using the Balanced Scorecard as a Strategic Management System," *Harvard Business Review,* 75-85 Jan.–Feb.1996.

[5] Kaplan, R. S. and Anderson, S. R., *Time-driven activity-based costing: a simpler and more powerful path to higher profits,* Harvard Business School Press, Boston, MA, 2007.

[6] "Management accounting tools for today and tomorrow" Available:
http://www.cimaglobal.com/Thought-leadership/Newsletters/Insight-e-magazine/Insight-2010/Insight-January-2010/Major-survey-benchmarks-management-accounting-tools/.. [Accessed Aug. 27, 2013].

[7] Mudde, P. A., & Sopariwala, P. R., "Examining southwest airlines' strategic execution – A strategic variance analysis," *Management Accounting Quarterly.* 20-32. Summer. 2008.

[8] Mutze, A. & van Ierland, D. "Time Driven ABC: nieuw in Nederland?," Available:
http://www.nl.atosconsulting.com/NR/rdonlyres/A2664E2D-727C-4B96-A362-72F0AA57AE4D/0/4447CM5_6_timedrivenabc.pdf. [Accessed Jun. 01, 2012].

[9] Rigby, D., & Bilodeau, B., "Management Tools and Trends 2007" Available:
http://www.bain.com.ua/bainweb/PDFs/cms/Marketing/Management%20Tools%202007%20BB.pdf. [Accessed Aug. 27, 2013].

[10] Shank, J.K. and Gonindarajan, V., *Strategic cost management: the new tool for competitive advantage,* New York: Free Press. 1993.

[11] Sharaf-Addin, H. H., Omar, N., & Sulaiman, S., "Target Costing Evolution: A Review of the Literature from IFAC's (1998) Perspective Model," *Asian Social Science;* 10 (9). 82-99. 2014.

[12] Souissi, M., "A Comparative Analysis Between The Balanced Scorecard And The French Tableau de Bord," *International Business & Economics Research Journal,* 7 (7). 83-86. Jul. 2008.

10

Systemic Evaluation of Semi-Electronic Voting System adopted in Nigeria 2015 General Elections

Omolaye P. O[1,*], Pius Daniel[2], Orifa A. O[3]

[1]Department of Electrical and Electronic Engineering, University of Agriculture, Makurdi, Benue State, Nigeria
[2]Department of Public Administration, Federal Polytechnic, Nasarawa, Nigeria
[3]Department of Business Education, Adeyemi College of Education, Ondo, Nigeria
*Corresponding author: email:donphylloyd1@yahoo.com

Abstract Nigeria's experience with paper-based balloting has produced challenges to election such as the snatching of ballot boxes and alteration of election results. Full-flesh Technology-based election most especially the use of Electronic Voting Machines will go a long way to arrest some of these electoral crimes. Therefore, in this research work, we review the tedious electioneering processes, voting technologies, foot note and solution to the rising perspective as a result of low turnout of voters during elections in all the six geo-political zones with a proper documentation. Hence, a proposed web-enabled voting system which inculcates the features and characteristics of electronic voting machine (*e*VM), Internet Voting (*i*-voting) and mobile voting (*m*-Voting) is proposed for enhanced participatory democracy that has attributes of free, fair and credible election in Nigeria and Africa as a whole.

Keywords: Nigeria, internet, i-voting, m-Voting, INEC, democracy

1. Introduction

"A system is said to be democratic in nature if, it permits only eligible voters to vote and it ensures that each eligible voter can vote only once [4]". There is a wide variety of different voting systems that are based on traditional paper ballots, mechanical devices, or electronic ballots [2,3]. In order to determine whether a system performs these tasks well, it is useful however, to develop a set of criteria for evaluating system performance. The criteria to be developed are such as accuracy, democracy, convenience, flexibility, privacy, verifiability and mobility [5]. Election is a process in which voters choose their representatives and express their preferences for the way that they will be governed. In this regard, voting refers to the actual process of casting ballots (on the assigned day of voting). Therefore, correctness, robustness to fraudulent behaviors, coherence, consistency, security, and transparency of voting are all key requirements for the integrity of an election process and also integrity, impartiality, transparency, professionalism, gender sensitivity are principles guiding the election officials to conduct free and fair election. [1]. People all over the world including the local and foreign observers started taking a hard look at their Independent National Electoral Commission (INEC) authentication equipment, long procedures to follow by the officials and ad-hoc staff, and trying to figure out how to improve on the issue of voting fraud and challenges such as deceased people voting,

voter impersonation, voting by proxy, voter suppression, voting not count, election rigging, snatching of ballot boxes and ballot papers, results being prevaricated and to cap it all the litigation after the election. All these challenges summed up to irregularity and instability in electoral process which tends to make the people to lose confidence in the electoral system of Nigeria.

The flaws of electoral act in most countries lead to election rigging, which constitutes a serious threat to democratic values in any liberal democracy. These flaws are inherent in most African States' Electoral Acts. These flaws affect Nigeria democracy with six Geo-political zones as shown in Figure 1.

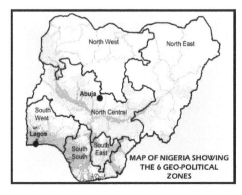

Figure 1. the map of Nigeria indicating the Six Geo-political zones

Nigeria's democracy is the most populous democracy in Africa with population of about 160 million. Nigeria is so giant that people say that as Nigeria goes, so goes

Africa. Therefore, much is expected from Nigeria in all ramifications. On 28 March 2015, after 4 years of tremendous preparation, Nigerians experienced its first Nigeria Semi-Electronic General Elections in which the country tapped partly from breakthrough of Information and Communication Technology (ICT) in part of the electoral process. The Semi-Electronic election process in this context is the act of using an electronic device for verification of eligibility of voters, vote with the use of ballot paper based system and counting manually, and then collation at top levels can be done with the use of e-collation platform. Nigeria 2015 Election, closely and keenly contested by two giant parties brought about the whole world turned and watched the electoral drama unfolding itself. Nigerians started wondering, "Wouldn't all our problems be solved if they just used Traditional based paper system, Semi-Electronic voting or full flesh Electronic voting systems?"

2. Literature Review

According to Macintosh which started that the most powerful symbol of a democracy is the citizen's involvement in the free and fair election of representatives to govern them. Macintosh continues to state that voting is seen as the act that currently defines the relationships between citizens, governments and democracy. Today, the internet has become a part of the daily life of many people around the world; no one could have foreseen how it would transform society three decades later [6]. Owing to the fast progress of computer and communication technologies, many advanced services have been developed to take the advantages of the techniques. Among these services, electronic voting is a popular one since every voter can finish her/his voting process securely and rapidly but here in Nigeria, the electoral process is termed as Semi-Electronic voting system with following activities and processes as shown in Figure 2.

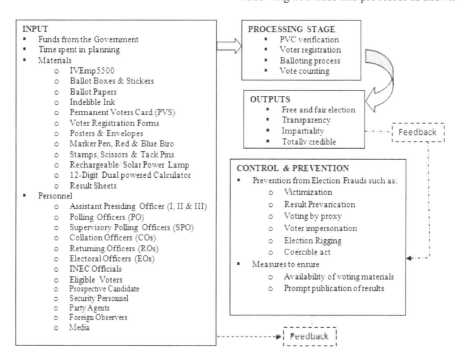

Figure 2. Nigeria Semi-Electronic Voting System

In [9,11], the author specified mainly on securing the voting system, by comparing the insecurities that exist in the manual voting system to that of the electronic voting system. Since the 1959 elections, which were the last to be supervised by the colonial authorities, all but one election has had its result contested. The only exception to this pattern was the June 12 1993 presidential election won by Chief M. K. O Abiola which was annulled by the Ibrahim Babangida military administration [7]. All the previous elections from 1999 till 2011 are purely manual but that of 2015 embraced some elements of ICT in action.

General Muhammadu Buhari, who contested the 2003 presidential polls on the platform of All Nigerian Peoples Party(ANPP), describes the election as "a dark period in our history" (Buhari, 2006) and Akume (2006) contends that the elections were "characterized by large scale malpractices including rigging at all levels" Given the massive irregularities that attended the 2003 elections and the consequent legitimacy crisis they engendered, the

2007 and 2011 polls presented an opportunity for both the government and the election authorities to restore public confidence in the election process [16,17]. The opportunity to make amends in 2007 was, unfortunately, squandered by the Obasanjo presidency and INEC. While the former exploited its control of state administrative resources (including using anti-graft agencies and the court to undermine the electoral ambition of opposition candidates), and the latter arbitrarily deployed its regulatory powers to exclude certain candidates from the ballot [7]. The process that led to the 2007 elections and their actual conduct was massively flawed. Thus, the outcome of the elections could hardly be regarded as representing the true wishes of the Nigerian voters.

Local and foreign election observer groups that monitored the 2007 and 2011 elections documented the irregularities and manipulation that attended the elections. The Transition Monitoring Group, a consortium of domestic observer groups, reported that the elections "were seriously marred by egregious irregularities and malpractices to the extent of not only compromising the integrity of the ballot in many states.

3. Review of Voting Technologies

a. Paper-Based Process: The process is a rigorous one because the process of validation before voter's ID will be issued involves a lot of paper work, appropriate training and time used to get the polling unit/station arranged according to specification. After voting, the counting of ballots will be looked after by another group of officers [14]. With all these steps, groups and procedures that are involved, the process can prove to be tedious, error prone and costly. Some introduction of technology currently in the Nigerian and Jamaican system, however, makes the process semi-electronic, but this is far from what could be really accomplished by a fully ICT integrated and driven process.

b. E-Voting: Electronic voting encompasses both electronic means of casting votes and counting of votes which can include punched cards, optical scan voting systems and specialized voting kiosk, transmission of ballots via telephones, private computer networks or the internet [12]. There are different types of electronic voting systems with the advent of technology to avoid electoral frauds like paper based electronic voting.

c. Direct Recording Electronic Voting System (DRE): This voting machine records votes by means of a ballot display provided with mechanical or electro-optical components that can be activated by the voter - typically buttons or a touch screen [13]; that processes data with computer software; and that records voting data and ballot images in memory components which produces a tabulation of the voting data stored in a removable memory component and as printed copy.

d. Public network DRE voting system: Internet voting systems have been used privately in many modern nations and publicly in the United States, the UK, Switzerland and Estonia. A public network DRE voting system is an election system that uses electronic ballots and transmits vote data, from the polling place to another location over a public network. Vote data may be transmitted as individual ballots as they are cast, or periodically as batches of ballots throughout the Election Day, or as one batch at the close of voting exercise.

e. Smart Card Voting(Token): With the use of the smart cards and kiosk there was a significant leap in voting technology, as persons were able to vote within their own comfort zone or that was the intension. The need for the various human security bodies was eliminated. This system however, has flaws on security aspect and voters could vote multiple times.

4. Nigeria 2015 General Elections

The just concluded 2015 Election propounded the laid down voting procedure follow [1]:

- Accreditation and verification of eligible voters using Emp5500 machine in the morning between the hours of 8 am and 1 pm.
- After accreditation and verification, followed strictly by the election proper at exactly 1:30 pm. The voters

will line up to cast their votes by thumb printing for the candidate of their choice based on party logo. The Presiding officer (PO) will count the number on the line and a security personnel will stand as the last person to avoid people joining unnecessarily

- After the last voter has voted, then voting process is said to be concluded, the Presiding officers in polling centers count the votes in the presence of all the party agents and some voters that are present.
- Following the completion of counting and recording of the votes on Forms EC. 8A and/or EC. 8A (I) and (II), the PO shall put the original completed form (statement of Result of Poll from the Polling Unit) in a tamper-proof envelope(s)
- The PO proceed immediately to the Collation Centre where election results shall be done at the levels depending on the type of election in the following order:
  - ♣ Registration Area/Ward (RA/Ward) – Collation for all Elections
  - ♣ Local Government Area – LGA (Collation for all Elections)
  - ♣ State Constituency (Collation and Declaration of State House of Assembly Elections)
  - ♣ Federal Constituency (Collation and Declaration of House of Representatives Elections)
  - ♣ Senatorial District (Collation and Declaration for Senatorial District Elections)
  - ♣ Governorship (Collation and Declaration for Governorship Elections)
  - ♣ Presidential (Collation and Declaration for Presidential Election)
- At state level, E-Collation may be employed where election type and date is selected, delimitation parameter such bas State, LGA, Ward and PU is allowed to be selected too before entering publishing result after confirmation.

After carefully check through all the procedures involved listed above, we concluded that this is purely manual electoral processes with element of electronic voting in the areas of accreditation, verification and e-collation.

5. Hardware: IVAS (Emp5500)

The hardware of IVAS is the physical component of the system that we can feel and touch. The acronym IVAS means INEC Voters Authentication System.

Figure 3. IVAS (Emp5500) device

This is a device designed purposely for electronic authentication of voters, supports both touch and keyboard input and configure to red contactless card and output (display) same on the LCD. The specification of the hardware adopts the following specifications [1]:

- Dual Core Cortex – A7 Central Processing Unit (CPU)
- ARM Ultra-Low Power Consumption
- Single core frequency of 1.2GHz
- Baseband Version – MOLY.WR8.W1315.MD.WG.V23
- System Version – ALPS.JBS.MP.VI.46
- Software Version – 14.1220.1
- Android Version – 4.2.2

The components/features include:

- Fingerprint Window
- Speaker and Indicator
- Display and Touch Pad
- Main Key Area
- Card Reading Area
- Battery (320mAh)
- USB Interface

Voter's cards are scanned along with the voter's fingerprint. The emp5500 machine compares both the fingerprints, if there is a match, indicates that the bearer of the card owns the card, and the converse if not true; before storing the voter Identification Number (VIN) with the authentication status.

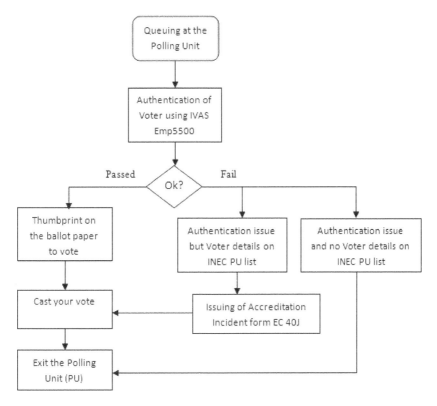

Figure 4. Semi-Electronic Process flow diagram

6. Data Analysis, Result and Finding

6.1. Data Analysis

The Data was based on 2015 General election in Nigeria across the six geo-political zones. The summary of the data obtained during 2015 election was presents in Table 1 of which the total number of eligible voters was Sixty-Six million, Eight Hundred and Seventy-Eight Thousand, and Four (**66,878,004**). The number of accredited voters and the total vote casted were Twenty-nine million, Five hundred and Eighty-Five Thousand, and Six hundred and Fifty-Two (**29,585,652**) and Twenty-Seven Million, Four Hundred and forty-Two Thousand, and Six hundred and Eighty-Four (**27,442,684**) respectively.

Table 1. The summary of the data obtained during 2015 election across the 6 geo-political zones

Geo-Political zone	Eligible Voters	Accredited Voters	Total Votes Casted
South-East	7,028,560	3,060,403	2,824,348
South-West	14,298,356	4,886,261	4,539,707
South-South	8,937,057	5,552,925	5,226,291
North-Central	7,675,369	4,293,232	3,970,735
North-East	10,038,119	4,083,354	3,783,920
North-West	10,900,543	7,709,477	7,097,683
	66,878,004	29,585,652	27,442,684

Table 2. Eligible Voters

		Frequency	Percent	Valid Percent	Cumulative Percent
	7028560	7028560	10.5	10.5	10.5
	7675369	7675369	11.5	11.5	22.0
	8937057	8937057	13.4	13.4	35.3
Valid	10038119	10038119	15.0	15.0	50.4
	14298356	14298356	21.4	21.4	71.7
	18900543	18900543	28.3	28.3	100.0
	Total	**66878004**	**100.0**	**100.0**	

Table 3. Accredites Voters

		Frequency	Percent	Valid Percent	Cumulative Percent
	3060403	7028560	10.5	10.5	10.5
	4083354	10038119	15.0	15.0	25.5
	4293232	7675369	11.5	11.5	37.0
Valid	4886261	14298356	21.4	21.4	58.4
	5552925	8937057	13.4	13.4	71.7
	7709477	18900543	28.3	28.3	100.0
	Total	66878004	100.0	100.0	10.5

Table 4. Total Votes Cast

		Frequency	Percent	Valid Percent	Cumulative Percent
	2824348	7028560	10.5	10.5	10.5
	3783920	10038119	15.0	15.0	25.5
	3970735	7675369	11.5	11.5	37.0
Valid	4539707	14298356	21.4	21.4	58.4
	5226291	8937057	13.4	13.4	71.7
	7097683	18900543	28.3	28.3	100.0
	Total	66878004	100.0	100.0	

Table 5. Summary of Statistical Report

	EligibleVoters	AccreditedVoters	TotalVotesCast
N	66878004	66878004	66878004
Valid Missing	0	0	0
Mean	12718984.19	5392762.13	4995356.40
Median	10038119.00	4886261.00	4539707.00
Std. Deviation	4543676.170	1594649.594	1461747.619
Range	11871983	4649074	4273335
Minimum	7028560	3060403	2824348
Maximum	18900543	7709477	7097683

7. Results and Discussion

From the summary table in Table 1, it was clearly observed and showed that the number of eligible voters is far higher than the responses during election period. The graphical representation of Table 1 is shown in fig 5(a), Figure 5(b) and Figure 5(c).

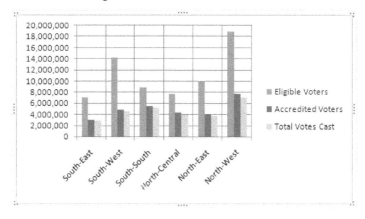

Figure 5(a). clustered column graph equivalent

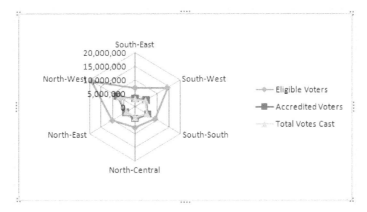

Figure 5(b). Radar graph equivalent

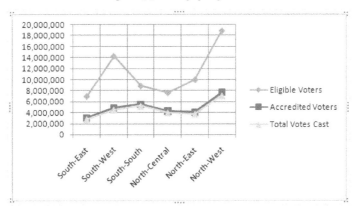

Figure 5(c). Line graph equivalent

8. Findings

From the result of data analysis, we arrived at the following conclusions:

- The voting procedure was cumbersome as voters had to be accredited first, and came back to vote later.
- Late arrival of election materials often trail elections conducted negatively.
- Manipulation of results in order to influence their outcome, manual counting error, allegations of violence, intimidation, ballot stuffing, under-age and multiple voting and complicity of the security agencies often trail elections conducted negatively.
- Too much money spent in conducting of 2015 general election.
- Some people believed the results were rigged in some states which resulted to post-election violence in some state.
- Majority of the eligible voters preferred alternative way of voting for future elections.
- Majority of the eligible voters believed that manual voting was not good enough for Nigerian elections.
- Majority of the eligible voters wanted an alternative to manual voting (electronic voting system)

Consequent to the findings above, we concluded that Nigeria needs alternative means of voting that will bring sanity into electoral processes such as follows:

- Cast-as-Intended, Counted-as-Cast and Verifiability
- One voter, One vote and Coercion Resistance
- Elimination of post-election violence in Nigeria
- Reduction of money spent on ballot papers and other materials
- Prevention of the use of hooligans, ballot hijacking, and imposition of candidates
- Reduction of staff to the minimal to avoid human errors as a result of manual counting

9. A Proposed Web-Enabled Voting System

A web-enabled voting system which inculcates the features and characteristics of electronic voting machine (EVM), Internet Voting (*i*-voting) and mobile voting (*m*-Voting) on a single module is proposed for enhanced participatory democracy that has attributes of free, fair and credible election in Nigeria. The proposed system in question inculcates electronic voting machine (EVM), Internet Voting (*i*-voting) and mobile voting (*m*-Voting) technologies into a single module using sophisticated and integrated software and hardware. The purpose of literature review conducted so far is to create an insight and technical solution that satisfies the functional requirements for the system. The functional specification produced during system requirements analysis is transformed into a physical architecture through system modeling and database design. Based on to the literature review conducted, the design of proposed web-enabled voting system must satisfy a number of competing criteria. This competing criterion gives an avenue for a free, fair, credible and confidential election as highlighted below:

- **Fairness**: No person can learn the voting outcomes before the tally
- **Eligibility**: Only eligible voters are allowed to cast their vote.

- **Uniqueness**: No voter is allowed to cast their vote more than once.
- **Uncoercibility**: No voter can prove how he voted to others to prevent bribery.
- **Anonymity**: There should be no way to derive a link between the voter's identity and the marked ballot.
- **Robustness**: A malicious voters cannot frustrate or disturb the election.
- **Accuracy**: All the valid votes should be counted correctly with tolerable extent of error
- **Efficiency**: The counting of votes can be performed within a minimum amount of time.
- **Confidentiality**: Ensuring that no one can read the message except the intended receiver.
- **Authentication**: Only the eligible and authorized voters can vote through the system
- **Integrity**: Votes should not be able to be modified, forged or deleted without detection
- **Audit Trail**: The system should provide the mechanism for audit trail which helps to verify that the votes are accounted correctly in the tally.
- **Transparency**: The election process should be transparent to the voters. Voters can clearly understand the mechanism of the electronic voting system and know whether their votes have been correctly counted.
- **Simplicity**: The system should be designed user friendly. It should also meet the need of the disabled and illiterate.
- **Democracy**: Permits only eligible voters to vote only once
- **Security**: Votes should not be manipulated during the whole process of voting.

10. Conclusion

To sum up the discussion above, this paper clarifies the requirements and key elements of cumbersome procedure lay by INEC, the review of voting technologies, the footnote associated with the existing voting system and argues for pro-active reforms to improve the quality of electoral politics in the country which in turn impacts on the quality of governance. Since, the legitimacy of electoral process and of the post-election regime is heavily contingent on the fairness and transparency of the transition process. Therefore, consequent to carefully subjecting the data to various analytical and quantitative tests, it is audible to the deaf and seeable to the blind that our recent elections have prompted calls for a reform of the voting system. Many ideas have been put forward and one of the recommendations is a web-enabled voting system, which tends to reduce the chaos that often ensues on Election Day.

11. Recommendations

1. The need to discard paper-based election should be included and not to be taken with the hand of levity in the reform agenda of electoral processes.

2. In this age of advanced communication technology, human elements in election management should be reduced to a barest minimum.
3. Another issue worthy of being on the reform agenda is that of enfranchising Nigerians resident outside the country.

References

[1]   INEC Manual for election Officials (2015): Funded by the European Union through the UNDP Democratic Governance for Development (DGD II) Project.

[2]   Vishal V. N (2014): "E-Voting Using Biometric". International Journal of Emerging Technology and Advanced Engineering www.ijetae.com (ISSN 2250-2459, ISO 9001:2008 Certified Journal, Volume 4, Issue 6, June 2014).

[3]   Okediran O. O., Omidiora E. O., Olabiyisi S. O.,Ganiyu R. A., Alo O.O., "A FRAMEWORK FOR A MULTIFACETED ELECTRONIC VOTING SYSTEM", International Journal of Applied Science and Technology Philadelphia, USA, Vol. 1 No.4, pp 135-142; July 2001.

[4]   Aditya, R., Byoungcheon L, Boyd, C and Dawson, E. "IMPLEMENTATION ISSUES IN SECURE E-VOTING SCHEMES", Proceedings of the Fifth Asia Pacific Industrial Engineering and Management Systems Conference 2004.

[5]   Maheshwari, A. "Two way authentication protocol for mobile payment system", International Journal of Engineering Research and Applications, Vol. 2, Issue4, July-August 2012.

[6]   Omolaye P. O., *Management Information Systems Demystified for Managers and Professionals*; pp. 167- 171. Selfers Publishers Ltd., Makurdi, Nigeria. 2014.

[7]   Animashaun, M.A. (2008b); "African Democracy and the Dilemma of Credible Elections." *Journal of Social Sciences*. Vol. 3 No 1. August.

[8]   Macintosh, A. (2004) Characterizing e-participation in policy-making. System Sciences, Proceedings of the 37th (C), 1–10. 2004 Retrieved from http://ieeexplore.ieee.org/xpls/abs_all.jsp?arnumber=1265300.

[9]   Manish K, Suresh K.T, Hanumanthappa. M, Evangelin G.D (2005), "Secure Mobile Based Voting System", Retrieved online at http:// www.iceg.net/2008/books/2/35_324_350.pdf on November 17th 2012.

[10] Boniface M., (2008), "A Secure Internet-Based Voting System for Low ICT Resourced Countries". Master of Information Technology Thesis, Department of Information Technology, Makerere University, Uganda.

[11] Jones D. W., (2001), "A Brief Illustrated History of Voting" Department of Computer Science, University of Iowa, USA.

[12] Keller, A. M., Dechert, A., Auerbach, K., Mertz, M., Pearl, A., and Hall, J.L., (2005) "A PC-based Open-Source Voting Machine with an Accessible Voter-Verifiable Paper Ballot," *Proceedings of the USENIX Annual Technical Conference*, U.S.A., p.52.

[13] Kohno, T., Stubblefield, A., Ribin, A. D., and Wallach, D.S, "Analysis of an Electronic Voting System," *IEEE Computer Society*, 2004, pp. 27-40.

[14] Yekini, N.A., Oyeyinka I. K., Oludipe O.O., Lawal O.N (2012): Computer-Based Automated Voting Machine (AVM) for Elections in Nigeria. International Journal of Computer Science and Network Security, VOL.12 No.5, May 2012.

[15] Animashaun K (2010): Regime character, electoral crisis and prospects of electoral reform in Nigeria. Journal of Nigeria Studies Volume 1, Number 1, Fall 2010.

[16] Amuta, C. (2008); "Still Nigeria Expects." The Nation. http://www.thenationonlineng.net. May 30, 2008.

[17] Egwu, S. (2007); "The Context and Lessons of the 2003 Elections in Nigeria" in Issac Albert, Derrick Marco and Victor Adetula (eds.), Perspectives on the 2003 Elections in Nigeria. Abuja: IDASA.

11

Structural-Functional Model of the Information Systems of City Planning

Vladislav ZAALISHVILI[1], Alexandr KANUKOV[2,*], Dmitry MELKOV[2]

[1]Laboratory of Engineering Seismology, Center of Geophysical Investigations of VSC RAS and RNO-A, Vladikavkaz, Russia
[2]Laboratory of Instrumental Monitoring of Hazardous Natural-Technogenic Processes, Center of Geophysical Investigations of VSC RAS and RNO-A, Vladikavkaz, Russia
*Corresponding author: akanukov@list.ru

Abstract   On the basis of modern the technologies information database of seismicity and seismic risks in information system designed for city planning is developed. System includes maps of detailed seismic zoning (DSZ) of North Ossetia-Alania and map of seismic microzonation (SMZ) of the territory of Vladikavkaz city.

Keywords: *seismicity, information system, database*

1. Introduction

Governments in all countries are obligated to ensure the work of the infrastructures of different forms to provide the comfort of vital activities and safety of citizens. Management of physical infrastructure requires the linkage of different systems and, correspondingly, informational infrastructure. Infrastructures of three-dimensional data (Spatial Data Infrastructures (SDI)) play important role, because information about the position of one or other object or another plays the key value in control of all systems, which are controlled and are governed by public authority, for example, such as roads, utility networks, systems of public health and others. Like the majority of the forms of infrastructure, SDI also ensure platform for the economic development of the country or region.

2. Objectives

According to city planning code of RF the information systems of the city planning (ISOCP) are the systematized set of the documented information about the development of territories, about their building, about the land sections, about the objects of capital construction and other necessary for the realization of city planning information [1]. In this definition the information system can be both the manual and automated.

In the wide understanding ISOCP - meta-system (system of systems) [2], which ensures the information support of the set of the diverse processes of subsistence and development of city. Such integrated system includes several classes of software:

- GIS (geographical information system),

- SED (system of electronic document turnover),
- DBMS (Data Base Management System),
- EAR (control system of electronic administrative regulations),
- CSCI (classification system and coding information), web- portal,
- and also organize access to SIEI (system of interdepartmental electronic interaction).

The purpose of conducting the information systems of the city planning is the provision of government, local authority, physical and legal persons the reliable information, necessary for the realization of city planning, investment and other economic activity, conducting land exploitation.

The information about the seismic danger and the seismic risk of the territories, which are basic in the building in the seismically dangerous regions, in our opinion, occupies special position.

Seismological studies for different purposes, including the tasks for the branch of construction, are carried out in our country already more than a century. The seismic danger assessment in this case, as a rule, is reduced to the calculation of maximally possible seismic actions, which must be considered with the building in the seismic regions. The value of seismic danger is shown in the specific parameters (marks) on the maps of the seismic zonation of one territory or another. In our country are three levels of the seismic zonation depending on tasks and necessary detail of seismic danger mapping:

- the general seismic zoning (GSZ) - for the entire territory of the country;
- detailed seismic zoning (DSZ) - for the limited areas and the separate regions;
- seismic microzonation (SMR) - for the cities, the populated areas and the construction sites.

As a result a series of studies in 2006-2010 yr. according to the seismic danger assessment the center of geophysical studies created the original maps of the detailed seismic zonation (DSZ) of republic North Osetia-Alaniya [3,4], the map of seismic microzonation (SMZ) of Vladikavkaz city [5,6]. The work on the composition of similar maps for other populated areas at present is conducted. It is obvious that the cartographic materials must correspond to the world level, presented to three-dimensional data and, in the first place, possess the possibility of the direct start in any contemporary information systems [7-13].

Thus, the purpose of our work consisted of the creation of the information database of seismicity and seismic risks in the information system for city planning.

3. Methods

The existing automated systems of city planning, cadaster system, and also other information resources were examined [14].

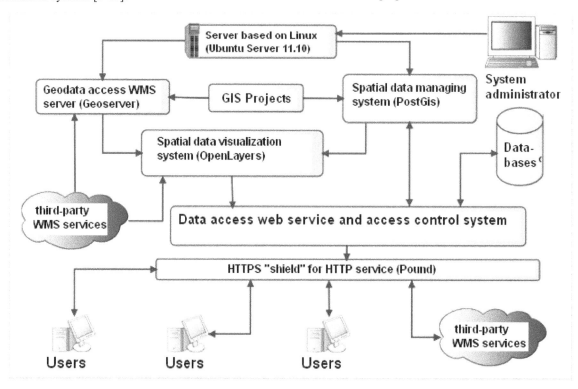

Figure 1. Structural-functional model of ISOCP

As a result of conducted investigations we have developed structural-functional model ISOCP, which makes it possible to create information system for the needs of user, with the retention of compatability with other products, built according to this model, and also with a number of the already existing systems (Figure 1).

For developing the web- service is selected the specification Web Map Service (WMS). Protocol WMS is the standard of the open geo-three-dimensional consortium – Open Geospatial Consortium (OGC) and is supported by the majority of applications [15]. On the basis of OGC specifications is created the large part of special software for developing the cartographic Web- services in the Internet. As the basis was selected Geoserver, as the product, which satisfies all necessary requirements, and also by compatibility with the Web- resource of united information system Seismic safety of Russia.

As the platform for the created program complex was selected the server, which works under control of the freely extended operating system Ubuntu Server 11.10.

4. Results

We developed the Web- interface of access and visualization of service data (on the basis of OpenLayers),

that possesses the necessary functional for the survey of the probabilistic maps of the seismic danger of RSO-A territory and the map of seismic microzonation for the mass building of the Vladikavkaz territory.

On main page it is necessary to pass authorization for obtaining the access to the data. Authorization has two-level, but it is transparent for the user. I.e., it is necessary to introduce only login/password, further system itself will conduct authorization not only on the Web- service, but also on Geoserver too.

Further loads the map of seismic microzonation of the Vladikavkaz territory (Figure 2a). On this page is realized the search for object with the address, with the highlighting of the corresponding section of map (Figure 2b).

Using navigation buttons on the map, it is possible to move away and to draw near objects, and also to be moved on it, in this case in the left lower angle there is located the scale rule, whose scale depends on degree of approximation to a map. Using the switches of the visibility of layers in the region of control it is possible to examine information user interested in, for example information about the cadastral survey (Figure 2b).

Each object on the map has extra information, in the form file or attributive information. As an example the information of the Vladikavkaz city building seismic risk database (Figure 2d) [16,17].

Figure 2. a) the main page of Web- service with the map of Vladikavkaz city; b) the realization of the function of the search for object with the address; c) the output of cadaster information; g) the database of the building seismic risk

Analogously the map of the detailed seismic zonation of the republic North Osetia-Alaniya territory is represented, with the appropriate possibilities.

For mapping of data are developed the corresponding SLD- styles. Using PostGis the function of the search for objects with the address is realized. Other new technologies, such as web 2.0, AJAX and other were used too [18,19].

The problems of safety are examined and the system of access to information and differentiation of the users rights is developed. Using encription protocol HTTPS we reduce to a minimum the possibility of the unsanctioned access to the data. The use of an asymmetric algorithm of coding RSA with a length of the key of 256 bits makes inadvisable the method of breaking by direct trial and error of key. The application of the signed certificate makes it possible to use maximum vulnerability of data link, making extremely complex the procedure of breaking.

5. Discussion

In conclusion it should be noted that in connection with the application of the latest technology and standards, there is a number of requirements, necessary for the correct work of Web-service. Survey must be achieved in the browser, which supports the standard of web 2.0. This makes work in the obsolete browsers impossible. The IE Explorer version are supported, beginning from the 6th version, Google Chrome, Opera 9 and above. The Mozilla Firefox is no supported. In the browser it is necessary to

include the support of JavaScript and the possibility to obtain and to store cookies (by default all browsers already have all disposed parameters).

The developed system is easily modernized and is the basis of the contemporary constantly supplemented information database of town-building activity for the investigated cities and the populated areas of North Ossetia uniting the results of all directions, which makes it possible to organically include the data in the federal All-Russian information system.

6. Conclusions

1. Geo-information systems (GIS) together with the systems of electronic document turnover (SED) are at present necessary component of state administration.
2. The adoption of city planning code led to the creation of many information systems of city planning (ISOCP). In this case the state cannot separate or introduce its own system ISOCP. This way is extremely ineffective, that blocks development and "self-" improvement of systems. At the same time, state can, and must regulate the protocols of the data exchange between the systems taking into account the requirements of safety, to develop the structures metadata, as for instance, this is already realized in the electronic system of "Roskadastr" (Russian land inventory).

3. By the force of practical need and demand the most flexible geo-information system proved to be the system of Roskadastr.

4. The developed structural-functional model of ISOCP makes it possible to create information system for the needs of user, with the retention of compatability with other products, built according to this model, and also a number of the already existing systems.

5. The possibilities provision of using the cadaster map on the protocol WMS (in the form WMS- service) made it possible to use data in many applications both civil services and particular users.

6. Protocols WMS and WFS are the standards of the open geospatial consortium (OGS) and are supported by the majority of applications.

7. The use of protocol WMS makes it possible to ensure access to the seismicity and the risks data in the form of information division both into its own developed products and into the products of third developers.

8. On the basis of contemporary information technologies is created the database of the initial seismicity of the different level (probabilistic maps DSZ and SMZ) of territory RSO-A (detailed seismic zonation) and Vladikavkaz city territory.

References

[1] City planning code of the Russian Federation, 29.12.2004 N of 190-FZ (accepted by GD FS RF 22.12.2004), *Parliamentary newspaper*, N 5-6, 2005.

[2] Mamysheva E.G., Zagoruyko A.E. Survey of technological platforms for the formation ISOCP *Control of the development of territory*, 3. 2010, 70-72.

[3] Zaalishvili V.B., Arakelyan A.R., Makiev E, Melkov D.A. To a question of the seismic zonation of the republic North Osetia - Alaniya territory in *the 1ˢᵗ international conference "dangerous natural and technogenic geological processes in the mountain and foothill territories of the North Caucasus"*, Vladikavkaz, September 20-22, 2007, Vladikavkaz, 2008, 263-278.

[4] Zaalishvili V.B., Dzeranov B.V. Estimation of the seismic danger in the territory of RNO-Alania in *Practical-scientific conference "Young scientists in the solution of the vital problems of science"*, Vladikavkaz, 2010, 342345.

[5] Zaalishvili V.B., Melkov D.A., Dzeranov B.V., Kanukov A.S. The seismic danger assessment in the urbanized territory on the basis of contemporary methods of seismic microzonation (based on the Vladikavkaz city example) in *Practical-scientific conference*

"Young scientists in the solution of the vital problems of science", Vladikavkaz, 2010, 348-351.

[6] Zaalishvili V.B., Melkov D.A., Dzeranov B.V. Modern seismic hazard assessment methods (in example territory of Vladikavkaz-city) //Proceedings of 14th European conference of earthquake engineering. 30August –0 3 September, Ohrid, republic Macedonia, 2010, 8 pp.

[7] Zaalishvili V.B. Rating estimation of the urbanized territories (theses of reports) in *V Russian national conference on the earthquake-proof building and the seismic zonation with the international participation*, Sochi, 2003, 64.

[8] Zaalishvili V.B. Seismic risk in the estimation of the directions of the historical center of Tbilisi reconstruction *The theory of construction and seismic stability*. IBM&S, GAS, Vol. 1, Tbilisi, 2000, 189-194.

[9] Zaalishvili V.B. Timchenko I.E., Chachava N.T., Lekveishvili M.N. Seismic risk and the reconstruction of historical center of Tbilisi (theses of reports) in *The III national conference on the earthquake-proof building and the seismic zonation*, Sochi, 1999, 140.

[10] Zaalishvili V.B. *Physical bases of seismic microzonation*, UIPE RAS, Moscow, 2000. 367.

[11] Zaalishvili V.B., Gogmachadze S.A., Zaalishvili Z.V., Otinashvili M.G., Shengeliya N.O. Method of the rating estimation of the territory for purposes of insurance in *The IV national conference on the earthquake-proof building and the seismic zonation*, Sochi, 2001, 166.

[12] Zaalishvili V.B., Melkov D.A., Kanukov A.S. The information system of city planning on the basis of the information database of seismicity and seismic risk *Informatization and connection*. ISSN 2078-8320, 5, 2012, 14-8.

[13] Zaalishvili Z.V., Melkov D.A., Korotkaia N.A., Dzeranov B.V. Rating estimation of the soil conditions of territory. Transactions of the I Caucasian International school-seminar of young scientists "Seismic danger and control of seismic risk in the Caucasus". Vladikavkaz, 2006.

[14] Geographical information system. URL: http://www.gisa.ru/13058.html (2.02.2011).

[15] The OGC's Role in Government & Spatial Data Infrastructure URL: http://www.opengeospatial.org/domain/gov_and_sdi.

[16] Balasanyan S.Yu., Nazaretyan S.N., Amirbekyan V.S. Seismic protection and its organization, Gyumri, "Eldorado" 2004, 436.

[17] Gogmachadze S.A., Zaalishvili Z.V., Otinashvili M.G., Shengeliya N.V. Rating estimation of the urbanized territory for purposes of insurance. *Theory of construction and seismic stability*, IBM&S, GAS. Tbilisi, 2003, 3, 46-54.

[18] OpenGIS® Web Map Server Implementation Specification. Version: 1.3.0. OpenGIS® Implementation Specification. OGC® 06-042. Ed. Jeff de la Beaujardiere. Date: 2006-03-15, 2006, 85. URL: http://portal.opengeospatial.org/files/?artifact_id=14416

[19] Styled Layer Descriptor profile of the Web Map Service Implementation Specification. Version: 1.1.0 (revision 4). OGC® Implementation Specification OGC 05-078r4. Ed. Dr. Markus Lupp. Date: 2007-06-29, 2007, 53. URL: http://portal.opengeospatial.org/files/?artifact_id=22364.

12

ICT Governance Drivers and Effective ICT Governance at the University of Rwanda

Jean Bosco Nk. Ndushabandi*, Agnes N. Wausi

School of Computing and Informatics University of Nairobi, Kenya
*Corresponding author: j.b.ndushabandi@ur.ac.rw

Abstract Investments in information and communication technology (ICT) based systems and processes are essential for business organizations. Yet many organizations have not been able to derive maximum benefit from their substantial spending on ICT. Some organizations have seen their systems end up as technical or organizational failures. This paper aims at examining the relationship between ICT governance drivers and ICT governance at the University of Rwanda. Adopting the actor network theory perspective to ICT in organizations, we developed a conceptual framework for a holistic approach to examine the ICT governance concept. Empirical data was collected via a survey questionnaire with the respondents being participants from the six colleges, representatives' central administration consisting of top and senior authorities, middle managers as well as academic and ICT staff, thereby enabling an institutional level unit of analysis. The findings revealed a significant positive relationship between ICT strategic alignment and ICT governance; a significant positive relationship between ICT performance management and ICT governance; a significant positive relationship between ICT resource management and ICT governance and a high and significant positive relationship between ICT strategic alignment together with ICT performance management and ICT resource management and ICT governance with ICT resource management being a better predictor of ICT governance than the ICT strategic alignment and ICT performance management. This research therefore recommends that while putting in place ICT governance structures it is important to get the support of top, senior and middle managers as well as involve all stakeholders in the development and implementation of ICT governance at the Institution.

Keywords: *ICT Governance, ICT Management, ICT Strategic Alignment, ICT Performance Management, ICT Resource management, Actor Network Theory*

1. Introduction

Universities around the world like other organizations have integrated ICT into their processes to communicate and share information among their community.

It is easy for University ICT project managers to know how much they spent on ICT initiatives, but very few universities, especially in developing countries realize full benefits of their investments. ICT projects are risky, and many fail to deliver on stated business objectives. Every organization has limited resources and more to do than the budget will allow [1].

ICT projects that often fail to deliver value are a major source of contention within organizations. It is for this reason that so much emphasis is placed on high quality ICT project management and ICT project managers paying closer attention to return on ICT investment.

Universities obtain a return value on their ICT investment not only in the form of cost savings but also by improving its global internal organization, user satisfaction, university image and outreach.

The Center for Information Systems Research (CISR) has shown that the top performing organizations generate up to 40% higher returns from their ICT investments than their competitors with weak ICT governance (ICTG) [2,3].

The term "governance" is essentially associated with accountability and responsibilities within an organization that pay particular attention to organizational structure, management mechanisms, and policies [4]. Many times, ICTG implementation fails due to ineffective institutionalization [5].

Researchers have contributed to the ICTG, with [6,7] suggesting two major frameworks for understanding ICTG implementation. While [6] revealed that organizations with superior ICT governance had 20% more profit than organizations with poor governance given the same strategic objectives, [7] emphasized on structures, processes and relational mechanisms as ICT governance arrangements.

However, the frameworks by [6,7] do not consider how ICTG emerges in organizations. To bridge this limitation, [8] goes beyond and examines best practices of ICTG and understanding how ICTG arrangements emerge in organizations and the social and technical contexts in which ICTG arrangements arise. They adopted [7] definition of ICTG because the definition acknowledges the relationship between corporate governance and ICTG, and stresses the importance of having well-balanced ICTG arrangements in organizations. ICTG processes, structures and relational mechanisms, need to be blended together in order to derive ICTG value to assist in achieving the business' ultimate goal [8].

The relationship mechanisms introduce the social aspect which is well defined in Actor-Network Theory (ANT) by stating that human actors are not the only actors that compose the social sphere, since non-human actors are also part of it [9]. Therefore, ANT's contribution to social theory is in the recognition that social actors and social relationships do not exist without non-human actors and if studied in isolation from each other, important dynamics can be missed [10].

Like many other Universities in the developing world, ICT contribution to the University of Rwanda service delivery improvement, could be coupled with ICT governance related concerns that include:

- Scattered and fragmented ICT initiatives and applications with the loss of synergies and economies of scale in and across the University.
- A lack of identified critical areas to which more focus can be directed for success, given the ICT resources and related knowledge and culture constraints.
- A lack of top and middle management support and active involvement of both ICT and University personnel in planning, implementing and monitoring ICT-enabled business applications.
- A lack of clear coordination controls and active ICT performance measures in and across the University for its major activities, computerization and support.
- The ineffective use of the available ICT professionals and difficulty in holding individuals accountable for their results, thus affecting the optimal use of ICT.
- Difficulties in managing cost-effectively constantly rising ICT investment including ICT applications and enabling infrastructure.
- The lack of a clear guide for ICT integration into University strategies and reform program.

Against this background, the study sought to investigate ICTG at the University of Rwanda, and thereby contributing to the understanding of ICT governance in Universities. The objectives of the study were:

1. To examine the relationship between ICT strategic alignment and ICT governance at the UR.
2. To examine the relationship between ICT performance management and ICT governance at the UR.
3. To examine the relationship between ICT resource management and ICT governance at the UR
4. To examine the relationship between ICT Strategic alignment together with ICT performance management and ICT resource management and ICT Governance at the UR.

2. ICTG Theoretical Perspectives

2.1. Actor Network Theory

Actor network theory (ANT) emerged during the mid 1980s, primarily with the work of Bruno Latour, Michel

Callon, and John Law. ANT is a conceptual frame for exploring collective socio-technical processes, where a particular attention focuses to science and technologic activity [11]. ANT has been used as a theoretical framework used in social studies of technology to explain the way technological artifacts are constructed in society [9].

Anchoring on ANT as a theoretical lens, [8] developed a model ,illustrated in Figure 1,to analyze how ICTG emerges and in what circumstances stable ICTG arrangements can be produced. The model links the interdependency between ICTG arrangements that are structures, processes and relational mechanisms with ICT infrastructure. Thus, the interaction between ICTG arrangements and ICT infrastructure serves as a foundation upon which to achieve business coherence and support the alignment of ICT strategy and business strategy [12]. In this case, ICTG arrangements and ICT infrastructure are actor-networks, but they can also be treated as actors.

ITG arrangements and IT infrastructure are both heterogeneous in the sense that they consist of interdependent elements of humans, organizational processes and technology. The interaction between ITG arrangements and ICT infrastructure can be explored through the lens of ANT because their development are not only limited to the critical role of technology, but also involves the human and social aspects. Thus, ITG arrangements and IT infrastructure are considered as a socio-technological phenomenon that highlights the enabling and restricting role of ICT in a socio-technical process [8].

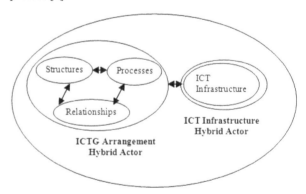

Figure 1. ICTG Arrangement and ICT Infrastructure [8]

2.2. ICTG Drivers and Outcomes

ICT has long been recognized as one of the most critical factors for an organization to increase its efficiency, competitiveness and innovation [13]. However, [13] argues that by merely investing in the state of the art ICT alone cannot ensure the realization of these benefits to an organization. As a consequence, the board of directors and top management need to understand the strategic importance of ICT and ought to put ICT governance firmly on their agenda. The overall objective of ICT governance, therefore, is to understand the issues around the strategic importance of ICT to enable the organization to sustain its operations and implement the strategies required to extend its activities into the future [14].

J.C. Henderson and N. Venkatraman introduced the concepts of business and ICT alignment and ICT governance in the early 1990's. The strategic alignment concept concerns with the idea to align business strategy with ICT strategy on one hand and align strategies with internal organization and processes on the other [15], and Henderson and Venkatraman argue that the inability to realize value from ICT investment is, in part due to the lack of alignment between ICT and business strategies [16]. [17,18] considered ICT governance as one of the twelve components of the strategic alignment model and suggested that ICT governance was concerned with how the authority for resources, risk, conflict resolution, and responsibility for ICT is shared among business partners, ICT management, and service providers. This is similar to the perception of other researchers, such as [6] and [19] that describe ICT governance as (a) the distribution of ICT decision-making rights and responsibilities among different stakeholders in the organization, and (b) the rules and procedures for making and monitoring decisions on strategic ICT concerns. The ICT Governance Institute is of the view that ICTG is the responsibility of the Board of Directors and executive management, and therefore an integral part of enterprise governance. Further ICTG consists of the leadership and organizational structures and processes that ensure that the organization's IT sustains and extends the organization's strategy and objectives [20,21].

The foregoing perspectives of ICTG lead to five main focus areas for ICT governance, all driven by stakeholder value, as illustrated by [21] in Figure 2. The focus areas are categorized as drivers (strategic alignment, resource management and performance measurement) and outcomes (value delivery and risk management).

ICT Resource Management

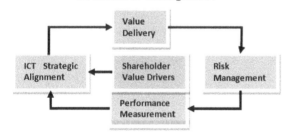

Figure 2. Five Focus areas for ICT Governance

2.3. ICT Governance Conceptual Approach

Based on the review of literature, we identified and considered three categories of factors that serve as drivers of ICT Governance: ICT Strategic alignment, Performance management, and ICT Resource management.

2.3.1. ICT Strategic Alignment

ICT strategic alignment focuses on ensuring the linkage of business and ICT plans; defining, maintaining and validating the ICT value proposition; and aligning ICT operations with enterprise operations, getting top and middle management support and ownership and ensures organization change strategy is established [15].

2.3.1.1. Clear ICT Strategy, Principles and Policies

IS Strategic planning relates to the long term direction an organization would like to take in leveraging technology for improving its business processes. The purpose of ICT

strategy is that enterprises can enhance their level of information system, based on the modern information technology, and provide better services for the management strategy [23,24]. Lack of involvement of the ICT executive in the creation of the business strategy indicates that there is a risk that the ICT strategy and plans will not be aligned with the business strategy.

2.3.1.2. Effective Alignment and Communication between ICT Strategy and Business Strategy

The alignment between business and ICT is one of important aspect of ICT governance. ICT-business alignment enables organizations to adhere to business objectives, and to maximize the value from ICT investment [7]. The assumption is that all organizations have a corporate or business strategy, and if they do not or at least if such a strategy is not written down, there is little with which to strategically align information technology. Furthermore, ICT cannot be viewed as different from business. A strategy for ICT can be formulated to fit the corporate strategy without regard to any other issues [25]. This implies that there should be a better communications between ICT strategy and business strategy to avoid poor understanding of the value or contribution the other provides.

2.3.1.3. Getting Adequate Top and Middle Management Support and Ownership

Top management must support and articulate the need for ICT governance and communicate its functionality within the context of the organization's strategy, structure and systems. Top management commitment for ICT related initiatives enhances ICT success by making ICT resources available, supporting and guiding the ICT functions. This requires top executives to act as business visionaries [26]. According to IT Governance Institute (ITGI) the standard assists top management to understand and fulfill their legal, regulatory, and ethical obligations in respect of their organizations' use of ICT. The lack of such support may see ICT resources having little effect on performance, even when substantial investments are made to acquire or develop the ICT resources [27].

2.3.1.4. Adequate Stakeholders' Involvement

The success of ICTG implementations requires the engagement of stakeholders with clear roles, goals and a shared understanding of the common agenda. Information Systems Audit and Control Association (ISACA) has defined a stakeholder as anyone, who has a responsibility for, an expectation from, or some other interest in the organization. Control Objectives for Information and related Technology Five (COBIT 5) on the other hand has not only defined the Stakeholder but also incorporates stakeholders as a vital and integral component throughout. [6] revealed that the more the organization involves key stakeholders, the more successful the governance of ICT becomes. As the primary role for organization is to create value for Stakeholders, then it is reasonable to see stakeholders actively involved in the governance of information technology as a strategic asset [28].

2.3.2. ICT Performance management

ICT performance measurement tracks and monitors strategy implementation, project completion, resource usage, process performance and service delivery, using, for example, balanced scorecards that translate strategy into action to achieve goals measurable beyond conventional accounting.

2.3.2.1. Good project Management Methodology

A project is conducted within a management environment that is created for the purpose of delivering one or more products, services or results according to a specified business case. PRojects IN Controlled Environments (Prince 2) a process-based method for effective project management has defined a project as: 'A temporary organization that is created for the purpose of delivering one or more business products according to an agreed Business Case'. The objective of the Project Management Methodology is that all projects are managed in accordance with a consistent and appropriate methodology throughout the duration of the project, ensuring sponsors expectations are met through a successful delivery against time, cost and quality parameters. The Project Management Methodology promulgates appropriate management and controls through the four phases of a project (1) Initiation & Approval (2) Governance & Planning (3) Execution & Control (4) Closure & Review.

2.3.2.2. Effective Performance Management Strategy

Performance management is a discipline that aligns performance with strategy using performance metrics. A strategy, which is part of business strategy development and execution, directed towards individual and team performance, focused on employee development, integrated with a formal performance appraisal component, directed by line managers, and assimilated with human resource and reward management systems [29]. Performance management is a four-step cycle that involves: creating strategy and plans, monitoring the execution of those plans, and adjusting activity and objectives to achieve strategic goals. This four-step cycle

revolves around integrated data and metrics, which provide a measurement framework to measure the effectiveness of strategic and management processes [30].

2.3.3. ICT Resource Management

Resource management is about the optimal investment in, and the proper management of, critical ICT resources which are applications, information, infrastructure and people. They are key issues related to the optimization of knowledge and infrastructure [21].

2.3.3.1. Sufficient Financial Support

ICT strategic planning is required to manage and direct all ICT resources in line with the business strategy and priorities. Many organizations have not been able to derive maximum benefit from their substantial spending on ICT. Therefore ICT is seen as cost center. A framework should be established and maintained to manage ICT-enabled investment programs and that encompasses cost, benefits, prioritization within budget, a formal budgeting process and management against the budget.

2.3.3.2. Adequate ICT skills & staff

Inefficient ICT resources, ICT staff with inadequate skills or staff burnout or dissatisfaction, these are ICT human resource issues that require effective oversight and good governance to ensure that people management and skills development is addressed effectively. As people are important assets, governance and the internal control environment are heavily dependent on the motivation and competence of personnel.

2.4. Conceptual Framework

Figure 3 represents a conceptual framework that integrates the factors that drive effective ICT governance in an organization to the ICT Governance concept and is used to formulate the study's hypothesis as:

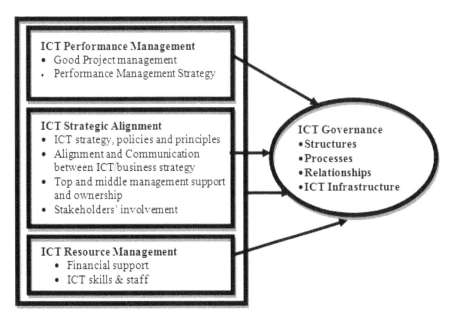

Figure 3. Conceptual Framework

H1: ICT Strategic Alignment has a significant positive influence on ICT Governance.

H2: ICT Performance Management has a significant positive influence on ICT Governance.

H3: ICT Resource Management has a significant positive influence on ICT Governance.

H4: ICT Strategic Alignment together with ICT Performance Management and ICT Resource Management have a significant positive influence on ICT Governance.

3. Methodology

3.1. Research Design

The research adopted a quantitative approach to analyze the correlated effect of the three drivers on ICT governance. The study population consisted of the public university in Rwanda; in this case, the University of Rwanda as it is the only public university in Rwanda. The unit of analysis was the institution as represented by the participants drawn from the six colleges, central administrations consisting of top and senior staff, middle managers, as well as Academic and ICT staff.

Following the objectives of this study, stratified purposive sampling was applied. The strata of interest in this case included; Top authorities (Vice Chancellor, Deputy Vice Chancellor for Administration and Finance and the Deputy Vice Chancellor for Academic and Research); Senior Authorities of the six colleges (six Principals); Middle managers (Director of Finance, Director Planning, Director Human resource, Deans and Project managers from each college and central administration here called headquarter), while academic staffs were mostly senior lectures who had occupied managerial positions. ICT staff were drawn those occupying departmental positions from each of the six college and central administration.

3.2. Data Collection

A self-administered questionnaire using five-point Likert scale ranging from "strongly disagree" to "strongly agree" was used to examine participants' responses to form the primary data. A paper based questionnaire was hand delivered to all the potential respondents. A total of 92 questionnaires were issued and 83 questionnaires were returned giving a response rate of 83/92=90.2%. Two questionnaires had invalid data and therefore could not proceed to the stage of analysis. The number of valid questionnaires that were analyzed further was 81.

3.3. Validity and Reliability Test

3.3.1. Reliability Test

The reliability was calculated using internal consistency technique, which is the internal consistency of the questionnaire that was determined through Cronbach's alpha coefficient to calculate the correlation of each item based on the mean inter-item correlation. The Cronbach's Alpha coefficient (α), should not, according to recommendations, be below 0.70 [31]. Results in the Table 2 bellow indicated that the questionnaire was reliable as observed from the Cronbach's Alpha values which were above 0.7 in either case respectively. The Alpha values meet acceptance standards for the research and reflecting a similarity in the research. Therefore; since, the Cronbach's alpha score for all items the instruments are above acceptable level of alpha (i.e. 0.70), the instruments employed in this study was reliable.

Table 1. Reliability Coefficient

Variables	Cronbach's Alpha	N of Items
Independent	.902	44
Dependent	.894	26

3.3.2. Validity Test

3.3.2.1. Validity of Instrument

For this study the researcher used the validity of instrument to measure the degree to which collected data were not reflecting any opinion or biases. In order to test the validity of the instruments, questionnaires were first scrutinized for consistency and a pre-test of the instruments done by distributing the questionnaire to four potential respondents representing middle managers, academic staff, and ICT staff. The pre-test results were used to correct the questionnaire.

3.3.2.2. Validity of Construct

Factor analysis using principal component analysis extraction method and varimax rotation method to determine the Eigen value and factor loading matrix of each item of the instrument was used to measure construct validity. The factor loading of items was evaluated using the criteria of Eigen value, and the results tabulated in Table 2.

Table 2. Validity of Construct

Variables of the study	Number of Items	Factor Analysis		
		Component	Eigen Value	Factor Loading
ICT Strategic Alignment	24	9	1.062	79.13%
ICT Performance Management	10	4	1.012	71.81%
ICT Resource Management	10	3	1.199	66.76%
ICTG Mechanisms	26	6	1.173	71.58%

Based on the results, the questionnaire employed in this study was considered as valid because of the factors loading for all items in the questionnaire were beyond the acceptable level which 50% cut -off points.

3.3.2.3. Validity of Content

The content validity of the study was assessed using factor analysis through Kaiser-Meyer-Olkin (KMO) and Bartlett's test. KMO value indicates the sampling adequacy of the study and KOM value should be above the bare minimum of .50 for all variables. The Bartlett's test also indicates the test of sphericity and significance level of the measurement instrument at $p<.50$. The KMO and Bartlett's test result are summarizes in the Table 3.

The KMO value of all variables is above the proposed cut-off level of KMO greater than .50 and the Bartlett's test of all variables of the study are 0.000, which are highly significant at P<.001. Therefore, the sample of the   study was considered as adequate.

Table 3. Content Validity

	KMO for sampling adequacy	Chi-Square (Approx)	Degree of Freedom	Sig.
ICT Strategic Alignment	0.681	1084.342288	276	0.000
ICT Performance Management	0.572	245.7586731	45	0.000
ICT Resource Management	0.783	301.8262671	45	0.000
ICTG Mechanisms	0.773	1476.775102	325	0.000

3.4. Data Analysis

The study adopted Descriptive statistics, Pearson's Correlation Coefficients and Multiple Regressions analysis to reduce, summarize, organize, evaluate and interpret the collected data. However before the statistical techniques were employed, the data collected was prepared. This was achieved through editing of data to detect errors, corrections done where possible edited, then, coded before being entered into computer software SPSS 16.0 for use with the quantitative techniques listed.

4. Findings and Discussion

4.1. Descriptive Analysis

The demographic features of the respondents was the general information in the study and included the gender, job position, and the duration the respondent has held the job position. The results obtained with their relevance to the study are discussed as follows:

4.1.1. Gender Distribution

The gender distribution of the respondents is illustrated in Table 5, and shows that most of the respondents were male representing 77.78% and the females representing 22.22%. This is true because females, since long, have been under represented in many disciplines despite the national policy of having at least 30% of women in all sectors in Rwanda.

Table 4. Gender Distribution

	Frequency	Percent
Female	18	22.2
Male	63	77.8
Total	81	100.0

In terms of gender distribution in relation to the job positions, results in Table 5 shows that among the 3 top authorities, there were no females; among the 5 senior authorities, 40% were women, while women represented 20% among the middle managers. For the academic and ICT staff, women respondents were 19.04% and 26.08% respectively.

Table 5. Females distribution per Job position at UR

	Job position at UR					Total
	Top Authority	Senior Authority	Middle Manager	Academic staff	ICT staff	
Female	0 0%	2 40%	6 20%	4 19.04%	6 26.08%	18 22.22%
Male	2	3	24	17	17	63
Total	**2**	**5**	**30**	**21**	**23**	**81**

4.2. Descriptive Cross-Tabulation Analysis

Cross-tabulation analysis was used to get a better understanding on how responses differed when considering the current job position against ICT strategic alignment, ICT performance management, ICT resource management and ICT governance mechanisms.

4.2.1. ICT Strategic Alignment

The experience of the respondents with ICT strategic alignment which comprised ICT strategy, principles and policies; alignment and communication between ICT/UR

strategies; stakeholder's involvement; and top and middle managers support; and ownership posted the following results.

a)   ICT strategy, Policies and principles

At the basic level of understanding and awareness, findings from Table 6 indicated that 98.76% agreed that the University should have an ICT Strategy or equivalent document. However, only 32% of total respondents indicated that they were aware about the University ICT strategy or equivalent document and 67.9% indicated that they either strongly disagreed, disagreed or they don't know about the university strategy or equivalent document, as shown on Table 7.

Table 6. ICT Strategy per Job Position

	The University should have an ICT strategy or equivalent document			Total
	Disagree	Agree	Strong Agree	
Top Authority	0	0	2	2
Senior Authority	0	0	5	5
Middle Manager	1	9	20	30
Academic Staff	0	4	17	21
ICT Staff	0	9	14	23
Total	1	22	58	81

The results from Table 7 is an indication that there might be a university ICT direction, but the challenge or problem may be how such a direction is communicated to different stakeholders or how stakeholders are involved or are participating in its development.

Table 7. ICT Strategy Awareness per Job Position

	Staff who are aware about the University ICT strategy or equivalent document					Total
	Strongly Disagree	Disagree	Don't know or N/A	Agree	Strongly Agree	
Top authority	0	0	0	1	1	**2**
Senior Authority	0	0	3	0	2	**5**
Middle manager	4	4	10	8	4	**30**
Academic staff	4	7	9	1	0	**21**
ICT staff	3	5	6	8	1	**23**
Total	11	16	28	18	8	**81**

With regards to knowing whether the ICT strategy had been approved by appropriate organs, we found that 96.3% strongly disagreed, disagreed or didn't know if the ICT strategy had been approved. This finding is tabulated in Table 8, and the findings confirmed the absence of a formally written ICT strategy. However we found that there was a draft of ICT strategic plan under development by a team of ICT professionals from different colleges under the leadership of the ICT Coordinator. This was corroborated by the documentation review as stated out in the report documented by [33]. The ICT strategic plan was initiated by ICT professional but not yet approved by the highest authorities and it needs further elaboration. The report continued to state that an active participation of heads of the colleges and administrative department should be included.

Table 8. Approved ICT Strategy per Job Position

	ICT strategy has been approved by the appropriate institutional ICT governance committee and by the Senior Management					**Total**
	Strongly Disagree	Disagree	Don't know or N/A	Agree	Strongly Agree	
Top Authority	0	2	0	0	0	2
Senior Authority	1	1	3	0	0	5
Middle Manager	13	2	14	1	0	30
Academic Staff	8	3	10	0	0	21
ICT staff	11	5	5	1	1	23
Total	33	13	32	2	1	81

b) Alignment and Communication between ICT/UR strategies

It is essential for the ICT strategy to be supported by and communicated to key stakeholders, and it should include and articulate the university objectives. Top and senior management should in turn communicate the university direction to which ICT should be aligned. We found that 100% of top and senior manager confirmed that the university direction to which ICT should be aligned is effectively articulated and communicated; while 54.3% strongly disagreed, disagreed or don't know about the direction to which ICT should be aligned, as summarized in Table 9. At the same time, 88.88% of respondent confirmed that the ICT strategy is not visible nor communicated across the university. This finding is tabulated in Table 10, a result that confirms the direction of ICT is not yet written and approved by appropriate organs.

Table 9. ICT Strategy is Articulated and Communicated

	Senior management articulates and communicates the University direction to which ICT should be aligned					Total
	Strong Disagree	Disagree	Don't know or N/A	Agree	Strong Agree	
Top Authority	0	0	0	1	1	2
Senior Authority	0	0	0	4	1	5
Middle Manager	14	2	4	8	2	30
Academic Staff	4	2	7	7	1	21
ICT Staff	5	4	2	7	5	23
Total	23	8	13	27	10	81

c) Stakeholders involvement

To become a success, the implementation of ICT strategy requires the engagement of stakeholders with clear roles, goals and a shared understanding of the common agenda. Findings from the study tabulated In Table 11 indicated that 90.12% strongly disagreed, disagreed or didn't know whether the ICT strategy and policies are communicated to internal or external stakeholders. In this context more effort should be put in place to engage all stakeholders in the development and implementation of ICT strategy and policies.

Table 10. ICT strategy is visible.

	ICT strategy is visible and clearly communicated across the institution to all personnel responsible for its deployment					Total
	Strong Disagree	Disagree	Don't know or N/A	Agree	Strong Agree	
Top authority	0	2	0	0	0	2
Senior Authority	3	1	0	1	0	5
Middle manager	17	10	2	1	0	30
Academic staff	11	5	3	2	0	21
ICT staff	5	7	6	3	2	23
Total	36	25	11	7	2	81

Table 11. Stakeholders Involvement

	Strategy and Policies are communicated to internal as well as external stakeholders					Total
	Strongly Disagree	Disagree	Don't know or N/A	Agree	Strongly Agree	
Top authority	0	1	0	0	1	2
Senior Authority	2	3	0	0	0	5
Middle manager	12	10	5	2	1	30
Academic staff	5	12	3	1	0	21
ICT staff	6	10	4	3	0	23
Total	25	36	12	6	2	81

4.2.2. ICT Performance Management

The ability of the University to manage ICT performance is based on how well the university addresses short-term and long-term ICT projects, decisions and control mechanisms. We sought to find out the experience of respondents in project management methodology and effective performance management strategy at the University.

a)   Good project management methodology

Regular monitoring of key ICT projects is a prudent management practice, and often requires regular progress reports from concerned project managers. Our findings from the study, and summarized in Table 12 indicated that only 35.8% of respondents agreed or strongly agreed that senior management obtained regular progress reports on major ICT projects while 64.2% have strongly disagreed, disagreed or didn't know that senior management obtained regular progress reports on major ICT projects. The distribution of the 35.8 % that reported positively to this question was as follows:100% of top authorities, 60% of senior authorities and 56.5% of ICT staff. These results show that more efforts have to be made to institute an ICT performance measurement framework where project management methodology should guide the university into evaluating and monitoring of ICT project implementation.

Table 12. Good Project Management

	Senior Management obtains regular progress reports on major ICT projects.					Total
	Strongly Disagree	Disagree	Don't know or N/A	Agree	Strongly Agree	
Top Authority	0	0	0	0	2	2
Senior Authority	0	2	0	2	1	5
Middle Manager	3	5	12	9	1	30
Academic staff	0	2	18	1	0	21
ICT staff	1	3	6	12	1	23
Total	4	12	36	24	5	81

4.2.3. ICT Resource Management

ICT strategic planning is required to manage and direct all ICT resources in line with the business strategy and priorities. ICT resources include financial, skilled staff and infrastructure.

a)   Sufficient Financial Resource

Allocation of financial resources is important for successful ICT projects. The study found out that 53.1% of the respondents confirmed that there was sufficient financial support from executive. On the other hand 46.9% strongly disagreed, disagreed or didn't know about the financial support from the executive. Of the 46.9%, we found 4 out of 5 senior authority level respondents who were of the same opinion with regards to ICT projects not having sufficient financial support from executive.

b) Skilled staff and infrastructure are made available.

The availability of ICT infrastructure and skills to support ICT projects is an enabler of successful implementations. As illustrated in Table 14, our findings were that 83.9% strongly disagreed, disagreed or didn't know whether skilled staff and infrastructure were made available to meet the required university strategy.

Table 13. Financial Resource

	ICT projects are getting sufficient financial support from Executive.					Total
	Strongly Disagree	Disagree	Don't know or N/A	Agree	Strongly Agree	
Top Authority	0	0	0	1	1	2
Senior Authority	1	1	0	2	1	5
Middle Manager	5	4	5	14	2	30
Academic Staff	5	6	2	7	1	21
ICT Staff	1	4	4	12	2	23
Total	12	15	11	36	7	81

Table 14. Skilled Staff and resource available

	ICT infrastructures and ICT skills are made available to meet the required University strategic objectives					Total
	Strongly Disagree	Disagree	Don't know or N/A	Agree	Strongly Agree	
Top Authority	0	1	0	0	1	2
Senior Authority	1	3	0	1	0	5
Middle Manager	9	12	1	8	0	30
Academic Staff	4	12	5	0	0	21
ICT Staff	6	11	3	2	1	23
Total	20	39	9	11	2	81

4.2.4. ICT Governance Mechanisms

a) Structure Mechanisms

The study findings in Table 15 showed that 81.5% strongly disagreed, disagreed or didn't know about institutionalization of structures that ensure accountability and flexibility to the ICT organizational needs, while only 18.5% strongly agreed or agreed that there were structures that ensure accountability and flexibility to the ICT organizational needs. Further, 18 96.3% of respondents confirmed that the CIO is not Board member, while 77.8% of respondent confirmed that there was no ICT organization structure and 93.8% of respondent confirmed that there was no ICT steering committee at the University of Rwanda.

Table 15. Structure Mechanisms

	Strongly Disagree	Disagree	Don't know or N/A	Agree	Strongly Agree
The UR has instituted structures that ensure accountability and flexibility to the ICT organizational needs.	22	30	14	11	4
The CIO is on Board	35	16	27	3	0
There is an ICT organization structure at the UR.	20	16	27	17	1
There is an ICT steering Committee at the UR	33	16	27	5	0

b) Process Mechanisms

The use of industry accepted ICT governance processes and tools was also assessed, and the results summarized in Table 16. The study found out that 97.5% of respondent strong disagreed, disagreed or didn't know about the ICT performance measurement using ICT Balanced Scorecard, in the same line 96.3% confirmed that ICT Governance Frameworks like COBIT or ITIL are not implemented and 96.3% of respondent strong disagreed, disagreed or didn't about any periodic assessment of ICT governance maturity at the University of Rwanda.

Table 16. Process Mechanisms

	Strongly Disagree	Disagree	Don't know or N/A	Agree	Strongly Agree
ICT Performance Measurement using ICT BSC	18	20	41	2	0
ICTG Frameworks like COBIT or ITIL are implemented.	19	21	38	3	0
ICTG maturity is assessed after a certain period.	43	9	26	3	0

c) Relational Mechanisms

Stakeholders' participation in ICT projects has been said to improve commitment and motivation for success. Our analyzed results depicted by Table 17 showed that 75.3% of respondent strong disagreed, disagreed or didn't know about the participation and collaboration between all stakeholders. Meanwhile 79.01% of respondent confirmed that informal meeting about general activities and directions were used between UR and ICT executives.

Further the results revealed that trainings are given to UR staff about ICT services at a rate of 68% of respondents while 66.7% of respondent strong disagreed, disagreed or didn't about the trainings given to UR ICT staff about UR direction. Finally, 90.2% of respondent strong disagreed, disagreed or didn't know about systems which were in place to share and distribute knowledge about ICTG framework and responsibilities.

Table 17. Relational Mechanisms

	Strong Disagree	Disagree	Don't know or N/A	Agree	Strong Agree
There is an active participation and collaboration between all stakeholders	13	41	7	19	1
There is a use of informal meeting between University and ICT executive/senior management about general activities and directions	3	2	12	46	18
Trainings are given to UR staff about ICT services	4	9	13	49	6
Trainings are given to UR ICT staff about the UR direction	11	18	25	26	1
Systems are in place to share and distribute knowledge about ICTG framework and responsibilities	23	32	18	6	2

d)   ICT infrastructure

Results for general knowledge about ICT infrastructure enabling ICT governance are illustrated in Table 18, and showed that 97.5% of respondent strongly agreed or agreed that ICT infrastructure is part of overall ICT governance but 82.7% of respondent strongly disagreed, disagreed or didn't know about standardized and integrated ICT infrastructure and systems that are in place to optimize costs and information flow across the UR

Table 18. ICT Infrastructure

	Strongly Disagree	Disagree	Don't know or N/A	Agree	Strongly Agree
ICT infrastructure is part of overall ICT governance	0	0	2	27	52
Standardized and integrated ICT infrastructure and systems are in place to optimize costs and information flow across the UR	42	16	9	9	5

4.2.5. Summary of Descriptive Results

The aim of the descriptive cross-tabulation analysis was to get a better understanding on how responses from respondents differ when considering their current job position. It has been shown that there is no formal written ICT strategy, but from the findings the university has a clear direction as it has been confirmed by top as well as senior authorities. The absence of a formal written and approved ICT strategy should not affect the ICT governance at the University of Rwanda if there was any. By having a strategic perspective, top and senior authorities should build up mechanisms of cascading the ICT strategy downward to middle managers as the one in charge of its deployment and implementation. Moreover, to become a success the ICT strategy during its implementation should have involvement of all stakeholders. Furthermore, findings have clearly shown that there is no sign of ICTG implementation or development at the University of Rwanda. Any of the ICTG arrangements are at the stages of development.

4.3. Multiple Regression Analysis

Multiple regression analysis was carried out in order to test the extent of impact of independent variables on the dependent variable. Thus, this multiple regression analysis was performed to address the stated hypothesis of this study, that are, to find out whether ICT alignment has a positive influence on ICT governance or not; ICT performance management has a positive influence on ICT governance or not; ICT resource management has a positive influence on ICT governance or not and whether ICT strategic alignment together with ICT performance management and ICT resource management have a positive influence on ICT governance or not.

H1: ICT Strategic alignment has a significant positive influence on ICT Governance

To assess the influence of ICT Strategic alignment on ICT Governance, linear multiple regression analysis was carried out. The result of the regression model is summarized in Table 19, and the ICT strategic alignment being the independent variables explains **41.8%** of the variance in the overall ICT governance which is the dependent variable. This value is significant as indicated by the F-value and the significance **(F=56.709, p=000)**. F ratio helps to assess the statistical significance of the overall regression models. The larger the ratio, the more the variance of the dependent variable is explained by the independent variable. The ratio found in this study indicates a low significant at **.000** levels. This level means that the chances that the results of regression model are due to random events instead of true relationship between variables are **0.0%**. This level is far lower than the standard level of **5%**.

Table 19. Regression on H1

1. Model summary					
Model	R	R Square	Adjusted R Square	F	Sig
1	.646[a]	.418	.411	56.709	.000[a]

2. Beta coefficients					
Model 1	Un-standardized		Standardized	t	Sig.
	B	Std. Error	Beta		
(Constant)	.657	.264		2.491	.015
ICTSA	.676	.090	.646	7.531	.000
Dependent Variable: ICTG					
a. Predictors: (Constant), ICTSA					

This is implies that the relationship between ICT strategic alignment and ICT governance is weak at **95%** which is the confidence level. From the results in Table 19; ICTSA is positively influencing the ICT governance with better coefficient $\beta>0$. Regression result show that ICT Strategic Alignment has a direct positive **(beta=0.676)** impact on ICT Governance.

Therefore, the first hypothesis (H1) of the study is accepted, which implies, the more there is an ICT Strategic Alignment at the University the more the effective ICT governance.

H2: ICT Performance management has a significant positive influence on ICT Governance.

To assess the influence of ICT Performance Management on ICT Governance, linear multiple regression analysis was carried out. The result of the regression model is summarized in Table 20 where the

ICT Performance Management (independent variable) explains **34.0%** of the variance in the overall ICT governance(dependent variable). This value is significant as indicated by the F-value and the significance (**F=40.681, p=000**). The **F** ratio found in this study indicates a low significant at **.000** levels. This level means that the chances that the results of regression model are due to random events instead of true relationship between variables are **0.0%**. This level is by far lower than the standard level of **5%** as defined by the probability of F in SPSS. This is implies that the relationship between ICT performance management and ICT governance is weak at **95%** which is the confidence level. From the same results in Table 20; ICTPM is positively influencing the ICT governance with better coefficient $\beta>0$. Regression result show that ICT Performance Management has a direct positive (**beta=0.617**) impact on ICT Governance. Therefore, the second hypothesis (**H2**) of the study is accepted, which implies, the more there is an ICT Performance Management at the University the more the effectiveness of ICT Governance.

Table 20. Regression on H2

1. Model summary					
Model	R	R Square	Adjusted R Square	F	Sig
1	.583[a]	.340	.332	40.681	.000[a]
2. Beta coefficients					
Model1	Un-standardized		Standardized	t	Sig.
	B	Std. Error	Beta		
(Constant)	.899	.273		3.288	.002
ICTPM	.617	.097	.583	6.378	.000
Dependent Variable: ICTG					
a. Predictors: (Constant), ICTPM					

H3: ICT Resource management has a positive significant influence on ICT Governance.

To assess the influence of ICT Resource Management on ICT Governance, linear multiple regression analysis was carried out. The result of the regression model is summarized in Table 21 where the ICT Resource Management (independent variable) explains **47.4%** of the variance in the overall ICT governance (dependent variable). This value is significant as indicated by the F-value and the significance (**F=71.206, p=000**). The **F** ratio found in this study indicates a low significant at **.000** levels. This level means that the chances that the results of regression model are due to random events instead of true relationship between variables are **0.0%**. This level is by far lower than the standard level of **5%** and implies that the relationship between ICT resource management and ICT governance is weak at **95%** which is the confidence level.

Table 21. Regression on H3

3. Model summary					
Model	R	R Square	Adjusted R Square	F	Sig
1	.689[a]	.474	.467	71.206	.000[a]
4. Beta coefficients					
Model1	Un-standardized		Standardized	t	Sig.
	B	Std. Error	Beta		
(Constant)	1.073	.188		5.712	.002
ICTPM	.607	.072	.689	8.438	.000
Dependent Variable: ICTG					
a. Predictors: (Constant), ICTRM					

Further from the findings listed in Table 21; ICTRM is positively influencing the ICT governance with better coefficient $\beta>0$. Regression result show that ICT Resource Management has a direct positive (**beta=0.607**) impact on ICT Governance. Therefore, the third hypothesis (**H3**) of the study is accepted, which implies that, the more there is ICT Resource Management at the University the more the effectiveness of ICT Governance.

H4. ICT Strategic alignment together with ICT Performance management and ICT Resource management they have a significant positive influence on ICT Governance.

To assess the combined influence of ICT Strategic Alignment together with ICT Performance Management and ICT Resource Management on ICT Governance, multiple regression analysis was carried out and the result of the regression model summarized in Table 22 where the combined effect of ICT Strategic Alignment together with ICT Performance Management and ICT Resource Management explains **56.0%** (R=.748, R²=.560) of the variance in the overall Structure mechanism. This value is highly significant as indicated by the F-value and the significance (**F = 32.601, p=000**). The **F** ratio found in this study indicates a low significant at **.000** levels. This level means that the chances that the results of regression model are due to random events instead of true relationship between variables are **0.0%**. This level is by far lower than the standard level of **5%** and implies that the relationship between the combined effect of ICT strategic alignment together with ICT performance management and ICT resource management and ICT governance is weak at **95%** which is the confidence level. Further, from the results listed in Table 22 the combined effect of ICTSA together with ICTPM and ICTRM is positively influencing the ICT governance with beta coefficient $\beta>0$. Multiple regression result shows that the combined effect of ICTSA together with ICTPM and ICTRM has a direct positive impact on ICT Governance.

Table 22. Regression on H4

5. Model summary					
Model	R	R Square	Adjusted R Square	F	Sig
1	.748[a]	.560	.542	32.601	.000[a]
6. Beta coefficients					
Model1	Un-standardized		Standardized	T	Sig.
	B	Std. Error	Beta		
(Constant)	.449	.244		1.842	.069
ICTSA	.371	.128	.355	2.903	.005
ICTPM	.016	.133	.015	.123	.903
ICTR	.411	,088	.466	4.662	.000
Dependent Variable: ICTG					
a. Predictors: (Constant), ICTSA, ICTPM, ICTRM					

Therefore, the fourth hypothesis (**H4**) of the study is accepted, which implies that, the more there is a combined effect of ICTSA together with ICTPM and ICTRM at the University the more the effectiveness of ICT Governance. Results further indicate that ICTRM (β= **.411**) are a better predictor of ICTG than ICTSA (β=**.371**) and ICTPM (β=**.016**).

To summarize the findings on the hypothesis formulated, both the correlation and regression analysis was employed and the summary findings illustrated in Table 23.

Table 23. Summary on Hypothesis

Hypothesis	Results	Status
H1: ICT Strategic alignment has a significant positive influence on ICT Governance.	**Correlation:** There is a significant positive relationship between ICT strategic alignment and ICT Governance (**r=.646; sig. p<.01**). **Linear Regression:** ICT Strategic Alignment has a direct positive impact on ICT Governance at **R^2=41.8%** and **Beta=0.676.**	Accepted
H2: ICT Performance Management has a significant positive influence on ICT Governance.	**Correlation:** There is a significant positive relationship between ICT Performance Management and ICT Governance (**r=.583; sig. p<.01**). **Linear Regression:** ICT Performance Management has a direct positive impact on ICT Governance at **R^2=34.0%** and **Beta=0.617.**	Accepted
H3: ICT Resource Management has a significant positive influence on ICT Governance.	**Correlation:** There is a significant positive relationship between ICT Resource Management and ICT Governance (**r=.689; sig. p<.01**). **Linear Regression:** ICT Resource Management has a direct positive impact on ICT Governance at **R^2=47.4%** and **Beta=0.607**	Accepted
H4: ICT Strategic alignment together with ICT Performance Management and ICT Resource Management they have a significant positive influence on ICT Governance.	**Correlation:** there was a significant positive relationship between ICT Strategic alignment together with ICT Performance management and ICT Resource Management and ICT Governance (**r=.730; sig. p<.01**). **Multiple Regression:** ICT Strategic Alignment together with ICT Performance Management and ICT Resource Management have a direct positive impact on ICT Governance at **R^2=56.0%** and **Beta =.355, .015, .466** respectively for ICTSA, ICTPM and ICTRM.	Accepted

5. Discussion

The presentation of the discussion is arranged in line with the objectives and findings of the study as follows:

1. To examine the relationship between ICT Strategic Alignment and ICT Governance

ICT Strategic alignment exists when business organization's goals and activities are in harmony with the information systems that support them. To address the alignment challenges, it is important for an organization to have a clear and in-depth view regarding its business goals and how IT goals and IT processes support those goals [7]. The findings do concur with the works of [34] who said that; the organization with the lower business-IT alignment results clearly had a lower IT governance implementation status, compared to the organization with the highest business-IT alignment. Extant literature has shown that ICT strategic alignment has identified success factors that are: mutual understanding of both business and ICT strategies between business and ICT managers and incorporation of this understanding into ICT planning and development [35]. Findings from [36] also showed that respondents were largely positive about IT alignment with the goal of the institution, with their study results showing that aligning IT goals with institutional goals and promoting an institutional view of IT were the most cited as drivers for pursuing IT governance; while the barrier is the lack of participation of all parties among others. The results of the University of Rwanda reported in this study in Table 11 also disclosed that 100% of top and senior manager confirmed that the university direction to which ICT should be aligned is effectively articulated and communicated. This implies that there is an involvement and a support from top and senior authorities. These findings are in line with those from literature stating that the support and the involvement of senior management can be achieved by instituting a senior management role in the IT decision making and monitoring process, demonstrating viable business value proposition from IT to gain the support of senior management, and motivating senior management to use IT actively [37]. However the results illustrated in Table 9, Table 10 and Table 11, whereby 54.3% strongly disagreed, disagreed or didn't know about the direction to which ICT should be aligned

on one hand; and on the other hand, 88.88% of respondent confirmed that the ICT strategy was not visible nor communicated across the university and that 90.12% strongly disagreed, disagreed or don't know whether the ICT strategy and policies are communicated to internal or external stakeholders indicate communication gaps across management levels. Thus more efforts should be put in place to engage all stakeholders in the development and implementation of ICT strategy and policies as it concurs with results that revealed that the stakeholders involvement can be achieved by establishing key stakeholders' responsibilities in the IT decision making and monitoring process and developing a common understanding among key stakeholders on shared IT/business goals and imperatives [37]. Therefore connected and integrated planning not only makes explicit what is important for both UR and ICT, but also helps to see how ICT can support future UR strategies and how future ICT developments can enable business decisions.

2. To examine the relationship between ICT performance management and ICT governance

The study's findings disclosed the existence of a significant positive relationship between ICT performance management and ICT governance as demonstrated in section 4.3. This implies that existence of ICT Performance Management at the University will result into an effective ICT Governance and lack of ICT Performance Management results into poor ICT Governance. Results from the survey showed that 100% of top authorities, 60% of senior authorities and 56.5% of ICT staff forming 35.8% of total respondents agreed or strongly agreed that senior management obtain regular progress reports on major ICT projects. These results show that more efforts have to be made to institute an ICT performance measurement framework where project management methodology should guide the university to evaluate and monitor ICT projects implementation. This is in line and supported by the conclusion that there is a benefit to organizations for implementing a tailored project management methodology and suggests that the greater the level of project management methodology tailoring, the greater the level of project success [38]. [39] continue arguing that using the data gathered, the following key points were observed: Projects managed without a defined project management methodology reported project success only 66% of the time while projects managed with a defined project management methodology reported project success at an average of 74%; while organizations using a fully tailored, or customized, methodology reported an 82% project success rate. Literature has also revealed that project success is measured based on "the triple constraints" or "the iron triangle" of time, cost and scope of objectives. These elements are mutually dependent; therefore, a change in one will have a resultant effect on at least one other element [40]. Furthermore [40] continue arguing that; project success should be measured in terms of completing the project within the constraints of scope, time, cost, quality, resources, and risk as approved between the project managers and senior management. Therefore ICT performance management should impact budget allocation. UR need to monitor and measure the performance of their ICT investments and use this as a guide for ICT budget allocation decisions.

3. To examine the relationship between ICT resource management and ICT governance

The study's findings illuminated the existence of a significant positive relationship between ICT resource management and ICT governance as demonstrated in section 4.3. This implies that existence of ICT resource management at the University will result into an effective ICT Governance and lack of ICT Performance Management results into poor ICT Governance. IT budget refers to IT spending or investment where with low investment, organizations do not expect immense progress in IT governance. The size of an IT function is characterized by number of IT employees. As demonstrated in the IT innovation literature, size of an IT department predicts IT adoption and the need to effectively manage IT resources so that they can enhance the business value of firms makes ICTG an important issue and yet an uneasy task [41]. Results from Table 133 have shown that 53.1% of respondents confirmed that there is a sufficient financial support from executive while results from Table 144 have revealed that 83.9% strongly disagreed, disagreed or didn't know whether skilled staff and infrastructure are made available to meet the required university strategy. Furthermore findings from literature also have confirmed that the most highly rated barriers to ICTG include lack of resources, lack of knowledge and skills and lack of awareness. Lack of time, human and financial resources remain the most salient factor among all organizations. The lack of knowledge and skills are more apparent in public sector organizations [42], and while the results were mixed, there is clear need for UR to be visibly seen in committing resources to ICT projects and communicate the decisions for stakeholder awareness.

4. To examine the relationship between ICT Strategic alignment together with ICT Performance management and ICT resource management and ICT governance

The study found the existence of a high significant relationship of the combination of ICT strategic alignment together with ICT performance management and ICT resource management and ICT governance as demonstrated in section 4.3. This implies that existence of ICT Strategic Alignment together with ICT Performance Management ICT Resource Management at the University will result into an effective ICT Governance and lack of them results into poor ICT Governance. As isolated component, results from section 4.3 showed that each component (ICT strategic alignment together with ICT performance management and ICT resource management) had a significant influence on ICT governance. Thus the University has to find ways to allocate ICT-related resources and to ensure ICT alignment for increased business value [43].

6. Recommendation

The UR needs to focus on putting in place ICT governance structures and respect them: to ensure that plans are developed and priorities set collectively; to ensure that all ICT related actions taken are consistent with university wide shared values, strategies and objectives; to ensure that risks are properly mitigated; and to ensure that investments made return the value expected. ICT governance should involve policies, plans, projects and priorities. ICT governance structures define roles, who does what in ICT and when, who advises those who make decisions and how and where that advice is provided. As a strategic and critical resource, ICT governance should be situated at multiple levels in the UR. On strategic level where the board and top as well as senior authorities are involved, on management level with involvement of middle managers and operational level with ICT and University management. This implies that at all these levels, UR community and ICT people need to be involved in the ICT governance process and be made to understand their individual roles and responsibilities. ICT performance measurement should include activities to ensure that the University's goals are consistently being met in an effective and efficient manner. Balances Scorecard is the appropriate one as it focuses not only on financial perspective but also on the customer perspective, internal operations and Innovation and learning. Last but not least, monitoring and assessing the adequacy of ICT resources (people, applications, technology, facilities and data) to ensure that they are capable of supporting the current and proposed ICT strategy is a key aspect of IT Governance at the University. Therefore, to achieve the above, the university should not only get the support from top, senior and middle managers but also involve all key stakeholders.

Acknowledgement

I would like to thank the University of Rwanda; the mother institution for funding this research through Swedish International Development Agency; and the School of Computing and Informatics, University of Nairobi where this research was carried out under the guidance of the Dr. Agnes Wausi, a senior faculty member of the School, and was involved in the study's design, data analysis and manuscript writing for this article.

References

[1] Gartner, "Executive Report Series Winning Asset Management Strategies. 8.0. IT Spending:How Do You Stack Up?," 2003 Gartner, Inc. and/or its affiliates, 2003.

[2]   Trusted_Advisor, "What would be a basic framework or model for establishing an effective IT Governance function?," David Consulted Group, 2013.

[3]   Weill Peter, "Don't just Lead, Govern: How Top-Performing Firm Govern IT," CISR Working Paper No. 341, 2004.

[4]   A. Al-Hatmi, Public IT Investment: The Success of IT Projects, Singapore: Pertridge Publishing, 2014.

[5]   R. Bhatia, "IT Governance Implementation Formulating and Presenting Practical Business Cases," ISACA JOURNALVOLUME 1, 2013.

[6]   Weill Peter & Ross Jeanne W, IT Governance: How Top Performers Manage IT Decision Rights for Superior Results,, Harvard busness School Publishing, 2004.

[7]   De Haes S. & Van Grembergen W., "An Exploratory Study into IT Governance Implementations and its Impact on Business/IT Alignment," Information Systems Management, vol. 26,, pp. 123-137, 2009.

[8]   Mohamad H. & A. Simon & N. Letch, "A Network Analysis of IT Governance Practices: A Case Study of an IT Centralisation Project," 23rd Australasian Conference on Information Systems Geelong, 2012.

[9]   B. Latour., Ressembling the Social: An Introduction to Actor Network Theory, New York: Oxford University Press Inc., 2005.

[10]   Whittle A. & Spicer A., "Is actor network theory critique?," Organization Studies, 29(4), pp. 611-629, 2008.

[11]   A-Ritzer, "ACTOR NETWORK THEORY," Encyclopedia.qxd, 2004.

[12]   Mohamad H. H.& Letch N.& Simon A., "The Role of IT Governance and IT Infrastructure in the Process of Strategic Alignment," 24th Australasian Conference on Information Systems, 2013.

[13]   &. M. A. S. Majed Alyahya, "A Conceptual Model for Business and Information Technology Strategic Alignment from the Perspective of Small and Medium Enterprises," International Journal of Business, Humanities and Technology Vol. 3 No. 7, 2013.

[14]   Luc Kordel, "IT Governance Hands-on:Using COBIT to Implement IT Governance," Information Systems Audit and Control Association: All rights reserved. www.isaca.org., 2004.

[15]   Henderson & Venkatraman, "Strategic Alignment: Leveraging information technology for transforming organizations,," IBM Systems Journal, Vol. 32, No. 1,, pp. 4-16, 1993.

[16]   Handerson & Venkatraman, "Strategic alignment: Leveraging Information technology for transforming organisations," Reprinted from IBM System Journal Vol38 No 2&3, 1999.

[17]   Luftman J.,   "Assessing   Business   Alignment   Maturity," Communications of AIS, Volume 4, Article 14, 2000.

[18]   J. B.-Z. T. D. R. &. R. E. H. Luftman, "IT governance: An alignment maturity perspective.," International Journal on IT/Business Alignment and Governance, 1(2), pp. 13-25, 2010.

[19]   Peterson R. R, "Information Strategies and Tactics for Information Technology Governance.," Strategies for Information Technology Governance, ed. W. Van Grembergen, Idea Group Publishing, Hershey, pp. 37-80, 2004.

[20]   ITGI, " Board Briefing on IT Governance," On-line available at www.itgi.org, 2001.

[21]   ITGI., "Board Briefing on IT Governance 2nd Edition," www.itgi.org and www.isaca.org, 2003.

[22]   VAN GREMBERGEN W, "Introduction to the Minitrack: IT Governance and its Mechanisms,," Proceedings of the 35 Hawaii International Conference on System Sciences (HICCS), IEEE., 2002.

[23]   Van Grembergen W.& S. De Haes & E. Guldentops., Structures, Processes and Relational Mechanisms for IT Governance,Van Grembergen, W. (Ed.),, Pennsylvania, USA: Strategies for Information Technology Governance, Idea Group Publishing, 2003.

[24]   W. &. D. H. S. Van Grembergen, "A research journey into enterprise governance of IT, business/IT alignment and value creation.," International Journal on IT/Business Alignment and Governance 1(1), pp. 1-13, 2010.

[25]   Steve Clarke., Information Systems Strategic Management an integrated approach, London: Routledge, 2001.

[26]   P. G. J. H. Acklesh Prasad., "ON IT GOVERNANCE STRUCTURES AND THEIR EFFECTIVENESS IN COLLABORATIVE ORGANIZATIONAL STRUCTURES," International Journal of Accounting Information Systems, vol. 13, no. 3, pp. 199-220, 2012.

[27]   Samuel D. L. & Aris B. S., "INFORMATION TECHNOLOGY GOVERNANCE: THE EFFECTIVENESS IN BANKING SECTOR," The Proceedings of The 7th ICTS, Bali,, 2013.

[28]   ISACA, "COBIT 5 ISACA's New Framework for IT Governance, Risk, Security and Auditing: An Overview.," COBIT @ ISACA, 2012.

[29]   Sherry Lee Price, Performance Management Strategies: A Competitive Advantage for High Technology Firms. A Study in the Okanagan Valley Region of British Columbia,, In partial fulfilment of the award of Doctor of Business Administration, Faculty of Business, University of Southern Queensland , 2006.

[30]   Wayne W. Eckerson, "performance management strategies: How to Create and Deploy Effective Metrics," First quarter 2009, TDWI best practices report, www.tdwi.org, 2009.

[31]   Abel Gitau Mugenda, Social Science Research Theory and Practice, Nairobi: Applied Research and Training Services, 2011.

[32]   &. R. R. G. Joseph A. Gliem, "Calculating, Interpreting, and Reporting Cronbach's Alpha Reliability Coefficient for Likert-Type Scales," in Midwest Research-to-Practice Conference in Adult, Continuing, and Community Education, Columbus, 2003.

[33]   TUDelft, "Assessment of the ICT status at University of Rwanda," UR SIDA, Kigali, 2015.

[34]   Steven de Haes et Al, "IT Governance and Business-IT Alignment in SMEs," ISACA Journal Volume 6, pp. 38-44, 2010.

[35]   Shankar B. C. at Al, "How Does Alignment of Business and IT Strategies Impact Aspects of IT Effectiveness?," International Journal of Applied Management and Technology Volume 12, Issue 1,, p. 1-15, 2013.

[36]   Ronald Y. & Judith B. C., "Process and Politics: IT Gogernance in Higher Education," EDUCAUSE CENTER FOR APPLIED RESEARCH, pp. 1-10, 2008.

[37]   Nkufa E & Rusu L., "Critical Success Factors for Effective It Governance in the Public Sector Organizations in Developing Country: The Case of Tanzania.," In proceedings of the European Conference on Information Systems., 2010.

[38]   U. Sekaran, RESEARCH METHODS FOR BUSINESS: A Skill-Building Approach. Fourth Edition, Danvers: Hermitage Publishing Services, 2003.

[39]   Sean Whitaker, "The Benefits of Tailoring Making a Project Management Methodology Fit," Project Management Institute, Inc, pp. 1-24, 2014.

[40]   Karessa C. & David W., "Improving performance in project-based management: synthesizing strategic theories," International Journal of Productivity and Performance Management, pp. 1-17, 2014.

[41]   Van Grembergen W & De Haes S, "A research journey into enterprise governance of IT, business/IT alignment and value creation.," International Journal on IT/Business Alignment and Governance 1(1), pp. 1-13, 2010.

[42]   Mohd Fairuz & Taizan Chan., "Barriers to Formal IT Governance Practice – Insights from a Qualitative Study," 46th Hawaii International Conference on System Sciences, pp. 1-10, 2013.

[43]   Jerry Luftman et al, "IT governance: An alignment maturity perspective.," International Journal on IT/Business Alignment and Governance, 1(2), pp. 13-25, 2010.

13

ASP: Advanced Security Protocol for Security and Privacy in Cloud Computing

Shyam Nandan Kumar[1,*], Amit Vajpayee[2]

[1]M.Tech-Computer Science and Engineering, Lakshmi Narain College of Technology-Indore (RGPV, Bhopal), MP, India
[2]Department of Computer Science and Engineering, Lakshmi Narain College of Technology-Indore (RGPV, Bhopal), MP, India
*Corresponding author: shyamnandan.mec@gmail.com

Abstract Security concern has become the biggest obstacle to adoption of cloud because all information and data are completely under the control of cloud service providers. To provide optimal services on cloud, this paper introduces a new distributed and scalable data sharing scheme for data owners in clouds that supports anonymous authentication. Proposed ASP (Advanced Security Protocol) protocol is a cryptographic access control protocol based on key-updating scheme referred to as Advanced Key Update (AKU). The main advantage of the AKU scheme its support for efficient delegation and revocation of privileges in hierarchies without requiring complex cryptographic data structures. Proposed ASP protocol also includes a new digital signature scheme that enables cloud providers to ensure that requests are submitted by authorized end-users, without learning their identities. User Revocation facility is also supported by proposed ASP. In this paper various existing approaches and issues related to data encryption and message authentications are also discussed. At last, experiment results are analyzed and performances are evaluated. The main aim of the paper is to provide more visibility and control to the end-users and close the gap between capabilities of existing solutions and new requirements of cloud-based systems.

Keywords: cloud computing, data sharing, decryption, encryption, concurrent access, distributed system, web, message signing and verification, data confidentiality, message authentication, cloud security

1. Introduction

Cloud computing is emerging from recent advances in technologies such as hardware virtualization, Web services, distributed computing, utility computing and system automation. It is continuously evolving and showing consistent growth in the field of computing [1]. With virtualization, one or more physical servers can be configured and partitioned into multiple independent "virtual" servers, all functioning independently and appearing to the user to be a single physical device. Such virtual servers are in essence disassociated from their physical server, and with this added flexibility, they can be moved around and scaled up or down on the fly without affecting the end user. The difference with cloud computing is that the computing process may run on one or many connected computers at the same time, utilizing the concept of virtualization [1]. With multiple users from different organizations contributing to data in the Cloud, the time and cost will be much less compared to having to manually exchange data and hence creating a clutter of redundant and possibly out-of-date documents. With social networking services such as Facebook, the benefits of sharing data are numerous such as the ability to share photos, videos, information and events. Google Docs provides data sharing capabilities as groups of students or

teams working on a project can share documents and can collaborate with each other effectively. This allows higher productivity compared to previous methods of continually sending updated versions of a document to members of the group via email attachments. Also in modern healthcare environments, healthcare providers are willing to store and share electronic medical records via the Cloud and hence remove the geographical dependence between healthcare provider and patient. Due to this need of Cloud Mining [5] and security over web [4] is gaining popularity.

Cloud computing providers offer their services according to several fundamental models [6]: infrastructure as a service (IaaS), platform as a service (PaaS), and software as a service (SaaS) where IaaS is the most basic and each higher model abstracts from the details of the lower models.

Layered architecture of cloud computing requires different levels of security considerations. In this work we are mainly concerned with the problem of identity management and access control in application and service level. In SaaS, users are provided access to application software and databases. SaaS users have less control over security among the three fundamental delivery models in the cloud [1]. In the PaaS models, cloud providers deliver a computing platform, typically including operating system, programming language execution environment, database, and web server. Application developers can develop and run their software solutions on a cloud platform without the cost and complexity of buying and managing the underlying hardware and software layers. PaaS application security comprises two software layers: Security of the PaaS platform itself (i.e., runtime engine), and Security of customer applications deployed on a PaaS platform [7]. PaaS providers are responsible for securing the platform software stack that includes the runtime engine that runs the customer applications. PaaS model aims to protect data, which is especially important in case of storage as a service. In case of congestion, there is the problem of outage from a cloud environment. Thus the need for security against outage is important to ensure load balanced service. The data needs to be encrypted when hosted on a platform for security reasons. Cloud providers manage the infrastructure and platforms that run the applications [1]. IaaS refers to the sharing of hardware resources for executing services, typically using virtualization technology. Potentially, with IaaS approach, multiple users use available resources. Unlike PaaS and SaaS, IaaS customers are primarily responsible for securing the hosts provisioned in the cloud. Customers of IaaS have full access to the virtualized guest VMs that are hosted and isolated from each other by hypervisor technology. Hence customers are responsible for securing and ongoing security management of the guest virtual machine (VM) [1]. However, finding an efficient and secure way to share partial data in cloud storage is not trivial. In a shared-tenancy cloud computing environment, things become even worse. Data from different clients can be hosted on separate virtual machines (VMs) but reside on a single physical machine. Data in a target VM could be stolen by instantiating another VM co-resident with the target one [2].

The fundamental factor defining the success of any new computing technology is the level of security it provides [1]. The three basic requirements of security: confidentiality, integrity and availability are required to protect data throughout its lifecycle. Data must be protected during the various stages of creation, sharing, archiving, processing etc. However, situations become more complicated in case of a public cloud where we do not have any control over the service provider's security practices [8].

To enable data access control in the Cloud, it is imperative that only authorized users are able to get access to data stored in the Cloud. Various access control models are in use, including the most common Mandatory Access Control (MAC), Discretionary Access Control (DAC) and Role Based Access Control (RBAC). All these models are known as identity based access control models. In all these access control models, user (subjects) and resources (objects) are identified by unique names. Identification may be done directly or through roles assigned to the subjects. These access control methods are effective in unchangeable distributed system, where there are only a set of Users with a known set of services [1,2]. In DAC, information may be accessed by unauthorized users because there is no control on copies of objects. MAC deals with information flow and solves this problem by attaching security levels on both users and objects. All users are required to obtain certain clearance to access objects. Security labels propagate to derivative objects, including copies. However, the policies in DAC and MAC are fixed and there is no room for flexible access control.

RBAC emerged due to increasing practitioner dissatisfaction with the then dominant DAC and MAC paradigms, inspiring academic research on RBAC. Since then RBAC has become the dominant form of access control in practice. In enterprise settings, we see the rise in demand for data outsourcing, which assists in the strategic management of corporate data [1,2,3]. It is also used as a core technology behind many online services for personal applications.

Cloud security is an evolving sub-domain of computer security, network security, and, more broadly, information security. It refers to a broad set of policies, technologies, and controls deployed to protect data, applications, and the associated infrastructure of cloud computing. Most Cloud service provider's provide basic key encryption schemes for protecting data or may leave it to the user to encrypt their own data. Both encryption and key management are very important to help secure applications and data stored in the Cloud [1,3]. The stored data must be protected against unauthorized access. Also, both the data and the access to data need to be protected from cloud storage service providers (e.g., cloud system administrators). In these scenarios, relying on password and other access control mechanisms is insufficient. Cryptographic encryption mechanisms [2,3,4] are typically employed. However, simply having encryption and decryption implemented in the cloud database systems is insufficient. In order to support both challenges, data should be encrypted first by users before it is outsourced to a remote cloud storage service and both data security and data access privacy should be protected such that cloud storage service providers have no abilities to decrypt the data, and when the user wants to search some parts of the whole data, the cloud storage system will provide the accessibility without knowing what the portion of the encrypted data returned to the user is about [1,2].

The Cloud however is susceptible to many privacy and security attacks. The biggest obstacle hindering the progress and the wide adoption of the Cloud is the privacy and security issues associated with it. Evidently, many privacy and security attacks occur from within the Cloud provider themselves as they usually have direct access to stored data and steal the data to sell to third parties in order to gain profit [1,2,3]. Care should be taken to ensure access control of the sensitive information. Performance of sharing and accessing applications should be improved.

The main aim of the paper includes:

- To provide more visibility and control to the end-users and close the gap between capabilities of existing solutions and new requirements of cloud-based systems.
- To introduce a new scalable and secure key-updating scheme for access hierarchies.
- To design and implement a scalable and privacy-preserving access control framework for existing untrusted cloud services. Proposed framework supports lazy revocation and access hierarchies.
- To present a signature scheme for Key-Policy Attribute-Based Encryption [15]. Using proposed signature scheme, users can prove that they own a key that its policy satisfies with a set of attributes, without revealing their identity or credentials.

The paper is organized as follows. Security issue with cloud model is given in Section 2. Literature Review is presented in Section 3. The mathematical background, Access policies and assumptions are detailed in Section 4. We present our privacy preserving access control scheme ASP in Section 5. Section 6 has the idea about Implementation and Operation of ASP protocol. The security is analyzed and computation complexity is discussed in Section 7. Conclusion and future work is provided in Section 8.

2. Security issue with Cloud Model

As cloud computing is achieving increased popularity, concerns are being voiced about the security issues introduced through adoption of this new model. The relative security of cloud computing services is a contentious issue that may be delaying its adoption [1]. Security issues have been categorized into sensitive data access, data segregation, privacy, bug exploitation, recovery, accountability, malicious insiders, management console security, account control, and multi-tenancy issues. Solutions to various cloud security issues vary, from cryptography, particularly public key infrastructure (PKI), to use of multiple cloud providers, standardization of APIs, and improving virtual machine support and legal support [1].

In a public cloud enabling a shared multi-tenant environment, as the number of users increase, security risks get more intensified and diverse. It is necessary to identify the attack surfaces which are prone to security attacks and mechanisms ensuring successful client-side and server-side protection [1,3,10]. Because of the multifarious security issues in a public cloud, adopting a private cloud solution is more secure with an option to move to a public cloud in future, if needed [1,13]. A few of the key security issues in a public cloud include:

- In case of a public cloud, the same infrastructure is shared between multiple tenants and the chances of data leakage between these tenants are very high. However, most of the service providers run a multitenant infrastructure. Proper investigations at the time of choosing the service provider must be done in order to avoid any such risk [1,8,46].
- The three basic requirements of security: confidentiality, integrity and availability are required to protect data throughout its lifecycle. Data must be protected during the various stages of creation, sharing, archiving, processing etc. However, situations become more complicated in case of a public cloud where we do not have any control over the service provider's security practices [1,8].

In a private cloud, customers have total control over the network. Private cloud provides the flexibility to the customer to implement any traditional network perimeter security practice. Although the security architecture is more reliable in a private cloud, yet there are issues/risks that need to be considered: A few of the key security issues in a public cloud include [1]:

- In a private cloud, users are facilitated with an option to be able to manage portions of the cloud, and access to the infrastructure is provided through a web interface or an HTTP end point. There are two ways of implementing a web-interface, either by writing a whole application stack or by using a standard applicative stack, to develop the web interface using common languages such as Java, PHP, and Python etc. As part of screening process, Eucalyptus web interface has been found to have a bug, allowing any user to perform internal port scanning or HTTP requests through the management node which he should not be allowed to do. In the nutshell, interfaces need to be properly developed and standard web application security techniques need to be deployed to protect the diverse HTTP requests being performed [1,47].

- Virtualization techniques are quite popular in private clouds. In such a scenario, risks to the hypervisor should be carefully analyzed. There have been instances when a guest operating system has been able to run processes on other guest VMs or host. In a virtual environment it may happen that virtual machines are able to communicate with all the VMs including the ones who they are not supposed to. To ensure that they only communicate with the ones which they are supposed to, proper authentication and encryption techniques such as IPsec [IP level Security] etc. should be implemented [1,48].

Private clouds are considered safer in comparison to public clouds; still they have multiple issues which if unattended may lead to major security loopholes. Hybrid cloud model is a combination of both public and private cloud and hence the security issues discussed with respect to both are applicable in case of hybrid cloud.

Various types of Attack on Cloud are increasing day by day. Some of the common attack can be consider as follows:

Cross Site Scripting (*XSS*) attacks: Cross-site Scripting (XSS) refers to client-side code injection attack wherein an attacker can execute malicious scripts (also commonly referred to as a malicious payload) into a legitimate website or web application. XSS is amongst the most rampant of web application vulnerabilities and occurs when a web application makes use of un-validated or un-encoded user input within the output it generates. In order for an XSS attack to take place the vulnerable website needs to directly include user input in its pages. An attacker can then insert a string that will be used within the web page and treated as code by the victim's browser [1,2,26].

XML Signature Wrapping Attacks: Using different kinds of XML signature wrapping attacks, one can completely take over the administrative rights of the Cloud user and create, delete, modify images as well as create instances [2].

Data Stealing Attacks: A term used to describe the stealing of a user account and password by any means such as through brute-force attacks or over-the-shoulder techniques. The privacy and confidentiality of user's data will be severely breached. A common mechanism to prevent such attacks is to include an extra value when authenticating. This value can be distributed to the right user by SMS and hence mitigate the likelihood of data confidentiality issues [2].

Flooding Attacks: A malicious user can send requests to the Cloud; he/she can then easily overload the server by creating bogus data requests to the Cloud. The attempt is to increase the workload of the Cloud servers by consuming lots of resources needlessly [2].

Passive Attacks: This type of attacks includes observation or monitoring of communication. A passive attack attempts to learn or make use of information from the system but does not affect system resources. The goal of the opponent is to obtain information that is being transmitted [3]. Types of passive attacks includes: *Traffic Analysis* and *Release of Message Contents.*

Cloud computing security issues include preserving confidentiality and privacy of data. Only encryption or authentication cannot give suitable security service. They having individual feature [1]. Confidentiality assures that private or confidential information is not made available or disclosed to unauthorized individuals over the clouds. A loss of confidentiality is the unauthorized disclosure of information. Message authentication assures that data received are exactly as sent (i.e., contain no modification, insertion, deletion, or replay). In many cases, there is a requirement that the authentication mechanism assures that purported identity of the sender is valid. It verifies the integrity of message [1].

To achieve confidentiality, integrity and authentication of data, there should be encryption and decryption along with message signature and verification. Data Confidentiality and Message Authentication together will give better security than single encryption or single authentication during data processing over the cloud. The data objects should never be updated by unauthorized clients and in order to achieve this limitation the system ensures that only correct and authorized client are able to perform the updates [1]. For optimal authentication, signing and verifying of message is need. Message authentication may also verify sequencing and timeliness.

3. Literature Review

When sensitive information is stored in cloud servers, which is out of user's control in most cases, risks would rise dramatically. Unauthorized users may also be able to intercept someone's data (e.g. server compromise).

Sahai and Waters proposed a new type of IBE – Fuzzy Identity-Based Encryption [14]. It is also known as Attribute-Based Encryption (ABE). In their work, an identity is viewed as a set of descriptive attributes. Different from the IBE, where the receiver could decrypt the message if and only if his identity is exactly the same as what specified by the sender, this fuzzy IBE enables the decryption if there are identity overlaps' exceeding a pre-set threshold between the one specified by sender and the one belongs to receiver. However, this kind of threshold-based scheme was limited for designing more general [1].

In Key-policy ABE or KP-ABE (Goyal et al. [15]), the sender has an access policy to encrypt data. Cipher-text is associated with a set of attributes, which partially represents the cipher-text's encryption policy. A writer whose attributes and keys have been revoked cannot write back stale information. The receiver receives attributes and secret keys from the attribute authority and is able to decrypt information if it has matching attributes. Unfortunately, with a drawback that the access policy is built into the secret key, the data owner in a KP-ABE scheme cannot decide the one who can decrypt the cipher text, and he can only choose a set of attributes to control the access of cipher texts. Besides, the access structure is a

monotonic access structure which cannot express the negative attribute to exclude the participants with whom the data owner does not want to share data. Subsequently, Ostrovsky et al. [16] proposed a scheme with a non-monotonic access structure where the secret keys are labeled with a set of attributes including positive and negative attributes [1].

In 2007, using a monotonic access tree as access structure, Bethencourt et al. [17] proposed the first CP-ABE construction. Their scheme can support flexible access control policies like the KP-ABE [15] scheme, but the security proof is in the generic group model. Cheung and Newport [18] provided a provably secure CP-ABE scheme which is proved to be secure under the standard model and their scheme supports AND gate on positive and negative attributes as its access policy. In 2011, Waters [19] proposed a new methodology for realizing CP-ABE under concrete and non-interactive cryptographic assumptions in the standard model. He expressed access control by a linear secret sharing scheme (LSSS) matrix over the attributes in the system (previously used structures can be expressed succinctly in terms of an LSSS). In this most efficient scheme, the cipher text size and the encryption/decryption overheads increase linearly with the complexity of the access formula. As a result, his scheme achieves the same performance and functionality as Bethencourt et al.'s [17]. Finally, Lewko et al. [20] recently leveraged the encoding technique from Waters's scheme [19] to propose an ABE scheme that achieves adaptive (nonselective) security. Their scheme is based on the Composite order groups, which results in some loss of practical efficiency when compared with Water's. Emura et al. [21] improved the efficiency and achieved hidden policies [1].

Multi-authority ABE schemes [22,23] can be divided into two types. One needs a central authority (CA, for short) which is used to guarantee the proper decryption and can also decrypt all cipher texts, such as schemes [22,24], while the other does not need a CA, such as schemes [25,26]. Paper [55] proposes the threshold-based key generation approach (TKGA) for ciphertext-policy attribute-based encryption (CP-ABE). TKGA is a multi-authority approach which utilize the technologies of functional encryption and (n, k)-secret sharing. TKGA could efficiently impede collusion attacks because no single authority can directly generate secret keys.

In 2009, Attrapadung and Imai [27] presented a new ABE scheme called the Dual-Policy ABE. Basically, it is a conjunctively combined scheme of Goyal et al.'s KP-ABE scheme [15] and Waters' CP-ABE scheme [19]. It allows simultaneously two access control mechanisms over encrypted data. One involves policies over objective attributes ascribed to data and the other involves policies over subjective attributes ascribed to user credentials. These two access control mechanisms can only allow either functionality above one at a time. What is more, the security proof is based on decisional bilinear Diffie-Hellman exponent (DBDHE) assumption [1].

To achieve the hierarchical access control and improve update efficiency, the revocable attribute based encryption scheme with hierarchical revocation based on multi-linear maps is proposed in [57]. Hierarchical attribute-based encryption scheme (HABE) [28] by combining a hierarchical identity-based encryption (HIBE) system and a cipher text-policy attribute-based encryption (CP-ABE) system, so as to provide not only fine-grained access control, but also full delegation and high performance. It supports a scalable revocation scheme by applying proxy re-encryption (PRE) and lazy re-encryption (LRE) to the HABE scheme, so as to efficiently revoke access rights from users. Based on the key-policy attribute-based encryption (KP-ABE), combined with the idea of hierarchical ID-Based encryption (HIBE), a hierarchical authority key-policy attribute-based encryption (HA-KP-ABE) scheme is presented in [58]. It uses hierarchical multi-authority to distribute private keys to users. Here private keys are computed for users according to random polynomials.

To make data sharing more efficient, proxy re-encryption (PRE) is proposed. Introduced by Mambo and Okamoto [29] and first defined by Blaze et al. [30], PRE extends the traditional public key encryption (PKE) to support the delegation of decryption rights. It allows a semi-trusted party called proxy to transform a cipher text encrypted under Alice's public key into another cipher text of the same plaintext intended for Bob. The proxy, however, learns neither the decryption key nor the underlying plaintext [1]. Paper [56] paper presents a novel cipher text-policy attribute-based multi-use unidirectional proxy re-encryption scheme. In this scheme, the tree access policy can be used to handle and (¡Ä), or (¡Å) and threshold (of) operators.

Digital content is easily spread out in the era of cloud computing. [53] Proposed a novel identity-based access control approach for digital content based on ciphertext-policy attribute-based encryption (iDAC). In iDAC, the access control still works even the digital content is duplicated to another content server. Moreover, only one copy of encrypted digital content is required to share with multiple users. This could efficiently reduce the overhead of content servers.

In [54], for achieving access control and keeping data confidential, the data owners could adopt attribute-based encryption to encrypt the stored data. Users with limited computing power are however more likely to delegate the mask of the decryption task to the cloud servers to reduce the computing cost. This scheme achieves security against chosen-plaintext attacks under the k-multi-linear Decisional Diffie-Hellman assumption.

4. Background Work

In this section, Access Policies, Mathematical Background, assumptions and KP-ABE [15] scheme are presented.

4.1. Assumptions

Following assumptions are made [2]:
1) The cloud is honest-but-curious, which means that the cloud administrators can be interested in viewing user's content, but cannot modify it. This is a valid assumption that has been made in [2,34]. Honest-but-curious model of adversaries do not tamper with data so that they can keep the system functioning normally and remain undetected.

2) Users can have either read or write or both accesses to a file stored in the cloud.
3) All communications between users/clouds are secured by Secure Shell Protocol, SSH.

4.2. Formats of Access Policies

Access policies can be in any of the following formats: 1) Boolean functions of attributes, 2) Linear Secret Sharing Scheme (LSSS) matrix, or 3) Monotone span programs. Any access structure can be converted into a Boolean function [2,35]. An example of a Boolean function is $((a_1 \wedge a_2 \wedge a_3) \vee (a_4 \wedge a_5)) \wedge (a_6 \vee a_7))$, where $a_1, a_2, ..., a_7$ are attributes. Consider an access structure for which there exists a linear secret-sharing scheme that realizes it. It is known that for every LSSS realizable access structure, there exist a monotone span program (MSP) that computes the corresponding Boolean functions and vice versa. Thus, such an access structure can be represented by a monotone span program.

Secret-Sharing Schemes: Secret-sharing schemes (SSS) are used to divide a secret among a number of parties. The information given to a party is called the share (of the secret) for that party. Every SSS realizes some access structure that defines the sets of parties who should be able to reconstruct the secret by using their shares.

Let $Y : \{0,1\}^n \rightarrow \{0,1\}$ be a monotone Boolean function [2,36]. A monotone span program for Y over a field F is an $l \times t$ matrix M with entries in F, along with a labeling function $a : [1] \rightarrow [n]$ that associates each row of M with an input variable of Y, such that, for every $(x_1, x_2 ..., x_n) \in \{0,1\}^n$, the following condition is satisfied:

$$Y(x_1, x_2, \ldots, x_n) = 1$$
$$\Leftrightarrow \exists v \in F^{l \times l} : v M = [1, 0, 0, \ldots, 0]$$
$$\text{and } (\forall i : x_{a(i)} = 0 \Rightarrow v_i = 0)$$

In other words, $Y(x_1, x_2, ..., x_n) = 1$ if and only if the rows of M indexed by $\{i \mid x_{a(i)} = 1\}$ span the vector $[1, 0, 0, ..., 0]$.

4.2.1. Access Tree

Let T be a tree representing an access structure. Each non-leaf node of the tree represents a threshold gate, described by its children and a threshold value. If num_x is the number of children of a node x and k_x is its threshold value, then $0 < k_x \leq num_x$. When $k_x = 1$, the threshold gate is an OR gate and when $k_x = num_x$, it is an AND gate. Each leaf node x of the tree is described by an attribute and a threshold value $k_x = 1$.

Here the parent of the node x in the tree is denoted by parent(x). The function att(x) is defined only if x is a leaf node and denotes the attribute associated with the leaf node x in the tree. The access tree T also defines an ordering between the children of every node, that is, the children of a node are numbered from 1 to num. The function index(x) returns such a number associated with the node x. Here the index values are uniquely assigned to nodes in the access structure for a given key in an arbitrary manner.

4.3. Mathematical Background

Bilinear pairings on elliptic curves is used. Let G be a cyclic group of prime order q generated by g. Let G_2 be a group of order q. We can define the map $e: G_1 \times G_1 \to G_2$. The map satisfies the following properties [3]:

1) $e(P^a, Q^b) = e(P, Q)^{ab}$ for all $P, Q \in G_1$ and $a, b \in Z_q$, $Z_q = \{0, 1, 2, ..., q-1\}$.

2) Non-degenerate: $e(g, g) \neq 1$.

Bilinear pairing on elliptic curves groups is used. The choice of curve is an important consideration because it determines the complexity of pairing operations.

4.4. Key Policy-Attribute Based Encryption (KP-ABE)

Key Policy - Attribute Based Encryption [15] scheme consists of four algorithms, proceeds as follows:

4.4.1. System Setup

This is a randomized algorithm that takes no input other than the implicit security parameter. It outputs the public parameters PK and a master key MK.

Let G_1 be a bilinear group of prime order p, and let g be a generator of G_1. In addition, let $e: G_1 \times G_1 \to G_2$ denote the bilinear map. A security parameter, k, will determine the size of the groups. We also define the Lagrange coefficient $\Delta_{i,s}$ for $i \in Z_q$ and a set, S, of elements in $Z_q : \Delta_{i,s}(x) = \prod_{j \in s, j \neq i}(x - j)/(i - j)$. We will associate each attribute with a unique element in Z_q^*.

Consider T be an access tree with root r. Consider T_x as the subtree of T rooted at the node x. Hence T is the same as T_r. If a set of attributes γ satisfies the access tree T_x, it can be denoted as $T_x(\gamma) = 1$. $T_x(\gamma)$ can be computed recursively as follows:

- If x is a non-leaf node, evaluate $T_{x'}(\gamma)$ for all children x' of node x. $T_x(\gamma)$ returns 1 if and only if at least k_x children return 1. If x is a leaf node, then $Tx(\gamma)$ returns 1 if and only if $att(x) \in \gamma$.

Define the universe of attributes $u = \{1, 2, ..., n\}$. Now, for each attribute $i \in u$, choose a number t_i uniformly at random from Z_q. Finally, choose y uniformly at random in Z_q. The published public parameters PK are

$$T_1 = g^{t1}, ..., T_{|u|} = g^{t|u|}, Y = e(g, g)^y$$

The master key MK is:

$$t_1, ..., t_{|u|}, y.$$

4.4.2. Encryption (M, γ, PK)

This is a randomized algorithm that takes as input a message M, a set of attributes γ, and the public parameters PK. It outputs the cipher text E.

To encrypt a message $M \in G_2$ under a set of attributes γ, choose a random value $s \in Z_q$ and publish the cipher text as:

$$E = (\gamma, E' = MY^s, \{E_i = T^s_i\}_{i \in \gamma}).$$

4.4.3. Key Generation (T, MK, PK)

This is a randomized algorithm that takes as input – Access Tree T (an access structure A), the master key MK and the public parameters PK. It outputs a decryption key D.

The algorithm outputs a key that enables the user to decrypt a message encrypted under a set of attributes γ if and only if $T(\gamma) = 1$. The algorithm proceeds as follows. First choose a polynomial q_x for each node x (including the leaves) in the tree T. These polynomials are chosen in the following way in a top-down manner, starting from the root node r.

For each node x in the tree, set the degree d_x of the polynomial q_x to be one less than the threshold value k_x of that node, that is, $d_x = k_x - 1$. Now, for the root node r, set $q_r(0) = y$ and d_r other points of the polynomial q_r randomly to define it completely. For any other node x, set $q_x(0) = q_{parent(x)}(index(x))$ and choose d_x other points randomly to completely define q_x.

Once the polynomials have been decided, for each leaf node x, we give the following secret value to the user:

$$D_x = g^{qx(0)/ti}, \text{ where } i = att(x)$$

The set of above secret values is the decryption key D.

4.4.4. Decryption (E, D, PK)

This algorithm takes as input - the cipher text E that was encrypted under the set γ of attributes, the decryption key D for access tree T (access control structure A) and the public parameters PK. It outputs the message M if $\gamma \in A$.

Decryption procedure is specified as a recursive algorithm. For ease of exposition, the simplest form of the decryption algorithm is presented. Let consider a recursive algorithm $DecryptNode(E, D, x)$ that takes as input the cipher text $E = (\gamma, E', \{E_i\}_{i \in \gamma})$, the private key D (we assume the access tree T is embedded in the private key), and a node x in the tree. It outputs a group element of G_2 or $\perp$.

Consider $i = att(x)$. If the node x is a leaf node then:

$$DecryptNode(E, D, x) = \text{Either } e(D_x, E_i)$$
$$= e(g^{qx(0)/ti}, g^{s.ti}) = e(g, g)^{s.qx(0)} \text{ if } i \in \gamma$$
$$\text{Or } \perp \text{ otherwise}$$

Now consider the recursive case when x is a non-leaf node. The algorithm $DecryptNode(E, D, x)$ then proceeds as follows:

For all nodes z that are children of x, it calls *DecryptNode(E, D, x)* and stores the output as F_z. Let S_x be an arbitrary k_x-sized set of child nodes z such that $F_z \neq \perp$. If no such set exists then the node was not satisfied and the function returns $\perp$.

Otherwise, compute following and return the result:

$$F_x = \Pi_{z \in sx} F_z^{\Delta i, s' x(0)} \quad , \quad \text{where} \quad i = \text{index}(z) \quad \text{and}$$

$$s'_x = \{\text{index}(z) : z \in s_x\}$$

$$= \Pi_{z \in sx} (e(g,g)^{s.qz(0)})^{\Delta i, s' x(0)}$$

$$= \Pi_{z \in sx} (e(g,g)^{s.qparent(z)(index(z))})^{\Delta i, s' x(0)} \text{ (by construction)}$$

$$= \Pi_{z \in sx} (e(g,g)^{s.qx(i)})^{\Delta i, s' x(0)}$$

$$= e(g,g)^{s.qx(0)} \text{ (using polynomial interpolation)}$$

The decryption algorithm simply calls the function on the root of the tree. It can be observed that *DecryptNode(E, D, x)* $= e(g,g)^{ys} = Y^s$ if and only if the cipher text satisfies the tree. Since, $E' = MY^s$ the decryption algorithm simply divides out Y^s and recovers the message M.

5. Proposed Methodology

In this section, ASP (Advanced Security Protocol) is presented which is a privacy-preserving cryptographic access control Protocol that enables end-users to securely store, share, and manage their sensitive data in untrusted cloud storage anonymously. ASP is scalable and supports lazy revocation. It can be easily implemented on top of existing cloud services and APIs. Its prototype can be demonstrated based on Amazon S3 [37] API.

Advanced Security Protocol (ASP) supports cryptographic key-updating scheme, referred to as AKU (Advanced Key Update) as well as Authentication and data Integrity scheme, referred to as AB-SIGN. The main advantage of the AKU scheme its support for efficient delegation and revocation of privileges in hierarchies without requiring complex cryptographic data structures. Authentication Scheme is attribute based which enables the verifier to ensure that a signature is produced by a sender/creator/writer whose access policy is satisfied by a set of attributes without learning the signer's identity.

First, a formal definition for secure key-updating schemes for hierarchical access is provided. Then, we give a concrete construction of a key-updating scheme based on ABE scheme. It supports both key revocation and hierarchical delegation of secret access keys.

5.1. Hierarchical KU Scheme: Model and Definition

Let $T = (V, E, O)$ be a tree that represent a hierarchical access structure. More general access class hierarchies in which partially ordered access classes are represented by a DAG are studied in [34]. In our work, we are only interested in a special case where DAG is a tree. Each vertex v_i in $V = \{v_0, v_1, v_2, \ldots, v_n\}$ corresponds to an access class. v_0 is the root and an edge $e = (v_i, v_j) \in E$ implies that v_i class is the parent of class v_j. O is a set of

sensitive data objects, each object o is associated with exactly one access class $V(o)$. In this model, any subject that can assume access rights at class v_i is also permitted to access any object assigned to a vertex that is a descendant of v_i.

Definition 1 The local time at vertex v_i is an integer t_i that increases (elapses) every time access rights of a subject to that class is revoked.

Definition 2 The global time associated with node v_i is a vector $T_i = (t_0, \ldots, t_i, \ldots, t_j)$ where t_j is the local time of jth vertex on the path from root to vertex v_i on the access tree T.

Two instances of global time are comparable only if the vertices that they belong to are identical or one of them is the ancestor of the other one; We say $T_i < T_j$ if and only if T_i and T_j are comparable and all common components of T_i are less than the corresponding components in T_j. Similarly, we define comparative operators $=,>,\leq$, and $\geq$.

Definition 3 A Hierarchical Key-Updating (*HKU*) Scheme consists of a root user and end users. An end user may be a reader, a writer, or both. There are five polynomial time algorithms *HKU = (Init, Derive, Encrypt, Decrypt, Update)* defined as follows:

- **Init** $(1^k, T)$ is a randomized process run by the root user which takes as input a security parameter k and an access hierarchy tree T and then generates and publishes a set of public parameters Pub and outputs the root key K_{v0}, $\perp$. It also initializes the state parameters including the value of local time at each vertex.

- **Derive** $(T, K_{(vi,Ti)}, v_j)$ is a randomized process run by the root user, reader or writer which using the private key $K_{(vi,Ti)}$ of v_i at time T_i derives a private key of target class v_j at its current global time T_j according to T. Derive computes the requested key only if v_i is an ancestor of v_j and $T_j = T_i$; otherwise, it outputs null ($\perp$).

- **Revoke** (T, v_i) run by the root user, reader or writer, increments the local time t_i of v_i by one, updates other state variables, and returns the updated tree T'.

- **Encrypt** (T, o_k) is a randomized algorithm called by writer that encrypts the data object o_k and returns the encrypted object C.

- **Decrypt** $(K_{(vi,Ti)}, C)$ is a deterministic process run by reader which takes a key and an encrypted object as inputs and returns the corresponding object in plaintext. This function can decrypt C only if it belongs to the same or a descendant of the access class that the key belongs to and the time that ok is encrypted at is less than or equal to T_i; otherwise, it outputs null ($\perp$).

Definition 3 is a generalization of the definition of key-updating schemes in [38] and the definition of key allocation schemes for hierarchies in [39]. If we assign to T a tree of depth 1 where its leaves are a set of groups (i.e., remove hierarchies), our definition reduces to a key-updating scheme defined in [38] and if we remove the update process and the time dimension, our scheme reduces to key allocation scheme for hierarchies defined in [39]. Intuitively, a hierarchical key-updating scheme is secure if all polynomial time adversaries have at most a negligible advantage to break the cipher-text encrypted with the current-time key of a target class, assuming that the adversaries do not belong to higher (ancestor) target classes in the hierarchy, or possess keys for earlier time periods. In this model the adversary chooses her target at the beginning of the game and then adaptively queries the scheme.

We define the security model of hierarchical key-updating schemes as follows:

Definition 4 A hierarchical key-updating schemes is secure if no polynomial time adversary A has a non-negligible advantage (in the security parameter k) against the challenger in the following game (HKU game):

Choosing target: The adversary declares an access object $\tilde{v}$ and a time instance $T_{\tilde{v}}$ that she wishes to guess its corresponding private key (i.e. $K'(v', T')$).

Setup: The challenger runs Init($1^k, T$), and gives the resulting public parameters Pub and T to the adversary.

Key-Extraction Query: The adversary adaptively queries the private keys of polynomial number of vertices at any time that she wishes subject to the restriction that either the queried vertices are not an ancestor of (or equal to) $\tilde{v}$ or the time instance that they are being queried at is earlier than or equal to $T_{\tilde{v}}$.

Challenge: The adversary submits two equal length objects o_0 and o_1 belonging to the access class $\tilde{v}$. The challenger flips a random coin b, and encrypts o_b for time $T_{\tilde{v}}$ and submits the result to the adversary.

The adversary issues more Key-Extraction queries.

Guess: The adversary outputs a guess b' of b.

Adversary's advantage is the probability that her guess is correct: $Adv_A = Pr[b' = b]$. The HKU scheme is secure if the adversary's probability compared to random guessing (1/2) is negligible.

5.2. AKU: Confidentiality Scheme

In this section, a concrete construction for HKU scheme called Advanced Key Update (AKU) is presented. This scheme is based on the use of bilinear map and the difficulty of the Decisional Bilinear Diffie-Hellman problem. Our solution is realized on top of the Key-Policy Attribute-Based Encryption scheme (KP-ABE) [15] and invokes KP-ABE operations including Setup ABE, KeyGen ABE for private key generation, Encrypt_ABE for data encryption, and Decrypt_ABE for decryption.

5.2.1. Init(1^k, T)

The root user runs the Setup Attribute Based Encryption process with 1^k as security parameter to generate ABE public parameters and the master key MK. Publishes the ABE public parameters as Pub$_{abe}$.

Invoke KeyGen_ABE procedure using MK as the secret key and "$L_0 = v_0$" as its policy. Outputs the result as the root key ($K_{(v0,\perp)}$ = Key-Gen_ABE(MK, $L_0 = v_0$)).

To each vertex in T adds a local time variable t_i initialized to zero.

5.2.2. Derive(T, $K(v_i, T_i)$, v_j)

It is run by a user (root user, reader, or writer) with secret key $K_{(vi,Ti)}$ at time T_i to obtain the private key for node v_j.

If class v_j is not a descendant of class v_i, or the time T_i is not equal to current time T_j associated with v_j, then return null. Otherwise, denote $(u_1, u_2, ..., u_n)$ as the list of vertices in the path from v_i to v_j; denote $(t_{u1}, t_{u2}, ..., t_{un}, t_{vj})$ on T as the list of current local time values of intermediate vertices (including v_j); and let d represent the depth of v_i.

The user performs the following operations:
1) Construct the access tree T' which corresponds to the following Boolean expression: ($L_d.v$ attribute represents vertex in d-th level, $L_d.t$ represents its current local time and $^\wedge$ is conjunction operator.).

$$(L_{(d+1)}.v = u_1 ^\wedge ..... ^\wedge L_{(d+n)}.v = u_n$$
$$^\wedge L_{(d+n+1)}.v = vj) ^\wedge$$
$$(L_{(d+1)}.t = T_{u1} ^\wedge ..... ^\wedge L_{(d+n)}.t = Tun$$
$$^\wedge L_{(vj)}.t \leq Tvj)$$

This Boolean expression restricts access to objects that belong to node vj or its descendants and are created at current time or before.

2) Denote the access tree of $K_{(vi,Ti)}$ by T. Using the procedure for delegation of private key in [15], add the access tree T' to the root of $K_{(vi,Ti)}$, increase its threshold by one, update and calculate the private parameters associated to the root according the protocol. In implementation section we provide more details on this procedure.

3) Output the resulting access tree and parameters as a private key $K_{(vj,Tj)}$ for v_j.

5.2.3. Encrypt(T, o_k)

Encryption of data is performed using key. Denote v_i as the access class that object o_k belongs to. ($v_i = V(o_k)$). Denote $(v_0, u_1, u_2, ..., u_n, v_i)$ as v_i's path and $T_i = (t_{v0}, t_{u1}, t_{u2}, ..., t_{un}, t_{vi})$ as its current time according to T. A writer encrypts o_k as follows:

The attribute set is used as the public key for encryption. Set the attribute set γ as follows:

$$\gamma = \{L_0.v = v_0, ..., L_n.v = v_n, L_{n+1}.v = v_i;$$
$$L_0.t = t_{v0}, ..., L_n.t = t_{un}, L_{n+1}.t = t_{vi}\}$$

Use ABE encryption procedure to encrypt o_k with attribute set γ and return the resulting encrypted object. ($C = Encrypt\_ABE(Pubabe, \gamma, o_k)$).

5.2.4. Decrypt($K_{(vi, Ti)}$, C)

After encryption of the data using key, we get cipher text that is transmitted to receiver end. Receiver or reader decrypts the cipher text as follows:

- If the encrypted object C does not belong to the same access class vi as the key $K_{(vi, Ti)}$ or one of its descendants, or the time when C is encrypted is later than the time T_i when the key is generated, then return null ($\perp$).

- Otherwise, run ABE decryption procedure and return its result as output $(o_k = \text{Decrypt\_ABE}(K_{((vi, Ti)}, C))$.

5.2.5. Revoke(T, v_i)

It is run by a user to increment the local time of v_i by one and then returns the updated tree T'.)

The correctness of AKU scheme follows the correctness of the key policy ABE scheme [15].

Theorem 1 Assuming the hardness of the Decisional BDH, AKU is a secure hierarchical key-updating scheme.

Proof 1 Sketch. It suffices to show that an adversary, who can play HKU game for AKU with non-negligible advantage, can also win KP-ABE game with a non-negligible probability, and thus break the security of KP-ABE and subsequently the Decisional BDH. Let A be an adversary who can win HKU game with non-negligible advantage $1/2 + \epsilon$. She can play KP-ABE Selective-Set model game as follows:

Init: A declares the set of attributes that corresponds to vertex $\tilde{v}$ and time $T_{\tilde{v}}$ as γ, the set of attributes that she wishes to be challenged upon.

Setup: This step is identical to Setup step in HKU game.

Phase 1: In this phase the adversary queries for the private keys for access structures (trees) T_j which correspond to that of keys that she would query in HKU game. Since, according to the protocol of HKU game, these keys belong to vertices that are not an ancestor of $\tilde{v}$ or their time is less than $T_{\tilde{v}}$, their access trees will not satisfy with attributes in γ (γ does not belong to T_j) and therefore they are legitimate queries.

Challenge: Identical to the Challenge step in HKU game.

Phase 2: Repeat Phase 1.

Guess: The adversary guesses b using the same strategy that she uses in HKU game. Since the data is encrypted under the same set of attributes and using the same procedure, she has the same non-negligible advantage to make the correct guess. This concludes our proof.

5.3. AB-SIGN: Authentication and Integrity Scheme

Proposed ASP protocol supports message authentication and data integrity using AB-SIGN scheme. Our design for AB-SIGN is based on the same technique introduced by by Moni Naor (Section 6 of [40]) for Identity Based Encryption and then extended in [41] for HIDS signature scheme. However, the original paper which introduces KP-ABE [15] does not present any signature scheme.

AB-SIGN scheme is an attribute based signature scheme which

1) Enable the readers to verify the integrity of data and ensure that it is produced by an authorized writer,

2) Enable the cloud service providers to validate incoming requests and block unauthorized accesses.

Definition 5 AB-SIGN is a signature scheme for KP-ABE [15] that it's signing and verification methods are defined as follows. Let's say that the signer has a key K for policy P, and wants to sign message M. The verifier needs to verify that the signature is generated by a signer whose key policy satisfies attribute set A:

Signature: From K derive a key (K') which corresponds to a policy which is the concatenation of P and $(@S = M)$ ($@S$ is a reserved attribute for signatures). Send the derived key to the verifier as the signature.

Signature Verification: Generate a random token and encrypt it using the attribute set $AU\{@S = M\}$ and then decrypt the result using a key which is equal to the signature. If the result is equal to the original token the signature is valid (i.e. the attribute set A satisfies the signer's key policy.)

To prevent an attacker from using the signature method to derive a valid access key, we need to reserve the attribute '$@S$' for signature.

Theorem 2: Assuming the hardness of the Decisional BDH, AB-SIGN is a secure signature scheme.

Proof 2: Enforceability of AB-SIGN scheme follows immediately from the security of KP-ABE scheme. In AB-SIGN, a signature is a derived key from the actual write access key. Therefore, based on the security of KP-ABE derive operation; the only entity who can generate the signature is the owner of the write access key. Moreover, security of derive operation guarantees that the verifier cannot guess the original access key from the derived key.

6. Implementation and Operation

The ASP protocol runs between the root user, end-user (reader or writer), and the cloud providers. The root user may be a system administrator in the data owner's organization, who can specify the access privileges of end-users. The end-users may further delegate their access privileges to other individuals for easy sharing. We achieve the revocation of privilege by encoding the validity period in the private keys of users and advancing time with respect to the target hierarchy or data object. Another advantage of our ASP framework for use in cloud storage is the support of anonymous access.

ASP protocol requires three repositories: *Meta-data Directory, Data Store* and *Key-store* as shown in Figure 1.

Meta-data Directory: All meta-data associated with hierarchies and data objects are maintained in this repository. ASP requires two properties for each object: Read Access Revision (RAR) and Write Access Revision (WAR). These two properties play the role of local time in AKU for read and write access, respectively. In order to compute Read/Write Access Revision Vectors (which correspond to global time instances in ASP), the cloud provider that hosts Meta-data Directory needs to provide an API for querying RAR and WAR values of multiple directories in a single request. All existing cloud-based databases (also known as 'NoSQL systems' or 'schema-free database' such as Amazon SimpleDB [43], Microsoft Azure SQL [42], and Google's AppEngine [44] database

(Bigtable [45])) satisfy this requirement and therefore qualify to host an ASP Meta-data Directory. For our experiments we use Amazon SimpleDB [43].

Data Store: This repository contains the actual content of each data object. Any cloud key-value based storage system such as Amazon S3 [37] can be used as ASP Data Store. In ASP, keys are hierarchical path name of data objects and values are the actual content of corresponding data objects. Cloud key-value storage providers are tuned for high throughput and low storage cost; these features make them a good candidate for ASP Data Store.

Key-store: Key-Store is a secure local repository which having all read/write access keys of end-users. Each key-store contains all public parameters as well as read/write access key entries of all data-objects and categories that the end user has access to. Each access key entry contains the following fields: object path, access type (read/write), granter's identity, and secret key. The Key-store provides an API that given user's credential and a path, returns the first key entry that its path is a prefix of the input path.

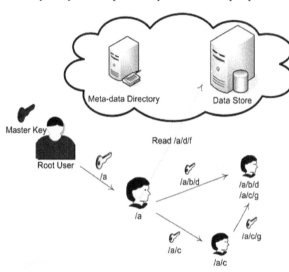

Figure 1. ASP Working Environment

All major participants of ASP protocol are shown in Figure 1. In ASP protocol, end-users can enforce access control on their own data without fully trusting or relying on the cloud providers. Here keys are distributed and managed in a distributed fashion. Solid arrows represent access delegation.

Working with ASP

- To work with ASP, the root user needs to follow the following steps:
- Sign up for cloud services required for hosting Meta-data Directory and Data Store.
- Run *Init* procedure according to AKU scheme to generate public parameters and the master key.
- Save the master key and public parameters in the root's Key-store.
- Share the public parameters with the cloud service providers that support ASP request authorization.
- Create an entry in Meta-date Directory that corresponds to the root directory. The WAR and RAR numbers of the root directory entry are initialized to zero.

6.1. ASP Operation

The basic operations supported by ASP include: write, read, delegate, and revoke. Each basic operation leads to calls to Meta-data directory and/or Data Store. Other operations such as create, remove, rename, update for directories and data objects can be defined similarly. AB-SIGN Scheme is needed before performing the basic operations to maintain the authenticity and data integrity. Requirement of AB-SIGN of ASP to perform operations enables cloud providers to block unauthorized request.

6.1.1. Write Operation

Figure 2 shows the idea about write operation using ASP protocol. To write into a specific data object, the end-user needs to perform the following steps:

1) Retrieve the required write access key from the local Key-store.
2) Query Meta-data directory to get read access revision (RAR) vector of the target object.
3) Using AKU scheme, encrypt the data by the retrieved RAR vector and its path.
4) Using AB-SIGN scheme, sign the data by his write access key.
5) Construct a key-value pair where the key is equal to the path of data object and the value is the encrypted data and corresponding signature. Store the pair in Data Store.
6) To prevent destructive writes by unauthorized users, the Data Store can query write access revision (WAR) vector of that object from the Meta-data Directory to validate the signature of request.

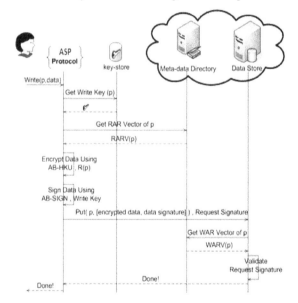

Figure 2. Write Operation

6.1.2. Read Operation

Figure 3 shows the idea about read operation using ASP protocol. To ensure the data is produced by an authorized writer, the reader needs to validate the corresponding signature using AB-SIGN signature scheme. Then the reader can decrypt the data using its read access key and AKU scheme. To read a specific data object stored using ASP protocol, the end-user needs to do the following steps:

1) Retrieve the required read access key from the local Key-store.

2) Using AKU scheme and the read access key, decrypt the encrypted data.
3) Using AB-SIGN signature scheme, validate the signature to ensure that data is produced by a user who has the proper write access.
4) Return the decrypted data.

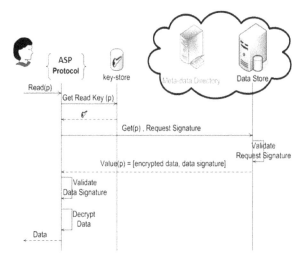

Figure 3. Read Operation

6.1.3. Delegation Operation

Delegation operation can be run by a user to authorize another user a subset of his access privileges as shown in Figure 1. It requires three input parameters: the identity of the delegate, the resource path, and access type (read/write). The steps required for this operation are listed below:
1) From the local Key-store, get the access key that matches the target resource path and access type.
2) Query Meta-date Directory to get the read/write access revision (RAR/WAR) vector of target resource.
3) Run Derive operation, as defined in AKU scheme, to generate the required access key.
4) Send the generated access key to the delegate through a secure communication channel.

6.1.4. Revocation Operation

This facility reduces the overhead on the data center by restricting fake user. To revoke a user's access on a specific directory or data object, the authorized user needs to make a signed request to the Meta-data Directory to increase the corresponding access revision number. To ensure the integrity of access revision numbers, these entries should be signed by the requester.

7. Analysis of Proposed Technique

In this section, some experimental results are provided which show the performance overhead of our ASP protocol.

Pre-computation and caching: As discussed in the previous sections, to overcome the limitation of fixed attributes, we adopted large universe construction of KP-ABE. However, in this construction the process of mapping an attribute to the bilinear group $G(i.e.\{1,0\}^* \to G)$ is very expensive (on average 22 ms per attribute). In our KP-ABE library every bit of a

numerical attribute gets translated into a symbolic attribute. For example, a 10-bit representation of the numerical attribute $li = 352$ gets translated into a list of symbolic attributes shown in Table 1.

Table 1. Symbolic representation of attribute $li = 352$
[li@0=1, li@1=1, li@2=0, li@3=0, li@4=0, li@5=1, l i@6=1, li@7=0, li@8=1, li@9=0]

Also, all numerical comparisons get translated into symbolic matching policies. For example, Table policy 2 corresponds to the numerical comparison $li < 356$.

Table 2. KP-ABE policy for $li < 356$
(2 li@9=0 (1 (2 li@7=0 (1 (1 (2 li@4=0 (2 li@3=0 (1 li@1=0 li@2=0))
) li@5=0) li@6=0)) li@8=0))

In ASP, every level of an object's path has two numbers associated with it – read access revision number and write access revision number. Therefore, these numerical attributes lead too many symbolic attributes which their mapping cost create a significant over-head. Since the value of each bit is either zero or one, we pre-compute the mapped values of these symbols and during the startup process load them into the framework. Moreover, at runtime, we cache the mapped value of each path segment in a hash table so that it can be reused. Using the described pre-computation and caching techniques, we were able to significantly reduce the computational cost associated with required KP-ABE crypto operations.

Security Process: In ASP the actual content of data is encrypted using either a symmetric-key or asymmetric-key encryption scheme based on user choice. And only the corresponding symmetric/asymmetric keys are encrypted by KP-ABE scheme. By default our framework uses AES (Advanced Encryption Standard) [4,12] for symmetric encryption with the default key length of 128 bits. Similarly, AB-SIGN signature scheme is performed on fixed-length digest of data. Our framework, by default, uses SHA-1 [4,11] as the digest hash function. SHA-1 generates 160-bit message digest of data.

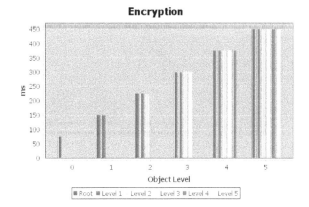

Figure 4. Encryption Analysis

The Figure 4 and Figure 5 show the overhead of encryption and decryption schemes while Figure 6 and Figure 7 show signature and sign verification schemes of ASP protocol on top of underlying symmetric-key encryption and hashing schemes. In our experiments numerical attributes are of size 10 bits.

Figure 4 shows how the cost of ASP encryption relates to the user's access level and hierarchy level of the data object. In KP-ABE the encryption time is only a function of number of attributes, which linearly increases as the object level increases. As a result, ASP encryption cost linearly increases as the hierarchy level of the object increases, but it is independent of the user's access level.

By contrast, as Figure 5 shows, decryption time is just a function of user's access level. That is because in KP-ABE, decryption time is a function of complexity of access structure that linearly increases as user's access level increases. Decryption time is independent of hierarchy level of the encrypted object.

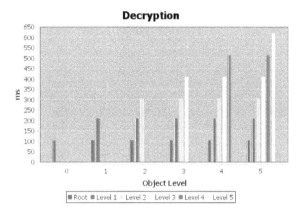

Figure 5. Decryption Analysis

Figure 6 and Figure 7 show the overhead of ASP signing and signature verification on signed objects in different hierarchy levels for users with different access levels respectively. In ASP, as Figure 6 illustrates, signature cost is independent of the hierarchy level of data objects; it only depends on access level of the user. This is because proposed AB-SIGN signature scheme is based on KP-ABE derive operation which its complexity linearly increases as the complexity of the access structures increases.

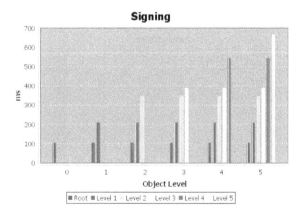

Figure 6. Message Signing Analysis

In AB-SIGN scheme, each signature verification operation requires KP-ABE encryption and decryption, therefore its computational cost depends on the user's access level as well as the hierarchy level of data object. Figure 7 shows how the time required for signature verification increases linearly as the access level of user decrease and the hierarchy level of data object increases

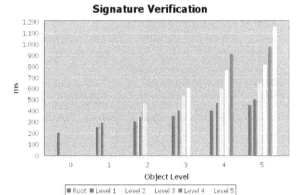

Figure 7. Signature Verification Analysis

Figure 8 and Figure 9 show the combined overhead cost of read and write operations in ASP. To perform ASP write operation, a user needs to encrypt and sign the data objects. The portion of cost below the white indicator is related to encryption and the rest is the cost associated with signature as shown in Figure 8.

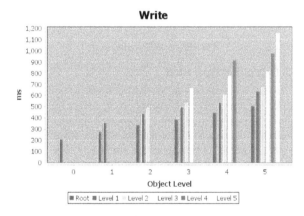

Figure 8. Write Operation Analysis

ASP read operation includes cost of decryption and signature verification. If we divide the graph given in Figure 9 by horizontal line, portion below and above of that line, shows the overhead cost for decryption and signature verification, respectively.

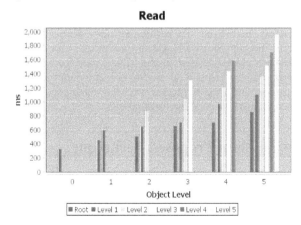

Figure 9. Read Operation Analysis

7.1. Complexity Analysis

In this section, we denote N as the number of attribute authorities, I as the size of the entire attribute set and X as the number of nodes in a tree T_p. Table 3 shows the complexity comparisons of proposed approach with existing approaches proposed in [9] and [26].

Table 3. Complexity Comparisons

Phase	Chase et al. [26]	Yu et al. [9]	ASP
System Setup	$O(1)$	$O(1)$	$O(1)$
KeyGen	$O(N + I)$	$O(X)$	$O(N + I)$
Encryption	$O(1)$	$O(1)$	$O(X \cdot K)$
Decryption	$O(N \cdot I)$	$O(max(X, I))$	$O(X)$
Revocation		$O(1)$	$O(X \cdot K)$

System Setup:

When the system is setup, ΠY^k is computed by any one of the authorities and sent to others, whose complexity is $O(N)$. Then, secret parameters xk's are calculated within the clusters. The complexity of that calculation is $O(C2 \cdot NC) = O(C \cdot N)$, but C is a constant number, so $O(C \cdot N) = O(N)$. Therefore, the total complexity is $O(N)$. However, since we have N authorities per system, the complexity per authority is $O(1)$.

KeyGen

In the Attribute Key Generation, $g^{\Sigma Vi}$ is computed by N authorities, and $D_i = H(att(i))^{ri} \cdot g^{\Sigma Vi}$ is computed for I times by one attribute authority. Therefore, the total complexity of Attribute Key Generation is $O(N2 + I.N)$. In the Aggregation of Two Keys, a user aggregates the I components, thus the computation complexity of this

operation is $O(I)$. So, the complexity per authority is $O(N+I)$.

Encryption

In this phase at every non-leaf node, a polynomial is chosen and k_{x-1} numbers are to be found to determine the polynomial, where x is the threshold value. Therefore, denoting the average threshold value to be K, the computation complexity of this process is $O(X.K)$.

Decryption

Decryption is a recursive algorithm, and it is executed exactly once at every node in a Breadth-First-Search manner, therefore the computation complexity of this process is $O(X)$.

Revocation

Revocation operation has the same complexity as the addition of Encryption and Decryption. Its complexity is $O(X.K)$.

The comparison between proposed ASP protocol and the different multi-authority schemes is shown in Tables 4 and 5. By $|U|$, $|A_U|$, and $|A_C|$, we denote the number of the universal attributes, the attributes held by user U, and the attributes required by the cipher text, respectively. I_U and I_C denote the index set of the authorities. By E and P, we denote one exponential and one paring operation, respectively. By L_{G1} and L_{G2}, we denote one element in group G1 and one element in group G2, respectively. N denotes the number of the authorities in the systems. Table 4 shows the ideas about operation cost for various MA-ABE schemes while Table 5 shows the working ideas comparison of existing MA-ABE technologies.

Table 4. Comparison of computational cost

Schemes	Authority setup	KeyGen	Encryption	Decryption
Chase's [22]	$(|U|+1)E$	$(|A_U|+1)E$	$(|A_C|+2)E$	$|A_C|E+(|A_C|+1)P$
Han et al.'s [23]	$(|U|+2N)E$	$(|A_U|+3|I_U|)E$	$(|A_C|+3)E$	$|A_C|E+(|A_C|+|I_C|+1)P$
Chase and Chow [26]	$(|U|+2N)E$	$(|U|+|I_U|^2)E$	$(|A_C|+2)E$	$|A_C|E+(|A_C|+1)P$
Our ASP	$(|U|+2N)E$	$(|U|+|I_U|^2+1)E$	$(|A_C|+3)E$	$|A_C|E+(|A_C|+1)P$

Table 5. Working Idea Comparison for MA-ABE

Scheme	Security Model	Used ABE	Cipher text Length	Central Authority	Authenticity
Chase's [49]	Selective	KP-ABE	$(|A_C|+1)L_{G1} + L_{G2}$	Yes	No
Han et al.'s [50]	Selective	KP-ABE	$(|A_C|+2)L_{G1} + L_{G2}$	No	Yes
Lin et al.'s [51]	Selective	FIBE	$(|A_C|)L_{G1} + L_{G2}$	No	No
Chase and Chow [52]	Selective	KP-ABE	$(|A_C|+1)L_{G1} + L_{G2}$	No	No
Our ASP	Selective	KP-ABE	$(|A_C|+2)L_{G1} + L_{G2}$	Yes	Yes

7.2. Security Analysis

In this section we state the security guarantees provided by ASP protocol.

Confidentiality: Our solution ensures that only the users who have the most recent version of the access key of the data object or one of its ancestor directories can decrypt it. The confidentiality of stored data is protected under our protocol because writers always encrypt the data objects by their path and most recent read access revision (RAR) vector according to AKU scheme. The cloud provider or other unauthorized users cannot gain any

information that helps them to guess the access key of unauthorized data objects.

Integrity: The integrity of stored data is preserved. This guarantee is realized by requiring writers to sign the data by their write access key using AB-SIGN scheme. We require readers to validate writer's signature to ensure that it is produced by an authorized writer (i.e. a user with write access to that data object or on of its parent directories). Because meta-data entries stored in the Meta-data Directory are also required to be signed by the end-users, any unauthorized change in Meta-data Directory is detectable by the reader.

Authenticity and Anonymity: The end users are anonymous to each other and to the cloud providers. The signatures used in proposed authorization do not contain any identify information. During the course of protocol, the end-users do not reveal any information about their credentials. AB-SIGN signatures bound to the data objects and requests; include only attributes related to the location and global time of those objects.

Collusion-resistance: Security of KP-ABE guarantees that unauthorized users and malicious cloud service providers cannot collude to guess access key to an unauthorized data object.

8. Conclusion and Future Work

As people are becoming more concerned about their privacy these days, the privacy-preserving is very important over the cloud. Security issues can be categorized into sensitive data access, data segregation, privacy, bug exploitation, recovery, accountability, malicious insiders, management console security, account control, and multi-tenancy issues. The three basic requirements of security: confidentiality, integrity and availability are required to protect data throughout its lifecycle. Data must be protected during the various stages of creation, sharing, archiving, processing etc. However, situations become more complicated in case of a public cloud.

In this paper, Advanced Security Protocol (ASP) is presented that supports Hierarchical Key-Updating scheme. This protocol illustrates how recent cryptographic schemes can be utilized to develop an effective client-side access control protocol for protecting confidentiality and integrity of data stored in untrusted cloud storage. Proposed ASP protocol also includes an attribute based signature(AB-SIGN) scheme that enables cloud providers to ensure that requests are submitted by authorized end-users, without learning their identities. Using the key-updating and signature schemes, proposed idea is developed, implemented, and evaluated. Presented protocol is a scalable cryptographic access control protocol for hierarchically organized data. Proposed ASP protocol achieves Confidentiality, Data Integrity and Authenticity as well as reduces the overhead on web by restricting fake users.

In future, work can be done on security systems for various web based services.

References

[1] Shyam Nandan Kumar, and Amit Vajpayee, "A Survey on Secure Cloud: Security and Privacy in Cloud Computing." American Journal of Systems and Software, vol. 4, no. 1 (2016): 14-26.

[2] Shyam Nandan Kumar, "Cryptography during Data Sharing and Accessing Over Cloud." International Transaction of Electrical and Computer Engineers System, vol. 3, no. 1 (2015): 12-18.

[3] Shyam Nandan Kumar, "DecenCrypto Cloud: Decentralized Cryptography Technique for Secure Communication over the Clouds." Journal of Computer Sciences and Applications, vol. 3, no. 3 (2015): 73-78.

[4] Shyam Nandan Kumar, "Review on Network Security and Cryptography." International Transaction of Electrical and Computer Engineers System, vol. 3, no. 1 (2015): 1-11.

[5] Shyam Nandan Kumar, "World towards Advance Web Mining: A Review." American Journal of Systems and Software, vol. 3, no. 2 (2015): 44-61.

[6] "The NIST Definition of Cloud Computing". National Institute of Standards and Technology. Retrieved 24 July 2011.

[7] Mather T, Kumaraswamy S, Latif S (2009) Cloud Security and Privacy. O'Reilly Media, Inc., Sebastopol, CA.

[8] A. Verma and S. Kaushal, "Cloud Computing Security Issues and Challenges: A Survey", Proceedings of Advances in Computing and Communications, Vol. 193, pp. 445-454, 2011.

[9] Shucheng Yu, Cong Wang, Kui Ren, and Wenjing Lou. "Achieving secure, scalable and fine-grained data access control in cloud computing". In Proceedings of the 29th conference on Information communications, INFOCOM'10, pp. 534-542, Piscataway, NJ, USA, 2010. IEEE Press.

[10] Wayne Jansen, Timothy Grance, "NIST Guidelines on Security and Privacy in Public Cloud Computing", Draft Special Publication 800-144, 2011.

[11] RFC 3174, US Secure Hash Algorithm 1 (SHA1) http://www.ietf.org/rfc/rfc3174.txt.

[12] Joan Daemen and Vincent Rijmen. Rijndael/aes. "In Encyclopedia of Cryptography and Security". 2005.

[13] Jon Marler, "Securing the Cloud: Addressing Cloud Computing Security Concerns with Private Cloud", Rackspace Knowledge Centre, March 27, 2011, Article Id: 1638.

[14] A. Sahai and B. Waters, "Fuzzy identity-based encryption", in EUROCRYPT, ser. Lecture Notes in Computer Science, vol. 3494. Springer, pp. 457-473, 2005.

[15] V. Goyal, O. Pandey, A. Sahai, and B. Waters, "Attribute-Based Encryption for Fine-Grained Access Control of Encrypted data," in Proceedings of the 13th ACM Conference on Computer and Communications Security (CCS '06). ACM, 2006, pp. 89-98.

[16] R. Ostrovsky, A. Sahai, and B. Waters, "Attribute-based encryption with non-monotonic access structures," in Proceedings of the 14th ACM Conference on Computer and Communications Security (CCS '07), pp. 195-203, November 2007.

[17] J. Bethencourt, A. Sahai, and B. Waters, "Ciphertext-policy attribute-based encryption," in Proceedings of the IEEE Symposium on Security and Privacy (SP '07), pp. 321-334, May 2007.

[18] L. Cheung and C. Newport, "Provably secure ciphertext policy ABE," in Proceedings of the 14th ACM Conference on Computer and Communications Security (CCS '07), pp. 456-465, November 2007.

[19] B. Waters, "Ciphertext-policy attribute-based encryption: an expressive, efficient, and provably secure realization," in Public Key Cryptography (PKC '11), pp. 53-70, Springer, Berlin, Germany, 2011.

[20] A. Lewko, T. Okamoto, A. Sahai, and B. Waters, "Fully secure functional encryption: attribute-based encryption and (hierarchical) inner product encryption," in Advances in Cryptology: EUROCRYPT 2010, vol. 6110 of Lecture Notes in Computer Science, pp. 62-91, Springer, Berlin, Germany, 2010.

[21] K. Emura, A. Miyaji, K. Omote, A. Nomura, and M. Soshi, "A ciphertext-policy attribute-based encryption scheme with constant ciphertext length," International Journal of Applied Cryptography, vol. 2, no. 1, pp. 46-59, 2010.

[22] M. Chase, "Multi-authority attribute based encryption," in Theory of Cryptography, vol. 4392 of Lecture Notes in Computer Science, pp. 515-534, Springer, Berlin, Germany, 2007.

[23] J. Han, W. Susilo, Y. Mu, and J. Yan, "Privacy-preserving decentralized key-policy attribute-based encryption," IEEE Transactions on Parallel and Distributed Systems, vol. 23, no. 11, pp. 2150-2162, 2012.

[24] V. Bozovic, D. Socek, R. Steinwandt, and V. I. Villanyi, "Multi-authority attribute-based encryption with honest-but-curious central authority," International Journal of Computer Mathematics, vol. 89, no. 3, pp. 268-283, 2012.

[25] H. Lin, Z. Cao, X. Liang, and J. Shao, "Secure threshold multi authority attribute based encryption without a central authority," Information Sciences, vol. 180, no. 13, pp. 2618-2632, 2010.

[26] M. Chase and S. S. M. Chow, "Improving privacy and security in multi-authority attribute-based encryption," in Proceedings of the 16th ACM Conference on Computer and Communications Security (CCS '09), pp. 121-130, Chicago, Ill, USA, November 2009.

[27] N. Attrapadung and H. Imai, "Dual-policy attribute based encryption," in Applied Cryptography and Network Security, pp. 168-185, Springer, Berlin, Germany, 2009.

[28] Guojun Wang, Qin Liu, Jie Wu and Minyi Guo, "Hierarchical attribute-based encryption and scalable user revocation for sharing data in cloud servers", 2011.

[29] M. Mambo and E. Okamoto, "Proxy cryptosystems: delegation of the power to decrypt ciphertexts," IEICE Transactions on Fundamentals of Electronics, Communications and Computer Sciences, vol. 80, no. 1, pp. 54-62, 1997.

[30] M. Blaze, G. Bleumer, and M. Strauss, "Divertible protocols and atomic proxy cryptography," in Proceedings of the International Conference on the Theory and Application of Cryptographic Techniques (EUROCRYPT '98), pp. 127-144, Espoo, Finland, 1998.

[31] Tatsuaki Okamoto and Katsuyuki Takashima, "Decentralized Attribute-Based Signatures" , Public-Key Cryptography – PKC 2013, Springer Berlin Heidelberg, pp 125-142.

[32] Xiaofeng Chen, Jin Li, Xinyi Huang, Jingwei Li, Yang Xiang and Duncan S. Wong, "Secure Outsourced Attribute-Based Signatures", pp: 3285-3294, IEEE, vol. 25, (2014).

[33] Wenyi Liu, Uluagac, A.S. and Beyah, R., "MACA: A privacy-preserving multi-factor cloud authentication system utilizing big data", IEEE Conference on Computer Communications Workshops (INFOCOM WKSHPS), 2014, pp. 518-523, Toronto, ON.

[34] S. Yu, C. Wang, K. Ren, and W. Lou, "Attribute based data sharing with attribute revocation" in ACM ASIACCS, pp. 261-270, 2010.

[35] A. B. Lewko and B. Waters, "Decentralizing attribute-based encryption", in EUROCRYPT, ser. Lecture Notes in Computer Science, vol. 6632. Springer, pp. 568-588, 2011.

[36] H. K. Maji, M. Prabhakaran, and M. Rosulek, "Attribute-based signatures", in CT-RSA, ser. Lecture Notes in Computer Science, vol. 6558. Springer, pp. 376-392, 2011.

[37] Amazon S3 . http://aws.amazon.com/s3/.

[38] Michael Backes, Christian Cachin, and Alina Oprea. "Secure Key-Updating for Lazy Revocation",. In Research Report RZ 3627, IBM Research, pages 327-346. Springer, 2005.

[39] Marina Blanton, Nelly Fazio, and Keith B. Frikken. "Dynamic and Efficient Key Management for Access Hierarchies". In Proceedings of the ACM Conference on Computer and Communications Security, 2005.

[40] Dan Boneh and Matthew Franklin. "Identity-based encryption from the weil pairing". SIAM J. Comput., 32: 586-615, March 2003.

[41] Craig Gentry and Alice Silverberg. "Hierarchical ID-based cryptography". In ASI- ACRYPT, pp. 548-566, 2002.

[42] SQL Data Services/Azure Services Platform. http://http://www.windowsazure.com.

[43] Amazon SimpleDB. http://aws.amazon.com/simpledb/.

[44] Google App Engine. http://appengine.google.com.

[45] Fay Chang, Jeffrey Dean, Sanjay Ghemawat, Wilson C. Hsieh, Deborah A. Wallach, Mike Burrows, Tushar Chandra, Andrew Fikes, and Robert E. Gruber. Bigtable: "A distributed storage system for structured data". In Proceedings of the 7th symposium on Operating systems design and implementation - volume 7, pp. 205-218, 2006.

[46] P. Sharma, S. K. Sood, and S. Kaur, "Security Issues in Cloud Computing", Proceedings of High Performance Architecture and Grid Computing, Vol. 169, pp. 36-45, 2011.

[47] Alessandro Perilli, Claudio Criscione, "Securing the Private Cloud", Article on Secure Networks, Virtualization.info. http://virtualization.info/en/security/privatecloud.pdf.

[48] Thomas W. Shinder, "Security Issues in Cloud Deployment models", TechNet Articles, Wiki, Microsoft, Aug, 2011.

[49] Craig Gentry, A FULLY HOMOMORPHIC ENCRYPTION SCHEME", PhD Thesis, STANFORD UNIVERSITY, September 2009.

[50] Cloud Security Alliance (2012), "SecaaS implementation guidance, category 1: identity and Access management". Available: https://downloads.cloudsecurityalliance.org/initiatives/secaas/SecaaS_Cat_1_IAM_Implementation_Guidance.pdf.

[51] Ron Rivest (2002-10-29). "Lecture Notes 15: Voting, Homomorphic Encryption.

[52] B. R. Kandukuri, P. V. Ramakrishna, and A. Rakshit, "Cloud security issues", in Proceedings of the IEEE International Conference on Services Computing (SCC '09), pp. 517-520, September 2009.

[53] Win-Bin Huang and Wei-Tsung Su, "Identity-based access control for digital content based on ciphertext-policy attribute-based encryption", International Conference on Information Networking (ICOIN), IEEE, pp. 87-91, Cambodia, 2015.

[54] Jie Xu, Qiaoyan Wen, Wenmin Li, Zhengping Jin, "Circuit Ciphertext-Policy Attribute-Based Hybrid Encryption with Verifiable Delegation in Cloud Computing", IEEE Transactions on Parallel and Distributed Systems, vol. 27, issue: 1, pp. 119-129, 2015.

[55] Win-Bin Huang, Wei-Tsung Su, and Chiang-Sheng Liang, "A threshold-based key generation approach for ciphertext-policy attribute-based encryption", Seventh International Conference on Ubiquitous and Future Networks (ICUFN), IEEE, pp. 908-913, Sapporo, 2015.

[56] Juanjuan Li, Zhenhua Liu, and Longhui Zu, "Chosen-Ciphertext Secure Multi-use Unidirectional Attribute-Based Proxy Re-Encryptions", Ninth Asia Joint Conference on Information Security (ASIA JCIS), IEEE, pp. 96-103, Wuhan, 2014.

[57] Han Yiliang, Jiang Di , Yang Xiaoyuan, "The Revocable Attribute Based Encryption Scheme for Social Networks", International Symposium on Security and Privacy in Social Networks and Big Data (SocialSec), IEEE, pp. 44-51, Hangzhou, 2015.

[58] Lin You, and Lijun Wang, "Hierarchical authority key-policy attribute-based encryption", IEEE 16th International Conference on Communication Technology (ICCT), pp. 868-872, Hangzhou, 2015.

14

Cloud Computing Adoption in Insurance Companies in Kenya

Pastor Meshack Akhusama[*], Christopher Moturi

School of Computing and Informatics University of Nairobi, Kenya
*Corresponding author: makhusama@gmail.com

Abstract Cloud Computing allows companies to access ICT-based services i.e. computer infrastructure, applications, platforms and business processes, via the internet. Cloud Computing is still at the infancy stage in Africa. Studies have indicated a lack of cloud based awareness, even among big organizations in Africa. Kenya just like any other African market is yet to fully adopt cloud based systems due to trust and security concerns. This study aimed at identifying the extent and characteristics of Cloud Computing adoption in insurance companies in Kenya. The study assessed Cloud Computing uses in terms of productivity applications, business applications (CRM, SaaS), infrastructure on-demand (storage, network, and server), finance applications, core business application, databases and desktop. The adoption of the Cloud Computing services in insurance companies was relatively low. The results obtained would assist in providing a roadmap for the best practices to improve Cloud Computing services in the insurance industry in Kenya.

Keywords: *Cloud Computing services, ICT in insurance, insurance in Kenya, TOE model*

1. Introduction

Cloud Computing (CC) or cloud refers to the delivery of on-demand computing resources over the internet on a pay-for-use basis. Cloud Computing relies on sharing computing resources rather than have personal devices or local servers handle applications. As a platform it supplies, configures and reconfigures servers. The servers can be physical machines or virtual machines. On the other hand, Cloud Computing describes applications that are extended to be accessible through the internet and for this purpose large data centers and powerful servers are used to host the web applications and web services. The phrase 'Cloud Computing' refers to a type of internet based computing where different services – such as storage, servers, and applications- are delivered to an organization's devices and computers through the internet [3]. The benefits of Cloud Computing as stated by different researchers make it more preferable to be adopted by enterprises i.e. Insurance companies. CC infrastructure allows enterprises to accomplish more efficient use of their IT hardware and software investments. Enterprises need to reflect on the benefits, drawbacks and the effects of Cloud Computing on their businesses and usage practices, to make decision about the adoption and use. In the enterprise, the adoption of Cloud Computing owes much on the maturity of organizational and cultural, including legislative, processes in the organization.

2. Literature Review

2.1. Key Issues in Cloud Computing

Cloud Computing acceptance is faced with a number of issues. These issues are in the areas of infrastructure, security, trust, legal and compliance and organizational challenges [2]. Linked to all these is the issue of trust between clients and vendors, because Cloud Computing calls for enterprises to trust vendors with the administration of their IT resources including data and availability. Most sources of information or data are vulnerable to misuse or use by unauthorized parties which normally calls for control measures in terms of permission of use by the relevant authorities [10]. The impeding situation is that these measures are normally not protective enough and therefore do not offer quite substantive security to the data and information on the cloud [9].

2.2. Obstacles Facing Cloud Computing Adoption

There a number of obstacles for Cloud Computing adoption that include business continuity and service availability, data lock-in, data confidentiality, data transfer bottlenecks, performance unpredictability, scalable storage, reputation fate sharing, and software licensing [1]. These obstacles can however, be transformed into opportunities for growth of Cloud Computing. [7]. identified the following: security, privacy, connectivity and open access, reliability, interoperability, independence from CSPs, economic value, IT governance, changes in the IT organization, and political issues due to global boundaries.

2.3. Cloud Computing in Financial Systems in Kenya

Kenya just like any other African market is yet to fully adopt cloud based systems [8]. However, financial systems are now embracing the cloud approach in Kenya and outsource some of the non core services. There are opportunities in Kenya provided by cloud computing just like other eveloping economies as reported by [6]. The Mpesa system is termed as a great innovation and a lot of countries are now trying to adopt the same.

2.4. Development of Cloud Computing in Africa

Cloud Computing is in the infant stage in Africa. Studies have indicated a lack of cloud based awareness, even among big organizations in Africa. According to a Gartner survey conducted among large enterprises in 2011, half the respondents in emerging markets either had not heard of Cloud Computing or did not know what it meant [5]. The market for the cloud in developing countries is currently small, but is expanding rapidly. In Kenya, cloud demands are high in the offshoring industry and technology hubs. In South Africa, the call center industry has been a fastest growing area for cloud based technology.

3. Methodology

A descriptive survey research design was used to investigate the adoption of Cloud Computing services in insurance companies. The area of study was Nairobi,

Kenya, where most of the insurance companies are situated. A total of 33 insurance companies were studied. The Chief Executive Officers and Chief Information Officers were the respondents. Structured questionnaire was used to collect data. The reliability of the questionnaire was carried out and the result shows alpha coefficient of 0.72. Data collection was by use of a questionnaires and observation

4. Results and Discussion

4.1. Introduction of Cloud Computing Services

Out of the 33 companies studied, one introduced Cloud Computing services in less than a year, eleven (11) introduced a year ago while twenty one (21) companies introduced the services more than a year. Since Cloud Computing is relatively new and expensive, most companies took slightly longer in adopting the services. Employees had not been fully trained to handle the Cloud technology.

Chi-square test results showed there was a relationship between Cloud Computing services applications (productivity applications, business applications (CRM, SaaS), application development/deployment platform, application development/deployment platform, finance applications, core business application, databases) and adoption rate of Cloud Computing since p- values were =.000 less than the alpha of 0.05

4.2. Adoption Rate of Cloud Computing Services

The findings showed 19 insurance companies were experimenting on Cloud Computing systems, while 9 were utilizing a combination of Cloud Computing services. The results are shown in Figure 1 below.

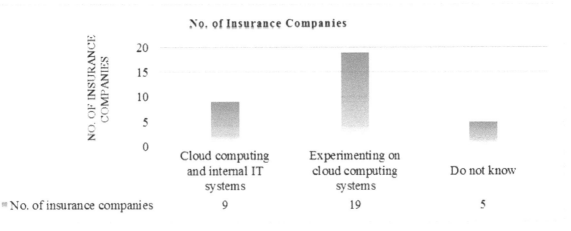

Figure 1. Level of Adoption of Cloud Service

4.3. Use of Cloud Computing Services

The findings show that 18 companies expected to use Cloud Computing services in productivity applications, business application development platform, infrastructure on-demand, databases and desktop. However, the

companies did not use finance applications and core business applications in Cloud Computing, may be due to levels of understanding and maintenance issues related to Cloud Computing systems. Figure 2 below shows the results of the findings.

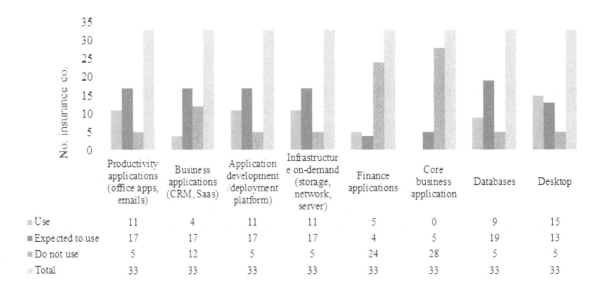

	Productivity applications (office apps, emails)	Business applications (CRM, Saas)	Application development /deployment platform)	Infrastructur e on-demand (storage, network, server)	Finance applications	Core business application	Databases	Desktop
Use	11	4	11	11	5	0	9	15
Expected to use	17	17	17	17	4	5	19	13
Do not use	5	12	5	5	24	28	5	5
Total	33	33	33	33	33	33	33	33

Figure 2. users and expectations to use Cloud Computing services

The study revealed that, most insurance companies used or expected to use Cloud Computing service applications, since these services offered the companies with unmatched flexibility in terms of usage policies and scalability. Data storage is one of the major resources that insurance companies moved to the cloud. With data storage on the cloud, the companies would pay for the volume of space consumed. Cloud Computing service were also used since they were cost effective and flexible in terms of resource utilization which leads to reduced operational costs as well as controlled financial spending on large scale upgrade.

Another reason for the use of cloud services was that, data was available when required. The insurance companies also used Cloud Computing services trust for its security and data integrity. It was noted that, using services led to the ability to work from anywhere and from multiple devices hence, resulting in innovative work cultures in insurance companies.

4.4. Factors Influencing Rate of Adoption of Cloud Computing Services

It was reported by (94%) of companies that security of data was very important and therefore, influencing rate of adoption in terms of keeping data safe and its integrity. Influence of infrastructure on rate of adoption was reported by (29%) of the companies studied, while (34%) indicated influence in the rate of adoption by hardware and software. 44% of the respondents noted that internet coverage influenced the rate of adoption since the Cloud Computing squarely depends on the internet coverage. Finally, (24%) respondents showed that standardization influenced rate of adoption, there was no clear standards set in the whole industry of insurance companies therefore, and the rate of adoption was low.

Significance level in our model is 0.000 which is less than 0.05 which indicates that our model is statistically significant in predicting adoption rate of Cloud Computing with our independent variables (Core business applications, infrastructure on-demand (storage, network, server), finance applications, productivity application, application development/deployment platform) business applications (CRM, SaaS) in the Insurance Company).

Table 1. Regression summary of adoption rate of Cloud Computing services

Model	Unstandardized coefficients		Standardized coefficients	t	Sig.	95.0% confidence interval for b	
	B	Std. Error	Beta			Lower bound	Upper bound
1 (constant)	1.16	.18		5.86	.000	.701	1.42
Productivity application	.17	.09	.26	1.97	.053	-.002	.340
Business applications (CRM, Saas).	-1.77	.18	-2.06	-9.98	.000	-2.12	-1.41
Infrastructure on-demand (storage, network, server)	1.79	.18	1.99	10.04	.000	1.44	2.15
Application development/deployment platform	.72	.13	.796	5.32	.000	.455	1.00
Finance applications	-.15	.10	-.123	-1.44	.153	-.355	.057
Core business Applications	.00	.02	.000	-.012	.990	-.036	.035

a. Dependent variable: rate of adoption of the Cloud Computing services.

The coefficient for productivity application (0.169) is not statistically significantly influence the adoption rate of Cloud Computing services from 0 because its p value of 0.053 slightly larger than 0.05. The coefficient for Business applications, (-1.769) is statistically significant

to adoption rate of Cloud Computing services, because its p-value of 0.000 is less than 0.05. The coefficient for Infrastructure on-demand (1.799) is statistically significant to adoption rate of Cloud Computing services, because its p-value of 0.00 is less than 0.05. The coefficient for application development/deployment platform (0.73) is statistically significant to adoption rate of Cloud Computing services its p-value of 0.00 is less than 0.05.

The coefficient for Finance applications, is .103. The intercept is not statistically significantly different to adoption rate of Cloud Computing services, from 0 because its p-value (0.153) is larger than 0.05. Financial applications were not very popular among the insurance companies and were not widely used may due to its complexity involved. Finally the coefficient for core business applications is (0.018). The intercept is not statistically significantly different to adoption rate of Cloud Computing services from 0 because its p-value (0.990) is much larger than 0.05. This implies that core business applications didn't influence the adoption rate of Cloud Computing services in the insurance companies.

4.5. Platforms used in Insurance Companies in Kenya

58% indicated that platform used included; software services (email, database access, back-up, enterprise application), Platform as a Service (PaaS) (use of operating systems, development environments, software's, packages). The platforms were user friendly and were being used for basic transactions on day to day terms. Lastly the Use of infrastructural (hardware, storage, network) resources (infrastructure-as-a -service) was reported by (52%) of the companies studied. The use of these platforms services enabled the insurance companies to turn ideas into innovations faster.

The model summary where the R value is .833 this indicated that 83 % of the variations observed in the dependent variables was caused by the independent variables. The other 17 % of variations observed may have been due to other factors not captured in the study.

The significance level in the model was 0.000 which was less than 0.05 which indicates that the model was statistically significant in predicting platform used with independent variables (testing on SaaS model, use of infrastructural resources, use of operating systems, development environments, software's, packages as a platform in the insurance company).

Table 2. Regression of the influence services on rate of adoption of Cloud Computing services

Model	Unstandardized Coefficients		Standardized Coefficients	t	Sig.
	B	Std. Error	Beta		
Constant	.563	.762		.739	.463
use of operating systems, development environments, software, packages (platform-as a-service) as a platform in the insurance company	1.438	.322	.842	4.462	.000
Use of infrastructural (hardware, storage, network) resources (infrastructure-as-a -service)	.563	.189	.333	2.976	.004
Testing on Saas Model	.438	.260	.258	1.684	.097

a. Dependent variable: Rate of adoption of the Cloud Computing services.

The use of operating systems, development environments, software, packages (platform-as a-service) as a platform in the insurance company was statistically significantly different from 0, its p-value 0.000 was less than 0.05. The coefficient for Use of infrastructural (hardware, storage, network) resources (infrastructure-as-a -service), was also statistically significant to the rate of adoption of the Cloud Computing services as its p-value of 0.004 less than 0.05. The coefficient for Testing on SaaS Model (0.438). The intercept is not statistically significantly different from 0 because its p-value (.097) is larger than 0.05. The testing on Saas does not influence the rate of Cloud Computing services in the insurance companies.

4.6. Cloud Computing Concerns

According to the study, it was observed that significance level in the model was 0.000, indicating that the model was statistically significant in predicting adoption rate of Cloud Computing with independent variables.

Table 3. Regression of the influence of concerns on the rate of Cloud Computing services

Model	Unstandardized Coefficients		Standardized Coefficients	t	Sig.
	B	Std. Error	Beta		
Constant	3.000	.812		3.696	.000
Immature technology as a concern in Cloud Computing services in company	1.276	.322	.435	3.959	.000
compliance issues a concern in Cloud Computing services in company	-1.276	.541	-.259	-2.360	.021

Dependent Variable: Rate of adoption of the Cloud Computing services.

The p value for immature technology as a concern in Cloud Computing services in insurance company was 0.000. Therefore, immature technology as a concern was statistically significant to the rate of adoption of Cloud Computing services. On the other had compliance issues are not statistically significant to the adoption rate of the Cloud Computing services since the p value is 0.21 which is greater than 0.05.

4.7. Technology Adoption Factors

The most statistically significant factor according to the regression model was insufficient or lacking technology and implementation with a beta coefficient of -.337 and a p value of 0.002 less than alpha 0.05 and the least contributing factor was insufficient security with a beta coefficient of -.348 with a p value of 0.578 greater than alpha 0.05. Other observations included insufficient legal (-1.072, p-value .005 less than 0.05) and insufficient/ lacking compliance (-1.420 and p value of .007 less than 0.05).

Table 4. Regression summary of the influence of insufficient services in adoption of Cloud Computing services

Coefficients'

Model	Unstandardized Coefficients		Standardized Coefficients	t	Sig.
	B	Std. Error	Beta		
Constant)	7.954	.838		9.490	.000
Insufficient security	-.348	.622	-.071	-.559	.578
Insufficient legal	-1.072	.371	-.365	-2.889	.005
Insufficient or lacking technology and implementation	-.695	.218	-.337	-3.188	.002
Insufficient/lacking compliance	-1.420	.511	-.288	-2.780	.007

a. Dependent Variable: rate of adoption of the Cloud Computing services.

4.8. Discussion

These finding may guide and provide a roadmap for the process of successfully adopting or migrating to Cloud Computing services for insurance companies in Kenya. This will address key issues associated with cloud migration such as those identified by [4].

The Technology-Organization-Environment (TOE) adoption model is proposed for customization in the development and implementation of the roadmap. This roadmap will address the following factors: technology (characteristics of available CC technology), organizational (structures and processes), and environmental (client, competitor, and regulations).

The TOE components are external environment representing the outside of the insurance companies. From the findings the external environment is supporting the adoption, through making technology reachable. Technology such as fiber optic is now widely available in the country. For any technology to be adopted external environment must be conducive. From the findings areas that had bad environments had a rough time in the adoption process this fosters better communication within the organization. The organization represents the insurance internal organization. For successful adoption then structures must exist. Based on the research the insurance companies that had some forms of structures made the adoption much easy. The insurance companies that adopted seamless had a defined business process and a way of introducing new technologies. For adoption to be successful a project plan is further to be adopted to make sure it captures all the areas.

The proposed roadmap would have four phases in the adoption of cloud computing project: analysis, planning, adoption, monitoring and evaluation. Analysis would use the TOE model to in the assessment of success and Hindrance factors, usability in the insurance and financial environment, insurance readiness to adopt, and the impacts on the insurance industry.

Planning is key as it manages all the resources needed to effectively run a technology adoption process. Planning makes availability of all the ingredients available and also shall specify the standards to be used. Materials needed and resources are planned as well as the infrastructure to be used.

The implementation would include application modules, application migrations, rollout, and change management. Adoption will involve many aspects based on the TOE model. This phase is a preparation phase for the actual migration of systems and/or applications selected to the cloud platform and infrastructure of choice. In this phase systems/ application integration is done to ensure that the candidate applications will be able to function with the internal applications that are not migrated.

At the monitoring and evaluation stage the Cloud Computing adoption project is now fully operational. However, contract and dealer management, training, testing and maintenance, user support and review should be ongoing for several months to years subsequent to launch. The system metrics or benchmarks developed and set based on the TOE model can be used as indicators of project success and should be monitored Security standards compliance, SLAs, regulatory requirements and compliance issues, IT governance best practices and cost management are desirable metrics that need to be monitored and evaluated. Documentation of lessons learnt and best practices during the project should be documented and communicated to all stakeholders.

5. Conclusion

Based on the study findings the following are the recommendation: Insurance Companies should invest more in the areas of Cloud Computing security, infrastructure, capacity building and personnel training. A roadmap based on discussion above to be fully developed and implemented in order to address all issue of concern that include but not limited to security, privacy, vendor lock, legal issues, technology maturity, compliance, integration with existing ICT and cost model. Further studies will be required to establish the Mobile Cloud Computing services that are suitable for service delivery in insurance and the financial sector. The impact of Cloud Computing services in insurance companies in Kenya requires more investigation.

Acknowledgement

The insurance companies that participated in the survey.

References

[1] Armbrust, M., Fox, A., Griffith, R., Joseph, A. D., Katz, R., Konwinski, A., ... & Zaharia, M. (2010). *A view of cloud computing.* Communications of the ACM, 53(4), 50-58.

[2] Buyya, R. (2009). *Market-Oriented Cloud Computing: Vision, Hype, and Reality of Delivering Computing as the 5th Utility.* CCGRID '09 Proceedings of the 2009 9th IEEE/ACM International Symposium on Cluster Computing and the Grid , 3622-3624.

[3] Foster, I., Zhao, Y., Raicu, I., & Lu, S. (2008, November). *Cloud computing and grid computing 360 degree compared.* In Grid Computing Environments Workshop, 2008. GCE'08 (pp. 1-10). IEEE.

[4] Khajeh-Hosseini, A., Greenwood, D., & Sommerville, I. (2010). *Cloud migration: A case study of migrating an enterprise it system to iaas. In Cloud Computing (CLOUD), 2010 IEEE 3rd International Conference on* (pp. 450-457). IEEE.

[5] Kim, W., Kim, S. D., Lee, E., & Lee, S. (2009). *Adoption issues for cloud computing. In Proceedings of the 7th International Conference on Advances in Mobile Computing and Multimedia* (2-5). ACM.

[6] Kshetri, N. (2010). *Cloud computing in developing economies. ieee Computer*, 43(10), 47-55.

[7] Mather, T., Kumaraswamy, S., & Latif, S. (2009). *Cloud security and privacy: an enterprise perspective on risks and compliance.* O'Reilly Media, Inc.

[8] Omwansa, T. K., Waema, T. M., & Omwenga, M. B (2014). *Cloud Computing in Kenya A 2013 Baseline Survey.*

[9] Wambu, C. W., & Irungu, D. N. (2014). *Does Adoption of Information Technology Improve Firm Performance?* A Survey of Firms Listed in the Nairobi Securities Exchange. Journal of Economics and Sustainable Development, 5(23), 112-117.

[10] Winkler, V. (2011). *Securing the Cloud: Cloud Computer Security Techniques and Tactics* . New York: Syngress.

15

An Institutional Perspective to Understand FOSS Adoption in Public Sectors: Case Studies in Ethiopia and India

Selamawit Molla Mekonnen[*], Zegaye Seifu Wubishet

Department of Informatics, University of Oslo, Oslo, Norway
*Corresponding author: selamawm@ifi.uio.no

Abstract This paper is aimed at understanding institutional influences on Free and Open Source Software (FOSS) adoption in public sectors. It explores strategies, policies, and technical infrastructure so as to harness FOSS as an alternative technical solution in organizations such as the health sector. The study was conducted in India/Kerala and Ethiopia following interpretive qualitative research tradition. Data was collected at micro and macro level. While the micro level explored the acceptance of specific FOSS in Kerala and rejection in Ethiopia, the macro level studied how institutions outside the health sector were drawn upon to legitimize decisions. Data collection was conducted while at the same time analyzing and refining the data to find common themes for both settings. Subsequently, the themes were categorized interpretively into regulative, normative and cultural-cognitive institutions as provided by Scott (2001). The result shows regulative and normative institutions influence FOSS adoption in public sectors positively and that integrating FOSS with the proprietary dominated public sector of developing countries should begin by cultivating the normative institutional aspect. The normative aspect focuses on issues related to FOSS education and professional associations. Moreover, the study shows, technology by itself can facilitate its own adoption once it has gained large installed base; expanding the institutional framework to include a technological element. Practically, the study contributes to our understanding of the field level challenges in realizing the potential of FOSS for the benefits of public sector organizations in general and health sectors in particular in developing countries.

Keywords: FOSS, institutional theory, Health Information Systems, public sector, institutional pillars

1. Introduction

Free and Open Source Software (FOSS) is also referred to as F/OSS, FOSS, or FLOSS to mean Free/Libre/Open Source Software. Throughout this paper, we prefer to use the term FOSS as a synonym for the others.

FOSS is a relative novelty within the context of developing countries in general and within their public health sector in particular. The key concept in FOSS is an unrestricted free access to software code, enabling the possibility to study, re-use, redistribute, rework, adapt or improve the programs without being dependent on commercial vendors. It represents a particular strategy to introduce Information and Communication Technologies (ICTs) in developing countries providing the potential to bridge the digital divide without license restriction [1,2,3,4]. It has also potential benefit for African countries to advance their outsourcing industry [5]. The FOSS license facilitates acquisition of software avoiding "the often lengthy and hectic bureaucratic processes, negotiations and associated corruptions apparent in public sector organizations"[[6] p.18] of developing countries.

Moreover, there are various other mentioned potential technical advantages arising from issues of system security and interoperability. While FOSS is flexible to respond to the continuous change in organizations, proprietary software are rigid for change [7] once public sectors take ownership of the software. However, realizing these advantages in practice is fraught with various challenges, including those that arise from institutional conditions and capacity, which often tend to favor proprietary software [8,9].

Given that FOSS applications, especially in the contexts of the public health sector in developing countries are in its infancy and surrounded by uncertainty, there are various institutional factors that are used to either enable or constrain its adoption and use. For example, some opponents of FOSS may raise lack of support for FOSS as a basis to reject it in its entirety. The focus of this paper is on understanding how institutions influence decisions to adopt or not FOSS applications. We believe such a line of inquiry is a contribution to IS research in helping to theoretically unpack the institutional shaping of the processes to introduce FOSS. Practically, this analysis contributes to our understanding of the field level challenges in realizing the potential of FOSS for the benefits of public sector organizations in general and health sectors in particular in developing countries.

More specifically, by doing this study, we seek to contribute to the following two research aims:

- To theoretically understand the constraining and enabling institutions around the adoption of FOSS in public sectors.
- To explore strategies to adopt -FOSS- and seamlessly integrate it with the existing proprietary dominated health care systems through a case analysis involving two developing countries.

The empirical focus of this paper is on the processes surrounding the introduction of the same FOSS based Health Management Information System (known as DHIS2) in India/Kerala and in Ethiopia. While presence of formal institutional mechanisms and support for FOSS in Kerala, India contributed for the acceptance of the DHIS2, the absence of the same, we argue, in Ethiopia contributed to its rejection. This micro level study of the implementation processes is complemented with a broader study in both these countries on the general perceptions and attitudes of key stakeholders towards FOSS and proprietary based systems and by studying the regulative and education systems.

2. Analytical Framework

In order to formulate strategies for applying FOSS based computer systems as an alternative solution for public sectors in general and health organizations in particular, we frame our theoretical perspective around the theory of neo institutionalism. Neo institutionalism emphasizes the analysis of institutional change in addition to stability, with a focus on the role of cognitive-cultural institutions [10]. This perspective is relevant to this paper as we seek to analyze how various institutional mechanisms contribute to institutionalizing proprietary based technological solutions in a particular setting, and to investigate mechanisms to deinstitutionalize or loosen them for creating a "middle way" platform. By "middle way" platform, we mean an institutional environment where both proprietary and FOSS based systems are taken into consideration when choosing a technological solution for public sectors.

In IS studies, institutional theory has been used for analyzing and understanding the impact of institutional pressures on the diffusion of IT innovation, the institutionalization process of software applications and the interaction between IT artifact and existing institutions [11]. However, IS studies are criticized for giving little emphasis on the interplay between the micro and macro institutions [12]. Building on IS studies that used institutional theory for understanding the impact of institutional pressure on IT adoption, we seek to fill this research gap by undertaking a multi-level analysis both at the macro and micro level.

Institutions are rule-rule like frameworks that constrain or enable human actions [10,13]. Institutions are mostly used in relation to stability, with quite few studies employing the notion to study changes (for the later cf. [14,15]). In this study, we used the institutional pillars [10] as an analytical framework to unpack the various institutions that shape the adoption of FOSS in the two

settings contributing to literature that intends to understand how to bring about change in highly institutionalized environment like the public sector. The analytical framework is discussed below.

2.1. Institutional Pillars/Elements

We use the concept of institutional pillars (elements)-regulative, normative and cognitive-cultural [10] as an instrument to understand the various institutions that influenced FOSS adoption. Those are briefly discussed below.

2.1.1. Regulative Institutions

Regulative institutions are those institutions that constrain and regularize behavior. They give importance to explicit regulatory processes such as rule setting, monitoring and sanctioning activities. Regulative Institutions are described as formal institutions as they are explicitly stated and there is a written point of reference in case of disagreement [13]. The primary mechanism of control is coercion and the expected response to regulative institutions is conformity [10] which gives a sense of I have to respond to coercive institutions [16]. The indicators for regulative institutions, as described in [10] are rules, laws and sanctions, which are used as an instrument for implementing and sustaining a technological solution or other practices.

2.1.2. Normative Institutions

As the name indicates, the chief concern of normative institutions is upholding values and norms. While values are related to the principles that are constructed to guide a certain behavior, norms specify how things should be to achieve defined goals and objectives. The mechanism for such systems is normative and the indicators are certifications and accreditation. While the underlying basis of legitimacy is moral governance, the basis for compiling to normative pressure is social or professional obligation. The logic for normative institutions is appropriateness [10]-as I ought to respond to normative pressures because it is morally right to do so [16].

2.1.3. Cultural-cognitive Institutions

The cultural-cognitive institutions emphasize the cognitive dimension of human existence that constitutes the nature of social reality and the frame through which meaning is constructed. While cognitive-cultural is about the construction of common meanings embedded in social routines, the normative gives relevance to social obligation and binding expectations, specified by standards or industry policies [17]. The behavioral reasoning towards change or continuing same institutional practice would be the feeling of I want to [16]. Although institutions are the byproducts of individuals' cognitions, institutional studies have given little attention to the cognitive part of those individuals and how that influence change processes in organizations [18]. By exploring the perceptions of individuals towards FOSS, in this paper, we tried to understand how the surrounding institutions shaped their perceptions.

Previously, this analytical framework was used to study the adoption and diffusion of cross-cultural inter-organizational information systems for financial transaction [19]. The authors found out that the rate of IT innovation adoption in Europe was high because of the strong presence of the three institutional pillars in Europe than in Taiwan. In the same vein, in this study, we argue the interplay of these three to provide legitimacy for acceptance or rejection of FOSS. Therefore, there is a need to study these institutions within and outside the health sector for bringing about institutional change that is sought to facilitate FOSS adoption. Institutional change constitutes deinstitutionalization and re-institutionalization [20]. Deinstitutionalization "takes place when established meanings and action in an organization are discredited, either as a result of competing meanings and actions or because they are seen as failing to contribute to the institutional existence" [[21] p.37]. Re-institutionalization represents an exit from one institutionalization and entry into another institutional form, organized around different principles or rules [20]. Political, functional and social pressures, both within and beyond organizations, are conditions for causing deinstitutionalization [22]. In addition, others suggest conflicting institutional logics during the introduction of IT in health public sector to stimulate change in institutions by providing room for understanding the pertinent institutions that hinder or facilitate the introduction [15].

Information systems research recommends a cultivation approach for deinstitutionalization. Cultivation is a concept, which is operationalized by implementers through sensitivity to the institutional environment, learning from past experiences [23], following a small step incremental change [24,25] and understanding change as a process [26]. The cultivation approach requires the act of institutional entrepreneurs to identify constraining and enabling institutions so as to bring about change in a highly institutionalized environment. The notion of institutional entrepreneurs refers to "the activities of actors who have interest in particular institutional arrangements and who leverage resources to create new institutions or to transform existing ones" [[27] p. 657]. Hence, institutional entrepreneurs are "those actors whom the responsibility for new or changed institutions is attributed" [[28] p. 1]. Next, we will present the research approach.

3. Research Approach

This is a qualitative research with a primarily interpretive stance to help us understand the phenomena under study through the meanings that people ascribe to them [29,30,31,32,33]. It has also elements of critical stance. The central idea in critical perspective is that "everything possesses unfulfilled potentiality, and human beings by recognizing these possibilities, can act to change their material and social circumstances. And this potentiality for acting to change is constrained by prevailing economic, political and cultural dominations" [[31] p.19]. Therefore, critical researchers argue that phenomenon cannot be understood just by asking participants as done within interpretivist traditions but also by being critical to existing status quo, which constrains the action of the human agency to bring about change [32]. Therefore, the researchers either initiate change as part of action research or they play role in highlighting the constraining and enabling factors for change initiators.

In IS, such studies "are aimed at producing and understanding the context of information system, and the process whereby the information system influences and is influenced by the context [[29] p. 4-5]. We started the empirical work with the assumption that there exist social, cultural and political constructions of institutionalized perceptions around why certain technological solutions have evolved to become de facto standards. Replacing or changing them requires the active use of strategies for de-institutionalization of constructed shared assumptions and other institutions. By examining the national policies, strategies and human capacity, our intention was to explore the link between macro level institutions and organizational tendencies to adopt FOSS.

The case is built upon two sub cases from Ethiopia and India. We believed taking two cases provide rich insights into the various institutional constraints both at macro and micro-levels. At the macro-level, the two contexts provide a study of contrasts where India is known as software outsourcing destination, while Ethiopia is little known in this regard globally. Various states in India have been proactive with respect to policy pronouncements of FOSS while little movement in this regard is seen in Ethiopia. Thus, we felt that the different institutions in the two countries would be the source for varying perceptions with respect to FOSS and proprietary software, and thus with different implications for the micro level implementation efforts. At the micro-level, the focus was the attempts to introduce the same DHIS2 software within the framework of the Health Information Systems Project [34] in the two countries, ongoing nearly simultaneously. HISP is a global network, which has the main node in the University of Oslo and has been engaged in developing and implementing the DHIS2 mainly for developing countries to digitize the routine health data. The network constitutes organizations and individuals that have expertise in health, software development, and organizational issues. The main objective of the program is to make information generated during health care provision to be used for action and planning through the use of FOSS based IT solution. DHIS is a java based FOSS product, which is database and platform independent and have been used in more than 30 [1] countries including at the level of nongovernmental organizations.

Data were gathered through fieldworks within a focused period between April to August 2007 and throughout 2015. HISP was running in Ethiopia from 2003-2008 and the researchers participated in introducing the DHIS2 to in the health sector before and in response to the tender for national electronic health management information systems. In Kerala, we generated most of the data using interviews. We got in contact with relevant stakeholders through HISP India members who were working in this organization. Our role in HISP Kerela action research was closer to what would call an "outside observant" [35]. The first author is an active member of the HISP action research and has been involved in the recent pilot testing of the FOSS based DHIS2 in Ethiopia. This involvement generates observation data, which is used to explore the current software adoption in Ethiopian public health sector. The researcher was specifically involved in customization of the software. In this process,

---

[1] https://www.dhis2.org/inaction.

the researcher was able to examine how the stable software governance structure of HISP and the expanded use of DHIS2 in many organizations may have influenced its acceptance for pilot testing.

The second author was involved as an action researcher during the phase in which Ethiopia rejected DHIS2. The second author was also a teaching staff in one of the universities in Ethiopia, which enabled him access data regarding supportive structure for FOSS in the education sector. Documents analyses and email correspondences with relevant informants were also conducted to explore the shift of policy in both settings and its implication to FOSS adoption in health organizations.

3.1. Data Collection Techniques

Interview data and other secondary sources were used as data collection techniques. Data was primarily collected through semi-structured interviews, and supplemented through the study of a vast variety of secondary materials such as policy documents, tender announcements, university curriculum, company brochures, and other related materials. Interviews were conducted with respondents drawn from various sectors including FOSS advocates, academic institutions, software developers, health organizations, and concerned government ministries and users (see table below for a summary of our respondents). The rationale for the selection of these respondents was their importance in the shaping of stakeholder perceptions and capacity towards FOSS and proprietary systems. For example, meetings with university staff helped to understand the emphasis given to FOSS in the informatics curriculum, which was felt to be an important mechanism for shaping the views of students towards these new technologies. Similarly, discussions with private sector software developers helped us to understand the various business models employed by firms to promote FOSS and how those are compared with proprietary systems. Overall, understanding these broader views, we believed would provide us richer analytical insights into the micro-level dynamics of the DHIS2 introduction in the two settings. The following table depicts the representation of respondents in both countries.

Table 1. Number of Respondents in India and Ethiopia

Ethiopia	
Organizations	No. of respondents
Ministry of Health and its consultants	4
ICT development Agency	2
Ethiopian Free and Open Source Network (EFOSNet)	3
Developers in the Health Information System Program in Ethiopia (HISP Ethiopia)	6*
Software Development Companies	2
Addis Ababa University (AAU) staffs	3
Subtotal	20
India	
Kerala Health Department	1
Academic institution (IIIT)	1
Different Software Developing Companies	8(1 from each)
Total Service Providers	4
Developers in the Health Information System Program in India (HISP India)	5
Subtotal	22
Grand total	42

* Three of the respondents were consulted using online chat.

In terms of operational details, interviews were mostly conducted on site, in the premises of the respondent. Typically, depending on time availability of the respondent, an interview would last from 30 minutes to 1 ½ hours. Both authors of this paper conducted interviews. Typically, the meeting started with us asking about the background of the respondents, their job responsibilities, their general views about FOSS/Proprietary software, and the respective challenges they have seen. The questions were deliberately kept open to enable the respondent talk freely about issues they considered relevant. However, with respect to the micro-level analysis, we were particularly focused around asking questions about the introduction of DHIS2, and what were the underlying reasons. This helped to interpret what kinds of perceptions were being brought into the discursive practices, and their role in legitimizing decisions. In both settings, the researchers asked questions and clarifications and extensive hand written notes were taken. The second author had re-written the notes in MS word; already making his own interpretations of the views of the interviewees, which was later, compared and complemented with the first author's hand written notes.

Document analysis was done on various sources such as curriculums of universities, software evaluation criteria applied by the health care managers in the two countries with respect to software selections. For example, the curriculum of technology related studies in one of the public universities was examined to understand the emphasis given to FOSS. Observations were also conducted in the computer laboratories and firms to get a sense of the workplace dynamics in different setting such as private firms in Kerala and public health care setting in both the countries.

3.2. Data Analysis

Data collection and analysis went hand-in-hand through an iterative process as two stages process of data constructions. Van Maanen (as cited in [35]) describes the two stage process involves first-order construction by the interviewees about the phenomenon and second-order data construction of the researcher based on the first order construction and using conceptual approaches (p. 75). The first-order data were constructed from interview results. As briefly mentioned above the data analysis started while collecting data giving us possibilities to ask other respondents on areas we noticed more clarifications. A thick description (ibid.) of the case was constructed for each setting primarily from the interview data and they were supplemented by other sources. These first-order constructs were studied independently and together to find recurrent themes or issues and grasp the whole picture of the phenomenon. Then, the data from the two settings were merged and the researchers interpretively categorized them into macro and micro level issues; which was further categorized into "meaning units" [36]. "Meaning units" is described as "part of the data that even if standing out of context, would communicate sufficient information to provide a piece of meaning to the reader" [[36] p. 153]. The case description was prepared using those meaning units by reducing redundancies and shortening the data into meaningful constructs of the researchers.

The second-order construction of data was performed, when the authors tried to make sense of the first-order data using concepts from institutional theory. Theories are used as sensitizing device so as we as researchers could expose the restrictive conditions of the status quo [37]. Meaning units from the previous constructs were categorized under the three institutional pillars and their implications to the adoption of DHIS2 were studied and analyzed. While doing this, we noticed that there was another institutional element, which could hinder and facilitate FOSS adoption. We recognized this fourth element as "technological element" and discussed and presented how these could be related to the adoption or rejection of DHIS2.

4. Case Description

The case study is structured in two main sections. The first section focuses on the macro level of the institutions we recognized to exist around FOSS and proprietary systems in the contexts of Ethiopia and Kerala respectively. The second section focuses on the micro-level, wherein we analyze the process of decision making around the introduction of the same FOSS application (DHIS2) in the respective health care settings in the two countries. In explicating this process, we seek to understand the kinds of institutional mechanisms that were drawn upon in taking and legitimizing decisions to reject the FOSS in one case, and how the same seemed to have been relatively deinstitutionalized in the other case.

4.1. Macro-Level: External Institutional Influences

In this section, we examine institutions related to policy, capacity and perception in the wider contextual settings of health care organizations in Kerala and Ethiopia.

4.1.1. Policy and FOSS Organizations Related Issues

In Ethiopia, the policy related institutions could be described as a "chicken and egg" situation where the lack of proactivity of the policy making body was attributed to the weak demand from the public sectors, who in turn felt they needed a policy framework in the first place to enable experimentation with these new technologies. The former Ethiopian Information and Communication Technology Development Agency (EICTDA), which was established in 2002, had the national mandate of formulating ICT policy, evaluating and monitoring ICT projects, developing frameworks for guiding the different public sectors including health. With respect to FOSS, a respondent in the agency said "*in our current policies and future strategies there is nothing about OSS but this doesn't mean that it cannot be modified.*" In further discussing the issue, we understood that there was an implicit view that adequate demand has not yet come from the user departments for modification, creating this "chicken and egg" situation. Recently, this organization is restructured and named Ministry of Communication and Information Technology (MCIT), established in 2010 and have the same mandate as the former EICTDA. We found comforting slight appropriation of both FOSS and proprietary solutions as one of the strategies for e-government solutions in the national ICT policy document.

It is described as "*adopt and implement an open policy for use of proprietary, free and/open source software systems in developing e-government solutions*" (MCIT, 2009).

Potentially, in Ethiopia, there could be other actors in the future who could influence and break the deadlock of this existing chicken and egg situation. A key actor in this context is the Ethiopian Free and Open Source Software network (EFOSSNet), a non-governmental organization established by a group of interested individuals with the mission of carrying out research and development activities related to FOSS. EFOSSNet had specific initiatives to build awareness about FOSS, which is believed to positively contribute to the introduction of FOSS to the public sector in the country. They were also involved with advocacy efforts with the government. An informant from the organization believed that in the long run there was no other option for developing countries like Ethiopia other than going FOSS route. However, as we saw in the case of the health care setting, the impact of advocacy of this group on policy was rather limited.

Another view at the policy level in Ethiopia was the assumption that development agenda of the country was only possible to be furthered by multinational companies. A senior higher official at the policy-making level argued as follows:

Fast social development was possible only by relating to big multinational companies, and it is not good to go against the storm. Microsoft and other proprietary businesses are currently dominant, and so why should health sector take the risk of going otherwise?

In contrast to Ethiopia, in Kerala, India, there were various formal policy related institutions that had been established to actively promote the adoption of FOSS in the state. While Kerala had a relatively high level usage of proprietary systems, although lower than the nearby states of Karnataka and Andhra Pradesh, the intention of the government to actively promote FOSS was evident. The state had formulated specific policy of supporting, using, and promoting FOSS systems in all public institutions, with ambitions as described by some to make it "God's own e-state." The Kerala State IT Mission, a governmental organization established to foster the process of IT adoption in general and FOSS in particular, had various initiatives to support policy implementation such as through training, the creation of manuals and other instruments.

Further, policy implementation support in Kerala for FOSS came through 5 semi-governmental institutions, referred to as Total Service Providers (TSPs), established with the objective of promoting alternative computing under the framework of Free, Libre and Open Source Software (FLOSS). They claimed to help the benefits of ICTs reach larger section of society, as well as to promote employment and development through FLOSS. They developed software for different organizations in the public sector and were also expected to support the implementation processes.

4.1.2. Capacity and Expertise around FOSS

Higher education institutions play a key role in shaping perceptions, attitudes and capacities towards new technologies and approaches. In Ethiopia, the educational condition with respect to FOSS was one of passivity. In one of the oldest and most reputable academic institution, the graduates with software/information systems education were not well exposed to FOSS paradigm. By studying some of the curriculum, and talking to and observing students at work in laboratories, we inferred a general lack of awareness towards FOSS and related technologies, and a distinct affinity towards Microsoft technologies. This also reflected by the fact that there is not significant contribution to open source projects from Ethiopia. We attributed this partly to the education system and the consequent job market, which is not taking equal emphasis for both types of technological solutions and partly to the infrastructural challenge-internet and power supply.

The shortage of FOSS skilled professionals in the market further contributed to the dominance of the proprietary based businesses. In contrast in India, where the software industry was booming on a global scale, there were private and public colleges offering courses also in FOSS based technologies to meet the industry demand. However, the demand for FOSS developers in the public sector was found to be poor. The situation was made worse by the strong private sector, which lured away people with expertise in FOSS technologies (like Java) based on high salaries, which the government sector could not match and making them focus on proprietary solutions. A developer in India said:

This reality affects the expansion of FOSS and if organizations go for it, they will suffer shortage of qualified professional. In my former institution, we had a FOSS program, which was used to train our own staff on it. But since the market was luring, qualified people frequently left that institution, and the attrition rate was high. Only few that were committed remained.

Respondents often cited the low level of awareness towards FOSS in the public sector as a reason for the slow uptake of FOSS applications. The mindset of decision makers were described as: *"those at the decision making level, whenever they think of a computer based system, they think of proprietary software companies."* The situation on the ground where there was a monopoly of Microsoft products and skills only related to its use, dictated the use of proprietary systems, making it hard to go for FOSS. The counter argument to the lack of capacity for FOSS made by technical people in both countries was that training is part of a normal system development process, be it FOSS or proprietary. Therefore, if there is no demand for FOSS products, there is no development and that it will not be easy to find expertise in FOSS related technologies. In relation to this, technical people argued that it was not difficult to get used to the FOSS habit, and *"it was easy to get used to new systems very fast"*, but there should be demand from the public sectors first.

On the other hand decision makers complained about the poor help desk support and reference points of FOSS products to resolve technical problems. Some software company managers in India complained on the absence of technical support that *"No one is to be hold accountable for failures and troubles, and also that you will not get everything in a packaged form"*. The technical people countered the claim by attesting that one could get such support online for FOSS, at the fastest possible speed, and even much better than in the case of proprietary systems. One Indian FOSS programmer also stressed that depending on the demand of the system, it was possible to get all required help.

4.1.3. Business Models and Cost Effectiveness of FOSS

In Kerala, an interesting contrast with respect to Ethiopia concerned the presence of many private sector software companies who were building feasible business models around FOSS products and services. However, as contrasted to "pure" FOSS models, these companies gave the source code only to the specific client, be it a government organization or private business, which then did not have the right to distribute or sell the code, depending on the agreement.

Given that firms in Kerala had for the last few years been engaged with the development of FOSS applications, they saw public sector settings, for example in health, to provide a rich potential business domain. They had thus developed sharp cost related arguments about the advantages of FOSS over proprietary systems. For example, the CEO of an open source software development company in Kerala noted:

In such countries applications for health institutions can be developed by amateur programmers for a reasonable cost or smaller software companies can offer them for a bearable cost. However the supporting platform, systems have to be bought from big multinational companies for huge amounts and with escalating cost as distribution increases. Such infrastructure related costs are really discouraging for public health institutions where there are hundreds of regional and district level branches.

A researcher and lecturer at a technology related educational college in Kerala stressed that the TCO (Total Cost of Ownership), when it comes to FOSS, was very small. Another software development company manager recalled that, "some public institutions do spend a great deal of money for proprietary systems and yet they fail; and others abandon computerization due to absence of the required money." Such respondents believed that FOSS products have cost advantage to public sectors. However, counter arguments with respect to costs were put forth my firms dealing with proprietary software. Another manager of such a firm in Kerala, said:

Many people acknowledges getting source code to be an advantage but the thing is who can understand what is written by others...it is just like trying to finish a fiction written by another author...do you think it is possible to do that?...trying this requires high cost....it is very much cost effective to start from scratch.

Related to cost, maintenance issues were raised as important factors for the adoption of FOSS. Firms dealing with FOSS argued that closed source systems required access to the source code for responding to maintenance needs and changing requirements. So it created a lock-in situation with the vendor who always needed to be there for help, always involving additional costs. This dependency, according to a faculty member, often built tensions into the contract, where the vendor claimed that the contract was over while the client demanded more needs to be incorporated. Such tensions were potentially avoided in FOSS; where the source code was available free. However, few respondents countered that FOSS was never for free, and there were always costs involved related to training, maintenance and upgrades. A member of FOSS association rationalized that costs were always involved, be it proprietary or FOSS but the issue is what is most costly especially for maintenance.

We also heard some moral arguments about the cost effectiveness of FOSS, that public money being spent by public sectors, such as in health should, be used righteously. One respondent in India said:

Government owned health systems get their fund from taxpayers or from donors that are meant to help solve different critical health problems. If the money that could have been used to alleviate serious health problems is invested in the supporting health information systems, given that there is other alternative, it will be unfair to the best and unjust to the worst. The only way to make sure that public money is properly used is using FOSS approach.

4.1.4. Licensing and Availability of Source Code

Regarding license, almost all respondents from both countries revealed that organizations or individuals in many developing countries do use pirated systems; else it would be nearly impossible to develop applications given the prohibitive licensing costs of proprietary systems. However, we did not find respondents being concerned regarding the use of pirated copies in public sectors. They rather thought it was fair to use pirate copies in the framework of social justice.

Access to source code was seen especially crucial to public sectors like health, where the requirements were seen to be dynamic. However, many respondents, especially in Ethiopia argued that the availability of source code became irrelevant without adequate support and documentations. On the other hand, software developers perceived access to source code as necessary means to build internal capacity, gain self-reliance, avoid lock-in problems (when a single supplier would manipulate them in a way they wanted). They also appreciated the possibility of modifying the source code internally to address changing requirements. Access to source code was also seen by some to be crucial to enable interoperability of systems. An official from Ethiopia indicated:

If all health institutions use OSS, information exchange and interoperability will be simple……especially public health institutions in developing countries who are getting to be part of e-governance systems. They are better off following open standards for better data sharing.

However, access to source code was also mentioned to compromise patient security and privacy in the health sector, which was countered by proponents. The counter argument was that FOSS provides more security technologically, as it allows users to add their own security mechanisms, and not be dependent on what was provided by vendors.

4.2. Micro level: Decision making around the adoption of DHIS

Our specific focus in this section is on describing the decision making process of the same FOSS based DHIS2 in the two empirical settings.

4.2.1. DHIS2 in Ethiopia

The Ministry of Health is the highest authority nationally, endowed with powers and responsibilities to expand health services and provide care to the broader population, especially to the disadvantaged segments of society. There are 11 regional bureaus that report to MOH.

Although the regions have a fair degree of autonomy, the decision of the regions is influenced by MOH including one related to technological choices.

Albeit in its early development stage, DHIS2 was presented to MOH in 2007/2008 for consideration as a national monitoring and evaluation tool. The value proposition was that such a system would help streamline health information systems and also would contribute to develop capacity within the country.

The first interesting aspect of the decision making process was the tendering process in which the criteria for applying were stipulated. It was stated that a preference would be given to MS based platform. Specifically, the tender document said:

FMOH has a preference for Microsoft Visual Basic / dotNet (commercial, with free distribution for standalone installations)

At the end of the evaluation, MOH decision was to reject DHIS2 because of two key reasons. First, DHIS2 did not meet the functional requirements of the MOH, and second the HISP team did not have adequate professional capacity to provide sustainable support. The letter received explicitly stated:

It is essential that the FMOH own the HMIS software. The DHIS software source code is publicly available; however ownership means more than access to source code. Practically speaking, ownership means that the FMOH needs access to software developers with the experience needed to modify the source code. There is no evidence that the skills to modify the source code are readily available in Ethiopia.

In response, the HISP team wrote to the MOH that with respect to functional requirements, it was an incorrect argument since they were never formally provided with the requirements. While acknowledging that their software currently was in the process of development, HISP argued that software development was a process, which necessarily needs to evolve through a process of mutual interaction between development and use. They thus needed to be given this opportunity of mutual interaction so that capacity within the country will be developed through the process. Further, HISP strongly refuted the claim of their lack of technical capacity, arguing that:

Capacity is never a given for any kind of technology or application but needs to be cultivated and nurtured in close collaboration between the user and development communities. Here again we would like to argue that we have both strong exiting capacity and a solid basis for its evolution and growth in the future shape by the needs of the health services.

Based on this letter and a subsequent meeting with officials, another opportunity was given to HISP to present their software. A new and much improved version of DHIS2 was then presented, which again was rejected by the MOH, who in their letter emphasized the technical functionality and the lack of human resource capacity as shortcomings to adopt the software.

Through this letter, HISP was formally informed that the DHIS2 had been rejected, and they should with immediate effect stop all development work. A copy of the letter was also sent to the regional health bureaus that HISP should no longer be active. Subsequently, while interviewing respondents about the relevance of FOSS more generally in Ethiopia, the respondent argued that

FOSS was not relevant to Ethiopia because of the lack of existing technical capacity in this regard. The respondent said: *"Most of the developers in Ethiopia do not know FOSS technologies and it is difficult for us to go for it".* When we pointed out to the same respondent the argument of FOSS to provide the health department with the ownership of the source code, which enables them to continuously modify the software to meet their changing requirements, the respondent countered:

The responsibility of the MOH is to provide sustainable and effective health care. Why should they be concerned about software?.......usually it is not easily to understand what is written by others...so the question is is it cheaper to start from scratch?...may be it is.

By this, the MOH went on employing another donor funded software company to develop the needed software from scratch than building what was started. However, we found the problem to revolve around the low awareness level of FOSS products and began to assess the various institutions that may be relevant to make FOSS products alternative solutions in the public sector of the country. Those were presented in the previous section. On another note, currently, MOH is pilot testing DHIS2.0 as the existing software is not responding to the needs of the health sector.

4.2.2. DHIS2 in Kerala

Kerala is a state in the southwestern India, with an estimated population of 32 million, which is close to half of the whole Ethiopian population. Relevant to our analysis, the following features of the state were pertinent:

- A history of communist governments whose anti-imperialist stance made them strongly anti-proprietary software and pro free software.
- A new Left government was voted into power in 2005, which explicitly made free software use as a formal government policy.
- The state has a history of strong community based involvement in various sectors including in public health, thus encouraging the need for grass root level workers to take control of their own information processing needs amongst other things.

The HISP initiative had started in India in 2000. Initially, HISP approached the health department of the Kerala state and proposed them a pilot project in one clinic, and permission was accorded to them. Six months on, as promising results were seen, HISP approached the health department again to extend the project to the whole district. Around the same time the very first version of the DHIS2 was released. HISP offered to buy 17 computers and facilitate this extension process, and since the state department saw no financial costs to them and that HISP had shown promise in their initial efforts, the permission was provided, and the first version of DHIS2 was deployed in 19 Block level clinics.

However, as this phase of the HISP effort started, they came to know the existence of a competing health management information system project going on through a large government owned computer firm that had previously been responsible for the development of the first supercomputer in the country. This project was funded through the European Commission, and was proposed to be built using a mainframe based architecture where there would be one application running and online

use of the system would be carried out through the district level. This application was built on a proprietary platform involving Oracle as the database and Visual Basic as the development language. The view of the implementers was that a centralized architecture was needed because the field level users were not ready for computerization, and the maintenance overheads were tremendous. The HISP model was completely in contrast for various reasons. Firstly, it was built completely on free software. Secondly, the implementation model focused primarily on the grass root level, where the field users were seen to be the most important users of information, and thus it was their capacity, which needed to be developed. And historically, the field level and bottom up implementation model was one, which very much historically inscribed the HISP philosophy as it had taken root in 1994 post-apartheid South Africa (Braa and Hedberg, 2002; Braa and Sahay, 2012).

As both projects were ongoing, and threatening to conflict with each other, the state authorities needed to take a decision on which project should be continued. Both parties were called for a formal evaluation, which was presided by the key decision maker of the state health department. During the evaluation, the government firm sketched out their model of implementation in which they argued for a centralized model. HISP in their evaluation emphasized its approach based on FOSS which they pointed out was supporting the state government policy of promoting the use of FOSS. They also emphasized that their model is empowering the field workers, and indeed they were very capable of running the system and meeting their information processing needs. As evidence, they showed a set of reports for the current month that had been generated by the field staff in the pilot sites they had been working in. This demonstration was well received by the health department, as again it resonated with the left government agenda of promoting grass root level democracy. Furthermore, HISP elaborated on the global HISP network, the expertise available, and how the software would be continuously upgraded and global best practices incorporated.

Table 2. Comparing Kerala and Ethiopia at Macro and Micro level

Macro		
Ethiopia	**Kerela**	
Weak policy support to FOSS	Strong policy support	
Weak awareness and support that is exacerbated by the poor information technology infrastructures	Strong political commitment and support for FOSS	
Weak FOSS professional association and other advocacy groups	Multiple governmental and non governmental organization promote FOSS	
IT and Information systems courses favor proprietary software	FOSS is covered equally in the education systems	
Shortage of FOSS skilled professionals	FOSS skilled professionals are available but inadequate	
Conflicting views regarding the cost advantage, maintenance and governance issues of FOSS	Conflicting views regarding the cost advantage, maintenance and governance issues of FOSS	
Micro		
Ethiopia	**Kerala**	
- Rejected DHIS in 2007 - In the process of adopting DHIS in 2015 after the software becomes stable and matured	The health department accepted DHIS2 in 2000 and worked with HISP to adapt and extend it to their needs	

Based on these presentations, HISP was evaluated over the government company, which was extremely large, well endowed with resources, and were supported through the formal machinery of the EU. In contrast, HISP was a small NGO, supported through university research funds, and with very limited resources. Currently, HISP is not supporting the DHIS2 software in Kerala. The state health department has taken the responsibility of maintaining and running the software by themselves after getting several years of support from HISP. The table (Table 2) presents a comparison of the various issues that influence FOSS adoptions in the two settings.

5. Analysis

In this section, we analyze the empirical data provided in the previous section using the analytical framework presented in section 2. In this analysis, we identified the various institutions from the wider context in which the health care sector is situated in to highlight their enabling and constraining role to the adoption of DHIS2.

5.1. The Regulative Institutions (have to)

The regulative institutions in this context include the ICT policies and the official tender documents that sanctioned or support FOSS based systems in the two settings, which are actively drawn upon to "cultivate a belief in the legitimacy" of one or the other [10]. These institutions can be coercive by nature and conforming to them is rewarding, while non-conformity can lead to sanctions and rejection.

In Ethiopia, the former EICTDA the organization responsible for ICT policy formulation for the public sector, created a draft policy, which reflected a bias towards proprietary software, and a consequent marginalization of FOSS. FOSS was not mentioned as an alternative technological solution for the public sector in the policy drafted in 2005. However, in our recent examination of the Ethiopian ICT policy document, we found that bias to be slightly corrected by presenting an enabling environment for both proprietary and FOSS as alternative technological e-government solutions. This gives a positive implication to the change of institutions by defining a fair environment for both technologies. Some individuals felt the regulative institutions to be constraining them from going in FOSS direction.

Another regulative institution that constrained the use of FOSS in Ethiopia was the tender document; which again was influenced by the old ICT policy. This institutional element was reflected and also drawn upon by the MOH evaluation criteria in tender document in which explicitly MS products were stipulated as the preferred choice of the MOH for building the national HMIS. In contrast, in Kerala, the policy environment, influenced by historical and political reasons, clearly favored FOSS. Consequently, at the micro level, while the presence of such regulative institution facilitated the acceptance of DHIS in Kerala, the lack of similar institutions in Ethiopia led to the rejection of the same software in the Ethiopian health care sector. This finding is consistent with the recent findings in [19] that attributed the low diffusion of Straight-Through-Processing (STP)- a type of inter organizational system in the financial industry- to the loose regulative mechanisms in Taiwan. The authors further claimed that the presence of such regulative pressure facilitated the uptake of the same technological solution in Europe. In the same vein, IS researchers have found out top-down approaches to be more successful when it comes to digital infrastructure evolution [38] that includes adoption and diffusion. Regulative institutions as a topic of the top-level management need to be compatible with the nature and approaches of FOSS if they have to be adopted. The case demonstrated two opposite regulative institutions in Kerala and Ethiopia. While the Ethiopian regulations enable proprietary software, the Kerala regulations enable FOSS.

5.2. The Normative Institutions (ought to)

The normative institutions include those institutions that provide principles and guidance regarding the ideology, use, methods, and technological frameworks for FOSS that create appropriateness for its use in organizations. Organizations that are engaged in setting the normative institutions in practice include the formal education sectors, training facilities, and professional association. While the presence of normative institutions for FOSS facilitates adoption, the absence of such institutional mechanisms hinders its adoption and further diffusion.

In Ethiopia, the bias towards proprietary software was reinforced by the nature of the informatics curriculum in the national university where FOSS technologies did not find a prominent place. Microsoft products were seen to have become "part of the furniture" [39], and limited alterative voices existed to challenge this status quo and create any form of political or functional pressure [22]. In India, while the Oslo university staff and students through HISP could serve for professionalizing the FOSS concept in the public sector, the same potential could not be created in Ethiopia. In addition, the education system, in Ethiopia, has not provided any strong enabling institutions, which could provide guidance and principles in the use of FOSS.

Further contributing to creating positive environment for FOSS and thereby facilitating the adoption of FOSS in Kerala was the presence of a professional organ called TPSs. These organs were actively developing and promoting working business models around FOSS use in the public sector. Furthermore, in Kerala, the university-based model of HISP was seen positively as it was associated with enabling the circulation of new knowledge and global best practices. In contrast, private companies in Ethiopia created a normative pressure for the use of proprietary based systems. That was further reflected clearly in the evaluation result of the MOH, where the lack of private firms providing FOSS expertise was taken as a basis to reject DHIS2. The only enabling normative pressure for FOSS in Ethiopia comes from EFOSSNet- the FOSS association. However, the pressure was rather weak to contribute for the deinstitutionalization of the institutional environment, which is favoring proprietary software.

Moreover, contributing to the constraining normative institutions for FOSS is the professional distinctions health professionals upheld. For example, informants in Ethiopia pointed out the health sector were expected to focus on health aspects to legitimize their argument that software development was the primary responsibility of software firms and not the health department. These software firms, driven primarily by the principle of profit making, tended to pursue development through MS products, which undeniably had higher commercial value to the firm than FOSS. In addition, health sector managers did not believe that it was important to obtain the source code as it was the job of software companies and not themselves to customize the application in the future. Focusing only on health was the normative mechanism by which the organizational role of the health sector was seen confined. We argue that while such kind of professional role distinctions are important, understanding the significance of technology in health, there is a need that the health care sector should also go beyond the health matters and be actively involved in the choices of technological solutions. In conclusion, the different normative institutions were found to be enabling for both FOSS and proprietary products in Kerala, while in Ethiopia they were enabling only the use of proprietary systems.

5.3. The Cultural-cognitive Institutions (want to)

The study found out conflicting personal believes regarding the theoretical values of FOSS in both Kerala and Ethiopia. In one hand, stakeholders who are involved in FOSS paradigm view FOSS to positively contribute to the good of the health or other public sectors. The mentioned advantages of FOSS by this group of stakeholders were cost, availability of source code and interoperability. On the other hand, the other group of stakeholders perceived FOSS to come with disadvantages of hidden costs, poor support, and lack of expertise in working with already developed code. The theory of potential advantages of FOSS, arguably had been realized in practice in Kerala, thus helping to reinforce and diffuse the positive perceptions. The absence of the same in Ethiopia meant that contradicting arguments of the advantages of proprietary software over FOSS could not be resolved. Further, in Ethiopia, the normative and regulative elements of institutions were dominants and contributed to the reinforcement and diffusion of mindsets that want to follow propriety software paradigm.

In Kerala, there was also a degree of ambiguity in this regard that while the policy makers favored FOSS, other respondents showed preference towards Microsoft products. However, this could also be seen as an advantage, where the option of using either FOSS or proprietary systems remains open, and one option was not closed at the expense of the other. In Ethiopia, we found a belief system by policy makers that leap forging the digital divide was possible only by relying on well-established proprietary companies like Microsoft, and maybe is best left to multi-national corporations. This was related to fear that there is less accountability to FOSS than proprietary software. However, research shows that FOSS projects/firms follow varied governance mechanisms [40] that make them equally accountable as firms with propriety software development model. The influence of this institutional aspect towards micro level adoption of FOSS appeared to be similar in both settings.

While those who are proponents of FOSS perceive FOSS to have more advantages over proprietary software, the opponents counter argued.

5.4. Technology as the fourth Institutional Pillar (ought to have)

In addition to the three institutional pillars [10], we argue that technology by itself can play a role for its own adoption through the notions of network effects and increasing returns (Hanseth, 2000) that are drawn upon an economic perspective of technology adoptions.

We recognize the DHIS2 under the FOSS model has now reached the stage of becoming a global de facto standard for health management information systems in developing countries. More than 30 countries have adopted the software within the 15 years development and implementation time. The value of the software has increased through network effects, which in turn has increased the functionality and importance of the software making it attractive to more users and challenging the constraining institutional elements for its adoption. From being a tool for an aggregated health data, it has now expanded to being a tool for patient-based data. The continuous testing of the software by the involved countries has also contributed to prompt fixing of bugs. The more the software is adopted, the more it becomes improved increasing the return value of the software to new adopters [41] (Arthur, 1989). This aspect shows the importance of micro level adoption of FOSS to simulate and pressure change in the wider institutional setting, which has been constraining to FOSS. This is especially relevant to late adopters like the current case of Ethiopia and its interest in piloting DHIS2. However, early adopters like Kerala do not see this kind of enabling pressure. In Kerala, the afro-mentioned three institutional elements were more relevant than the technological pressure. To be consistent and complementing the typology of institutions (as discussed in section 2), we view the indicator for technological institutions with respect to adoption to be the presence of large installed base (number of user adopted the software). The basis for positive response towards such technological pressure would be the increasing return. While the technological pressure is enabling in Ethiopia as late adopter, it was constraining for Kerala as early adopter.

The following table presents a simplified version of how the complex institutional environment enables and constrains the adoption of FOSS in the Kerala and Ethiopia.

Table 3. Institutional Influences on FOSS adoption in public sectors

Institutional pillars	Kerala		Ethiopia	
	Constraining	Enabling	Constraining	Enabling
Regulative	NO	YES	YES	NO
Normative	NO	YES	YES	NO
Cultural-cognitive	YES	YES	YES	YES
Technology	YES	NO	NO	YES
FOSS adoption	**YES**		**YES**	

The table shows the combination of enabling normative and regulative institutions facilitates the adoption of FOSS in public sector organizations. The table suggests also, in the absence of regulative and normative institutions, the technology facilitates FOSS adoption once it has gained large installed base. However, in the latter case, the FOSS nature becomes irrelevant and the adoption process takes relatively longer time. Therefore, we argue that the viable approach for FOSS adoption in public sector is strengthening the regulative and normative institutions in favor of FOSS.

6. Practical Implications: the "middle way"

The Kerala case highlights a stage of how certain de-institutionalizing forces regulative and normative has helped to erode the legitimacy of the previously established institutions of proprietary systems and slowly cultivate and include one based on FOSS.

Politically, in Kerala the historically existing communist governments have explicitly rejected proprietary systems. Consequently, in 2005, the new government formulated a policy explicitly guiding government departments to adopt FOSS. These policies have faced a strong inertia at user level to practically realize the policy vision for two basic reasons. This is because there are no sanctions against the use of proprietary system, and human actors feel uncertain to make a change from a system they have been used to for many years. So, despite the policy, we saw most of the health facilities using MS products. The only FOSS based application in the health sector was the DHIS2 software, which is running on MS-Windows, despite also having the option of being run on Linux.

Scholars such as [13] emphasizes the need to incrementally bridge the gap between the formal institutions (the ICT policy) and the informal constraints (e.g. capacity and norms) on the ground. As the education system produces more FOSS aware students, and the private sector provides more opportunities for them to work in FOSS, cultivation [42] towards integrated IT platform can be seen to be ongoing in Kerala. This then contributes to the gradual changeover of systems in the public health sector as well. Moreover, the government has established the intermediary organizations (TPSs) to facilitate public sector user departments to changeover to FOSS solutions, a process, which will further accelerate the changeover. In this context, the state government can be seen to be acting as an institutional entrepreneur and placing their power and resources to facilitate this process of change cultivation.

However, in this paper we are not trying to promote the sole use of FOSS in the public sector, as history with respect to existing proprietary systems is part of our reality, and needs to be addressed, and more proactively taken advantage. In both countries, stakeholders acknowledge the advantages and disadvantages of both systems, and thus we believe a proposal that facilitates the integration of FOSS with the already existing proprietary based systems and work practices would be more appropriate than positioning one over the other. In Ethiopia, the current scenario is not visible to enable this integration, and requires working with normative institutions such as introducing explicit FOSS education in the current education system. We have noticed an initial technological pressure, which might result in change in the margins of the complex institutional environment. However, an important step towards widespread incremental change

towards integrating FOSS with proprietary software could come by cultivating the normative institutions which are vital in creating awareness, moral obligations and changing the negative perceptions towards FOSS.

As the Kerala example shows, intermediary organizations like the TPS need to play a more active role in facilitating change processes and it can be taken as a lesson for the Ethiopian health care sector. More importantly, the current practices of public sector organizations such as tendering need to be expanded in scope so that both FOSS and proprietary systems can bid for, be evaluated, and may the "best system win". The Ethiopian tender example where one option was shut out, we believe limits the opportunities of the public sector organization to take advantage of current technological developments.

The integration approach we propose thus involves more than a technical solution, but related to practices both at the level of decision making and also at the level of use. The DHIS2 use in Kerala provides a nice example of this, since while the application is based on FOSS technologies and is platform independent, at the clinics it is run on Windows keeping sensitively in mind the users preferences and capacities. However, the platform independence of the application provides the users with the option of a change over to another platform whenever and whatever the user chooses. The following figure depicts the "middle way" we are proposing.

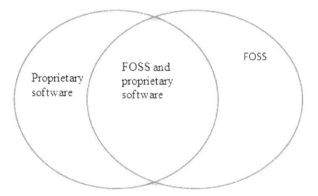

Figure 1. The "middle way" for both FOSS and proprietary software

7. Conclusions

While there is a significant amount of rhetoric about the potential of FOSS applications to overcome the digital divide and to enhance the quality of services delivery, there are challenges to put this rhetoric into practical benefits that can accrue good results. There is lack of sound evidence that bring the macro-micro dynamics together so as to support the understanding of the real challenges in the wider institutional environment and their implication to FOSS adoption. The institutional perspective taken in this paper emphasizes the need to unpack and understand the macro-level regulative, normative and cultural- institutions in various settings to cultivate change process to create an environment that takes into account both FOSS and proprietary systems as preferred IT solutions for the public sector. In relation to this, the macro level institutions: policy, education system, stakeholders' perceptions, and role of mediating agencies have all been identified as being important actors in enabling (and also constraining) these processes of change. Furthermore, at the micro-level the introduction of FOSS to an organization can stimulate change towards deinstitutionalizing the various institutional aspects that favors proprietary software. However, cultivating change towards a "middle way" technological platform, we argue, would be more sustainable if FOSS is properly introduced in the education system. A radical change can be achieved in the regulative institutions. Public sectors use of FOSS solution by itself can stimulate change in the education and regulative institutions.

Even though, we make such analytical distinctions of institutions for clarity, in reality, these are all intermingled and that they should be recognized as influencing each other.

By taking both macro- and micro level institutional analysis of the case studies, we contributed to the expansion of the analytical framework of institutions. The research set out with the assumption that FOSS adoption is more influenced by the surrounding institutions and that "network effects" may not have influence in FOSS adoption in public sectors if not combined with other institutional mechanisms. Network effects means "a product may simply be more valuable to each buyer; the more others have the product or service" [[43] p.7]. As a result, we took a sociological institutional perspective to study those influences. By doing so, we tried to understand how stakeholders in organizations create meaning drawn upon institutional aspects to legitimize their rejection or acceptance of FOSS. However, following upon the case through time shows that technology by itself creates also pressure for its adoption once it gets large installed base, consequently creating enabling environment for its adoption. Therefore, we recommend, future IS studies that seeks to apply this analytical framework to take into account the fourth institutional pillar to have a more comprehensive analytical tool in their study.

Concluding on a more positive note, we would like to emphasize that FOSS needs to be actively taken into the agenda of public sector digitization efforts in developing countries. However, this agenda should not be built upon utopian idealism but on the practical needs. FOSS like proprietary systems is never "fully" free as there are always costs involved in their customization, capacity building and maintenance. However, by eliminating the license costs, it is significantly "more free" than proprietary systems and it fosters innovation as the source code is accessible. Thus, there is a need to carefully evaluate the pros and cons of the different options, and make informed choices keeping the broader aims in mind of building sustainable, scalable systems that can effectively contribute to improve service delivery in the public sector.

Acknowledgement

We acknowledge all respondents in Ethiopia and India.

References

[1] Cook, I. and G. Horobin, Implementing eGovernment without promoting dependence: Open source software in developing countries in Southeast Asia. Public Administration and Development, 2006. 26(4): p. 279-289.

[2] Cook, I. and G. Horobin, Implementing eGovernment with out promoting dependence:open source software in developing countries in Southeast Asia. Public Administration and Development, 2006. 26(4): p. 279-289.

[3] Camara, G. and F. Fonseca, Information policies and Open source Software in developing Countries. Journal of the American Society for Information Science and Technology, 2007. 58(1): p. 121-132.

[4] Scacchi, W., et al., Understanding Free and Open Source Software Development Porcesses. Software Process Improvement and Practice, 2006. 11: p. 95-105.

[5] Abbott, P., How can African countries advance their outsourcing industries: An overview of possible approaches. The African Journal of Information Systems, 2013. 5(1): p. 2.

[6] Mengesha, N.T., Technology Capacity Development through OSS Implementation: The Case of Public Higher Education Institutions in Ethiopia. The African Journal Of Information Systems, 2010. 2(1): p. 2.

[7] Effah, J. and G. Abbeyquaye, How FOSS Replaced Proprietary Software at a University: An Improvisation Perspective in a Low-income Country. The African Journal of Information Systems, 2014. 6(1): p. 2.

[8] Twaakyondo, H.M. and J.H. Lungo, Open source software in health information systems: Opportunities and challenges. Tanzania Journal of Engineering and Technology, 2008. 2(1): p. 36-45.

[9] Sheikh, Y.H. and A.D. Bakar, Open Source Software Solution for Healthcare: The Case of Health Information System in Zanzibar, in e-Infrastructure and e-Services for Developing Countries. 2011, Springer. p. 146-155.

[10] Scott, W.R., Institutions and organizations. 2001: Sage Thousand Oaks, CA.

[11] DeVaujany, F., et al., Applying and theorising institutional frameworks in IS research. Information Technology & People, 2014. 27(3).

[12] Pishdad, A., et al. Identifying Gaps in Institutional Theory. in Proceedings of the 25th Australasian Conference on Information Systems, 2014. Auckland, New Zealand.

[13] North, D.C., Institutions, institutional change and economic performance. 1990: Cambridge university press.

[14] Greenwood, R., R. Suddaby, and C.R. Hinings, Theorizing change: The role of professional associations in the transformation of institutionalized fields. Academy of management journal, 2002. 45(1): p. 58-80.

[15] Sahay, S., et al., Interplay of institutional logics and implications for deinstitutionalization: case study of HMIS implementation in Tajikistan. Information Technologies & International Development, 2010. 6(3): p. pp. 19-32.

[16] Palthe, J., Regulative, Normative, and Cognitive Elements of Organizations: Implications for Managing Change. Management and Organizational Studies, 2014. 1(2): p. p59.

[17] Hsu, C., Y.-T. Lin, and T. Wang, A legitimacy challenge of a cross-cultural interorganizational information system. European Journal of Information Systems, 2015. 24: p. 278-294.

[18] Suddaby, R., Challenges for institutional theory. Journal of Management Inquiry, 2010. 19(1): p. 14-20.

[19] Hsu, C., Y.-T. Lin, and T. Wang, A legitimacy challenge of a cross-cultural interorganizational information system. European Journal of Information Systems, 2015. 24(3): p. 278-294.

[20] Jepperson, R.L., Institutions, institutional effects, and institutionalism. The new institutionalism in organizational analysis, 1991. 6: p. 143-163.

[21] Avgerou, C., Information systems and global diversity. 2002: OUP Oxford.

[22] Oliver, C., The antecedents of deinstitutionalization. Organization studies, 1992. 13(4): p. 563-588.

[23] Grisot, M., H. O., and A. Thorseng, Innovation of,in,on infrastructures: articulating the role of architecture in information infrastructure evolution. Journal of the Association for Information Systems, 2014. 15(special issue): p. 197-219.

[24] Hanseth, O. and E. Monteiro, Understanding information infrastructure. Unpublished Manuscript, Retrieved on 6th September from http://heim. ifi. uio. no/~ oleha/Publications/bok. pdf, 1998.

[25] Aanestad, M. and T.B. Jensen, Building nation-wide information infrastructures in healthcare through modular implementation

strategies. The Journal of Strategic Information Systems, 2011. 20(2): p. 161-176.

[26] Dahlbom, B. and L. Mathiassen, Computers in context: The Philospphy and Practice of System Design. 1993, Cambridge, Massachusetts: Blackwell Publisher

[27] Maguire, S., C. Hardy, and T.B. Lawrence, Institutional entrepreneurship in emerging fields: HIV/AIDS treatment advocacy in Canada. Academy of management journal, 2004. 47(5): p. 657-679.

[28] Hardy, C. and S. Maguire, Institutional entrepreneurship. The Sage handbook of organizational institutionalism, 2008: p. 198-217.

[29] Walsham, G., Interpreting information systems in organizations. Vol. 19. 1993: Wiley Chichester.

[30] Walsham, G., Doing interpretive research. European journal of information systems, 2006. 15(3): p. 320-330.

[31] Orlikowski, W.J. and J.J. Baroudi, Studying information technology in organizations: Research approaches and assumptions. Information systems research, 1991. 2(1): p. 1-28.

[32] Klein, H.K. and M.D. Myers, A set of principles for conducting and evaluating interpretive field studies in information systems. MIS quarterly, 1999: p. 67-93.

[33] Creswell, J.W., Research design: Qualitative, quantitative, and mixed methods approaches. 2013: Sage publications.

[34] Braa, J., E. Monterio, and S. Sahay, Networks of action: sustainable health information systems across developing countries. . MIS quarterly, 2004. 28: p. 337-362.

[35] Walsham, G., Interpretive case studies in IS research: nature and method. European Journal of information systems, 1995. 4(2): p. 74-81.

[36] Elliott, R. and L. Timulak, Descriptive and interpretive approaches to qualitative research. A handbook of research methods for clinical and health psychology, 2005: p. 147-159.

[37] Walsham, G., What is Interpretive Research? . (n.d), University of Oslo: Retrieved from http://www.uio.no/studier/emner/matnat/ifi/INF5740/h04/.../Lecture_1.pp.

[38] Henfridsson, O. and B. Bygstad, The Generative Mechanisms of Digital Infrastructure Evolution. Mis Quarterly, 2013. 37(3): p. 907-931.

[39] Silva, L. and J. Backhouse. Becoming part of the furniture:the institutionalization of information systems. in IFIP TC8 WG 8.2 international conference on information systems and qualitative research. 1997. Philadelphia: Chapman & Hall, Ltd.

[40] Wubishet, Z., Conceptualizing the Governance of Free and Open Source Software Development: A Framework Based on Case Studies of Three Software Projects in Norway, in Department of Informatics. 2011, Norway: Oslo.

[41] Arthur, W.B., Competing technologies, increasing returns, and lock-in by historical events. The economic journal, 1989. 99(394): p. 116-131.

[42] Aanestad, A., Cultivating Networks: Implementing Surgical Telemedicine., in Department of Informatics. 2002, University of Oslo: Oslo.

[43] Farrell, J. and G. Saloner, Standardization, compatibility, and innovation. The RAND Journal of Economics, 1985: p. 70-83.

16

Analyse the Risks of Ad Hoc Programming in Web Development and Develop a Metrics of Appropriate Tools

Manish Gubhaju*, **Ali Al-Sherbaz**

The University of Northampton, Northampton, United Kingdom
*Corresponding author: manishgubaju@hotmail.com

Abstract Today the World Wide Web has become one of the most powerful tools for business promotion and social networking. As the use of websites and web applications to promote the businesses has increased drastically over the past few years, the complexity of managing them and protecting them from security threats has become a complicated task for the organizations. On the other hand, most of the web projects are at risk and less secure due to lack of quality programming. Although there are plenty of frameworks available for free in the market to improve the quality of programming, most of the programmers use ad hoc programming rather than using frameworks which could save their time and repeated work. The research identifies the different frameworks in PHP and .NET programming, and evaluates their benefits and drawbacks in the web application development. The research aims to help web development companies to minimize the risks involved in developing large web projects and develop a metrics of appropriate frameworks to be used for the specific projects. The study examined the way web applications were developed in different software companies and the advantages of using frameworks while developing them. The findings of the results show that it was not only the experience of developers that motivated them to use frameworks. The major conclusions and recommendations drawn from this research were that the main reasons behind web developers avoiding frameworks are that they are difficult to learn and implement. Also, the motivations factors for programmers towards using frameworks were self-efficiency, habit of learning new things and awareness about the benefits of frameworks. The research recommended companies to use appropriate frameworks to protect their projects against security threats like SQL injection and RSS injection.

Keywords: PHP, ASP.NET, programming frameworks, MVC, ad-hoc programming

1. Introduction

The study focuses on the application developers who are mainly stuck within the ad hoc programming rather than framework programming and the role of frameworks in risk management process of large web based projects. It also highlights what actually the frameworks in application development means and the advantages and weaknesses of using them.

1.1. Research Background

Today, the easiest and fastest way to fetch information is getting 'on line'. The Internet Technology has become one of the most powerful advancements in the history of Technology [1]. The web is today known as World Wide Web (WWW) that has a huge influence in every sector of our lives and society [2]. In the past, the World Wide Web was only limited to email, transfer of files and data storage but now it has become a driving force for the success of any organization [3]. It has become the most powerful tool

for business promotion and communication. There is rarely anything left that can't be found on the web. All these information are found in the websites and these websites are developed by the web developers. There are different types of programming languages available for the web application development. Just like we use different types of languages in our daily life to communicate with other people, developers use different type of programming languages to communicate with the web server through the web [1]. So, to make programming more structured frameworks were developed. Frameworks are a set of structured software that developers can use, extend and customize to suit their application. It is a reusable mechanism that allows the developers to break down an application into a set of connecting objects [4]. Frameworks are usually not very different from OOP (Object Oriented Programming). It's just a reuse of a code that is already made for you in advance. In other words the web application framework can be defined as "*A reusable software system with general functionality already implemented*".[5], p.68

There is always a risk for failure of project if ad hoc programming is used. The ad hoc programming is just fine if you are a beginner but we have found that even most of the professional developers try to adopt this type of programming.

A survey done by Cutter Consortium (2000) cited in [5] showed that the top problems for the large scale web projects failure were as follows:
- Failing to meet up the needs of businesses (84%)
- Delay in the project plan (79%)
- Lack of budget (63%)
- Poor and inadequate functionality (53%)
- Poor quality of deliverables (52%)

The above results of the survey clearly show that two out of five problems for project failure were quality of programming and functions. When you are doing a large project with a number of developers working on it, it is not possible to meet the targets unless you follow a proper framework. Ad hoc programming for large projects can lead to a situation from where one can never come out and later have to restart the project. Frameworks have predefined functions and have specific locations for saving the different types of files.

1.2. Research Question

The research aims to investigate the following question:

Why do programmers avoid frameworks in favour of ad hoc program development and how can they be motivated towards using frameworks to minimize the risks of web projects?

1.3. Aims and Objectives

The major purpose of this research is to analyse the risk involved in large web development projects and find out the reasons behind programmers choosing ad hoc programming rather than the framework programming. The major aims and objectives of this paper are as follows:

Aims:
- Help organizations to minimize the risks involved in developing large web projects.
- Motivate Web Developers towards using the proper frameworks while programming.

Objectives:
- Identify the different frameworks of web applications.
- Evaluate the impacts of frameworks on web programming and evaluate their benefits and drawbacks in the web application development.
- Identify and analyse the risks of web projects due to ad hoc programming.
- Identify the methods through which risks can be managed for large web development projects by the use of proper frameworks.
- Investigate the motivation of programmers to engage with frameworks.
- Define methods to encourage programmers towards using the frameworks.

2. Literature Review

Before identifying the impacts of programming frameworks on web development, it is very important to review the theories on World Wide Web (WWW), web application development and web programming.

2.1. Internet and the World Wide Web (www)

Internet is nothing but a set of interconnected networks through which high speed data are being exchanged between servers and other connecting computers [6]. An author describes the need for internet in the following way: *"Why do people want to be 'on the Internet?' One of the main reasons is simple freedom. The Internet is a rare example of a true, modern, functional anarchy."(Sterling, 1993 cited in [7]*, p.579).

Today, the world is at our finger tips for the first time ever. We can find the information about anything using the internet and computer. From setting up a video conference to online shopping, listening to music, watching videos all can be done by entering into world's largest computer network - the Internet [8]. Internet is one the most important need for human beings today but a very few people know about the history of internet. The internet was first developed in 1969 by Advanced Research Projects Agency (ARPANET) for the US Defence Department to exchange scientific information. Later in 1970s and 1980s protocols like file transfer protocol (FTP) were developed to transfer files over the internet. After the wars, more features like electronic mail (e-mail), UseNet groups were added to the internet and were made publically accessible. Finally in 1991, the World Wide Web (WWW) was developed that allowed web contents to be accessed using the hyperlinks. Delphi was the first Internet Service Provider (ISP) in 1993 and there were only 133 sites at that time. The number increased to 3000 in 1994 and more than 2.2 billion in 1998 [6].

2.2. Web Application Development Static and Dynamic Websites

Web applications or websites can be developed depending upon the type of website either static or dynamic. Static websites are those in which a new page has to be uploaded in the server to change the content of the website. They are developed using HTML code. So if something needs to change in the webpage then the HTML code has to be changed itself. Static websites are usually built for small websites with fewer pages and were mostly used in the past [9]. The figure below gives a brief overview of how data are fetched from the web server and displayed in the clients' browsers.

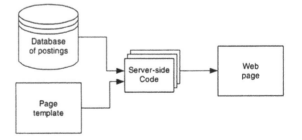

Figure 1. Static website architecture [10]

In Dynamic websites, contents are generated dynamically. The contents like text and images are stored in a database rather than static HTML pages and formatting instructions are placed in the webpage [11]. When a user requests a page, the pages are constructed on demand i.e. the code or instruction pulls the data from the database which combines with the layout to produce the output page and display in the client's screen [10].

The figure below shows the functionality of dynamic websites.

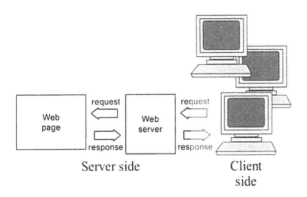

Figure 2. Dynamic website architecture [10]

2.3. Introduction to Frameworks

Programming frameworks are set of structured code, classes, libraries, and run-time environments that allow developers to efficiently and quickly develop applications with a good standard [12]. Frameworks help developers to build more cleaner, secure and maintainable applications which are the key reasons behind more developers switching from old ad-hoc style of programming to framework-based programming [13]. Frameworks are the tools for developing any applications and tools play a vital role in building any application in any language. They provide an ease of maintaining the software on a long term basis making the lives of developers and mangers better [14]. There are many web programming frameworks available in the market and some of them are very popular among the developers.

2.3.1. Popular Web Development Frameworks

There are altogether more than 100 web programming frameworks available in PHP, ASP.NET, JSP, Perl, Python, Ruby, and ColdFusion and below are some of the most popular ones in terms of usability and flexibility.

Zend Framework

Zend framework is an integrated software platform that provides scalability and reliability to the applications built in PHP. It was jointly announced by Zend Technologies, Inc and IBM. Zend helps to deliver PHP intelligence by fixing some of the major problems in PHP applications such as run-time and database errors [15].

CodeIgniter

CodeIgniter (CI) is a powerful PHP framework that is based on Model-View-Controller (MVC) web development [16]. The author believes CodeIgniter has changed his relationship between his clients and the web development. As the codes are organized, it makes the documentation easy and shortens the project completion time [16]. As of [17], they believed that CodeIgniter is a

tool for making PHP easy to use and implement. CI is very easy to install and free which makes it more desirable to use. But its not recommended for those who are weak in OOP (Object Oriented Programming) in PHP or who like to write all of their code rather than using pre built solutions [17].

CakePHP

CakePHP is a well-documented PHP framework that provides a broad architecture for developing and maintaining web applications. CakePHP has a wide range of features that are suitable for beginners as well as experienced developers [18].

The figure below shows how the three components of MVC in CakePHP work together.

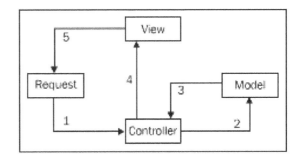

Figure 3. MVC architecture [12]

The objective of MVC in CakePHP is to separate the operations into models for interacting with the database using queries, views for taking inputs from the user and giving output and controller for controlling the whole program flow and generating the output by the help of models. Using MVC errors can be debugged easily. Suppose, if you are getting errors related to your query or database, the problem is usually in the model section as all the database related files are kept in there. The CakePHP is also very handy framework if you are doing a big project in a group because the developers already know where the files are stored and is everyone has to follow the same pattern [19].

ASP.NET MVC framework

According to [20], ASP.NET MVC is a framework by Microsoft that was developed to overcome the weaknesses of traditional ASP.NET programming and built clean and effective web applications using the model-view-controller (MVC) architecture. This view has also been supported by the work of [21]. The framework mainly emphasizes on the clean architecture, testability, and design patterns. The ASP.NET MVC 3 was released recently in 2011 which is the latest version of the framework.

2.4. Advantages and Disadvantages of Using Frameworks in Web Application Development

Framework programming is now known as the most modern technique for developing web applications. But like any other technology it has few disadvantages that can't be denied. The negative impacts that the frameworks have in web development are far less compared to its positive impacts. Frameworks will be the next big thing in the world of web development in the near future. Frameworks help to build dynamic websites much quicker than normal programming and minimize repetitive tasks. The following sections further enlighten the positive and negative impacts of frameworks on web programming [22].

2.4.1. An Approach to Improve Reuse in Web Applications

The need for code reusability has been aroused due to complexity of application and time taken to build web applications like ecommerce sites and other web applications. Building a web application quicker and free of bugs is the most important thing to keep in mind while developing websites. This is only possible if a proper architecture is followed and navigations like landmarks and indexes are used [23]. Frameworks contain scripts that have already been developed, used, tested by other developers that can be effectively used to save time and money. Hence, the web application frameworks contain most of the above mentioned attribute to help web developers build bug free and quality applications quickly and effectively.

2.4.2. Code Acceleration and Optimization

Web code optimization is a very essential part of web development in today's faster growing web industry. As the authors believe *"A crucial part of developing successful web applications is optimizing the files that comprise them. Speed optimization affect show users perceive the efficiency and fluidity of an application."* [24], p.420.

2.4.3. Improve Web Security and Lower the Risks of Hacking

Website security has always been a hot topic for last few years. There are literally so many examples of websites hacked because of weak scripting. On October 13, 2005 a security flaw in myspace.com resulted in over one million friend request to its creator's profile. Similarly, a security flaw in PayPal website allowed hackers to steal credit card numbers of thousands of users [25]. As in [26], SQL injection has been one of the most common attacks in the world of internet for last 10 years but yet it has not been clearly understood by web developers and security professionals

2.4.4. Disadvantage: Framework Code Overhead, Application Performance and Loss of Understanding

Although frameworks have lots of advantages, it also has some weaknesses. Frameworks consists of large number of classes, libraries and other reusable codes for the functions like connecting to the database, caching, authentication and security features which can create a large code overhead. This will be applied for each and every application built in that framework. For large projects it will not matter a lot but it is a big disadvantage for small projects where millions of unnecessary lines of code will have to be written instead of few codes [27].

The heavy lines of codes for interacting with the database can affect the performance of the application and force it to slow down. There are different other aspects in which the frameworks can harm the performance of the application. For example caching function is a good one for running complex codes but it can slower down the

server's performance because of its complex caching system [28].

2.5. Ad-hoc programming: Leading a Project Towards Risks

As in [21], the author categorizes software into two types: good software and bad software. A good software is the one that has no flaws, well optimized, without any repetition of code and most importantly works as you want it to be worked and can be maintained easily. As in [29], the author sees software change as an essential part of software development life cycle and an important task for the developers. There are basically four reasons for the change of software. Firstly because we need to add new features to the software, secondly if we need to fix any bug in the software. Thirdly, to make improvements on the design and lastly for the optimization of code or database querys.

On the other hand, a bad software is one which is very difficult to maintain and doesn't work as you projected. A badly written software has properties like inflexibility, dullness, fragility, recurrence and needless complexity. An inflexible software is one which needs a lot of changes if one change has to be made in it. Dullness means a software that is difficult to understand. If a software breaks into lots of places for a small change its called a fragile software. Recurrence means repetition of same code which results in increased code execution time and occupies extra space. Lastly, a complex software is the one which is needlessy written in too many lines which could be done within few lines of code [21].

2.6. Future of Web Application Frameworks

The world is moving more towards frameworks not only in the field of web development but in other fields of technology. The framework based software engineering is growing rapidly because of its concept on re-use. It is always good to follow an architectural approach to start any task. Developing software has always been a complex activity and the more complex thing for developers has been ensuring that the software built works correctly without any flaws. Therefore, the concept of frameworks is one of the best solutions to get rid of all these problems [30].

Reviewing the benefits of web application frameworks, the future of frameworks seems to be more bright in the field of web application development. The awareness about the benefits of using the frameworks is the important factor for motivating the web developers towards using the frameworks. Apart from these self-efficiency and self belief are the other factors that can motivate the web developers. One can never experience the benefits of a service unless and until he or she uses it.

3. Research Methodology

This section provides the literature on research techniques and describes the methods that were used by the author to collect the primary data to answer the research question.

3.1. Introduction

A research process is not something which is performed when you feel like doing it; it should follow a certain process which must be sequential and generalized [31]. There are different methods for collecting primary data for a research and the researcher has to decide which methods to use to collect information through primary sources. Some of the popular methods of data collection are observation, questionnaire, experiment and survey. But still the methods used depend upon the type of data required to answer the research problem [32].

3.2. Research Approach

Depending upon the design of the research, the research approach mainly uses either inductive approach or deductive approach. Inductive approach is the one in which data is collected first and then theory is developed as a result of the data analysis. Conversely, in deductive approach theory or hypothesis is first developed and then a research strategy is designed to test the hypothesis [33]

In deductive research, data is collected to see whether the hypothesis is true or false. It uses 'top-down' approach in which prediction is made at first and then evidence is asked for to either support or disconfirm the statement. For example a researcher might predict that class with smaller number of students would result in greater number of students in learning compared to large number of students. If after comparing the results between the smaller and larger number of students, the class with smaller number of students show a greater learning then the hypothesis would be supported else would be rejected. However in inductive research, the researcher first collects the data, observes the phenomenon, systematically analyses the data and finally builds an abstraction of the phenomenon that was being studied [34].

As the author had not predicted any statement or hypothesis upfront but wanted to find the answers for why programmers avoided frameworks in favour of ad-hoc program development and how they can be motivated towards using the frameworks, an inductive approach was selected. Primary data was collected using different methods like survey and interview which are described later in this section and was analysed to build a theory.

3.3. Qualitative versus Quantitative Research Methods

The selection of qualitative and quantitative methods for research depends upon the objective of the research and previous experience of the researcher [32]. Qualitative research is mainly used to gain the in-depth knowledge about any topic or understand the phenomenon about which very less is known (Marshan-Piekkari and Welch, 2004 cited in [32]). Qualitative research is very suitable for studying organizations, groups and individuals. Qualitative methods are mainly recommended for inductive and exploratory research as they lead to building hypothesis and statements.

On the other hand in quantitative research method, findings are arrived at by statistical methods. The major difference between qualitative and quantitative research methods is that quantitative research is based on measurement and qualitative is not (Layder,1993; Bryman and Bell, 2003 cited in [32]). Quantitative research uses numbers and statistics, and seeks measurements that can

be easily replicated by other researchers. In this type of method the role of the researcher is to mainly observe and measure [35].

The research has been chosen to get the in-depth knowledge about the risks of using ad-hoc program development and find the answers to why programmers avoid frameworks and their motivation towards using the frameworks. Also, the research does not really use any statistics or measurements. Hence, the research is based on both qualitative and quantitative methods of data collection. A survey was conducted to collect the quantitative data from the programmers to analyse their behaviour and approach towards frameworks, and the qualitative data was collected by interviewing managers from different companies to analyse the risks of ad-hoc programming to their firm.

3.4. Research Strategy

Research strategy is nothing but a general plan for answering the research question. It specifies the sources from where data are collected and the constraints that the author will have inevitably. The research strategy justifies why a particular organization, group or staff was chosen to talk or interview. Furthermore, the justification should depend upon the research question and objectives. The research strategies used in research are usually experiment, survey, case study, grounded theory, ethnography and so on [33].

The research strategy that was chosen by the author was basically the survey and interviews. Survey method was chosen to examine the nature of the programmers. It was chosen to investigate the web developers' relation with web application frameworks and find out the possible reasons for them being or not being engaged with different web development frameworks. Since, the author himself had worked as a web application developer in Peoples Information Technology located in Kathmandu, Nepal and had lots of friends in Nepal working in the same field; most of the developers that were surveyed belonged to Nepal. Time was the major constraint for using this method because developers were very busy with their jobs. So, it took about a month to collect data using the different data collection methods which are mentioned in section 3.6.

Interview was another research strategy chosen by the author to collect qualitative data. The reason for choosing this strategy was to get in-depth knowledge about how the IT project managers viewed the benefits and risks of using frameworks in projects. Some of the major constraints of using this strategy were time and money. The IT project managers had very limited time to talk about different subjects in details. On the other hand, the rate of telephone calls from UK to Nepal was quite expensive.

3.5. Sampling

Collecting data is an essential part of any research which is independent of the research question(s) or objectives. However, it is not possible to collect data from all user groups due to some constraints like time, money and accessibility. For this purpose sampling is used in which a particular sample group is focused from the whole population of users. Probability and non-probability sampling are the most common types of sampling methods. In probability sampling data are collected from random samples and in non-probability, samples are collected from targeted samples [33].

As the research for mainly based on web application development and web application frameworks, basically web programmers were targeted for the research purpose. Therefore non-probability sampling method was used in which web programmers from different parts of the world were surveyed. Most of the developers were from Nepal. Also, in the research, managers and Chief Technical Officers were involved who had previous experiences with web application development. Proshore Nepal, Smart Tech Ideas, National Technology Centre and Peoples Information Technology were the major companies in Nepal from which most of the developers were surveyed for the research.

3.6. Data Collection

Data for the research was collected in two phases. The first phase was conducting a semi-structured interview for collecting qualitative data. Telephone interview method was used for the interview process in which 8 people were interview out of which 2 were Chief Technical Officer, 4 were IT Project Managers, 1 was senior web developers, 1 was junior web developers. Hand notes were used to record important answers of the interview. The interview was feasible because the author had friends in the companies mentioned in 1.5. Therefore, the date and time for the interview was set through the author's friends. Also, some of the developers and managers were very close friends of the author. The interview with Chief Technical Officers and Managers had 5 questions and was about 15 minutes long. The interview with web developers had 4 questions and was about 10 minutes long.

The second phase was collecting the quantitative data using survey strategy. Questionnaire method was used for data collection. The questionnaires were designed using the tool Google Forms included in the Google Docs. It was a structured questionnaire which was designed based on the literature in section 2. Also, for the users' convenience the questionnaire was uploaded in a live webpage. The author used an online questionnaire method in which 70 developers were invited to fill the questionnaire out of which 50 developers responded. Most of the respondents were from Nepal and others were from United Kingdom, United States, Japan, and Australia. The data obtained were analysed using the Microsoft excel software.

3.7. Reliability and Validity

Reliability and Validity are the two important fundamentals of any measurement procedure and are common in quantitative research but it has now been reviewed in qualitative research as well [36]. A research is considered reliable only if the results of the research are consistent over time and can be reproduced to be used under similar methodology (Joppe, 2000 cited in [36]). According to Kirk and Miller (1986 cited in [36]), there are three types of reliability in quantitative research. The first one is that the measurement should be stable over time. Secondly, the measurement should be similar within a period of time and third is the degree in which the measurement is repeated should be same.

Validity determines whether the findings are really about what they appear to be about. It is concerned with the truthfulness of the results of the research. In simple words validity is nothing but the accuracy of measurement of the data [33].

To maintain reliability and validity in the measurement of data, the survey was conducted only within the programmers and managers who had experience in web application development. The questions and options in the questionnaire were designed with the aim of collecting accurate data to answer the research question and the questions clearly showed that the survey was only for people with explicit knowledge in web programming. Furthermore, the interviewees were managers and developers who were reliable and from whom proper information could be obtained to generate valid measurements.

4. Data Analysis and Findings

4.1. Evaluation of Interviews

The responses of the interviews from different levels of professionals from the companies namely Proshore Nepal, Smart Tech Ideas, National Technology Centre and Peoples Information Technology are analysed and categorised according to the designation of the interviewees. Responses of the interviews from individuals belonging to the same designation are discussed under same heading and are compared to draw necessary conclusions.

4.1.1. Interviews with the Chief Technical Officers of Proshore Nepal and Peoples Information Technology

Planned interviews were conducted over telephone with two Chief Technical Officers, one from Proshore Nepal and the other from Peoples Information Technology. Both the companies are reputed companies of Nepal in the field of Web Application Development. Five questions were asked with each interviewee and the duration of each interview was approximately 15 minutes. Quite interesting and remarkable data were produced from the interview in understanding the characteristics of developers and impacts of using frameworks.

4.1.2. Interview with Chief Technical Officer of Proshore Nepal

The first question that was asked was about the company background, number of employees and their expertise. The Chief Technical Officer said that the company was established in Netherlands, Nepal and United Kingdom in 2009 and since then have been serving clients from all parts of the world. Their development team is mainly located in Nepal and the marketing team is located in Netherlands and United Kingdom. He further added that the company mainly specializes in developing websites, web shops, online applications in PHP and ASP.net, and also mobile applications. There are around 40 employees currently working in Proshore Nepal among which most of them are PHP developers and others are ASP.net programmers, web designers and data entry staffs.

The second question asked was whether they use frameworks for web application development. In reply to this question, he said that they use frameworks but not for all the projects. He basically asks developers to use frameworks for less skilled projects and medium size projects. He further added that he does not encourage developers to use frameworks for skilled and very large projects because they don't have all the functions required for skilled projects and sometimes internal bugs in the libraries of the frameworks are hard to find and fix. He was again asked about the frameworks that they mainly use and why. In reply he said they mainly use cakePHP and CodeIgniter for building web applications in PHP and ASP.NET MVC framework for building web applications in ASP.NET. He added they use cakePHP and CodeIgniter because they are easy to learn and implement than other frameworks like Zend framework. Also, these frameworks help them to develop applications faster because of the features like automatic database and module generator and MVC architecture.

The third question was asked about the benefits and vulnerabilities of using frameworks. In response to this question he said that the benefits of using frameworks were that it helped them to develop web applications faster due to their pre-built and pre-tested functions. Frameworks have good documentation which helps developers to understand the project done by other developers quickly and help them to work as a team. Furthermore, he said that the major vulnerabilities of using frameworks were that it was not suitable for very small projects because of its code overhead and also not suitable for skilled projects as bugs were difficult to track and fix if occurred within the library functions.

The fourth question asked to the interviewee was how comfortable were the developers with using frameworks and why they avoided frameworks. He replied that the developers who have not used frameworks even once try to avoid frameworks but those who have already used frameworks before are comfortable with it. He further added using frameworks requires deep knowledge of OOP (Object Oriented Programming) and not all the developers are good at it so I would say the comfort zone depends upon the nature and self-efficiency of the developers. So, lack of knowledge and experience are the reasons they avoid frameworks.

The last question asked was how successfully the projects were delivered to the clients on time and the risks to the web projects. He said that not all projects are delivered successfully but most of them are delivered. He further added hacking is one of the major risks to the web projects. Last year three out of ten auction sites developed by our programmers were hacked by some Italian hackers group and this year two auction websites were hacked. We use our in-house framework for developing auction websites.

4.1.3. Interviews with the IT Project Managers of Proshore Nepal, Peoples Information Technology, Smart Tech Ideas and National Technology Center

Altogether four IT Project Managers were interviewed. The responses of the interviews with IT project managers of different companies are discussed and compared in the section below. Most of the responses of project managers matched with each other while few were contradictory.

The first question was about their role in their company. The replies were common stating their roles included

assigning projects to the web programmers, assisting them understand the requirements and debugging the code. Further roles included documentation of project requirements and completion schedule, and also interacting with the clients to fulfill their needs.

The second question was whether they used frameworks for web application development or not and which frameworks they used the most and why. The project managers from Proshore Nepal and Smart Tech Ideas said that they mainly used cake PHP and Code Igniter for PHP, and ASP.NET MVC for ASP.NET. They said they liked these frameworks because they were based on MVC architecture which made the code look clean, managed and easy to debug. The manager from National Technology Centre said they used Yii Framework because it was easy to learn and implement for developers and had easy GUI interface for creating automatic models, controllers and forms. On the other hand, Project Manager from Peoples Information technology said they don't use frameworks so frequently because they are difficult to learn and implement.

The third question was about benefits and vulnerabilities of using frameworks. The managers said clean coding, code reusability, error handling and logging, good documentation as some of the major benefits. The manager from Smart Tech Ideas said that he finds the in-built cache functions of frameworks as the major benefits to programming as it make the website run fast in the browser. The vulnerabilities were that frameworks were not suitable for all projects due to code overhead and limited library functions.

The fourth question that was asked was whether developers were comfortable with frameworks and why they avoided them. From the responses of the managers it can be evaluated that it's not only the experience that motivates developers to use frameworks but self-belief and awareness about the benefits of programming are the major factors.

The final question was how successfully the projects were delivered to the client and identifying the risks to web projects. The analysis of the responses showed that companies like Proshore Nepal and Smart Tech Ideas who used frameworks seemed to have better customer satisfaction in delivering project than the other two who relied more on ad-hoc programming. Hacking due to security holes and flaws in programming seemed to be the common answer from all the managers as the major risks to web projects.

4.1.4. Interviews with the Junior Web Developer of Proshore Nepal

Short telephone interviews of 10 minutes each were conducted with the Junior Web Developer of Proshore Nepal. The interview analysed the things like the prospective of developers towards frameworks, encouraging and discouraging factors for using frameworks and so on.

When first question was asked about the years of experience he had, he replied that he has about 6 months of web development experience.

The second question asked to the Junior Web Developer was whether he used frameworks for web application development. He replied that he started using them two months after he started his job in Proshore

Nepal. When asked why he uses them, he further answered it saves his time as applications are developed quickly using frameworks and he doesn't need to worry about things like security, code optimization and cache.

The third question was the factors that motivated him towards using frameworks in his working environment. He replied that he didn't know about frameworks at all when he joined the company. After doing ad-hoc programming for 2 months, his project manager held a workshop for them. The workshop was about the use and benefits of using frameworks. They were then trained for using the CodeIgniter framework. So according to him, motivation from the project manager was one of the crucial factors for using frameworks. Lastly he added: "Once I was aware of the benefits of using the CodeIgniter framework, I learned the CakePHP and Yii framework then started implementing in the projects".

The last question was choosing the best framework in PHP or JSP. He replied he has just used three PHP frameworks till now: CodeIgniter, CakePHP and Yii, and thinks CakePHP is the best framework because it is simple, has wide range of features and easily understood by beginners.

4.2. Evaluation of Questionnaires

The data was collected from 50 developers and were analysed. The result of the survey showed that out of 50 developers 34 developers were from Nepal, 2 were from Australia, 3 were from Japan, 6 were from United Kingdom and 5 were from United States (Appendix II). The majority of the respondents are between age 26 to 40 years and the rest are aged between 18 to 25 years.

The results of the questionnaires are divided into the following categories:

- Understanding the trends of Web application development.
- Ad-hoc programming Versus Framework programming.
- Motivation for programmers towards using frameworks.
- Project risks and solutions.

4.2.1. Understanding the Trends of Web Application Development

From the researcher's point of view it is very important to look at the issues like how a project is carried out in an organisation and issues in doing it.

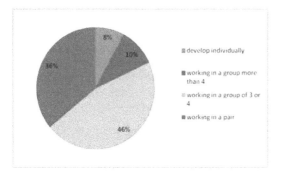

Figure 4. Pie chart showing how big web projects are developed

When asked how they usually developed big web projects in their company, as shown in Figure 4, out of 50

respondents 46% said that they develop big web projects in a group of 3 or 4 and 36% developed working in a pair. Only 8% developed individually and 10% developed in a group more than 4. The result shows that web application development is about team work and developers usually work as a team to accomplish large web applications.

The table below shows the results of the survey in which respondents who answered the question "To what level do you agree or disagree on the most common problems that you face while developing a web project in a group using ad-hoc programming?"

Table 1. Results showing the common problems while developing a web project

	1 Definitely disagree	2	3	4	5 Definitely agree
Assign modules to individuals	10%	12%	50%	16%	12%
problem understanding the classes and functions created by others	10%	14%	20%	10%	46%
problem locating files created by others	6%	10%	24%	54%	6%
communication problem	4%	8%	22%	54%	12%
problem integrating the modules that are completed	4%	12%	26%	48%	10%
problem executing the files due to bugs in libraries created by others	6%	12%	12%	22%	48%
problem preparing a documentation	4%	10%	28%	46%	12%

The above table result shows that 46% of respondents strongly agree with the fact that problems caused by ad-hoc programming while working in a group are problem understanding the classes and functions created by others and 48% agree they have problem executing the files due to bugs in libraries created by others. The results also show that Developers face some problems in locating files created by others and communication problems. The result shows some of the drawbacks of ad-hoc programming.

These problems can hugely affect the performance of the developers on completing the web projects in any organisation because a lot of developers' time is wasted in the above mentioned tasks.

4.2.2. Ad-hoc Programming Versus Framework Programming

When asked how long have they been in the web development profession, mmong the 50 respondents, 38% respondents were developers with three to four years of experience. The second highest percentage was 26% having experience more than four years. Only 14% of the developers surveyed where one to two years of experience. This result shows that the survey has covered developers with all ranges of experiences.

Developers were asked whether they used any frameworks for web application development. It was not surprising to see 66% respondents says "Yes" when asked if they used frameworks or not. But was quite unusual to see 26% not using frameworks at all and 0% not being unable to comment which means they have not heard about the web development frameworks.

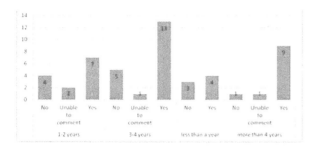

Figure 5. Bar diagram showing the percentage of respondents who used or did not use frameworks.

When the results of question no. 5 and question no. 6 were analysed, it showed that the number of developers using frameworks were not only experienced developers and those not using frameworks were not only of 1-2 years' experience. The result shows experience is not so important factor for the motivation of developers towards using frameworks.

The following table shows the ratings in percentage for PHP frameworks in terms of functionality and relevance.

Table 2. Ratings in percentage for different PHP frameworks

	1 Least relevant	2	3	4	5 Most relevant
Zend Framework	2%	6%	40%	16%	10%
CodeIgniter	0%	4%	16%	20%	38%
CakePHP	4%	4%	10%	28%	30%
Yii Framework	6%	6%	14%	32%	14%

Similarly, the following table shows the ratings in percentage for ASP.NET frameworks in terms of functionality and relevance.

Table 3. Ratings in percentage for different ASP.NET frameworks

	1 Least relevant	2	3	4	5 Most relevant
ASP.NET MVC Framework	4%	2%	6%	10%	20%
DotNetNuke	4%	2%	20%	12%	2%
OpenRasta	4%	8%	22%	6%	0%
MonoRail	4%	8%	24%	4%	0%

4.2.3. Motivation for Programmers Towards Using Frameworks

To find out the main motivation factors for programmers towards using frameworks, they were asked to select the reasons for developers being stuck in ad-hoc programming.

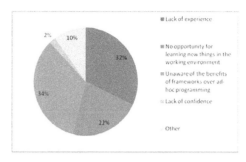

Figure 6. Pie Chart showing results of the reasons for developers being stuck in ad-hoc programming.

The chart above shows that 34% respondents said the reason behind web developers being stuck in ad-hoc programming is unaware of the benefits of frameworks over ad-hoc programming. About 32% thought because developers had not much experience and 22% said they had not opportunity for learning new things in the working environment.

When asked to select the motivation factors for web developers towards using frameworks, a majority of 50% respondents said web developers can be motivated towards using frameworks by making them aware about the benefits of frameworks. About 36% said self-efficiency and habit of learning new things are the motivation factors towards using them. About 8% and 6% said motivation from project managers and work experience as the motivation factors respectively.

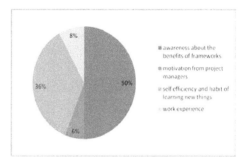

Figure 7. Pie Chart showing the results of the motivation factors for programmers towards using frameworks.

4.2.4. Project risks and Solutions

Projects can be in risk due to various factors. To know more about risks in real development respondents were asked rate the most common problems due to which web projects fail. The table below shows the results.

Table 4. Results of the most common problems due to which web projects fail

	1 Strongly disagree	2	3	4	5 Strongly agree
Client Dissatisfaction	10%	10%	14%	54%	12%
Lack of requirement analysis	8%	4%	12%	10%	66%
Security problems	6%	16%	52%	12%	14%
Lack of testing	2%	4%	18%	26%	50%
Project not completed before deadline	2%	10%	22%	56%	10%
Poor scripting and documentation	12%	10%	20%	20%	38%

When respondents from different parts of the world were asked if the use of frameworks made their project secure, fast and clean without putting in much effort, 74% respondents said 'yes' (as shown in Figure 8). Only 12% said 'No' and 14% respondents were unable to comment on it.

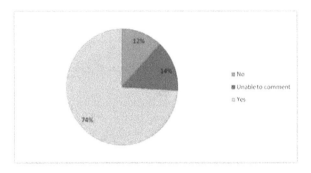

Figure 8. Results showing the responses of developers towards using frameworks.

Figure 9 shows that the number of respondents that said 'yes' has outnumbered those who disagreed in all the countries. Also, all the respondents surveyed from Australia and Japan said they agree with the question 16. This shows that developers from all parts of the world are aware of the benefits of using frameworks.

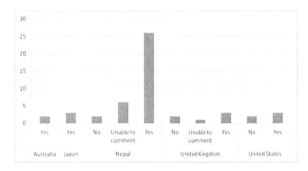

Figure 9. Results showing the responses of developers from different countries towards the benefits of using frameworks.

5. Discussion

From the interview with the Chief Technical Officer of Proshore Nepal it was found that frameworks are best if used with large projects and at the same time should not be used for developing very high skilled projects because if bugs are present in any library functions then they are very hard to debug and fix. Code reusability was discussed as one of the major advantages of using frameworks in the literature review (2.4.1). Frameworks contains scripts and libraries that has already been developed, used and tested by other developers and makes the process of application development faster according to Schwabe et al. (2001). Similar results were found from the interview with the Chief Technical Officer of Proshore Nepal i.e. frameworks help to develop web applications faster because of its pre-built and pre-tested libraries. Other advantages like error logging, better documentation and in-built cache functions were found out from the interview with the managers of Smart Tech Ideas and Proshore Nepal (4.1.2).

From the results of the survey done on the trends of web application development (4.2.1), it was found that big web projects are mostly developed by working in a group of three or four. Furthermore, Table 1 shows that the common problems that developers face while working in a group using ad-hoc programming are mainly problem executing the files due to bugs in libraries created by others, problem understanding the classes and functions created by others, problem locating files created by others, problem integrating the modules that are completed and communication problem. The one and only solution for solving all these problems are using frameworks. Frameworks like CodeIgniter, CakePHP, Yii, ASP.NET MVC are based on MVC architecture. Developers do not have to worry about locating files created by others because all the files must be saved in the particular MVC folders as discussed in the literature review (2.3.1.3). Also, while using frameworks users do not have to create any functions or libraries as they are already present in the frameworks so there are fewer chances of bugs and the documentation can be used to understand the in-built libraries. Therefore it was found out that frameworks are best for solving problems that are created while developing applications in a group.

The vulnerabilities of ad-hoc programming were found out from the evaluation of interviews with managers and the result of the surveys. From the interview with the project manager of Peoples Information Technology who relied on ad-hoc programming rather than framework programming, it was found out that they received frequent complaints from clients about the bugs and security holes in their applications. Also, another complaint was that the websites were very slow. On the other hand, very few complaints about these issues were received according to the manager of Proshore Nepal who used frameworks for developing websites. This shows ad-hoc programming is a process of building very poor software. Walther as in [21] has described the differences between a good and a bad software which is explained in more detail in the literature review (2.5). Ad-hoc programming is surely a major factor for project failure as 38% respondents strongly believe that poor scripting and documentation is one of the common problems due to which web projects fail (Table 4).

From the survey results and the evaluation of interviews, it was found out that use of frameworks are the best solutions for minimizing the risks of web projects and making it secure, fast and clean without putting in much effort. About 74% agreed with this statement as shown in Figure 8. Also, the respondents who agreed were not only from Nepal but from other parts of the world like Australia, Japan, United Kingdom and United States (Figure 9).

6. Conclusions and Recommendations

6.1. Research Conclusion

From the results and findings of the research it can be concluded that the main reasons behind web developers avoiding frameworks are that they are difficult to learn and implement. Also, due to code overhead problem most developers do not use it for small web projects. From the interview with some of the developers, it was found out that some developers are stuck with ad-hoc programming because they do not have opportunity to learn new things in their workplace. The results showed that frameworks should not be used to develop very high skilled web applications because they do not contain very high skilled libraries and bugs are difficult to fix if present. On the basis of the results of the interviews and survey, it can be concluded that the major motivation factors for web developers towards using frameworks are awareness about the benefits of frameworks, self-efficiency and habit of learning new things and last but not the least motivation from project managers. Even junior web developers were found using frameworks because they were motivated by their senior managers. Experience does play a vital role in learning and implementing the frameworks quickly but it is not an essential factor. Furthermore, the major risks of using ad-hoc programming were risks of project failure due to bugs, security holes and client dissatisfaction. Frameworks help to lower the risks of web project failures and increase the efficiency of web applications. Pre-built and pre-tested functions protect the web applications against threats like SQL injection and RSS injection. The in-built cache functions help to execute the codes faster so that websites load faster in the user browsers. In simple words, frameworks make your web project secure, fast and clean without putting in much effort. On the basis of the outcomes of the interviews and survey the best PHP frameworks are CodeIgniter, CakePHP and Yii; and the best ASP.NET framework is ASP.NET MVC framework.

6.2. Recommendations

The overall results of the survey and interviews with managers and developers of different web development companies of Nepal, lead us to the following recommendations that may help web development companies and senior managers to improve the quality of the web applications that they develop and increase client satisfaction.

The results of the research found out that some developers were stuck in ad-hoc program development because they were not given opportunity to learn new things and were not supported by senior managers. The author's recommendations to the senior managers of the web development companies is that developers should be given chance and time to explore their knowledge and should be motivated towards learning new technologies.

Most companies have problem assigning task to the developers and even big projects are given to develop single handed. The results of the survey showed that usually big projects are done in a group of three or four. This helps to concentrate developers in particular modules which speed ups the development time. So, it can be recommended to the managers of software companies to use groups of 3 or 4 to develop big projects.

The results highlighted hacking due to poor scripting as the major threat to web applications till date and also use of frameworks make projects secure, fast and clean without putting in much effort. Therefore author's recommendation is highlighting the use of frameworks to minimize the security risks like SQL injection and RSS injection, and increase performance of web applications.

6.3. Research Limitations

Although the research was successful in achieving its goals, there were some respondents who were subjective with their answers. Also, the interviewees were not so open and hesitated to give the interview. Another limitation of the research was that the interview was conducted over telephone due to which very long conversation could not be done with the interviewees. Furthermore, managers and Chief Technical Officers were so busy with their schedule that it was very difficult to manage time for them on the phone and were unable to hang up on the phone for very long period of time. The author tried to make full use of the data collected and analysed most of the data but it's human nature that sometimes all things cannot be observed by a single person so some information can be inadvertently ignored.

6.4. Future Research

Similar research can be carried out by using the qualitative and quantitative data from the software companies of different counties other than Nepal. As we know that the interviewees belonged to Nepal and most of the developers surveyed were from Nepal. The motivation factors for developers in other countries might be totally different and the way web applications are build may vary from that of Nepal. Therefore it would be very interesting to know the trends of building web applications in the other countries and analyse the motivation factors of developers towards using frameworks.

References

[1]   Shah, D. N. (2009) A Complete Guide to Internet and Web Programming. New Delhi: Dreamtech Press.

[2]   Kappel, G., Prill, B., Reich, S. and Retschitzegger, W. (2006) Web engineering: the discipline of systematic development of web applications. Chichester: John Wiley and Sons, Ltd.

[3]   Lu, M.T. and Yeung, W.l. (1998) A framework for effective commercial Web application development. Internet Research: Electronic Networking Applications and Policy. 8 (2), 166-73.

[4]   Henney, K. (2010) 97 Things Every Programmer Should Know [e-book] Sebastopol: O'Reilly Media. Available from: University of Northampton website <http://www.northampton.ac.uk> [Accessed 5th August 2011].

[5]   Kappel, G., Prill, B., Reich, S. and Retschitzegger, W. (2006) Web engineering: the discipline of systematic development of web applications. Chichester: John Wiley and Sons, Ltd.

[6]   Todd, S. (1999) A guide to the Internet and World Wide Web. Structural Survey. 17 (1), 36-41.

[7]   Ingram, P. (1996) Web developments and the Internet. Computers and Geosciences. 22 (5), 579-84.

[8]   Gralla, P. (1998) How the Internet works. 4th ed. Indianapolis: Que Corporation.

[9]   Banks, M. (2005) OCR AS GCE Applied ICT Double Award. Oxford: Heinemann Educational Publishers.

[10]   Camilleri, M. and Sollars, V. (2003) Information and communication technologies and young language learners. Kapfenberg: Council of Europe Publishing.

[11]   Severdia, R. and Crowder, K. (2009) Using Joomla: Building Powerful and Efficient Web Sites. Sebastopol: O'Reilly Media.

[12]   Bari, A. and Syam, A. (2008) CakePHP Application Development. Birmingham: Packt Publishing.

[13]   Vaswani, V. (2010) Zend Framework, A Beginner's Guide. New York: McGraw-Hill Companies.

[14]   Coggeshall, J. and Tocker, M. (2009) Zend Enterprise PHP Patterns. New York: Springer-Verlag.

[15]   Taft, D.K. (2005) Zend delivers PHP Intelligence. eWeek. 22 (3), 30.

[16] Thomas, M. (2008) Professional CodeIgniter. Indianapolis: Wiley Publishing, Inc.

[17] Argudo, J. and Upton, D. (2009) CodeIgniter 1.7. Birmingham: Packt Publishing.

[18] Iglesias, M. (2011) CakePHP 1.3 Application Development Cookbook. Birmingham: Packt Publishing.

[19] Golding, D. (2008) Beginning CakePHP: From Novice to Professional. New York: Springer-Verlag.

[20] Freeman, A. and Sanderson, S. (2009) Pro ASP.NET MVC 3 Framework. New York: Springer Science Business Media.

[21] Walther, S. (2010) ASP.NET MVC Framework Unleashed. New York: Pearson Education, Inc.

[22] Bella, L.L. (2011) Careers in Web Development. New York: The Rosen Publishing Group.

[23] Schwabe, D., Rossi, G., Esmeraldo, L. and Lyardet, F. (2001) Web Design Frameworks: An Approach to Improve Reuse in Web Applications. Web Engineering 2000. 2016 (10), 335-52.

[24] Hasan, S.S. and Issac, R.K. (2011) An integrated approach of MAS-CommonKADS, Model–View–Controller and web application optimization strategies for web-based expert system development. Expert Systems with Applications. 38 (1), 417-28.

[25] Khare, R. (2006) Network Security and Ethical Hacking. Beckington: Luniver Press.

[26] Clarke, J. (2010) Web Application Security. New York: Springer-Verlag.

[27] Softcov (2008) Softcov [online] Available from: http://www.softcov.com/programming-and-testing/advantages-and-disadvantages-of-several-major.html [Accessed 29th October 2011].

[28] Trejder (2010) Advantages and Disadvantages of Framework Programming - Yii Framework Forum [online] Available from: http://www.yiiframework.com/forum/index.php?/topic/14300-advantages-and-disadvantages-of-framework-programming/ [Accessed 29th October 2011].

[29] Feathers, M.C. (2005) Working Effectively with Legacy Code. New Jersey: Pearson Education.

[30] Sinnott, R.O. (1998) Frameworks: the future of formal software development?. Computer Standards and Interfaces. 19 (7), 375-385.

[31] Dawson, C.W. (2005) Projects in Computing and Information Systems. Harlow: Pearson Education Limited.

[32] Ghauri, P. and Gronhaug, K. (2010) Research Methods in Business Studies. Harlow: Pearson Education Limited.

[33] Saunders, M., Lewis, P. and Thornhill, A. (2003) Research Methods for Business Students. Harlow: Pearson Education Limited.

[34] Lodico, M.G., Spaulding, D.T. and Voegtle, K.H. (2010) Methods in Educational Research: From Theory to Practice. 2nd ed. San Francisco: Jossey-Bass.

[35] Thomas, R.M. (2003) Blending qualitative and quantitative research methods in theses and dissertations. California: Corwin Press.

[36] Golafshani, N. (2003) Understanding Reliability and Validity in Qualitative Research. The Qualitative Report. 8 (4), 597-607.

17

A Survey on Multi Criteria Decision Making Methods and Its Applications

Martin Aruldoss[1,*], T. Miranda Lakshmi[2], V. Prasanna Venkatesan[1]

[1]Department of Banking Technology, Pondicherry University, Puducherry, India
[2]Department of Computer Science, Research and Development Centre, Bharathiyar University, Coimbatore, India
*Corresponding author: jayamartin@yahoo.com, cudmartin@gmail.com

Abstract Multi Criteria Decision Making (MCDM) provides strong decision making in domains where selection of best alternative is highly complex. This survey paper reviews the main streams of consideration in multi criteria decision making theory and practice in detail. The main purpose is to identify various applications and the approaches, and to suggest approaches which are most robustly and effectively useable to identify best alternative. This survey work also addresses the problem in fuzzy multi criteria decision making techniques. Multi criteria decision making have been applied in many domains. MCDM method helps to choose the best alternatives where many criteria have come into existence, the best one can be obtained by analyzing the different scope for the criteria, weights for the criteria and the choose the optimum ones using any multi criteria decision making techniques. This survey provides the comprehensive developments of various methods of FMCDM and its applications.

Keywords: *multi criteria decision making, fuzzy, MCDM, TOPSIS, best choice, decision making*

1. Introduction

In our day today life, so many decisions are being made from various criteria's, so the decision can be made by providing weights to different criteria's and all the weights are obtain from expert groups. It is important to determine the structure of the problem and explicitly evaluate multi criteria. For example, in building a nuclear power plant, certain decisions have been taken based on different criteria. There are not only very complex issues involving multi criteria, some criteria may have effect toward some problem, but over all to have an optimum solution, all the alternatives must have common criteria which clearly lead to more informed and better decisions.

Multi Criteria Decision Making is pertaining to structure and solve decision and planning problems involving multiple criteria. The main objective of this survey is to support decision makers where there are huge choices exist for a problem to be solved. Typically, it is necessary to use decision maker's desire to differentiate between solutions [1] where there is no unique optimal solution for these problems. Solving the problem can be interpreted in different ways. It could correspond to choose the "best" alternative from a set of alternatives (where "best" can be interpreted as "the most preferred alternative" of a decision maker). Another interpretation of "solving" is to choose a small set of good alternatives, or grouping alternatives into different preference sets. An extreme interpretation is used to find all "efficient" or "non-dominated" alternatives.

The problem becomes more complex when many criteria exist for the alternatives. A unique optimal solution for an MCDM problem can be obtained without the desired information incorporation. An optimal solution's idea is often put back by the set of non-dominated solutions. A non-dominated solution has the property that without sacrificing at least one criterion it is not possible to move away from it to any other solution. Therefore, the decision maker can easily able to choose a solution from the non-dominated set. Otherwise, the decision maker could not do worse in any of them and could do better in terms of all the criteria. However, the set of non-dominated solutions is too large to present to the decision maker for their final choice.

This survey on multi criteria decision understands the need of MCDM, many works have been proposed in determining the best optimal solution for a problem using different methods in it, and each of the MCDM method has its uniqueness. Many applications uses MCDM in determining the flaws in the system, these flaws can be managed by using appropriate method for solving the problem.

The rest of the paper organized as follows, in section 2 discuss about the prior research on MCDM methods and its applications and section 3describes the research opportunities and section 4 concludes the paper.

2. Prior Research

In spite of incomplete information fuzzy logic allows decision making with estimated values. It should be noted that a decision may be incorrect and can be later improved when additional information is available. Of course, a complete lack of information will not support any decision making using any form of logic. For complex problems, conventional methods (non-fuzzy) are usually depend on mathematical approximations (E.g. linearization of nonlinear problems), which leads to poor performance and very expensive. Under such circumstances, fuzzy systems often outperform conventional MCDM methods. Many works have been done in various fields like banking, general purpose, student and teacher performances, water resource location and many. In this case the alternatives

and criteria have been collected and the evaluation of the criteria has been done to choose the best alternatives. MCDM structures complex problems by considering multi criteria explicitly, which leads to more informed and better decisions.

2.1. Methods of MCDM

MCDM methods have been applied to different applications and find the best solution to choose the best alternative. The Figure 1 depicts the hierarchical view of MCDM methods and its types. The widely used MCDM methods have been described in following headings.

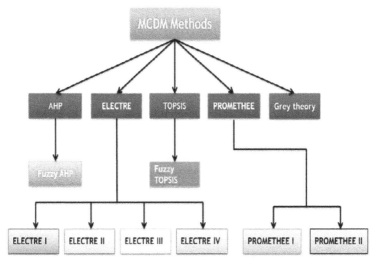

Figure 1. Hierarchical structure of MCDM Methods

2.1.1. Analytic Hierarchy Process

The basic idea of AHP is to capture experts' knowledge of phenomena under study. Using the concepts of fuzzy set theory and hierarchical structure analysis a systematic approach is followed for alternative selection and justification problem. Decision-makers usually find that it is more confident to give interval judgments than fixed value judgments. When a user preference is not defined explicitly due to fuzzy nature this method can be applied. AHP includes the opinions of experts and multi criteria evaluation; it is not capable of reflecting human's vague thoughts. The classical AHP considers the definite judgments of decision makers, thus the fuzzy set theory makes the comparison process more flexible and capable to explain experts' preferences. The Analytic Hierarchy Process (AHP) decomposes a difficult MCDM problem into a systematic hierarchy procedure [2]. The final step in the AHP method deals with the structure of an m*n matrix (where m is the number of alternatives and n is the number of criteria's). Using the relative importance of the alternatives a matrix is constructed in terms of each criterion. Analytic Hierarchy Process (AHP) is based on priority theory. It deals with the complex problems which involve the consideration of multi criteria/alternatives simultaneously.

2.1.2. Fuzzy Analytic Hierarchy Process

Fuzzification of Analytic Hierarchy Process (Fuzzy AHP) is used in conventional market surveys, etc. AHP, several products and alternatives are evaluated, by means of pairwise comparisons, the weight of each item evaluation and the evaluation values for each product and

alternatives are found for each item evaluation, but the result of pairwise comparisons are not 0,1, but rather the degree is given by a numerical value [3]. In fuzzy AHP, the weight is expressed by necessary measure or possibility measure, and in addition, the conventional condition that the total of various weights 1 can be relaxed.

2.1.3. TOPSIS

The TOPSIS method assumes that each criterion has a tendency of monotonically increasing or decreasing utility which leads to easily define the positive and the negative ideal solutions. To evaluate the relative closeness of the alternatives to the ideal solution Euclidean distance approach is proposed. A series of comparisons of these relative distances will provide the preference order of the alternatives. The TOPSIS method first converts the various criteria dimensions into non-dimensional criteria similar to ELECTRE method [4] The concept of TOPSIS is that the chosen alternative should have the shortest distance from the positive ideal solution (PIS) and the farthest from the negative ideal solution (NIS). This method is used for ranking purpose and to get the best performance in multi criteria decision making. FUZZY TOPSIS method is used to evaluate the criteria in each region and then all the criteria have been ranked based on the region.

2.1.4. ELECTRE

ELECTRE (Elimination EtChoix Traduisant la REalite´) is one of the MCDM methods and this method allows decision makers to select the best choice with utmost advantage and least conflict in the function of various criteria. The ELECTRE method is used for choosing the best action from a given set of actions and was later referred to as ELECTRE I. Different versions of ELECTRE have been developed including ELECTRE I, II, III, IV and TRI. All methods are based on the same fundamental concepts but differ both operationally and according to the type of the decision problem [5]. Specifically, ELECTRE I is intended for selection problems, ELECTRE TRI for assignment problems and ELECTRE II, III and IV for ranking problems. The main idea is the proper utilization of "outranking relations". ELECTRE creates the possibility to model a decision process by using coordination indices. These indices are concordance and discordance matrices. The decision maker uses concordance and discordance indices to analyze outranking relations among different alternatives and to choose the best alternative using the crisp data.

2.1.5. Grey Theory

Grey Theory has a high mathematical analysis of the systems which are partly known and partly unknown and is defined as "insufficient data" and "weak knowledge".

When the decision-making process is not obvious Grey Theory examines the interactional analysis, there exist a great number of input data and it is distinct and insufficient. In the recent years, many decision making problems uses Grey Theory methodology in a successful manner [6].

Above listed MCDM methods have been applied widely to find best alternative when choices and criteria are high. These methods have been selected according to nature of the decision making. For selection of best ELECTRE have been applied, for ranking TOPSIS have been applied which chooses the best and Grey theory have been applied to chose the best where complete data is not available. The next section discusses about applications of these Fuzzy MCDM methods.

Apart from the MCDM methods which are listed, many other MCDM methods are available which have been listed below with its purpose, advantages and disadvantages. The suitability of each method and problem in which it can be applied has been described in Table 1. The merits and demerits of various MCDM methods have been described in Table 1 as follows.

Table 1. MCDM methods with its merits and demerits

Sl. No	MCDM Methods	Description	Advantages	Disadvantages
1.	Analytic hierarchy process (AHP)	It also includes pair wise comparison of different alternatives for different criterion.	1. Flexible, intuitive and checks inconsistencies 2. Since problem is constructed into a hierarchical structure, the importance of each element becomes clear. 3. No bias in decision making	1. Irregularities in ranking 2. Additive aggregation is used. So important information may be lost. 3. More number of pair wise comparisons are needed
2	Analytic Network Process(ANP)	AHP builds the decision problem from arrangement of different goals, criteria and alternatives and pair wise comparison of the criteria to obtain the best alternative	1. Independence among elements is not required. 2. Prediction is accurate because priorities are improved by feedback.	1. Time consuming 2. Uncertainty – not supported 3. Hard to convince decision making
3.	Data envelopment analysis (DAE)	DAE is a method where it is used to find the efficiency of combination of multi inputs and multi outputs of the problem.	1. Multiple inputs and outputs can be handled. 2. Relation between inputs and outputs are not necessary. 3. Comparisons are directly against peers 4.Inputs and outputs can have very different units	1.Measurement error can cause significant problems 2. Absolute efficiency cannot be measured. 3. Statistical tests are not applicable. 4. Large problems can be demanding.
4	Aggregated Indices Randomization method (AIRM)	This method solves the complex problem where uncertainty occurs which has incomplete information for the problem to be solved.	1. Non-numeric, non-exact and non-complete expert information can be used to solve multi criteria decision making problems. 2. Transparent mathematical foundation assures exactness and reliability of results.	It aims only at complex objects multi-criteria estimation under uncertainty.
5.	Weighted Product model(WPM)	Alternatives are being compared with the other by the weights and ratio of one for each criterion.	1. Can remove any unit of measure. 2. Relative values are used rather than actual ones.	No solution with equal weight of DMs
6.	Weighted Sum Model (WSM)	It is used for evaluating a number of alternatives in accordance to the different criteria which are expressed in the same unit.	Strong in a single dimensional problems	Difficulty emerges on multi-dimensional problems
7.	Goal Programming	Goal programming is a division where it has more than one objective which conflicts with each other, and by arranging the goals or target have to be achieved by minimizing the irrelevant information.	1. Handles large numbers of variables, constraints and objectives. 2. Simplicity and ease of use	1. Setting of appropriate weights. 2. Solutions are not pair to efficient.
8.	ELECTRE	It is used to select the best choice with maximum advantage and least conflict in the function of various criteria	Outranking is used	Time consuming
9.	Grey analysis	This methods deal with all incomplete data and to overcome the deficiencies of other methods.	Perfect information has a unique solution	Does not provide optimal solution.

Table 1 has described advantages and disadvantages of each of the MCDM method. The next section describes various applications of Fuzzy MCDM methods from the literature.

2.2. Applications of FMCDM

FMCDM is used in various domains such as banking, performance elevation, decision making in different organization, safety assessment, multi choice general purpose problems, and etc. This section discuss about the various FMCDMS methods and its application domains.

2.2.1. Fuzzy MCDM Applications

Fuzzy occurs in various business organizations when multiple choices are available to take the best decision. For example for supplier selection for an organization is one of the multi criteria decision making problem which includes both quantitative and qualitative factors [7]. In order to choose the best supplier it is essential to make a

trade-off between these tangible and intangible factors some of which may conflict. The process of determining the suitable suppliers, who are capable of providing the right quality product or services at the right price at the right time and in the right quantities to the buyers, is one of the most critical activities for establishing an effective supply chain. To solve this various FMCDM methods such as TOPSIS, ELECTRE and AHP have been applied. ELECTRE is used to reach close to the positive and get move off from negative points.

Safety issues are really at the core of marine engineering. In marine engineering the safety comes on, how the crew members understand the urge of risk and how the members effectively manage it is very important [8]. For this purpose fuzzy techniques such as TOPSIS, ELECTRE, and AHP have been applied to find best safety measures. Fuzzy MCDM methods also have been applied in areas such as location planning [9], revision of OWA operator problems [10] etc., which are described in Table 2.

Table 2. FMCDM applications in business domain

Application	Alternatives	Criteria	Problem	Techniques	Best alternative
Location planning for urban distribution centers under uncertainty [9]	3 Different Areas A1 A2 A3	1.Accessibility 2.Security 3.Connectivity to multimodal transport 4. Costs 5.Environmental impact 6. Proximity to customers 7. Proximity to suppliers 8. Resource availability	Location planning for urban distribution centers is vital in saving distribution costs and minimizing traffic congestion arising from goods movement in urban areas.	TOPSIS	A1 >A3 >A2. A1 is the best area
Revising the OWA operator problems under uncertainty (A case study) [11]	1. Sahand 2. Shahriar 3. Kalghan 4.Germichai 5. Givi 6. Taleghan 7. Talvar 8. Galabar 9. Sanghsiah 10. Soral 11. Siazakh 12. Bijar	1.Allocation of water to prior usages 2.Number of beneficiaries 3.Supporting other projects 4.Benefit/cost 5.Range of environmental impacts 6.Publicparticipation 7.Jobcreation	In finding the most robust alternative among these seven criteria	FSROWA Fuzzy-Stochastic-Revised Ordered Weighted Averaging (FSROWA) method is applied.	Germ chai project is the most preferred project
Enhancing information delivery in extended enterprise networks [27]	P1, P2, P3, P4, P5 (information receivers)	1. partner's price range 2. partner's interest to information 3. partner's product range	To find the best supplier for mold and die manufacturing concern, the product price range, the information receiver's interest and the product range are often considered by enterprises.	FMCDS	P2
Evaluating anti-armor weapon using ranking fuzzy numbers [28]	1. Dragon 2. Milan and 3. Sword (weapon systems)	1. basic capability 2. fight capability 3.logisticmaintenance 4. electronic system	Fuzzy multi criteria decision support procedure is applied to non-quantitative factors where decision making is complex.	Fuzzy multi attribute decision making	Sword
Evaluation suppliers in supply chain management [7]	1.Suppiler 1 2.Suppiler 2 3.Suppiler 3 4.Suppiler 4 5.Suppiler 5	1.Urgent delivery 2.On time delivery 3.Ordering cost 4.Warranty period 5.Product price 6.Financial stability 7.Delivery lead time 8.Accessibility 9.Reliability 10.Transportation cost 11.Rejection of defective product 12.Cost ot support service 13.Testability	Supplier selection, the process of determining the suitable suppliers who are able to provide the buyer with the right quality products and/or services at the right price, at the right time and in the right quantities.	TOPSIS	Supplier 3

A fuzzy multi-criteria decision making model for supplier selection [12]	1.Saudi Arabian for Packaging Industry (SAPIN), 2.Arabian Can Industry (ACI), 3. ZA Turkish Supplier 4. Al-Watonga for Containers Manufacturing (CMC)	1.unit price and payment terms 2.delivery terms 3.supplier factory capacity 4.shipping method 5.lead time 6.location of can supplier 7.technical specifications 8.Services and communications with the supplier 9.compensationfor waste 10,major customers with the same business 11.certificate of Supplier	For the selection of cans supplier/Suppliers at Nitrides Factory in Amman-Jordan to demonstrate the proposed model.	1.Modified fuzzy DEMATEL model, 2.A modified TOPSIS model	SAPIN
Examine the use and application of MCDM techniques in safety assessment [29]	3 DIFFERENT COMPNANY 1.C1 2.C2 3.C3	1.Cost-control 2.Detailed information about the crewmembers and their behavior 3.availability of presenting data per ship 4.comparsion with industry 5. Planning, preview and scenarios of risk management.	To enhance safety by mitigating risks and increasing the reliability of a system.	1.TOPSIS 2.ELECTRE 3.AHP	C2
Multi-criteria decision making approach based on immune co-evolutionary algorithm with application to garment matching problem [13]	65 trousers with the same color, style and material for female are studied	waist girth (W), hip girth (H), and trousers length (L)	To solve the large scale garment matching problem where Size fitting problem is a main obstacle to large scale garment sales and online sales because it is difficult to find the fit garments by the general size information	co-evolutionary immune algorithm for the MCDM model	The product which satisfies the "CUSTOMER SATISFACTION and SERVICE QUALITY " the most
An incident information management framework based on data integration, data mining, and multi-criteria decision making [14]	1.Beijing 2.Tianjin 3.Hebei 4.Chongqing 5.Xinjiang(31 provinces)	1.Percentage of areas covered to total areas 2. Percentage of areas affected to total areas (Drought Flood Hailstorm Frost)	A case study on agro meteorological disasters that occurred in China between 1997 and 2001. This case study demonstrates that the combination of data mining and MCDM methods can provide objective and comprehensive assessments of incident risks.	TOWA operator, cluster analysis, grey relational analysis, and TOPSIS	Chongqing
Assessment of health-care waste treatment alternatives using fuzzy multi-criteria decision making approaches [15]	1.Incineration 2. Steam sterilization 3.Microwave 4. Landfill	1.Economic 2.Environmental 3.Technical 4.Social	The objective of this research is to propose multi-criteria decision making techniques for conducting an analysis based on multi-level hierarchical structure and fuzzy logic for the evaluation of HCW treatment alternatives.	fuzzy MCDM methodology, hierarchical distance-based fuzzy MCDM algorithm	Landfill
Comparative analysis of multi-criteria decision making methodologies and implementation of a warehouse location selection problem [6]	1. Warehouse A 2. Warehouse B 3. Warehouse C 4. Warehouse D	1.Unit price 2.Stock holding capacity 3.Average Distance to shops 4.Average distance to main suppliers 5.Movement Flexibility	To compare the MCDM methods and implementation of a warehouse location selection problem	AHP, TOPSIS, ELECTRE and Grey Theory	WAREHOUSE
Health- Safety and Environmental Risk Assessment of Refineries Using of Multi Criteria Decision Making Method [16]	Power plant 1. location 1 2. location 2 3. location 3 4. location 4	1.environment of the power plant, 2.health-safety risks, 3.technological risks, 4.the affected environment risks	To find the best location for the implementation of the power plant using the AHP	AHP	Location 3

Mathematical analysis of fuel cell strategic technologies development solutions in the automotive industry [17]	1.Professional manpower on industrial & semi-industrial scale 2.Professional manpower on laboratory scale 3.Know-how on industrial & semi-industrial scale 4.Know-how on laboratory scale 5.Hardware on industrial & semi-industrial scale 6.Hardware on laboratory scale	1. Power density 2. Efficiency system of fuel cells 3. Fuel type (Including the effect on fuel cells operation, process stages, availability, cost, safety and environment considerations) 4. Life time and preserving fuel cells 5. Operational heat, start-up period, reaction period and response of fuel cells 6. Security and confidence	The analysis of fuel cell strategic technology in the automotive industry using TOPSIS	TOPSIS	Professional manpower on laboratory scale

*[12] - Unit price and payment terms (C1), delivery terms (C2), supplier factory capacity (C3), shipping method (C4), lead time (C5), location of can supplier (C6), technical specifications (C7), certifications (Regular and International) (C8), services and communications with the supplier (C9), compensation for waste (C10), printing complies to design and color (C11), easy open and spoon leveling (C12), testing methods for packaging materials and available tests from supplier (C13), variation of dimensions (C14), stretch wrapping and clean separators, pallet size and height (C15), major customers with the same business (C16), certificate of supplier materials (C17), SAPIN - Saudi Arabian Packaging Industry, ACI - Arabian Can Industry, CMC - Containers Manufacturing.

*[14] - Incident information management framework consists of three major components. The first component is a high-level data integration module in which heterogeneous data sources are integrated and presented in a uniform format. The second component is a data mining module that uses data mining methods to identify useful patterns and presents a process to provide differentiated services for pre-incident and post-incident information management. The third component is a multi-criteria decision-making (MCDM) module that utilizes MCDM methods to assess the current situation, find the satisfactory solutions, and take appropriate responses in a timely manner

*[15] -Sub criteria: Economic: Capital cost, Operating cost, Environmental: Solid residuals and environmental impacts, Water residuals and environmental impacts, Air residuals and environmental impacts, Release with health effects. Technical: Reliability, Volume reduction, Need for skilled operators, Occupational hazards occurrence impact, Treatment effectiveness, Level of automation, Occupational hazards occurrence frequency. Social: Adaptability to environmental policy, Land requirement, Public acceptance obstacles

Table 2 describes some the application of Fuzzy MCDM in various disciplines. In some applications uncertainty in decision making arises, so fuzzy multi criteria decision making is chosen to solve this issue. The criteria used in urban distribution centers such as security, accessibility, cost, and environment [9]. The sensitivity analysis is performed to determine the influence of criteria and weights on location planning is applied to find the suitable locations. The selection of location for placing the watershed which is using the new method FSROWA is introduced to combine the Fuzzy and Stochastic features into a revised OWA operator, for choosing the effective place for the location of the water shed [10]. To search the best place for urban Centre distribution all the places are ranked based on criteria.

The co-evolutionary immune algorithm for the multi-criteria decision making (MCDM) model, is used for the model to solve the large scale garment matching problem. Size fitting problem is a main obstacle to large scale garment sales and online sales because it is difficult to find the fit garments by the general size information. This study regards the fit garment matching problem as a MCDM model with the constraints of size satisfaction. An immune co-evolutionary algorithm is used to search the fit garments from the candidate garments in the stock [33]. Health-care waste (HCW) management is a high priority environmental, public and health concern in developing countries. The management and treatment of HCW are gaining more attention with the rising awareness. The proposed decision approaches enable the decision-makers to use linguistic terms, and thus, reduce their cognitive burden in the evaluation process. By using MCDM, the evaluation of multi-level hierarchical structure and fuzzy logic for HCW treatment can be obtained [15].

An effective incident information management system deals with several challenges. Decision makers have to detect variance and extract useful knowledge. Different services to satisfy the requirements of different incident management phases. Multi-criteria decision-making assess the current situation, finds the satisfactory solutions, and takes appropriate responses in a timely manner [14].To compare the performance of different MCDM methods such as AHP, TOPSIS, ELECTRE (I, II, IS, III, IV and A), Grey theory a case study on warehouse selection have been selected and different characteristic of each method is discussed [6].

AHP method is used in the analysis of the health - safety and environmental risk assessment of refineries for the location of the power plant, the risk factor such as health-safety risk, technology risk, etc., have been considered [16]. To select best strategic technology for the fuel cell in the automotive industry TOPSIS have been applied [17].

From all these works, different methods have been used for different applications where each of the method has its own characteristics in finding the best alternatives. The applications which are developed to solve multi choice problems and FMCDS methods which are chosen provides better performance in cases such as supplier chain management in business applications, safety assessment in marine engineering, watershed location and urban distribution centers in public sectors.

2.2.2. FMCDM in Banking

To process the mortgage or loan applications banks have a fixed set of criteria. After going through the criteria the decisions are made rigidly by the bank officers. This process can be made easier and more efficient using fuzzy logic. Nowadays, banks are increasingly turning to intelligent banking solutions like artificial intelligence to screen out many loan applications to make the final recommendation and approval. Banks can save valuable man-hours and dedicate the resources to other productive one by means of using these approaches. Therefore, it improves the bank processes efficiency and lowers the operating cost for the bank. Table 3 describes some of the bank applications which describe FMCDS.

Table 3. FMCDM applications in banking domain

Application	Alternatives	Criteria	Problem	Techniques	Best alternative
Banking performance based on Balanced Scorecard.[18]	Three banks 1.C Bank, 2.S Bank, and 3.U Bank	1. Finance 2. Customer 3.Internal Process 4. Learning and Growth	To rank the banking performance and improve the gaps with three banks as an empirical example.	The three MCDM analytical tools of 1. SAW, 2. TOPSIS, 3. VIKOR	"U Bank"
Fuzzy performance evaluation in Turkish Banking Sector using Analytic Hierarchy Process and TOPSIS.[19]	The largest five commercial banks of Turkish Banking sector are examined and these banks are evaluated in terms of several financial and non-financial indicators	**Financial criteria:** 1. Asset quality 2. Capital adequacy 3. Liquidity 4. Profitability 5. Income and expenditure **Non Financial criteria:** 1.Pricing 2.Marketing 3.Productivity 4.Delivery services	To maintain the performance of the banking system since the economy is changing rapidly.	1.Fuzzy sets and fuzzy numbers 2.FAHP 3.TOPSIS	Customer satisfaction and Service quality have been evaluated for commercial banks.
The impact of 3D e-readiness on e-banking development in Iran: A fuzzy AHP Analysis. [30]	1. Human resource readiness 2. Top management readiness 3. Strategy readiness 4. Structure readiness 5. Technology readiness	1. organizational e-readiness 2. industry e- 3. macro environmental e-readiness	New information technologies and emerging business forces have triggered a new wave of financial innovation–electronic banking (e-banking).	Fuzzy AHP	Top management readiness and strategy readiness

Table 3 describes the various applications of Fuzzy MCDM in banking sector. However, intelligent banking systems has seen its usefulness enhanced with breakthroughs in technology such as fuzzy logic, there is still a need of human interpretation that must be used in dealing with sensitive transactions. It is a still a long way before intelligent banking system can do away with human interaction at all levels. Fuzzy logic allows a computer to reach a decision based on a myriad of factors with different levels of importance [21]. Rather than a yes or no answer, fuzzy logic application reaches a decision based on the weight given to the factors. The artificial intelligence in the application will compare all the potential results both positive and negative before coming to a final conclusion. Fuzzy logic applications using artificial intelligence often make use of neural networks to process the task.

Banking is the sector where fuzzy may occur many times, to overcome this fuzzy MCDM is applied. The fuzzy multi criteria decision making is very much useful in banking application and the performance evaluation of banks has important results for creditors, investors and stakeholder's since it determines banks' capabilities to compete in the sector and has a critical importance for the development of the sector [19].

The threat for E-Banking is identifying any phishing websites in real-time is really a complex and dynamic problem involving many factors and criteria [22]. The banking and financial industry is transforming itself in unpredictable ways powered in an important way by advances in information technology. Methods like TOPSIS, AHP, FAHP, FBCC and FSBM have been applied in e-banking.

In credit limit allocation model for banks all the criteria have been identified and each criteria assign weight by the experts group, and then criteria have been grouped in region wise [23]. The FUZZY TOPSIS method is used to evaluate the criteria in each region and then all the criteria have been ranked. Liner programming assigns credit risk concentration limits to the regional heads such that the total value of capital from all location (TVCA) becomes maximum.

The studied works gives an overview of applications of FMCDM where the different methods have been applied and used. Fuzzy is a technique which is widely used where uncertainty occurs, where the judgment of the result is not clear and optimal, the fuzzy weights have been assigned to each criterion and they have been evaluated. In banking sector FMCDM is used to overcome the uncertainty which was the drawback of the system. It is also being used in E- Banking where users often tend to have problem or dilemma in selecting the links where there is a threat of hacking the passwords through spam mails and hence fuzzy have been applied to identify the phishing web sites and links. The below sections explains about the performance evaluation of MCDM applications.

2.2.3. Fuzzy MCDM in Performance Evaluation

Not only general domains, the Fuzzy MCDM methods also applied to evaluate the performance of organization. Table 4 describes FMCDM methods to evaluate the performance of organizations. By applying COPRAS-G method the performance of a teacher has been computed. This method is adapted to utilize numerical scores in the form of interval marking. Common methodologies reported in past research can handle quantitative numerical score. These methods cannot consider interval making assigned to a particular item whereas COPRAS-G method overcomes this drawback [24].

In Evaluation of training performance of administrative instructors fuzzy set theory is applied to measurement the

performance. AHP is applied to obtain criteria weight and for ranking TOPSIS is applied. To evaluate decision alternatives involving subjective judgments made by a group of decision makers, fuzzy MCDM approach is used. A linguistic rating method is used for making absolute judgments and a pair-wise comparison process is used to help individual decision makers to make comparative judgments [4].

Table 4. FMCDM in Performance evaluation

Application	Alternatives	Criteria	Problem	Techniques	Best alternative
Application of MCDM approaches on teachers' performance evaluation and appraisal	5 teachers' T1 T2 T3 T4 T5	1.Interaction with students 2.Time taken for Problem solving (decision making) 3.Depth of knowledge in own field 4.Dedication, Punctuality and involvement 5.Pedagogy of teaching	To find the best teachers using MCDM technique. The performance and appraisal of each teacher are done separately.	COPRAS-G	T3
Training Performance Evaluation of Administration Sciences Instructors by Fuzzy MCDM Approach [4]	4 Instructor Instructor A Instructor B Instructor C Instructor D	1.Teaching style, 2.Individual features and social relation, 3.Knowledge level, 4. Observance of educational regulations 5.Educational tools.	To find the best trainee and the performance of the administrative science instructors	FMCDM	Instructor A
Power customer satisfaction and profitability analysis using MCDM [26]	A1, A2 A3 A4	cost, reliability, availability, maintainability and power quality	To investigate appropriate tools (MCDM) aiding decision makers to achieve their goals.	Analytic Hierarchy Process (AHP)	A2
Multi-criteria decision-making method based on interval-valued intuitionist fuzzy sets. [27]	1. A car company; 2. A food company; 3. A computer company; 4. An arms company.	1.The risk analysis; 2. The growth analysis; 3. The environmental impact analysis	To find the best company for investment of money in the 4 company using the interval valued intuitionist fuzzy sets.	interval-valued intuitionist fuzzy information	A2 >A4 >A3 >A1

*[26] - Alternative 1 (A1): Corresponds to the actual state of the electric power system under study, Alternative 2 (A2): Faults detectors are installed at each substation; consequently the time to fault research is reduced. Alternative 3 (A3): To alternative 2 (A2), are added remote control switches on outgoing MV lines to reduce the number of customers concerned by a failure. Alternative 4 (A4): Some overhead circuits are undergrounded and sections of the aging cables are replaced by new ones (are concerned the sections with a number of joints exceeding the threshold value).

The performance evaluation is used to measure the performance of the employee in the organization. Evaluations are utilized to determine whether the employee meets the certain criteria and to recommend appropriate follow-up actions. During the evaluation of performance uncertainty occurs, so MCDM approach is applied to measure the performance issues. In Teachers performance evolution many alternatives and criteria are applied to analyze the performance of teachers and best teacher is identified using COPRAS-G. In the same way to analyze the training administrative instructor's performance various criteria such as the knowledge level, problem solving skills and cognitive abilities have been considered [4].

Consumer demands for electrical energy are increasingly growing, because this energy is present in all the fields of human activity. The alternatives are technical and the organizational measures often taken in planning and operation phases of electrical power systems is to investigate appropriate tools (multi-criteria decision making methods) aiding decision makers to achieve the goals like customer satisfaction and profit making [26]. Multi-criteria decision-making method based on interval-valued intuitionist fuzzy sets which is used for determining the best company(a car company, a food company, a computer company, an arms company) to invest the money to obtain more profit [16].

3. Findings of Survey

Multi criteria decision making and its applications have been discussed in this survey. The multi criteria decision making is one of the powerful tool for obtaining the best choice for a complex decision making situations using various methods such as Fuzzy AHP, ELECTRE, TOPSIS, Grey theory etc. The evaluation of the criteria and ranking the criteria to find the best alternative have been found using MCDM techniques. The outcome of this survey has been described below.

3.1 MCDM is the Powerful Technique for Decision Making

The MCDM is used in many application such as performance evaluation, warehouse location, supplier selection, supply chain management, Assessment of health-care waste treatment, Banking performance, e-banking, teachers' performance and in various multi choice selection process. The decision making in all these application is efficient and best alternative have been found. Table 5 describes about various applications of MCDM techniques.

Table 5. Application of MCDM

MCDM Applications		
Banking performance	Performance mgmt.	Selection process
Business performance	Partner selection	Risk mgmt.
Automotive industry	Environment assessment	Mold and Die Industry
Education	Health care	Marine egg.
Financial investment decisions	Financial ratios and business performance	Manufacturing systems
Demand forecasting	Material selection	Bioinformatics

The performance of the MCDM is very high in the business organization which is used to solve the complexity of the problem. MCDM is used in all real world application such as warehouse location, environment assessment. The performance of the organization is developed by better solution which can be obtained by MCDM. In the business, the collections of relevant information have been done, to provide the better solution for the problem. The relevant information is very useful in the making the decision in the complex problem which occurs in the organization. The methods of MCDM are unique in there characteristic, which can be used in the certain problem that suits there characteristic. For example, the TOPSIS method, that has chosen the best alternative based on a maximization of the distance from the negative ideal point and minimization of the distance from the positive ideal point. Grey theory methods, examines the interactional analysis when the decision-making process is not clear, there are a great number of input data and it is discrete and insufficient data.

3.2. Fuzzy MCDM Application and Fuzzy MCDM Methods

The fuzzy multi criteria techniques have been applied in various fields such as Banking sectors, issues such as urban distribution centers, water shed allocation, safety assessment, and performance evolution of business organizations. The statistical report for the some of the areas in which multi criteria decision making is used is described in Table 6.

Table 6. Domain Vs. FMCDS application

S.No.	Banking	Business	Environment assessment	Performance evaluation
1	To evaluate Banking performance based on Balanced Scorecard	To find the best supplier for mold and die manufacturing concern in the enterprises	Location planning for urban distribution centers	To find the best teachers using MCDM technique. The performance and appraisal of each teacher are
2	To analysis performance of the banking system during economy is changing rapidly	Finding the best supplier who is able to provide the right quality products and/or services at the right price with the right quantities and at the right time.	In finding the most robust alternative among these seven criteria for water planet location	To find the best trainee and the performance of the administrative science instructors
3	To detect the phishing mails	Supplier selection, in selecting the best suppliers who are able to provide the buyer with the right quality products	To enhance safety by mitigating risks and increasing the reliability of a system.	To find the best company for investment of money in the 4 company using the interval valued intuitionist fuzzy sets.
4	New information technologies and emerging business forces in banking	For the selection of cans supplier/Suppliers at Nitrides Factory in Amman-Jordan	Evaluation of HCW treatment alternatives	to investigate Appropriate tools (multi-criteria decision making methods) aiding decision makers to achieve these goals
5	Data envelopment analysis (DEA) mainly utilizes envelopment technology to replace production function in microeconomics	-	Implementation of a warehouse location selection problem	-
6	-	-	To find the best location for the implementation of the power plant using the AHP	-
Contr.	5	4	6	4

Table 6 describes the analysis report of the multi criteria techniques which is widely used in various applications. Table 6, also describes the clear essence of the domains in which MCDM is applied. Most of the multi criteria based problems fuzzy MCDM approach is applied due to its capability of solving uncertainty issues and it gives the best determination for the decision makers, so that MCDM method is used in many domains. Each MCDM method is chosen according to difficulty of the problem. Table 7 describes about most widely applied methods in multi criteria decision making and these methods are ranked based on its applicability and usage in various domains.

Table 7. MCDM Methods and its usage

S. No	MCDM Methods	Contributions
1	FMCDM	5
2	TOPSIS	9
3	FAHP	6
4	VIKOR	2
5	ELECTRE	5
6	Others	3

A graph is plotted to indicate the usage of MCDM methods in the various applications in the survey work. Most widely applied methods in decision making problem such as TOPSIS, ELECTRE, FAHP, FMCDM, VIKOR and there are others methods such fuzzy DEMATEL,

FSROWA, Fuzzy BCC, Fuzzy SBM etc have been   applied in few works.

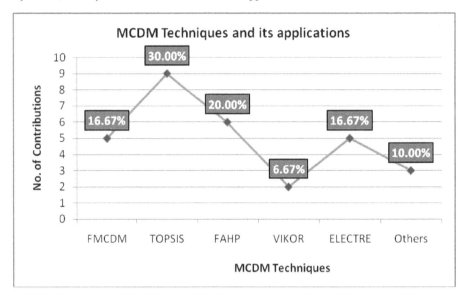

Figure 2. MCDM methods and its contributions

From the Figure 2 it known that TOPSIS method is applied mostly in many applications. The next is FMCDM method that has been used in the fuzzy application for solving the uncertainty. A Fuzzy MCDM is an approach for evaluating decision alternatives involving subjective judgments made by a group of decision makers. A pair-wise comparison process is used to help individual decision makers to make comparative judgments, and a linguistic rating method is used for making absolute judgments. The other methods are Fuzzy BCC, Fuzzy SBM, FSROWA and COPRAS-G. This survey outlines research opportunities in MCDM, the features of MCMD can be applied to any domain when multiple choices are available for decision making. The next sub section discuss the difference between fuzzy AHP methods,

3.3. Comparison of AHP and Fuzzy AHP

Analytic hierarchy process AHP is a method used for ranking purpose in selecting the best one when the decision maker has multiple criteria. This method helps the decision makers to select a better alternative from all by satisfying the minimal score to rank each decision alternative based on how well each alternative meets them. Fuzzy AHP, where it helps the human to make quantitative predictions as they are not well versed, but they are equally better in making quantitative forecasting. The uncertainty occurs during the judgments where in turn in consistency arises in between the alternatives.

Fuzzy pair wise comparisons states that there are many criteria's but if any criteria has a less important among all then it can be weighed as zero unlike other methods. Though that criterion is handled for the decision making process, if it has no importance when compared to all others. In the classic AHP method, deterministic values and operations do not permits such a situation "having zero weighed", but if a criterion is evaluated as less than all of the others, then the numerical weight of the criteria will be near to zero. Fuzzy AHP can merely ignore the criteria that have less importance whereas the classic AHP where it will be given with so weight. This can also be an advantage for fuzzy-AHP presenting additional

information for decision maker that there is no difference between the existence and nonexistence of such a criterion. Therefore, the decision maker can focus on more important criteria.

Classical and fuzzy methods are not the rivals with each other at same conditions. The important point is that if the information / evaluations are certain, classical method should be chosen; if the information / evaluations are not certain, fuzzy method should be chosen. In recent years, because of the uniqueness of information and decision makers, probable deviation should be integrated to the decision making processes, and because of that for each decision making method, a fuzzy version is developed. Fuzzy AHP method is a natural result of this necessity. Linguistic and subjective evaluations take place in questionnaire form. Each linguistic variable has its own numerical value in the predefined scale. In classical AHP these numerical values are exact numbers whereas in fuzzy AHP method they are intervals between two numbers.

3.4. Comparison of ELECTRE, TOPSIS and GREY THEORY

TOPSIS method selects the best alternative by minimizing the distance from the positive ideal point and maximizing the distance from the negative ideal point, was not only applied to areas such as performance evaluation but also applied to problems such as selection of production processes and flexible manufacturing systems, within the operation management scope. Similarly, ELECTRE methods (ELECTRE I, IS, II, III, IV, A) selects the best alternative by means of all alternatives pairwise comparison; within the decision problems, especially has been applied to solve the issues present in environmental valuation and environmental management.

Grey Theory has a high mathematical analysis of the systems which are partly known and partly unknown and is defined as "insufficient data" and "weak knowledge". When the decision-making process is not obvious Grey Theory examines the interactional analysis, there exist a great number of input data and it is distinct and insufficient. In the recent years [6], many decision making problems such as financial performance evaluation, supplier selection facility layout selection, demand forecasting and material selection uses Grey Theory methodology in a successful manner.

3.4.1. The Main Process

Using different calculation methods, decision making methodologies are separated from each others. The steps required separating from other decision making methods and the important solution algorithm are named as the core process [6].

TOPSIS:

In TOPSIS methodology, the distance calculation from the positive ideal and the negative ideal solutions of each alternative draws attention. The algorithm for TOPSIS method is as follows,

Step 1: By using the alternatives m and criteria n we calculate the normalized values (R_{ij})

$$R_{ij} = \frac{A_{ij}}{\sqrt{\sum_{i=1}^{m} A_{ij}^2}} \quad i = 1,2,3...m, j = 1,2,...n \quad (1)$$

Step 2: The normalized values can be obtained by giving weights to the criteria (V_{ij})

$$V_{ij} = W_j * A_{ij}, i = 1,2,3...m, j = 1,2,...n \quad (2)$$

Step 3: The best performance (s^+) and worst perform (s^+) for every ideal alternative is determined.

$$s^+ = \left\{v_{1j}, v_{2j}, v_{3j}..., v_{mj}\right\} = \left\{\max v_{ij} \, for \forall j \in n\right\} \quad (3)$$

$$s^- = \left\{v_{1j}, v_{2j}, v_{3j}..., v_{mj}\right\} = \left\{\min v_{1j} \, for \forall j \in n\right\} \quad (4)$$

Step 4: For all the criteria, every alternatives distance to the best alternatives (D_i^+) using (3) and worst alternative (D_i^-) using (4)

$$D_i^+ = \sqrt{\sum_{j=1}^{n} (v_{ij} - s_j^+)^2} \quad for \, i = 1,2,...m \quad (5)$$

$$D_i^- = \sqrt{\sum_{j=1}^{n} (v_{ij} - s_j^-)^2} \, for \, i = 1,2,..m \quad (6)$$

Step 5: The positive ideal solution (C_i) is calculated using (5) and (6).

$$C_i = \frac{D_i^-}{D_i^- + D_i^+} \quad i = 1,2,...m \, and \, 0 \le C_i \le 1$$

The biggest (C_i) value is chosen as best selection and solution for the MDCM problem is obtained through TOPSIS.

ELECTRE:

While ELECTRE I and ELECTRE II methods are differs from the other methods through the determination of concordance and discordance matrices for each criterion and alternative pair. ELECTRE III method

differs from the other methods and it is based on the principle of fuzzy logic and uses the preference and indifference thresholds while determining the concordance and discordance indexes. The algorithm for the ELECTRE I method is given as,

The first two steps are same as TOPSIS. The weighed normalized values are calculated using the equation (1) and (2).

The C_{kl} concordance matrix elements is calculated,

$$C_{kl} = \sum_{j \in C_{kl}} W_j .$$

The D_{kl} discordance matrix element is calculated,

$$D_{kl} = \frac{\max\left\{V_{kj} - V_{ij}\right\} j \in D_{kl}}{\max\left\{\left|V_{kj} - V_{ij}\right|\right\} j \in V_j} \quad \text{Concordance} \quad \text{threshold}$$

(C_{avr}) and discordance threshold (D_{avr}) is calculated.

The last step, according to the condition $C_{kl} \ge C_{avr}$ and $D_{kl} \ge D_{avr}$ is calculated and the best alternative is selected.

GREY THEORY:

Step 1: The data set are created based on the criteria $C_0 = \left\{C_1, C_2, C_3, \cdots\right\}$

Step 2: $C_i = \left\{C_{i1}, C_{i2}, C_{i3}, \cdots\right\}$ comparison data is determined which shows the performance values of each alternatives against the criteria, where i=1,2,3..k, where k defines the alternative number.

The maximum performance indicator of the criteria is calculated as follows,

$$V_i(l) = \frac{V_i(l) - \min V_i(l)}{\max V_i(l) - \min V_i(l)} \quad (7)$$

The minimum performance indicator of the criteria is calculated.

$$V_i(l) = \frac{\max V_i(l) - V_i(l)}{\max V_i(l) - \min V_i(l)} \quad (8)$$

The optimum value performance indicator of the criteria is calculated

$$V_i(l) = 1 - \frac{\left|V_i(l) - U_i\right|}{\max\left|V_i(l) - U_i\right|} \quad (9)$$

The normalized data is calculated from equations (7), (8) and (9).

Step 3: The distance between data sets are calculated using $\Delta_i = \left(\left|d_{01} - d_{i1}\right|, \left|d_{02} - d_{i2}\right| \cdots \cdots \left|d_{0m} - d_{im}\right|\right)$ with global maximum (Δ_{max}) and global minimum (Δ_{min}).

Step 4: Each data point in difference set is changed into Grey Relational Coefficient. Grey Relational Coefficient of the data point "j" in difference set "i" is calculated using the formula:

$$C_i \gamma_i(j) = \frac{\Delta_{min} + \xi \Delta_{max}}{\Delta_i(j) + \xi \Delta_{max}}$$

$\Delta_i(j)$, Δ_i is the j. value in the difference set. Coefficient n is a value between 0 and 1, and is used to decrease the effect of Δ_{max}, which is the extreme value in the data set. This coefficient is taken as 0.5 in most problems.

Step 6: The grey relational grade of alternative (i) is calculated:

$$r_i = \sum_{n=1}^{m} \left(\gamma_i(n) * w(n) \right)$$

The criteria are ranked according to their grey relational grade, the priority ranking is obtained and best alternative is selected.

3.4.2. Number of Outranking Relationship and its Type

Many number of pair wise comparison matrix exist which leads to a disadvantage of AHP and the opportunity of carrying out the methodology is prevented when the number of alternative and criteria are huge. ELECTRE I and TOPSIS methodologies needless input is compared with AHP and the necessity of pairwise comparison is eliminated.

3.4.3. The Consistency Control

One of the most important advantages of AHP is the limitation of consistency. In methods like TOPSIS, ELECTRE I and ELECTRE II the consistency is not controlled. Furthermore, since it is necessary to make pairwise comparisons in all the levels of hierarchy, as the number of alternatives and criteria gets increased, it gets harder to perform AHP for more complex problems. On the other hand, AHP can be easily performed without regarding the applied data evaluation of alternatives based on criteria either is qualitative or quantitative. Based on its simplicity in perception and its usage TOPSIS method gets attention. For a problem with huge number of alternatives and criteria's, TOPSIS and ELECTRE methods can be performed easily.

4. Research Directions in MCDM

To provide the decision-maker with the ability to look into the future, and to make the best possible decision based on past and present information and future predictions is the true goal in integrated decision-making system. In the case of sustainable development, to predict in advance the risk and vulnerability of populations and infrastructure to hazards, both natural and man-induced. This requires that data be transformed into knowledge, and the consequences of information use, as well as decision-making and participatory processes, be analyzed carefully. The use of fuzzy will give only an approximate solution for problem is the conclusion obtained from the survey works. The use of fuzzy is to analyze the quantitative and qualitative data for any application. The different methods under FMCDM help us to perform may subtasks between where evaluation and ranking are done by different methods. Each method has its own uniqueness. This is how fuzzy in analyzing an application. In previous works the mapping of information has been done where what information is needed for which users, for e.g., Government needs a lots of information when compared to other users like customers, management etc, so the

further work can be enhanced by sending information to the users via correct medium and right time. The work to be done is to customize the correct information, where a student as a customer can get enough information regarding the educational loans. The visualization is mainly used to attract the users to get accessed often.

Fuzzy MCDM methods can be applied for information delivery in banking sector. In banking, loads of information's are obtained for various users like customers, government, management etc. so it's essential to deliver the correct information to the users in the way they want, each users might have they own perception of information to be delivered to them, so in banking the various needs of the users can be obtained by having many interviews from different users, making them to fill certain applications and questionnaire where they might able to capture the needs of each individual type of users, by this way the need of information delivery in banking can be improved to provide a better performance to them by customizing the information. Here comes the uncertainty in the information delivery for the user. For each user the information varies and content of the information also varies. Finding the best user and delivering right information and in user preferred channel should be delivered. The level of information also varies where different users need different information and the level of security also varies. This uncertainty problem can be solved by using FMCDM methods, which is used to provide the right information to right user in right time.

5. Conclusion

This survey finds opportunities in multi criteria decision making where decision making involves multiple choices. Fuzzy multi criteria decision making is used in many applications like Banking, performance evaluation, safety assessment and other multi criteria domains. FMCDM is applied to domains in which we need to evaluate more alternatives and multiple criteria and from that select the best alternative. According to the problem and its domain the MCDM methods have been selected. Very limited work has been applied using multi criteria decision making. This survey is concerned for banking where uncertainty occurs often in decision making. Fuzzy based MCDM is suitable for approximate problem spaces. Thus FMCDM can be applied to analyze quantitative and qualitative data of any application to arrive the solution. As it is known already there are many methods under MCDM each having its own scope of performance, the method have to be chosen in such a way for different problems that have to be solved.

References

[1] Albayrak, E., Erensal, Y. C. (2005). "A study bank selection decision in Turkey using the extended fuzzy AHP method". Proceeding of 35th International conference on computers and industrial engineering, Istanbul, Turkey.

[2] Aldlaigan, A.,Buttle, F.A.(2002). "A new measure of bank service quality". International Journal of Service Industry Management, Vol. 13, pp. 38-362.

[3] Business Credits (2006). "Non financial data can predict future profitability". BusinessCredits, Vol 108, Nbr. (4), pp.57.

[4] Nikoomaram.H, M.Mohammadi, M. JavadTaghipouria and Y. Taghipourian(2009). "Training Performance Evaluation of Administration Sciences Instructors by Fuzzy MCDM Approach". Tehran, Iran.

[5] Yusuf Tansellç, (2012) "Development of a credit limit allocation model for banks using an integrated Fuzzy TOPSIS and linear programming". Expert System with Applications. Vol. 39(5), pp. 5309-5316.

[6] TuncayOzcan, NumanCelebi,(2011) "Comparative analysis of multi-criteria decision making methodologies and implementation of a warehouse location selection problem". Vol. 38, pp.9773-9779.

[7] Mohammad SaeedZaeri, Amir Sadeghi, Amir Naderi,etal.,(2011). "Application of multi criteria decision making technique to evaluation suppliers in supply chain management", African Journal of Mathematics and Computer Science Research Vol. 4 (3), pp.100-106.

[8] Schinas O.(2007) "Examining the use and application of Multi - Criteria DecisionMaking Techniques in Safety Assessment", International Symposium on Maritime Safety, Security & Environmental Protection, Athens.

[9] Anjali Awasthia, S.S. Chauhanb, S.K. Goyalb(2000). "A multi-criteria decision making approach for location planning for urban distribution centers under uncertainty" CIISE, Montreal, Canada.

[10] T.C. Chu, (2002) "Facility location selection using fuzzy TOPSIS under group decisions", International Journal of Uncertainty, Fuzziness and Knowledge-Based Systems Vol. 10 (6), pp. 687-701.

[11] MahdiZarghami, FerencSzidarovszky(2011) "Revising the OWA operator for multi criteria decision making problems under uncertainty a Faculty of Civil Engineering ", Tabriz 51666-16471, Iran.

[12] DoraidDalalah, Mohammed Hayajneh, FarhanBatieha,(2011) ."A fuzzy multi-criteria decision making model for supplier selection", Expert Systems with Applications Vol. 38, pp. 8384-8391.

[13] Yong-Sheng Ding, Zhi-HuaHu, Wen-Bin Zhang,(2011). " Multi-criteria decision making approach based on immune co-evolutionary algorithm with application to garment matching problem", Expert Systems with Applications Vol. 38, pp.10377-10383.

[14] Yi Peng, Yong Zhang, Yu Tang, Shiming Li, (2011). "An incident information management framework based on data integration, datamining, and multi-criteria decision making ", Decision Support Systems Vol. 51, pp.316-327.

[15] MehtapDursun, E. ErtugrulKarsak,MelisAlmulaKaradayi,(2011). "Assessment of health-care waste treatment alternatives using fuzzymulti-criteria decision making approaches", Expert Systems with Applications Vol. 38, pp.10377-10383.

[16] SaharRezaiana, Seyed Ali Joziba,(2012) "Health- Safety and Environmental Risk Assessment of Refineries Using of Multi Criteria Decision Making Method", APCBEE Procedia Vol.3 , pp. 235-258.

[17] KeivanSadeghzadeh, Mohammad BagherSalehi (2011). "Mathematical analysis of fuel cell strategic technologies development solutions in the automotive industry by the TOPSIS multi-criteria decision making method" , International journal of hydrogen energy Vol. 3 6, pp.13272-13280.

[18] Hung-Yi Wua, Gwo-HshiungTzenga,b, Yi-Hsuan Chen c(2011). "A fuzzy MCDM approach for evaluating banking performance based on Balanced Scorecard", Taiwan.

[19] Nese YalcınSecme, Ali Bayrakdaroglu, CengizKahramanb, (2007). "Fuzzy performance evaluation in Turkish Banking Sector using AnalyticHierarchy Process and TOPSIS". Expert Systems with Applications, Vol. 36, pp.11699-11709.

[20] Ashton, C. (1998). "Balanced scorecard benefits Nat West Bank". International Journal of Retail and Distribution Management, Vol. 26(10), pp.400-407.

[21] Tsai, W. H., Yang, C. C., Leu, J. D., Lee, Y. F., & Yang, C. H. (2001). "An Integrated Group Decision Making Support Model for Corporate Financing Decisions". Group Decision and Negotiation, 1-25.C.T. Chen, A fuzzy approach to select the location of the distribution center, Fuzzy Sets and Systems ,Vol. 118 , pp. 65-73.

[22] S.Y. Chou, Y.H. Chang, C.Y. Shen, (2008). "A fuzzy simple additive weighting system under group decision making for facility location selection with objective/subjective attributes", European Journal of Operational Research Vol. 189 (1) 132-145

[23] Avijit Mazumdar (2010) "Application of multi-criteria decision Making (MCDM) approaches on teachers Performance evaluation and appraisal".

[24] Chen, C.W.E.,(2000). "Extensions of the TOPSIS for group decision-making under fuzzy environment". Fuzzy Sets and Systems vol. 114, pp.1-9.

[25] RabahMedjoudj, DjamilAissan, Klaus Dieter Haim, (2013)." Power customer satisfaction and profitability analysis using multi-criteria decision making methods",Electrical Power and Energy Systems Vol. 45 , pp.331-339.

[26] V. Lakshmana Gomathi Nayagam, S. Murali krishnan , Geetha Sivaraman,(2011). "Multi-criteria decision-making method based on interval-valued intuitionistic fuzzy sets", pp.1464-1467.

[27] H.C.W. Lau, Christina W.Y. Wong·, P.K.H. Lau, K.F. Pun, B. Jiang, K.S. Chin (2003) "A fuzzy multi-criteria decision support procedure for enhancing information delivery in extended enterprise networks.",Vol.16,pp.1-9.

[28] Shu-Hsien Liao, and Kuo-Chung Lu (2002), "Evaluating Anti-Armor Weapon Using Ranking Fuzzy Numbers", Vol. 11(1), pp.33-48.

[29] Mahammad Haghighi, Ali Divandari, Masoud Keimasi(2010) "The impact of 3D e-readiness on e-banking development in Iran: A fuzzy AHP analysis." Vol. (37), Issue 6, pp.4084-4093.

[30] Anderson, W., Jr., Cox, J. E. P., &Fulcher, D. (1976). "Bank selection decisions and marketing segmentation". Journal of Marketing, Vol. 40(1), pp. 40-45.

[31] Arshadi, N., Lawrence, E. C. (1987). "An empirical investigation of new bank performance". Journal of Banking and Finance, Vol. 11(1), pp.33-48.

[32] Ashton, C. (1998). "Balanced scorecard benefits Nat West Bank". International Journal of Retail and Distribution Management, Vol. 26(10), pp.400-407.

[33] Athanassopoulos, Giokas, D. (2000). "On-going use of data envelopment analysis in banking institutions". Evidence from the Commercial Bank of Greece. Interfaces, Vol. 30(2), pp.81-95.

[34] Bauer, P. W., Berger, A. N., Ferrier, G. D., & Humphrey, D. B. (1998). "Consistency conditions for regulatory analysis of financial institutions": A comparison of frontier efficiency methods. Journal of Economic and Business, Vol. 50(2), pp.85-114.

[35] Beccalli, A. (2007). "Does IT investment improve bank performance? Evidence from Europe". Journal of Banking & Finance, Vol. 31, pp.2205-2230.

[36] Caballero, R., Cerda, E., Munoz, M.M., Rey, L., (2004). "Stochastic approach versus multi objective approach for obtaining efficient solutions in stochastic multi objective programming problems". European Journal of Operational Research 158, pp.633-648.

[37] Changchit, C., Terrell, M.P., (1993)."A multi-objective reservoir operation model with stochastic inflows". Computers and Industrial Engineering Vol. 24 (2), pp.303-313.

[38] Chen, S.J., Hwang, C.L., (1991). "Fuzzy Multiple Attribute Decision making". Springer- Verlag, Berlin.

[39] MaherAburrous, M.A. Hossain, Keshav Dahal, FadiThabtah(2008). "Intelligent phishing detection system for e-banking using fuzzy data mining ". Jordan.

[40] Kuo-Liang Lee, Shu-Chen Lin, (2008) "A fuzzy quantified SWOT procedure for environmental evaluation of an international distribution centre", Information Sciences Vol. 178 (2), pp.531-549.

[41] J.J. Buckley, (1985). "Ranking alternatives using fuzzy numbers", Fuzzy Sets Systems Vol. 15 (1), pp. 21-31.

[42] Torra, V., Godo, L., (1997). "Averaging continuous distributions with the WOWA operator". EFDAN' 97, Germany.

[43] Torra, V., Narukawa, Y., (2007). "Modelling Decisions: Information Fusion and Aggregation Operators". Springer, Berlin.

[44] Yusuf Tansellç, (2012) "Development of a credit limit allocation model for banks using an integrated Fuzzy TOPSIS and linear programming". Expert System with Applications. Vol. 39(5), pp. 5309-5316.

[45] ErgünEraslan, Yusuf Tansellç, (2011). "A Multi-Criteria Approach for Determination of Investment Regions: Turkish Case". Industrial Management and Data Systems Vol. 111(6).

[46] Yusuf Tansellç, Mustafa Yurdakul,(2010). "Development of a quick credibility scoring decision support system using fuzzy TOPSIS". Expert Systems with Applications Vol. 37(1), pp. 567-574.

18

Decision Making Problem in Division of Cognitive Labor with Parameter Inaccuracy: Case Studies

Jin Huan Zhang, Khin War War Htike, Ammar Oad, Hao Zhang[*]

School of Information Science and Engineering, Central South University, Changsha, Hunan, P.R. China
*Corresponding author: hao@csu.edu.cn

Abstract Scientific communities will be more effective for society if scientists effectively divide their cognitive labor. So one way to study how scientists divide their cognitive labor has become an important area of research in science. This problem was firstly discovered and studied by Kitcher. Later on, Kleinberg and Oren pointed out that the model proposed by Kitcher might not be realistic. We investigate the impact of the imprecise parameter in project selection results. In this paper, we further our study on this issue. We study the policy of decision making problem based on the modified division of cognitive labor model with the assumption that a scientist is aware of the existence of the imprecise parameters and provide the detailed analytical results. And we provide a decision rule to minimize the possible loss based on error probability estimation.

Keywords: cognitive labor, imprecise parameters

1. Introduction

The best known approach for modeling congnitive labor has been created by Philip Kitcher [1,2] and Michael Strvens [3,4]. Kitcher proposed that the progress of science will be optimized when there is an optimal distribution of cognitive labor within the scientific community. However, the main argument of the model proposed by Kitcher has made many assumptions that might not be realistic.

The division of cognitive labor model is a procedure by which scientists calculate their expected rewards. Scientists calculate their marginal contribution to the probability of the success of project and then uses this information to estimate the expected reward and payoff. They assumed that scientists are utility-maximizes, the division of cognitive labor among a number of pre-defined projects, (distribution assumption) every scientist knows the distribution of cognitive labor before they choose what project to work on and finally (success function assumption) each project has a success function, and takes the units of cognitive labor as input and the mainly objective is probabilities of success of project.

Kitcher found that, when scientists made their decisions out of their personal interests for awards, the result might be even better than the pure one. Kitcher employed a mathematical model to support his argument. We got a lot of lessons from past experiences because the seemed mostly unlikely projects (or theory) might be proved to be the correct one in the end. Kitcher mentions in his work, that when those high-minded goals are replaced by baser motives such as thirst for fame, some scientists will automatically choose the second project towards the improvement of the total probability of success.

The main argument of division of cognitive labor model is that the assumptions of the model are not realistic. In division of cognitive labor model, Kitcher and Strevens used a representative-agent approach that means they assumed that every individual agent who is exactly the same situation as all the others. In this research, we keep only the representative agent approaches like Kitcher because we emphasize only about success function assumption with parameter inaccuracy. Like Gilbert said, we overrate or underrate the odds that it will occur. And hence we overrate or underrate the actual value of the gain [5]. He gave a lot of examples to prove that there are errors at the odds and value of gain when we decide what the right thing is to do.

In this paper, we introduce perturbation into the basic model parameters and studied the policy decisions with its impact on the original distributions. The theoretical and experimental results demonstrate that, under the provided conditions, the distributions are different from those obtained in the ideal case.

The rest of the paper is organized as follows. In section II, the related works are introduced. We study analytically the policy decisions under the division model with imprecise parameters and derive the close-form conditions in section III. Section IV bestows some experimental results for a number of cases. Finally, section V concludes the paper.

2. Related Works

In this section, we presents others work which is related to this research. We examine and review some of the existing solutions on different aspects of division of cognitive labor model in science. The idea of division of cognitive labor model, due to Kitcher, is one of the most striking features of modern social community.

However, in recent time there are many researches that are pointing out the weakness of Kitchers model. There are a large number of approaches for learning the structure and community of social network. Nowadays, most of young scientists and agents are facing with decision problem. They choose a method or make a decision according to their own past experience, and also following their peer or neighbors. Bala and Goyal presented a very general model in economic [6]. Langhe and Grieff studied the division of cognitive labor in science [7]. They generalized that Kitchers conclusion about the division of cognitive labor in science is not robust against changes in his single standard view to multiple standards.

In recent times, Jon Kleinberg and Sigal Oren proposed an idea to improve the social optimum in scientific credit allocation [8]. They adapted Kitcher model and showed that the misallocating scientific credit mechanisms might be a good way to obtain the social optimality. However, at [8] they built the credit allocation model to choose one among projects of varying levels of importance and difficulty of projects.

The division of cognitive labor is one of the most conspicuous model in modern social community. There are a large number of approaches for learning the structure and community of social network. The division of cognitive labor model has also been argued by Weisberg and Muldoon's epistemic landscape approach [9] and Zollman's epistemic networks approach [10,11]. In [9], they considered the original model in [1] is too ideal, e.g., all the agents know the distribution of cognitive labor at all times and division of cognitive labor model is not robust to change in the distribution assumption. They built robustness model, where agents actually calculate their marginal contributions to their project success using a specific function.

In recent time, most of young scientists and agents are facing with decision problem. They choose a method or make a decision according to their own past experience, and also following their peer or neighbors. Social network community have been studied in a number of domains; in economic, Bala and Goyal presented a very general model [12] and also another class of approaches to simple model of herd behavior, see work by [13,14]. They also study social network community by following the basic model of DeGroot [15] with the setting of individual agents are connected in social network and update their beliefs repeatedly taking into account the averaged weight of their neighbors' opinions can arrive a shared opinion [16,17,18].

We reviews some of the existing solutions and on different aspects of analyzing theories developed by prior studies in the area of social science, hhowever, they do not provide any detailed theoretical analysis or remedy on the impact of the variation on model parameters [19]. We recently modeled the impact of imprecise parameters theoretically and we provide detailed analytical results for this issue [20].

3. Theoretical Analysis

The fundamental equation of division of cognitive labor model built by Kitcher is as follows [1]:

$$p_i(n) = \rho_i(1 - e^{-kn}) \tag{1}$$

In this equation, ρ_i and k are all parameters and $k \geq 0$ is called the responsiveness. And assume that there are N scientists (denoted by $S_i, i = 0, 1, ..., N$) working on M projects (denoted by $PJ_i, i = 0, 1, ..., M$. $p_i(n)$ represents the probability of success when n scientists are working on PJ_i.

Each scientist is assumed to choose a project that maximizes his/her probability of success. When a project is successful, all scientists working on it would equally share the credit. From the aspect of each scientist, the principle of choice is assumed to be based on the reward that he/she might receive, i.e., a scientist would choose a project with the largest reward $p_i(n_i)/n_i$.

Kitcher provided analytical results in [1] for the basic model. However, in reality, it is not possible that model parameters are known precisely by each scientist. In this paper, we only consider the case when the parameter ρ_i deviates from its true value.

Although we conducted theoretical analysis on the impact of imprecise parameters [13], we do not give the right decision that a scientist should do in this situation. In this paper, we would focus on the decision making issue based on analytical models for some special cases.

3.1. One Scientist and Two Projects Case

For this case, the scientist is denoted by S1 and two projects are denoted by PJ1 and PJ2. The general model in Eq.1 can be rewritten as follows:

$$p_1(1) = \rho_1(1 - e^{-k})$$

$$p_2(1) = \rho_2(1 - e^{-k})$$

In real applications, the estimated model parameters $\hat{\rho}_1$, $\hat{\rho}_2$ might not be the true values. If we assume the measured ρ_2 contains some perturbation, i.e., $\hat{\rho}_1 = \rho_1$, $\hat{\rho}_2 = \rho_2 + x$ where x is the added perturbation, and the above equations can be rewritten as [13]

$$\hat{p}_1(1) = \rho_1(1 - e^{-k})$$

$$\hat{p}_2(1) = (\rho_2 + x)(1 - e^{-k})$$

Naturally, the perturbation x would have great impact on this model. When $\hat{p}_2(1) > \hat{p}_1(1)$, S1 will switch from PJ1 to PJ2 due to better estimated success probability. We use P_e to represent this probability of error, which can be denoted by the following equation:

$$P_e = P(PJ1) \cdot P(PJ2 | PJ1) + P(PJ2) \cdot P(PJ1 | PJ2)$$
$$= P(PJ1) \cdot P(\hat{p}_2(1) > \hat{p}_1(1) | PJ1)$$
$$+ P(PJ2) \cdot P(\hat{p}_1(1) > \hat{p}_2(1) | PJ2)$$

It can be rewritten as:

$$P_e = P(PJ1) \cdot P(x > \rho_1 - \rho_2 | PJ1)$$
$$+ P(PJ2) \cdot P(x < \rho_1 - \rho_2 | PJ2)$$

It can be further rewritten as:

$$P_e = P(PJ1) \cdot \int_{\rho_1 - \rho_2}^{+\infty} f_1(x) dx + P(PJ2) \cdot \int_{-\infty}^{\rho_1 - \rho_2} f_2(x) dx$$

It can be seen that P_e is a function of $\rho_1 - \rho_2$. In order to make the minimum probability of miscarriage justice, the above formula does derivation on $\rho_1 - \rho_2$ as:

$$\frac{\partial P_e}{\partial(\rho_1 - \rho_2)} = -P(PJ1)f_1(\rho_1 - \rho_2) + P(PJ2)f_2(\rho_1 - \rho_2).$$

So that the value of the derivative to zero, we obtain:

$$\frac{P(PJ1)}{P(PJ2)} = \frac{f_2(\rho_1 - \rho_2)}{f_1(\rho_1 - \rho_2)}$$

Without generality, we assume $\rho_1 > \rho_2$ and $f_1(x) = f_2(x)$. The scientist would choose a project with much larger reward. If the scientist would choose project PJ 1, the probability of error is written as:

$$P_{e1} = P(\hat{p}_2(1) > \hat{p}_1(1)) = P(x > \rho_1 - \rho_2) = \int_{\rho_1 - \rho_2}^{+\infty} f(x) dx$$

Otherwise, when the scientist would choose project 2, the probability of error is:

$$P_{e2} = P(\hat{p}_1(1) > \hat{p}_2(1)) = P(x < \rho_1 - \rho_2) = \int_{-\infty}^{\rho_1 - \rho_2} f(x) dx$$

If random variable x follows the uniform distribution, i.e.,

$$f(x) = \frac{1}{b - a} (a \le x \le b)$$

We obtain:

$$P_{e1} = \int_{\rho_1 - \rho_2}^{+\infty} f(x) dx = \int_{\rho_1 - \rho_2}^{+\infty} \frac{1}{b - a} dx$$

$$P_{e2} = \int_{-\infty}^{\rho_1 - \rho_2} f(x) dx = \int_{-\infty}^{\rho_1 - \rho_2} \frac{1}{b - a} dx$$

(1) If $\rho_1 - \rho_2 \le (a + b)/2$, $P_{e1} \ge P_{e2}$ would hold. The scientist would choose project 2 due to better estimated success probability.

(2) If $\rho_1 - \rho_2 > (a + b)/2$, $P_{e1} < P_{e2}$ would hold. The scientist would choose project 1 to get much more reward or success probability.

If random variable x follows the normal distribution, i.e.,

$$f(x) = \frac{1}{\sqrt{2\pi}\delta} e^{(x-\mu)^2/(2\delta^2)}$$

We obtain:

$$P_{e1} = \int_{\rho_1 - \rho_2}^{+\infty} f(x) dx = \int_{\rho_1 - \rho_2}^{+\infty} \frac{1}{\sqrt{2\pi}\delta} e^{(x-\mu)^2/(2\delta^2)} dx$$

$$P_{e2} = \int_{-\infty}^{\rho_1 - \rho_2} f(x) dx = \int_{-\infty}^{\rho_1 - \rho_2} \frac{1}{\sqrt{2\pi}\delta} e^{(x-\mu)^2/(2\delta^2)} dx$$

(1) If $\rho_1 - \rho_2 \le \mu$, we have $P_{e1} > P_{e2}$. In this case, the scientist would choose project 2 to work due to better estimated success probability.

(2) If $\rho_1 - \rho_2 > \mu$, $P_{e1} < P_{e2}$ would hold. The scientist would choose project 1 to get much more reward or success probability.

3.2. Two Scientists and Two Projects Case

For this case, two scientists are denoted by S1 and S2; two projects are denoted by PJ1 and PJ2, respectively. The distribution between scientists and projects could be <2, 0>, <0, 2> and <1, 1> three cases. Without parameter perturbations, S1 and S2 would not both choose PJ2, i.e., the stable distribution cannot be < 0, 2 > for the case $\rho_1 > \rho_2$.

Next, we would do analysis from the two aspects of personal and social with parameter perturbations. Without generality, we assume the measured ρ_2 contains some perturbation, i.e., $\hat{\rho}_1 = \rho_1$, $\hat{\rho}_2 = \rho_2 + x$ where x is the added perturbation.

(1) If the distribution is <2, 0>, the success probability or reward of scientists S1 and S2 working on project PJ1 is written respectively as:

$$p_1(2) = \rho_1(1 - e^{-2k})/2$$

The aggregate probability of success is:

$$p_a = \rho_1(1 - e^{-2k})$$

For the case with parameter perturbations, the estimated success probability is as follows:

$$\hat{p}_1(2) = \rho_1(1 - e^{-2k})/2$$

$$\hat{p}_2(2) = (\rho_2 + x)(1 - e^{-0k})/2 = 0$$

The aggregate probability of success is:

$$p_a = \rho_1(1 - e^{-2k})$$

Obviously, the parameter perturbations would not have impact on estimated success probability and the aggregate probability of success.

(2) If the distribution <0,2> holds, the success probability or reward of scientists S1 and S2 working on project PJ2 is written respectively as:

$$p_2(2) = \rho_2(1 - e^{-2k})/2$$

The aggregate probability of success is:

$$p_a = \rho_2(1 - e^{-2k})$$

The estimated success probability due to parameter perturbations is written as:

$$\hat{p}_2(2) = (\rho_2 + x)(1 - e^{-2k})/2$$

The aggregate probability of success is:

$$p_a = (\rho_2 + x)(1 - e^{-2k})$$

(3) If the distribution is <1,1>, the success probabilities of scientist S1 working on project PJ1 and scientist S2 working on project PJ2 are written respectively as:

$$p_1(1) = \rho_1(1 - e^{-k})$$

$$p_2(1) = \rho_2(1 - e^{-k})$$

The aggregate probability of success is:

$$p_a = \rho_1(1-e^{-k}) + \rho_2(1-e^{-k})$$

With parameter perturbations, the corresponding estimated probability of success are as follows:

$$\hat{p}_1(1) = \rho_1(1-e^{-k})$$

$$\hat{p}_2(1) = (\rho_2 + x)(1-e^{-k})$$

The aggregate probability of success is:

$$p_a = \rho_1(1-e^{-k}) + (\rho_2 + x)(1-e^{-k})$$

In general, we assume $\rho_1 > \rho_2$ and the scientist S1 would choose one project to work firstly. If the scientist S1 chooses the project PJ1, the scientist S2 would choose the project PJ1 or the project PJ2. The error probability of the scientist S2 choosing the project PJ1 or the project PJ2 is computed respectively by:

$$P_{e1} = P(\hat{p}_2(1) > \hat{p}_1(2)) = P(x > \rho_1(1+e^{-k})/2 - \rho_2)$$

$$= \int_{\rho_1(1+e^{-k})/2-\rho_2}^{+\infty} f(x)dx$$

$$P_{e2} = P(\hat{p}_1(2) > \hat{p}_2(1)) = P\left(x < \rho_1\left(1+e^{-k}\right)/2 - \rho_2\right)$$

$$= \int_{-\infty}^{\rho_1\left(1+e^{-k}\right)/2-\rho_2} f(x)dx$$

If random variable x follows the uniform distribution, i.e.,

$$f(x) = \frac{1}{b-a}(a \leq x \leq b)$$

We obtain:

(1) If $\rho_1(1+e^{-k})/2 - \rho_2 \geq (a+b)/2$, we obtain $P_{e1} \leq P_{e2}$. For this case, the scientist S2 would choose project PJ1 to work due to better success probability or reward. And the aggregate probability of success is:

$$p_{a1} = \rho_1(1-e^{-2k})$$

(2) If $\rho_1(1+e^{-k})/2 - \rho_2 < (a+b)/2$, $P_{e1} > P_{e2}$ would hold. The scientist S2 would choose project PJ2 to work on. The aggregate probability of success is:

$$p_{a2} = \rho_1(1-e^{-k}) + (\rho_2 + x)(1-e^{-k})$$

Next, it is also meaningful to study from the social aspect, i.e., if the scientist S2 would choose one of project to work on due to his/her better personal reward or success probability, is it the CO-distribution? For the distribution <2, 0>, only if $p_{a1} \geq p_{a2}$, it is the CO-distribution. When $p_{a1} \geq p_{a2}$, $x \leq \rho_1 e^{-k} - \rho_2$ should hold. And the random variable x follows the uniform distribution, i.e., $a \leq x \leq b$.

Hence, the inequality $a < \rho_1 e^{-k} - \rho_2 \leq b$ should hold.

Considering the inequality $\rho_1(1+e^{-k})/2 - \rho_2 \geq (a+b)/2$, the scientist S2 would make the choice for the benefit of both personal and social interests.

If random variable x follows the normal distribution, i.e.,

$$f(x) = \frac{1}{\sqrt{2\pi}\delta}e^{(x-\mu)^2/(2\delta^2)}$$

Similarly, we obtain:

If $\rho_1(1+e^{-k})/2 - \rho_2 \geq \mu$, the inequality $P_{e1} \leq P_{e2}$ would hold. The scientist S2 would choose project PJ1 due to better personal reward.

If $\rho_1(1+e^{-k})/2 - \rho_2 < \mu$, $P_{e1} > P_{e2}$ holds. S2 will make a choice on PJ2. If S2 would choose PJ1 due to better success probability, while making the distribution <2,0> be the co-distribution, the inequality $x \leq \rho_1 e^{-k} - \rho_2$ should hold.

From the above analysis, we know that when the perturbation item x would meet certain conditions both the personal and social better success probability could be satisfied.

3.3. One Scientist and M Projects Case

Without generality, let we assume the probabilities of success for M projects satisfy $p_1 > p_2 > p_3 > ... > p_M$. S1 will choose PJ1 with the highest probability of success. If $p_i(i > 1)$ contains perturbation item x, S1 will make the choice according to the following computation.

$$P_{ej} = P(PJj \mid PJ1) = P(P(PJj) > P(PJ1)) \quad j = 1, 2, 3, ..., M$$

The scientist S1 would choose project j only if P_{ej} is much smaller than others.

4. Simulation

We study the policy decision based on the modified division of cognitive labor model with the detailed simulation results. We would like to provide the probability of error when the scientist S2 chooses the projects with the assumption of parameter inaccuracy at the projects' probability of success. In this simulation experiment, the parameter values are as follows: $\rho_1 = 0.9, \rho_2 = 0.5, k = 0.4$ and the parameter inaccuracy x is set in random value between 0 and 1.

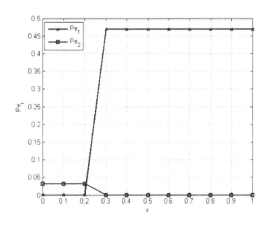

Figure 1. The error probability of the scientist S2 choosing the projects if x follows the uniform distribution

Figure 1 shows the probability of error according to the scientist S2 choice. When the scientist S1 is working in project PJ1, there are 2 ways to choose for scientist S2; he would follow <1,1> or <2,0> distribution. According to the result showing in Fig. 1, there would be only too small error probability if scientist2 chooses the project PJ2.

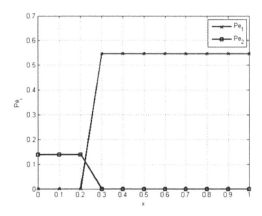

Figure 2. The error probability of the scientist S2 choosing the projects if x follows the standard normal distribution

Figure 2 shows that the error probability for scientist S2 with the assumption of parameter inaccuracy x follows the standard normal distribution. If scientist S2 chooses the project PJ1 to work together with scientist S1, he/she could get the probability of error over 0.5.

5. Conclusions

In this paper, we offer decision making rules in the division of cognitive labor with theoretical analysis on the impact of parameter perturbations. Due to the complexity involved in modeling the general case, we mainly focus on several special cases with a small number of scientists and projects. The analytical results demonstrate that when we assume the existence of parameters inaccuracy, we would choose the project that minimizes the error probability.

Acknowledgement

The work is supported by National Natural Science Foundation of China (No.61003033) and Specialized Research Fund for the Doctoral Program of Higher Education (No.20100162120018), the Hunan soft science project (2010ZK3061), Central Universities Fundamental Research Funds for the project (2012QNZT063).

References

[1]   P. Kitcher, "The division of cognitive labor, journal of philosophy," *The Journal of Philosophy*, vol. 87, no. 1, pp. 5-22, 1990.

[2]   P. Kitcher, "The advancement of science," *New York: Oxford University Press*, 1993.

[3]   M. Strevens, "The role of the priority rule in science", *Journal of Philosophy*, vol. 100, no. 2, pp. 55-79, 2003.

[4]   M. Strevens, "The role of the matthew effect in science," *Studies in the History and Philosophy of Science*, vol. 37, pp. 159-170, 2006.

[5]   D. Gilbert, "Buried by bad decisions," *Nature*, pp. 275-277, 2011.

[6]   V. Bala and S. Goyal, "Learning from neighbours," *Review of Economic Studies*, pp. 595-621, 1998.

[7]   DL.Rogier and G.Matthias, "Standards and distribution of cognitive labor," *Logic Journal of the IGPL*, 2009.

[8]   J.Kleinberg and S.Oren, "Mechanisms for (mis)allocating scientific credit," *Proceedings of the 43rd annual ACM symposium on Theory of Computing*, 2011.

[9]   M. Weisberg and R. Muldoon, "Epistemic landscapes and the division of cognitive labor," *Philosophy of Science*, pp. 37:159-170, 2009.

[10] K. J. Zollman, "The communication structure of epistemic communities," *Philosophy of Science*, vol. 74(5), pp. 574-587, 2007.

[11] K. J. Zollman, "The epistemic benefit of transient diveristy," *Erkenn*, vol. 72, pp. 17-35, 2010.

[12] Bala, Venkatesh and Sanjeev Goyal. "Learning from neighbours." Review of Economic Studies, pp. 595-621, 1988.

[13] Banerjee, A. V. "A simple model of herd behavior." The Quarterly Journal of Economics, 107 (3), pp. 797-817, 1992.

[14] Welch, I. "Sequential sales, learning, and cascades." The Journal of Finance, 47(2), pp. 695-732, 1992.

[15] M. H. DeGroot. "Reaching a consensus." J. American Statistical Association, 69, 118-121, 1974.

[16] B. Golub and M.O. Jackson. "Naive learning in social networks: Convergence, influence and the wisdon of crowds." American Econ. J.: Microeconomics, 2000.

[17] P. M. DeMarzo, D. Vayanos and J. Zweibel. "Persuasion bias, social influence, and unidimensional opinions." Auarterly Journal of Economics, 118(3), 2003.

[18] M. O. Jackson. "Social and Economic Networks." Princeton University Press, 2008.

[19] R. Muldoon and M.Weisberg, "Robustness and idealization in models of cognitive labor synthese," Synthese, vol. 183, pp. 161-174, 2011.

[20] K. W. W. Htike and H. Zhang, "Theoretical study of division of cognitive labor with imprecise model parameters," CSSS, pp. 4094-4097, 2012.

19

Application of Infrastructure as a Service in IT Education

Li Chao*

Math and Computer Science, University of Houston-Victoria, Victoria, United States
*Corresponding author: chaol@uhv.edu

Abstract This paper considers cloud service development to support hands-on practice in IT education. For IT education, cloud services can be used to reduce cost, enhance security, and provide flexibility. This paper presents a case study to illustrate how cloud services can be used to support hands-on practice for IT courses. It also provides a five-step development strategy to develop cloud based computer labs for various types of IT courses.

Keywords: cloud, infrastructure as a service, software as a service, platform as a service

1. Introduction

In IT education, students improve their problem solving skills through hands-on practice. For hands-on practice, computer labs are the key component in the teaching and learning of information technology. For IT education programs to be accredited, the Board for Engineering and Technology (ABET) requires that computer labs must be implemented (ABET, 2010). On the other hand, it is always a challenging task to develop and manage computer labs to meet different hands-on requirements for various types of IT courses (Chao, 2008). There are three major challenges: lab upgrade and reconstruction, meeting the lab requirements by different IT courses, and lab security. The IT curriculum changes rapidly to catch up with the IT industry. The changes in the IT curriculum require the computer labs to be upgraded accordingly. For many education institutions, the frequent upgrade of computer labs is a real burden due to lack of funding, manpower, and IT skills. The IT education curriculum consists of various subjects which require different technologies. Often, the computer lab designed for one IT course may not be used by other IT courses. For example, the computer lab configured for teaching networking is not suitable for teaching database development. The students in the networking class may alter the network set up so that the front-end applications cannot access the database server. Therefore, it is a challenge to meet the requirements from different types of IT courses. Lab security creates another challenge. To learn the skills for managing computer systems and networks, the students should be allowed to reconfigure the network in the lab for hands-on practice. They must be given the administrator's privilege. The IT service department at an education institution has great concern about giving students the administrator's privilege. Therefore, additional security measures need to be enforced to protect the institution's internal network from the students with the administrator's privilege.

The newly developed cloud computing technology may provide a better solution in dealing with the challenges in IT education. Cloud computing is a computation platform from which users can subscribe computing resources such as networks, servers, storage, applications, and services provided by a cloud provider. By subscribing computing resources, it is not necessary for users to develop their own IT infrastructure for IT services. Cloud providers make computing resources available to subscribers. Cloud computing users only pay for what they have subscribed. By using computing resources provided by a cloud provider, subscribers do not have to develop their own IT infrastructure. Without developing their own IT infrastructure, the subscribers are able to lower the cost and speed up the development of their own projects.

Education institutions can greatly benefit by cloud computing. Some of the IT courses may require a large number of servers to support hands-on practice. For example, a Software Project course may require 10 servers to support a project developed by a group students. If there are 10 groups of students in a Software Project class, the class will need 100 servers to support the hands-on practice. On the other hands, these 100 server do have to be on all the time. As soon as the students complete the assignments. These servers can be turned off. The is very common scenario in IT education. Therefore the nature of cloud computing fits the needs of IT education very well. At UC Berkeley, the Amazon Web Service (AWS) cloud has been used to support the IT infrastructure for the Software Project course (Fox, 2009). Each class subscripts a large number of servers at the beginning of the hands-on practice. The subscription will be released as soon as the submission deadline is passed.

More studies have been done to investigate the application of cloud computing in education. Cloud computing can play a significant role in student-centered practices (Chang and Guetl, 2010). The experimental can greatly benefit from the features of cloud computing. Cloud computing provides an leaning environment that particularly suitable for the leaning learning behavior, habits and styles of Generation Y. Berenfeld and Yazijian (2010) demonstrate, in their report, how the cloud computing technology was used in constructing a global lab for teaching and learning of environmental science. Cloud computing is gradually replacing the traditional way of providing software for higher education (Nicholson, 2009). Once a higher education institution is cloud powered, the cost on developing and managing the IT infrastructure can be significantly reduced. In addition, the cloud based IT infrastructure is highly flexible and agile. The features of cloud computing provide a new way to implement online teaching and learning in IT education. The cloud computing technology has the potential to meet various lab requirements of different IT courses (Chao, 2011).

This paper focuses on a case study to illustrate how the cloud computing supports the hands-on practice in IT education. Based on the requirements of IT education, this paper identify the cloud computing technology that best fits each type of IT courses.

2. Cloud Services for IT Education

As described by Velte, Velte, and Elsenpeter (2009), cloud computing runs under two different platforms, public cloud and private cloud. In a public cloud, the cloud provider is a third party company such as Amazon's Elastic Compute Cloud (EC2) or Microsoft Windows Azure. As a subscriber of the public cloud, the subscriber pays for the usage of computing resources provided by the cloud provider. As a contrast to the public cloud, a private cloud is built into an educational institution's existing IT infrastructure. The IT department of the educational institution serves as the cloud provider. The subscribers may include instructors and students. Both the provider and subscribers are working within the educational institution. Public as well as private cloud computing can provide three types of cloud services (Cloud Weeks, 2010).

Software as a Service (SaaS): This cloud service allows educational institutions to subscribe to online software hosted by a cloud provider. If proprietary software is used, educational institutions need to pay for the usage of the software. Some of the well known software packages provided by SaaS are Google Apps and Microsoft Office 365. IT courses that require hands-on practice on certain computer software, such as programming or multimedia development software, SaaS is adequate to get the job done. If the required software is available from a public cloud provider, education institutions do not have to do much. If it is not available, we can subscribe to a server from a cloud provider and install the required software. In most cases, the cost of subscribing to one server is affordable. Another option is to develop a private cloud to provide such a service.

Platform as a Service (PaaS): This service provides a Web-based application development platform. It can be used by an IT course to design, develop, test, deploy, upgrade, and host Web-based applications. It allows application developers to form a community to carry out collaborative work on a project. Server operating systems, databases, middleware, Web servers, and application development environments are provided remotely by PaaS providers. Microsoft Windows Azure is this type of service. IT courses that require hands-on practice on a client-server structure, such as database systems or application development courses, PaaS is the one to use. The PaaS service provided by Windows Azure is suitable for the database systems and application development courses. In addition, Microsoft provides a free solution development kit for developing database applications. Education institutions can also provide PaaS through a private cloud. PaaS provides an ideal platform for group projects. It enhances interaction among students and instructors.

Infrastructure as a Service (IaaS): This cloud service provides an IT infrastructure that consists of servers, networks, data storage and other necessary tools properly configured to form a virtual computing environment that fulfills the hands-on practice requirements of an IT course. Microsoft Windows Azure and Amazon Web Service (AWS) provide this type of service. It is a great challenge to support the courses that require hands-on practice on the server side, such as system administration and network management courses. These IT courses require the reconfiguration of operating systems and networks. There are many such courses in the IT curriculum. IaaS provided by a public cloud may not be the solution. A networking class may need to subscribe virtual servers for a semester. Each student may need to have 3 or more servers to create a local network environment. For many small education institutions, the subscription cost is too high. IaaS provided by a public cloud has another drawback. It is not easy for students to reconfigure the server's IP address, which will disconnect the students' access to the cloud. For IT courses such as networking or system administration, we should consider supporting IaaS with a private cloud or hybrid cloud.

The advantage of cloud service is particularly useful for supporting lab activities in the teaching and learning process. To catch the trend of the fast changing IT industry, computer labs are upgraded frequently and it takes a great deal of effort and resources to implement the changes. Cloud based computer labs can greatly benefit from the flexibility and agility offered by the cloud computing technology. By teaming up with IBM, cloud architecture to support learning and research has been developed at North Carolina State University (NCSU) (Stein, Ware, Laboy, & Scha_er, 2013). The strong support from the industry leader IBM and from NCSU IT service has made NCSU's cloud project very successful. However, many education institutions may lack the support from the IT industry. Due to the shortage of funding, skilled technicians, and "know-how", frequent updates of research infrastructure and computer labs can become a burden to these education institutions. Even with the above difficulties, these higher education institutions can still find a way to implement cloud services as shown in the case study. To support education, major cloud vendors provide education price for their products. For example, the VMware Academic Program (VMAP) package provided by VMware includes vSphere, Workstation, vCloud Suite, and other software for an annual subscription fee of $250 for education institutions. DreamSpark provided by Microsoft is a program that supports technical education. It provides Microsoft software for learning, teaching and research purposes. Amazon also provides Education Grants Program which allows instructors and students to apply for free usage credits. With the free usage credits, instructors and students can use Amazon Cloud to teach IT courses, conduct research, and experiment with new projects. In addition to the support from these well-known IT companies, education institutions can also consider using open source products such as Open Stack.

With these education programs, even a small education institution is able to implement its cloud services. The intention of this paper is to facilitate small education institutions in establishing their own cloud services with the resources provided by an education program mentioned above. This paper will first investigate the requirements by IT education. Then, it will identify the cloud technology that can be applied to IT education. The emphasis will be given to the cloud solution for the IT infrastructure which is used to support cloud based computer labs.

3. Case Study

For IT education, the development of cloud services can be done through a five-step solution model which includes requirement analysis, design, development, implementation, and evaluation. The following is the sample requirements for computer labs by different IT courses.

Gaming Network Architecture: It requires the SaaS service which provides the open source software such as Python and Unreal. It is desired that the software are available anytime and can be access from anywhere.

Internet Computing: It requires the SaaS service which provides open source application software such as Apache, MySQL, Perl, and Firefox as application software.

Object-Oriented Programming: It requires the SaaS service which provides programming software such as Java Development Kit (JDK).

Networking: It requires the IaaS service which provides IT infrastructure including multiple subnets, gateways, server operating systems, and software such as Web server, email server, and software for routing and directory service.

Security Management: It requires the IaaS service which provides IT infrastructure including subnets, proxy servers, firewalls, DMZ architecture, server operating systems, as well as security management software.

Software Engineering: It requires the PaaS service which provides a collaboration platform including server operating system, database management software, application development software.

In the design phase, the virtual lab is represented with a logical model which can be used to verify if the hands-on practice requirements have been met. Figure 1 is a sample logical design representing an hybrid cloud service which can be used to support all types of courses in IT education.

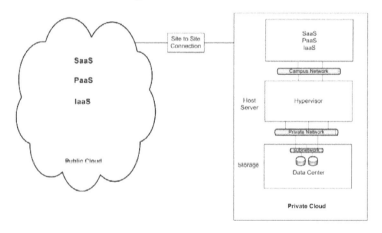

Figure 1. Hybrid Cloud Services

IT education can benefit from all these services. For teaching courses using application software such as Web application development, the SaaS service should be subscribed. Courses such as Software Engineering can benefit from the PaaS service. IaaS is necessary for the development of virtual computer labs. The IaaS service allows students to create and manage their own networks.

The designer has several choices of public clouds. Among them, Amazon (2010) is a pioneer that popularized the cloud computing platform. As early as the year 2006, the beta version of Amazon Elastic Compute Cloud (EC2) was made available to the public by Amazon (Barr, 2006). Amazon designed the AWS in Education program to help the academic community get a quick start on leveraging Amazon Web Services (AWS). The AWS in Education program provides educational institutions with teaching grants, research grants, and project grants.

Since then, cloud computing has begun to change the way of online computing. Many other public clouds became available on the market such as:

1. Blue Cloud by IBM which assists educational institutions in moving from traditional IT infrastructure to cloud based IT infrastructure by offering the IBM Cloud Academy (IBM, 2009),

2. App Engine by Google which supports educational institutions with the Google Apps for Education program (Google, 2010), and

3. Microsoft Windows Azure which offers a cloud solution to educational institutions (Microsoft, 2011). The educational institutions can subscribe services including IaaS, PaaS, and SaaS.

There are also several packages for developing private cloud. To name a few, consider the following commonly used cloud management software:

1. Cloud Director is a cloud management suite provided by VMware. It can be used to build hybrid clouds by integrating a public cloud with a private cloud built with VMware products. VMware provides Cloud Connector for migrating virtual machines between private and public clouds.

2. Microsoft System Center 2012 can be used to develop private clouds hosted by System Center Virtual Machine Manager (SCVMM). It provides App Controller for configuring, deploying, and managing virtual machines and services across private and public clouds.

3. Another popular cloud management platform is Eucalyptus. With Eucalyptus, users can manage multiple cloud providers. Eucalyptus provides an API which is fully compatible with the Amazon API.

4. Open Stack is an open-source cloud management platform for deploying clouds. Open Stack is built to support various public clouds such as Amazon Web Services and Windows Azure. Open Stack supports commonly used hypervisors such as KVM and Xen for developing the virtualized IT infrastructure.

As described in the design phase, the SaaS and PaaS provided by a public cloud provider are ideal for handling courses such as web development or database system development. For courses such as networking or system administration, the IaaS provided by a private is an ideal choice. In the process of developing virtual labs, the cloud services can be used for creating virtual machines with virtual images designed for different IT courses. Figure 2 shows virtual machines provided by the IaaS of a private cloud.

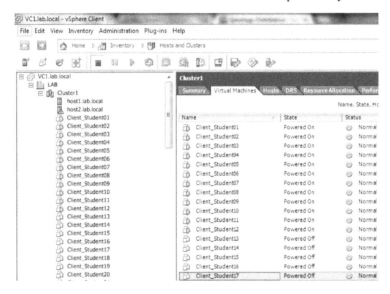

Figure 2. Virtual Machines

In the implementation phase, the instructors tested the virtual lab to make sure that all the lab activities can be performed in the lab which can be accessed anytime and anywhere as long as the Internet is available. Figure 3 illustrates the Windows Azure Management Portal for remotely accessing the virtual machines designed for a mobile application development class. Through the Internet connection, students can access the mobile service anytime and anywhere.

Instructors can also develop their own application interface for mobile devices. Figure 4 illustrates the interface for students' social network.

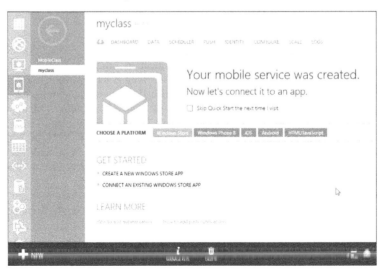

Figure 3. Windows Azure Portal

Figure 4. Interface for Uplaoding Pictures

To remotely access the cloud services, the access mechanism can be created either through the Web browser as shown in Figure 5, or through the open source graphic desktop sharing software such as Virtual Network Computing (VNC) as shown in Figure 6.

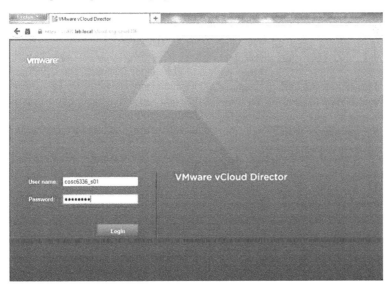

Figure 5. Browser-based Remote Access Interface

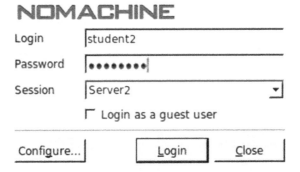

Figure 6. Virtual Network Computing Interface

One of the main tasks in the implementation phase is to provide tutoring service. To help students remotely access the cloud service, detailed instruction is necessary. Figure 7 illustrates lab logon instructions for the students.

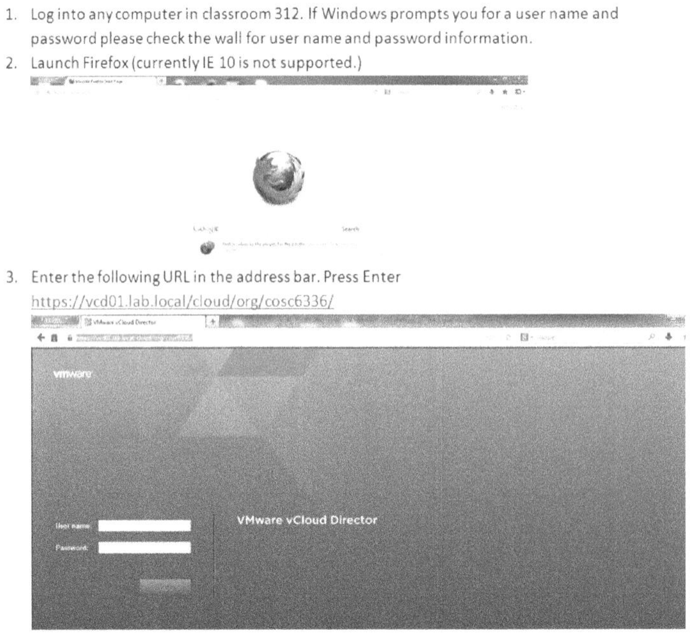

1. Log into any computer in classroom 312. If Windows prompts you for a user name and password please check the wall for user name and password information.
2. Launch Firefox (currently IE 10 is not supported.)

3. Enter the following URL in the address bar. Press Enter
   https://vcd01.lab.local/cloud/org/cosc6336/

Figure 7. Lab Instructions for Accessing Cloud Services

In this case study, the cloud-based learning environment was successfully implemented for the IT courses such as networking, database system development and web application development. As for the evaluation of the cloud-based learning environment, brief surveys were conducted for the students and instructors who had participated in the cloud-based teaching and learning. As an example, when the students in the cloud database development class were asked if they liked or disliked the cloud-based learning environment, 100% of the students liked the convenience, flexibility, scalability, and availability of the cloud-based learning environment. When asked if it took less time to complete their assignments in the cloud-based learning environment, 82% of the students said yes. 18% of the students preferred the traditional lab environment where they could easily get help from their instructors. 100% of the students were engaged in the collaboration during the project development. When asked if they would be able to use cloud computing for their work or learning, 97% of the students said yes. The reactions from the instructors were also very positive. They liked to use the cloud-based environment for developing course materials and doing research. 87% of the instructors also liked the cloud-based environment where they could conveniently help the students. It shows that it cost the university's IT service department almost nothing for class support. During the entire semester, the learning environment was available to the students 100% of the time.

As another example, a brief post class survey was conducted for a network management class. The result shows that 100% of students liked the convenience of the online virtual lab. 15% of the students stated that the hands-on practice in the virtual lab took more time due to lack of the face-to-face help from the instructors. 93% of the students considered the hands-on skills important for their career. 85 % of the students had worked with other students collaboratively. These students may also have contacted the technical support of the public cloud provider or contacted the instructor for help. The instructors agreed that lab preparation time had been reduced and it was easier to manage the online virtual lab.

4. Conclusion

This paper discusses the development of a cloud-based learning environment in IT education. With resources provided by the academic support programs or open source products, even a small education institution can develop their own cloud services. It is possible to replace some of the physical computer labs on campus with the cloud-based learning environment. The cloud based virtual computer lab has great usability, flexibility, as well as affordability.

References

[1] ABET, "Criteria for accrediting engineering programs," Available: http://www.abet.org/Linked%20Documents-UPDATE/Criteria%20and%20PP/05-06-EAC%20Criteria.pdf. [Accessed June 26, 2010.]

[2] Chang, V., and Guetl, C., "Generation Y learning in the 21st century: Integration of virtual worlds and cloud computing services." In Z. Abas et al. (Eds.), *Proceedings of Global Learn Asia Pacific 2010* (pp. 1888-1897). Chesapeake, VA: AACE. 2010.

[3] Chao, L, *Strategies and technologies for developing online computer labs for technology-based courses*. Hershey, PA: IGI Global, 2008.

[4] Fox, A, "Cloud computing in education," Available: http://inews.berkeley.edu/articles/Spring2009/cloud-computing. [Accessed July 26, 2010.]

[5] Nicholson, J. L, "Cloud computing: Top issues for higher education," Available: http://www.universitybusiness.com/viewarticle.aspx?articleid=1342 [Accessed July 26, 2010.]

[6] Stein, S., Ware, J., Laboy, J., & Schaffer, H. E, "Improving K-12 pedagogy via a Cloud designed for education," *International Journal of Information Management*, 33 (1), 235-241. 2013.

[7] Chao, L, Cloud technology and its application in IT education. In M. Koehler & P. Mishra (Eds.), *Proceedings of Society for Information Technology & Teacher Education International Conference 2011* (pp. 3053-3056). Chesapeake, VA: AACE. 2011.

[8]   Cloud Weeks, "Cloud computing – demystifying SaaS, PaaS and IaaS," Available: http://www.cloudtweaks.com/2010/05/cloud-computing-demystifying-saas-paas-and-iaas. [Accessed September 16, 2010.]

[9]   Velte, T., Velte, A., & Elsenpeter, R., *Cloud computing, a practical approach*. New York: McGraw-Hill Osborne Media. 2009.

[10]   Amazon,   "AWS   in   Education,"   Available: http://aws.amazon.com/education [Accessed July 15, 2011.]

[11]   Barr,   J.,   "Amazon   EC2   Beta." http://aws.typepad.com/aws/2006/08/amazon_ec2_beta.html [Accessed July 16, 2009.]

[12]   Microsoft,   "Cloud   computing   for   education,"   Available: http://www.microsoft.com/education/solutions/cloudcomputing.aspx. [Accessed July 15, 2011.]

[13]   IBM,   "Introducing   the   IBM   Cloud   Academy,"   Available: http://www.ibm.com/solutions/education/cloudacademy/us/en. [Accessed September 16, 2010.]

[14]   Google,   "Gmail,   Calendar,   Docs   and   more,"   Available: http://www.google.com/a/help/intl/en/edu/index.html   [Accessed September 16, 2010.]

20

Cloud Computing: A New Era in the Field of Information Technology Applications and its Services

Anwar Mohd. Mansuri[1,*], Prithviraj Singh Rathore[2]

[1]Department of Computer Science and Engineering, MIT Mandsaur, Mandsaur, India
[2]Department Master of Computer Application, MIT Mandsaur, Mandsaur, India
*Corresponding author: anwar.iter@gmail.com

Abstract Cloud computing is the computing that provides virtualized IT resources as a service by using Internet technology. In cloud computing, a customer lends IT resources as needed, uses them, get a support of real-time scalability according to service load, and pays as he/she goes. Cloud computing is becoming an adoptable technology for many of the organizations with its dynamic scalability and usage of virtualized resources as a service through the Internet. Cloud computing uses the Internet and central remote servers to maintain data and applications. As know that at present the e- ccommercee services opportunity to utilize pay-as-you-go resources together with their own and shared resource in the fields of IT. In this paper shows that the cloud computing plays an important role in the fields of Information Technology services and its applications and it is helpful to provide the data to the customer. The results show that the comparison of cloud services and normal services of Information Technology applications.

Keywords: cloud computing, SasS, distributed data base, cloud storage, big data

1. Introduction

Cloud computing has been an important term in the world of Information Technology (IT). Cloud computing is a kind of computing which is highly scalable and use virtualized resources that can be shared by the users. Users do not need any background knowledge of the services. A user on the Internet can communicate with many servers at the same time and these servers exchange information among themselves. The concept of cloud computing offers in the IT sector a way to increase IT capacity and add on the fly capabilities without investing in new infrastructure, new training, or licensing new software. There is no need to setup, configure and manage large physical installations of hardware and networks. This technology allows much more efficient computing by centralizing storage, memory, processing and bandwidth. In cloud computing big data tool utilize the big data and provide the solutions. Cloud computing techniques to estimate costs for service dependency and to monitor costs associated with typical scientific applications. Recently, cloud computing has been considered as an emerging model which aims at allowing customers to utilize computational resources and software hosted by service providers. Cloud computing promises to eliminate obstacles due to the management of IT resources and to reduce the cost on infrastructure investments. Cloud Computing refers to both the applications delivered as services over the Internet and the

hardware and systems software in the datacenters that provide those services. The services themselves have long been referred to as Software as a Service (SasS), so we use that term. Providers apply online ordering and payment via browser-based applications for selling Utility Computing and Application Service Providing . Hence, a very important aspect in Cloud Computing is E-commerce applied to the above-mentioned services. Other works introduce the service types infrastructure, platform and software for cloud-based services. Cloud-based infrastructure provides access to virtualized hardware located on the Internet.

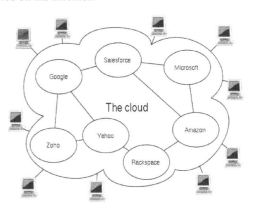

Figure 1. Cloud Computing and its Service Provider

It can be the ability to rent a virtual server, load software on it, turn it on and off at will, or clone it ten times to meet a sudden workload demand. It can be storing and securing immense amounts of data that is accessible only by authorized applications and users. the nature of cloud computing and how it builds on established trends while transforming the way that enterprises everywhere build and deploy applications.

2. Cloud Characteristics

This are some features, commonly associated with clouds. A customer can be an individual lab, a consortium participant, or a consortium.

- Resource outsourcing: Instead of a consumer providing their own hardware, the cloud vendor assumes responsibility for hardware acquisition and maintenance.
- Utility computing: The consumer requests additional resources as needed, and similarly releases these resources when they are not needed. Different clouds offer different sorts of resources, e.g., processing, storage, management software, or application services [6].
- Large numbers of machines: Clouds are typically constructed using large numbers of inexpensive machines. As a result, the cloud vendor can more easily add capacity and can more rapidly replace machines that fail, compared with having machines in multiple laboratories. Generally speaking these machines are as homogeneous as possible both in terms of configuration and location.
- Automated resource management: This feature encompasses a variety of configuration tasks typically handled by a system administrator. For example, many clouds offer the option of automated backup and archival. The cloud may move data or computation to improve responsiveness. Some clouds monitor their offerings for malicious activity.
- Virtualization: Hardware resources in clouds are usually virtual; they are shared by multiple users to improve efficiency. That is, several lightly-utilized logical resources can be supported by the same physical resource.
- Parallel computing: Map/Reduce and Hadoop are frameworks for expressing and executing easily-parallelizable computations, which may use hundreds or thousands of processors in a cloud.

Figure 2. Essential characteristics of Cloud Computing

3. Layers of Cloud Computing

To understand the cloud computing three layers are described:

3.1. Software As A Service (SaaS) As Application Layer

SaaS provider dispose the applied software unified on their server, the user can subscribe applied software service from the manufacturer through Internet .The Provider supply software pattern through Browser, and charge according to the quantity of software and using time. The advantage of this kind of service pattern is that the provider maintains and manages software, supplies the hardware facilities, the users can use software everywhere when they own the terminal which can log in Internet. Under this pattern, the users can use the corresponding hardware, the software and the maintenance service via the Internet, by paying some rents rather than liking traditional pattern which made users to spend much funds on them. This is the most benefit business pattern of the network application. For small business, SaaS is the best way to use advanced technology. At present, Salesforce.com is famous company for providing these services, so as Google Doc and Google Apps.

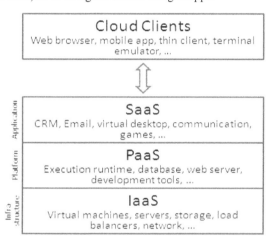

Figure 3. Architecture layers of Cloud Computing

3.2. Platform As A Service (PaaS) As Platform Layer

PaaS takes develop environment as a service to supply. This layer provides a platform for creating applications. PaaS solutions are essentially development platforms for which the development tool itself is hosted in the Cloud and accessed through a browser. With PaaS, developers can build Web applications without installing any tools on their computers and then deploy those applications without any specialized systems administration skills. .It is a kind of distribution platform server, the manufacturers supply service to the users, such as develop environment, server platform and hardware resources, and the users customize and develop their own application and transfer to other customers. Google App Engine is the representative product through their server and Internet.

3.3. Infrastructure As A Service (Iaas) As Infrastructure Services Layer

In this layer of IaaS, servers, network devices, and storage disks are made available to organizations as services on a need-to basis. IaaS takes infrastructure which is made of many servers as a measurement service to the customers. It integrates memory and I/O devices, storage and computing ability into a virtual resources pool, and provides storage resources and virtualization service for the whole industry. This is a way of hosted hardware, and the customer pays when they use the hardware. For example, Amazon Web Service and IBM Blue Cloud all rent the infrastructure as a service. The advantage of IaaS is that the user only need low cost hardware and rent computing ability and storage ability according to his need, greatly reduced cost of the hardware. Currently, Microsoft has been offering IaaS services, either through its own infrastructure or that of its partners.

4. Technologies Used in Cloud Computing

Cloud computing systems use many technologies of which the programming model, data management, data storage, virtualization are the key technologies:

4.1. Virtualization

Virtualization is a method of deploying computing resources. It separates the different levels of the application system including hardware, software, data, networking, storage and so on, breaks the division among the data center, servers, storage, networking, data and the physical devices, realize dynamic architecture, and achieves the goals of managing centralized and use dynamically the physical resources and virtual resources, improving the flexibility of the system, reducing the cost, improving the service and reducing the risk of management. In computing, virtualization means to create a virtual version of a device or resource, such as a server, storage device, network or even an operating system where the framework divides the resource into one or more execution environments. Even something as simple as partitioning a hard drive is considered virtualization because you take one drive and partition it to create two separate hard drives. Devices, applications and human users are able to interact with the virtual resource as if it were a real single logical resource.

4.2. Distributed Storage

In order to ensure high credibility and economy, cloud computing adopts distributed storage to save data, using redundancy storage to ensure the reliability of stored data and using high credible software to make up the readability of the hardware, therefore providing the cheap and credible mass distributed storage and computing system. The data storage system of cloud computing are Google File System (GFS) and Hadoop Distributed File System (HDFS) which is developed Hadoop team. GFS is a distensible distributed file system. It is used in large and distributed applications which need to access mass data. HDFS is a distributed file system which is applicable to running on commodity hardware. It is very similar to the existing distributed file system, but also with a significant difference.

4.3. Parallel Programming Model

To enable users efficiently to use cloud computing resources and more easily enjoy services that cloud computing adopts Map Reduce programming model,

which decomposes the task into multiple subtasks, and through two steps (Map and Reduce) to realize scheduling and allocation in the large-scale node. Map Reduce is a parallel programming system developed by Google. It puts parallelism and fault tolerance, data distribution, and load balance in a database. Map Reduce system mainly consists of three modules: client, master and worker. The client is responsible for submitting parallel processing assignments composed by the users to master node. Map Reduce is mainly used in mass data processing. One of the features of the task scheduling strategy is scheduling priority the task the node which the data belong.

4.4. Data Management

Cloud computing needs to process and analyze mass and distributed data, therefore, data management technology must be able to efficiently manage large data sets. Data items are ordered according to the sequence of keyword in the dictionary, with each row dynamically delivered to Tablets. To ensure the high scalability of data structure, adopts three-level hierarchical way to store location information.

5. Service offered of Cloud Computing

Various services offered cloud computing in differentfieldslikei.e.ITEducationSectore.Storage,Govt.Organization, Online marketin,E-Commerse etc.Cloud computing can describe services being provided at any of the traditional layers from hardware to applications. Clouds shift the responsibility to install and maintain hardware and basic computational services away from the customer (e.g., a laboratory or consortium) to the cloud vendor.

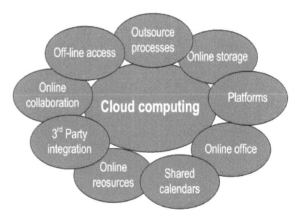

Figure 4. Services of Cloud Computing

To compete with open source products leading vendors like VMware now include higher-level services, such as configuration management, workload orchestration, policy-based allocation, and accounting.

6. Conclusion and Results

This paper introduces the definition of could computing and its main service offered in IT and other fields, summarizes the characteristics, and focused on the key technologies such as the data storage, data management and programming model. The ultimate goal of cloud computing is to provide calculation, services and applications as a public facility for the public, So that people can use the computer resources just like using water, electricity, gas and telephone. Cloud computing is a kind of computing paradigm that can access conveniently a dynamic and configurable public set of computing resources (e.g. server, storage, network, application and related service), provided and published rapidly and on-demand with least management and intervention. And in this paper we also show how cloud computing is better in various aspects like cost, customer and employee. The success of the cloud computing model depends hugely on the ability of cloud providers to keep promises made to users.

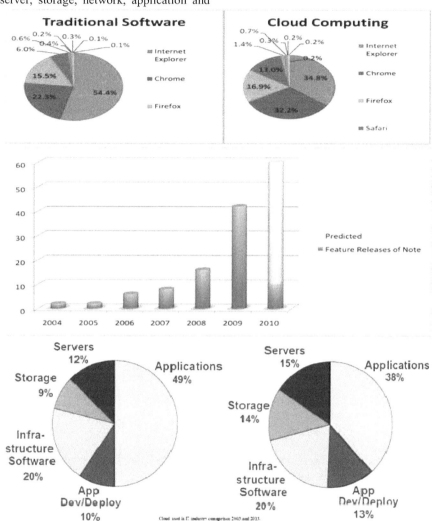

Figure 5. Results

The above result shows the industry results of cloud computing uses over 2009 to 2013 is improvise the revenue by product/service types using IT infrastructures. As a survey of for cloud computing application in 2009 17.5 billion revenue and in 2013 45 billion revenue generated by using cloud IT product/service.

Acknowledgement

Thanks to My family and my friends to encourage of this work. And I also thanks to my wife with always support of working with new technologies.

References

[1] Vaquero L. M., Rodero-Merino L, Caceres J., Lindner M. A break in the clouds: towards a cloud definition. In: ACM SIGCOMM, editor. Computer communication review 2009. New York: ACM Press; 2009. p. 50-5.

[2] Boss G, Malladi P, Quan D, Legregni L, Hall H. Cloud computing, 2009. http://www.ibm.com/developerswork/webspherezones/hipods/libr ary. html.

[3] Peter Mell, Timothy Grance. The NIST Definition of Cloud Computing (Draft). NIST. 2011. http://www.production scale.com/home/2011/8/7/the-nist-definition-of-cloud-Computingdraft.html#axz z1X0xKZRuf.

[4] Cloud Security Alliance. Security guidance for critical areas of focus in cloud computing (v 2.1). Decemeber, 2009.

[5] VMware. Inc. Understanding full virtualization, paravirtualization and hardware assist. Technical report, VMware, 2007.

[6] Amazon. Amazon elastic compute cloud (Amazon EC2). 2009. http://aws.amazon.com/ec2/.

[7] SANJAY GHEMAWAT; HOWARD GOBIOFF; PSHUN-TAK LEUNG. The Google file system. Proceedings of the nineteenth ACM symposium on Operating systems principles. Oct. 2003.

[8] Aymerich, F. M. Fenu, G. Surcis, S. An approach to a Cloud Computing network. Applications of Digital Informationand Web Technologies, 2008.

[9]   Anderson NR, Lee ES, Brockenbrough JS, Minie ME, Fuller S, Brinkley J, et al. Issues in biomedical research data management and analysis: needs and barriers. JAMIA 2007; 14: 478-88.

[10] Foster I, Kesselman C. Globus: a metacomputing infrastructure toolkit. Int J Supercomput Appl 1998; 11: 115-29.

[11] Moore RW, Rajasekar A, Wan M. Data grids, digital libraries, and persistent archives: an integrated approach to sharing, publishing, and archiving data. Proc. IEEE 2005; 93: 578-88.

[12] Iskold A. Reaching for the sky through the compute clouds. Availableat: http://www.readwriteweb.com/archives/searching_for_the_sky_th rough_compute_clouds.php.

[13] Amazon Web Services Simple Monthly Calculator. Available at: http://calculator.s3.amazonaws.com/calc5.html.

[14] D. Owens, Securing elasticity in the cloud, Communications of the ACM 53 (2010) 46-51.

[15] P. Watson, A multi-level security model for partitioning work flows over federated clouds, in: Cloud Computing Technology and Science (CloudCom), 2011 IEEE Third International Conference on, 2011, pp. 180 -188.

[16] Webhosting Unleashed (2008), 'Cloud Computing Services ComparisonGuideavailableat, http://www.webhostingunleashed.com/whitepaper/cloud computing comparison.

[17] Golden, B (2009), 'The Cloud as Innovation Platform: Early Examples'availableat, http://www.nytimes.com/external/idg/2009/06/18/18idg the cloud as innovation platform early- Examples 24294. html.

[18] Armbrust, M; Fox, A; Griffith, R; Joseph, AD; Katz, RH; Konwinski, A; Lee, G; Patterson, DA; Rabkin, A; Stoica, I & Zaharia, M (2009), 'Above the Clouds: A Berkel ey View of CloudComputing'.TechnicalReporNo.,UCB/EECS2009availableat, http://www.eecs.berkeley.edu/Pubs/TechRpts/2009/EECS200928. html.

[19] Challengers (2009), 'Final Research Agenda on Core and Forward Looking Technologies' available at http://challengers org.eu/index.php/Download document/5701.CHALLENGERS Research Agenda and Roadm FinalVersio January 2009.html.

[20] Wikipedia, 'CloudComputing'availableat, http://en.wikipedia.org/wiki/Cloud_computing.

[21] Golden; B. (2009), 'Capex vs. Opex: Most People Miss the Point AboutCloudEconomics'availableat, http://www.cio.com/article/484429/Capex_vs._Opex_Most_Peopl e_Miss_ the_Point_About_Cloud_Economics.

[22] Fellows, W. (2009), 'The State of Play: Grid, Utility, Cloud' availableat http://old.ogfeurope.,eu/uploads/Industry%20Expert%20Group/FE LLOWS_CloudscapeJan09WF.pdf.

[23] DeCandia, G.; Hastorun, D.; Jampani, M.; Kakulapati, G.; Lakshman, A.; Pilchin, A.; Sivasubramanian, S.; Vosshall, P. & Vogels, W. (2007), 'Dynamo: Amazon's Highly Available KeyvalueStore'availableat, http://s3.amazonaws.com/AllThingsDistributed/sosp/amazondyna mososp2007.pdf.

[24] Amrhein, D. & Willenborg, R. (2009), 'Cloud computing for the enterprise, Part 3: Using WebSphere CloudBurst to create private clouds'availableat http://www.ibm.com/,developerworks/websphere/techjournal/090 6_amrhein/0906_amrhein.html.

[25] CISCO, "Cisco Cloud Computing Data Center Strateg y, Architecture,andSolutions", http://www.cisco.com/web/strategy/docs/gov/CiscoCloudComputi ng_WP.pdf.

[26] Cloud Computing Use Cases White Paper, http://groups.google.com/group/cloud computing use cases.

[27] D. Nurmi, R. Wolski, C. Grzegorczyk, G. Obertelli, S. Som an, L. Youseff, and D. Zagorodnov. Eucalyptus: A Technical Re- port on an Elastic Utility Computing Architecture Linking Your Programs to Useful Systems. Technical Report 2008-10, UCSBComputer Science, 2008.

[28] C. Clark, K. Fraser, S. Hand, J. G. Hansen, E. Jul, C. Limpach, I. Pratt, and A. Warfield. Live migration of virtual machinesIn Proc. of NSDI' 05, pages 273-286, Berkeley, CA, USA, 2005. USENIX Association.

[29] yoob, I., Zarifoglu, E., Modh, M., Farooq, M. (2011) "Optimally Sourcing Services in Hybrid Cloud Environments", US Patent Filed 13/373,162.

21

Gender and Age Comparison of Information Communication and Technology Usage among Ghanaian Higher Education Students

Samuel NiiBoi Attuquayefio[1,*], Hillar Addo[2]

[1]Information Technology Department, Methodist University College, Accra Ghana
[2]Information Technology Department, University of Professional Studies Accra, Ghana
*Corresponding author: samuel_attuquayefio@yahoo.com

Abstract The paper attempts to explore gender and age differences in intention to use ICT and ICT usage, by students of higher educational institutions in Ghana. Cross-sectional survey designed was employed for the data collection. The study was carried on 950 Ghanaian higher educational students. We use the t-test statistics to investigate the difference among groups. There was no difference in intention to use ICT between male and female student. However, there were significance differences in the use of ICT among gender, male students actually use the ICT for learning and research more than their female counterpart. There were mixed results in the use of ICT between the young and the old students, however, there was no significant difference in the use of ICT for learning and research. Promoters of ICT usage in higher education must institute measures that could bridge the gap between male and female ICT use behaviour. Self confidence building programs must be organized for the female student so that can comfortably communicate with their peers and lecturers.

Keywords: *intention to use ICT, ICT usagez*

1. Introduction

All over the world, administrators of higher educational institutions have incorporated ICT into teaching and learning so as to enhance and facilitate academic work. Although there are varying ICT application in various institutions across different country, studies in these phenomena show varying results in the extent of ICT usage among different age and gender groups. This paper sought to investigate the extent to which Ghanaian students' intention to use ICT and usage behaviour is different between gender (male and female) and age (old and young).

Khalid Mahmood [6] explored the gender, subject (academic discipline) and degree (graduate vs. undergraduate) differences in access, use and attitudes toward information and communication technology (ICT) of the students of the University of the Punjab. The findings from the study suggest that Male and female students are different in using various ICT based services such as Internet, email and chat. Male students use these services more than female students. With regards to use of search engine and searching databases for academic purposes, the findings of Gurol suggested that male student were more effective than the female students. This findings reinforces the stereotype claim that girls have negative attitudes towards computers and are reluctant to use them Milan Kubiatko and Halakova [8].

However, on the contrary, the results of Neil [10] in the investigation of differences in undergraduates academic use of the internet, found that female students are more likely to use the internet to seek for academic information than the male students. Inoue suggested that students' portray positive attitude in the use of ICT and found no gap in students' perception of ICT usage attitude. Owusu-Ansah [9] investigated or verified whether gender affects the use of Information and Communication Technology (ICT) facilities among academics the findings of the study suggested that there is no gap in the usage of ICT for both male and female.

Although Bennett, Maton, and Kervin [2] suggested that young people have been immersed in technology all their lives, a condition, that filled them with sophisticated technical skills and learning preferences for which traditional education was unprepared. The findings from this research suggest that there is no significant difference in the use of ICT between young and old student. Also, Neil [10], in his quest to investigate the differences in undergraduate' academic use of the internet found no gap between young and old students.

In view of the varying findings from the use of ICT among gender and age groups of students from higher educational institution, hence, the following questions were formulated to address the objective of the study.

- Is there any significance difference in male and female students' intention to use ICT for learning and research?
- Is there any significance difference in male and female students' ICT use for learning and research?
- Is there any significance difference in young and old students' intention to use ICT for learning and research?
- Is there any significance difference in young and old students' ICT use for learning and research?

2. Methodology

To achieve the objective of the study, the research questions were address through quantitative methods where cross-sectional survey designed was used to elicit data from a large number of students through questionnaire. Purposive sampling scheme was employed for this study. The questionnaires were administered at three private universities and three public universities in Ghana. The public universities include University of Ghana (UG), Kwame Nkrumah University of Science and Technology (KNUST) and University of Cape Coast (UCC). The private universities include Methodist University College, Ghana (MUCG), Accra Institute of technology (AIT) and Central University College (CUC). The questionnaires were administered by the researcher and a representative from each institution. The representatives were trained by the researcher on how to administer the questionnaire.

A total of 1500 questionnaires were administered and 972 were received. However, only 955 were useful responses. Seventeen (17) of the responses were not engaging (i.e. respondents ticked the same number for all items). They were not included in the sample size. Table 1 presents details of the survey (quantity of questionnaires administered, received and response rate) from each of the 6 institutions chosen for the survey. The response rates from the institutions portrayed in Table 1 were very satisfactory since a 30% response rate is considered acceptable.

Table 1. Summary of Data Collection

Institution	Questionnaire Administered	Questionnaire Received	Response Rate (%)
UG	500	305	61.0
KNUST	300	170	56.6
UCC	200	104	52.0
CUC	150	82	54.7
MUCG	200	152	76.0
AIT	150	142	94.7
TOTAL	1500	955	63.7

Analyzing survey data is an important and exciting step in the survey process. It is the time that important facts about respondents may be revealed, uncover trends that might not otherwise have known existence, or provide irrefutable facts to support your plans.

Although, this seems like an obvious thing to do, many surveyors think that they can skip this step and dive right in to data analysis. In this study, a quick review of the response of the survey was checked to find out flaws, before committing hours of time in analyzing the data.

During the quick review, every question was examined to see if the results were intelligible. This instinctive check of the data uncovered issues with the survey. A quick review of the data also help understood whether the respondents were appropriate subjects or capture a representative sample of all students. In addition the quick review enabled the researcher to identify and highlight problems associated with the survey instrument and also showed areas were detailed data analysis can be focused.

It is important that before a researcher examines quantitative data to test hypotheses the data is put in a form that is suitable for capturing into a data analysis software. Data coding is systematically reorganizing raw data in a format that is machine readable (i.e. easy to analyse using computer [12]). Responses received from representatives were checked for errors and inconsistencies. The responses were also numbered serially as and when checking was completed. Codes were assigned to each item by combining the sub-title code and the item number. These codes were used as variable names in Statistical Package for Social Sciences (SPSS). Data extracted from responses were entered into SPSS according to the serial numbers assigned to the questionnaire by the researcher to facilitate easy retrieval of questionnaire when errors were detected during editing.

Data captured into SPSS were screened and anywhere errors occurred, the corresponding questionnaire was retrieved to ascertain the veracity of the error before the necessary corrections were executed. This exercise was undertaken to ensure that data entry errors were eliminated. Descriptive statistics such as minimum and maximum from SPSS were used to determine responses on variables which were out of range. The variance on each case was also examined to determine cases which were not engaging (i.e. respondents providing the same response to all variables per a case).

Descriptive and inferential data analysis techniques were utilized. SPSS version 16 was used for all the analysis. The selection of these software packages was based on the flexibilities and vast functionalities it provides in handling the aforementioned analysis. In addition, many scholars have employed these software in their studies successfully [1,3,11]. Hence the researcher considered it more appropriate for this study.

The researcher employed descriptive data analysis to investigate the general awareness and usage of ICT in higher educational institutions. It was also carried out across the available data to unveil any hidden pattern. The results of the descriptive analysis are presented in section 3.0.

The independent-samples t-test, was applied, to compare the mean scores of two different groups of students in relation to intention to use ICT for learning and research and usage behaviour. It provides information on whether there is a statistically significant difference in the mean scores for two groups. In statistical terms, the test investigates the probability that the two sets of scores came from the same population. The characteristics on which the comparisons were carried on include gender (male and female), age (young and old) and the continuous variables in this instance are intention to use ICT and ICT usage behaviour.

Techniques in this section assume that samples are obtained from populations of equal variances [13]. This means that the variability of scores for each of the groups is similar. To test this, SPSS performs the Levene test for equality of variances as part of the t-test and analysis of variances analyses. According to [13], if a significance value of less than .05 is obtained, it suggests that variances for the two groups are not equal, and there is violation of the homogeneity of variance assumption. However, for t-tests, SPSS provides two sets of results, for situations where the assumption is not violated and when it is violated.

Assessing differences between groups from a report generated by SPSS, two values under the column labelled Sig. (2-tailed) are provided for equal variance and unequal variance.

According to [13],

- Choose whichever value is applicable to the Levene's test result.
- If the value in the Sig. (2-tailed) column is equal or less than .05, then there is a significant difference in the mean scores on the dependent variable for each of the two groups.
- If the value is above .05, we conclude that there is no significant difference between the two groups.

3. Presentation of Results

Table 2 shows the results of the age distribution of the students sampled. Majority of Large number of students were below 25 years. They constitute 53.8 % of the

students sampled. 31.5% and 10.7 % of the students sampled were between the ages 25 to 34 and 35 to 45 respectively. Only 4% of the students sampled were 46 years and above. In order to use the sample t-test, ages of the respondents were reclassified as young and old. Students whose ages were below 35 years were classified as young and those who were 35 years and above were classified as old students. 85.3% of the respondents were classified as young and 14.7% were classified as old (See Table 3).

Table 2. Age Distribution of Students

		Frequency	Percent	Valid Percent	Cumulative Percent
Valid	Below 24 years	514	53.8	53.8	53.8
	25-34 years	301	31.5	31.5	85.3
	35-45 years	102	10.7	10.7	96.0
	46 years	38	4.0	4.0	100.0
	Total	955	100.0	100.0	

Table 3. Reclassification of Ages of students

		Frequency	Percent	Valid Percent	Cumulative Percent
Valid	Young(Below 35 years)	815	85.3	85.3	85.3
	Old(35 years and above)	140	14.7	14.7	100.0
	Total	955	100.0	100.0	

The distribution of gender presented on Table 4 demonstrates that males comprised 52.7% per cent of the sample size while females comprised of 47.3% per cent.

Table 4. Gender Distribution of Students

		Frequency	Percent	Valid Percent	Cumulative Percent
Valid	Male	503	52.7	52.7	52.7
	Female	452	47.3	47.3	100.0
	Total	955	100.0	100.0	

A cross tabulation of age and gender portray that respondents below 24 years were made up of male (51.4%) and female (48.6). Between ages 25 to 34 years the percentages of males and females were 56.8% and 43.2% respectively. In the next age classification, 35 to 45 years, there were 102 respondents and 47.1% were males and 52.9% were females. Students who were 46 years and

over at the time of data collection were 38 in number, comprised of 20 males (52.6%) and 18 females (47.4%). Clearly apart from the ages between 35 and 45 where females' percentage was high, in the other groups, females' percentages were very low compared to the males. (see Table 5 for details)

Table 5. AGE * GENDER Cross tabulation

			GENDER		Total
			Male	Female	
AGE	Below 24 years	Count	264	250	514
		% within AGE	51.4%	48.6%	100.0%
		% within GENDER	52.5%	55.3%	53.8%
		% of Total	27.6%	26.2%	53.8%
	25-34 years	Count	171	130	301
		% within AGE	56.8%	43.2%	100.0%
		% within GENDER	34.0%	28.8%	31.5%
		% of Total	17.9%	13.6%	31.5%
	35-45 years	Count	48	54	102
		% within AGE	47.1%	52.9%	100.0%
		% within GENDER	9.5%	11.9%	10.7%
		% of Total	5.0%	5.7%	10.7%
	46 years	Count	20	18	38
		% within AGE	52.6%	47.4%	100.0%
		% within GENDER	4.0%	4.0%	4.0%
		% of Total	2.1%	1.9%	4.0%
Total		Count	503	452	955
		% within AGE	52.7%	47.3%	100.0%
		% within GENDER	100.0%	100.0%	100.0%
		% of Total	52.7%	47.3%	100.0%

It is also evident in the in Table 6 that the percentage of older female students was greater than males students, however, for younger students the percentage respondents was higher for males than females.

Table 6. Age grouped as young and old * Gender Cross tabulation

			GENDER		Total
			Male	Female	
Age	Young	Count	435	380	815
		% within Age	53.4%	46.6%	100.0%
		% within GENDER	86.5%	84.1%	85.3%
		% of Total	45.5%	39.8%	85.3%
	Old	Count	68	72	140
		% within Age	48.6%	51.4%	100.0%
		% within GENDER	13.5%	15.9%	14.7%
		% of Total	7.1%	7.5%	14.7%
Total		Count	503	452	955
		% within young	52.7%	47.3%	100.0%
		% within GENDER	100.0%	100.0%	100.0%
		% of Total	52.7%	47.3%	100.0%

Having examined the responses from the students, the researcher compared the responses of groups in relation to students' intention to use ICT for learning and research and usage behaviour. Characteristics that were grouped include gender (male and female) and Age (young and old).

Comparing male (503) and female (452) responses toward intention to use ICT and ICT usage, equal variance was assumed for all items for both continuous variables except for situations where students use ICT to search for research data. The Levene's Test for Equality of Variances significant value was .05, hence equal variance not assumed figures where used as suggested by Pallant [13].

Table 7 presents details of independent-sample T-test from SPSS for gender on the two continuous variables. There was no significant difference in the scores for male (M=4.89, SD =1.93) and female (M=4.65, SD=1.98); t(953) =0.146, p=.884 on intention to use ICT more when learning in class. The results also showed that there was no significant difference in the scores for male (M=4.10, SD =2.10) and female (M=3.74, SD=2.05); t(953)=1.147, p=.252 on intention to use ICT for forum discussion. Furthermore, the results showed that there was no significant difference in the scores for male (M=5.21, SD=1.90) and female (M=4.94, SD=2.03); t=(953)=1.174, p=.241 on intention to use ICT for more learning materials. The results again showed that there was no significant difference in the scores for male (M=5.32, SD=1.78) and female (M=5.12, SD=1.87); t(953)=.962, p=.336 on intention to use ICT to enhance knowledge. In comparing male and female intentions to use ICT to contact lecturers,

the results showed that there was no significant difference in the scores of male (M=4.60, SD=2.10) and female (M=4.13, SD=2.14) t(953)=1.691. p=.091.

On the other hand, there were some significant differences in the mean scores of male and female response in ICT usage. The results clearly shows that there was significant difference in the scores for male (M=5.44, SD=1.63) and female (M=5.32 SD=1.63); t(953)=2.162, p=.009 on students usage of ICT to communicate with their lecturers. There was also significant difference in the mean scores for male (M=5.95, SD=1.33) and female (M=5.84, SD=1.51); t(953)=2.146, p=.032 on the use of ICT to search for information for research. The results further show that there was also significant difference in the mean scores for male (M=5.39, SD=1.80) and female (M=5.19, SD=1.87); t(953)=3.426, p=.001 on the use of ICT to contact peers and forum discussions. However, there were also no significant difference in the mean scores for male (M=6.16, SD=1.31) and females (M=6.08, SD=1.47); t(953)=1.70, p=.001 and male(M=5.21, SD=1.85) and female (M=5.19, SD=1.88); t(953)=1.88, p=.06 on the use of ICT to enhance their knowledge and for their studies respectively.

The mean scores for males on the items which were significant exceeded that of female respondents. Thus the findings suggest that male respondents use the ICTs provided by their institution, to communicate with their lecturers, search for information for research, contact peers and have forum discussions more than the female subjects.

Table 7. Independent Samples Test for two Age Groups

Items	Levene's Test for Equality of Variances		t-test for Equality of Means				
	F	Sig.	T	df	Sig. (2-tailed)	Mean Difference	Std. Error Difference
E11: I intend to use ICT more when learning in class	0.08	0.781	0.146	953	0.884	0.018	0.121
E12: In tend to use the ICT more for forum discussion	0.21	0.647	1.147	953	0.252	0.121	0.106
E13: In tend to use the ICT more for learning materials	3.84	0.05	1.174	904.236	0.241	0.109	0.093
E14: I intend to use the ICT more for enhancing my knowledge	0.58	0.445	0.962	953	0.336	0.086	0.09
E15: I intend to use the ICT more for lecturer contact and receiving advice	0.47	0.492	1.691	953	0.091	0.201	0.119
F11: I use the ICTs provided by my institution for my studies	1.59	0.208	1.88	953	0.06	0.239	0.127
F12: I use the ICT provided by my institution to communicate with my lecturers	0.02	0.901	2.612	953	0.009	0.351	0.134
F13: I use the ICT provided by my institution to search for information for my research	3.09	0.079	2.146	953	0.032	0.273	0.127
F14: I use the ICT provided by my institution to enhance my knowledge	0.37	0.346	1.699	953	0.09	0.201	0.118
F15: I use the ICT provided by my institution to contact peers and forum discussions	0.59	0.444	3.426	953	0.001	0.47	0.137

Subjects were divided into two age groups, namely old (35 years and over) (815) and young, (below 35 years). There were 140 and 815 old and young respondents respectively. Groups' responses toward the continuous variables, intention to use ICT and ICT usage were compared using independent samples T-test from SPSS. The results were presented Appendix C, Table 5.21. The results show that there were no significant difference in the use of ICTs by the two age groups for learning and research. However, there was significant difference in the mean scores for young (M= 5.14, SD =1.93) and old (M=4.76, SD=2.12); t(953)=2.08, p=.038 on intention to use the ICT for learning materials. Another significant difference occurred in the mean scores for young (M=5.28, SD=1.80) and old (M=4.94, SD=1.95); t(953)=2.04, p=.041 on groups intention to use ICT for enhancing their knowledge.

The finding suggested that younger students' intention to use ICT provided by their institutions for learning materials and enhance knowledge, exceeds that of the older students

Table 8. Independent Samples Test for two Age Groups

| | Levene's Test for Equality of Variances | | t-test for Equality of Means | | | | | | |
	F	Sig.	t	df	Sig. (2-tailed)	Mean Difference	Std. Error Difference	95% Confidence Interval of the Difference	
								Lower	Upper
I intend to use ICT more when learning in class	3.77	0.05	1.652	953	0.099	0.296	0.179	-0.06	0.648
In tend to use the ICT more for forum discussion	2.94	0.09	-1.12	953	0.262	-0.214	0.19	-0.59	0.16
In tend to use the ICT more for learning materials	4.33	0.07	2.08	953	0.038	0.374	0.18	0.021	0.726
I intend to use the ICT more for enhancing my knowledge	0.91	0.34	2.043	953	0.041	0.34	0.166	0.013	0.667
I intend to use the ICT more for lecturer contact and receiving advice	0.04	0.85	-0.06	953	0.949	-0.012	0.195	-0.4	0.37
I use the ICTs provided by my institution for my studies	0.3	0.59	1.588	953	0.113	0.27	0.17	-0.06	0.603
I use the ICT provided by my institution to communicate with my lecturers	0	0.97	0.193	953	0.847	0.029	0.149	-0.26	0.322
I use the ICT provided by my institution to search for information for my research	3.88	0.05	1.779	953	0.075	0.231	0.13	-0.02	0.486
I use the ICT provided by my institution to enhance my knowledge	0.35	0.56	1.303	953	0.193	0.165	0.127	-0.08	0.414
I use the ICT provided by my institution to contact peers and forum discussions	0.79	0.37	-1.04	953	0.3	-0.174	0.168	-0.5	0.156

4. Discussion

The results clearly suggest that gender gap exist in ICT usage among students of higher educational institution. Male students, on the average use the ICTs provided more often to communicate with their lecturers, search information for research, and contact peers for forum discussions more than the female students. The findings also suggest that male students are more confident to interact with others through the ICT provided than the females. On the other hand one could also say that the female student feel shy to interact or fear of being able to do it. Since there are no significant differences in their intention to do it. It also reinforces the stereotype claim that girls have negative attitudes towards computers and are reluctant to use them Milan and Halakova [8]. This result corroborates Gurol whose findings suggested that male student with regard to use of search engines and searching databases for academic purposes were more effective than the female students. A study by Khalid [6] in Pakistan supports the results. The results also agree with Venkatesh and Moris [14] who suggested that male students are more assertive, impatient and goal oriented. Female students may like to use the traditional library system for research information.

However, other past studies assert that there is significant difference in the use of ICT by male and female students. For example the results of Neil [10] in the investigation of differences in undergraduates academic use of the internet, found that female students are more likely to use the internet to seek for academic information than the male students. Owusu-Ansah [9] suggested that there is no gap in the usage of ICT for both male and female. On the contrary, a study by Inoue [5] suggested that students' portray positive attitude in the use of ICT and found no gap in students' perception of ICT usage attitude.

Although Bennett, Maton, and Kervin [2] suggested that young people have been immersed in technology all their lives, a condition, that filled them with sophisticated technical skills and learning preferences for which traditional education was unprepared. The findings from this research suggest that there is no significant difference in the use of ICT between young and old student. This finding agree with the results of Neil [10], in his quest to investigate the differences in undergraduate' academic use of the internet which actually contradicts the results by [7]. However, some significant differences were established in the intention to use ICT for learning materials and use of ICT to enhance their knowledge. The findings from the research suggest that younger students' intention to use ICT provided for learning materials and enhance knowledge exceeds that of the older students. This may be attributed to the fact that the older students have already made their intention but the younger students are now getting more information hence they want to dig deep for information. It could be that older students are skillful and active in the use of the ICTs hence majority did not intend to use it for their learning materials and knowledge.

The results confirm earlier study Glenda Gay, Sonia Mahon, Dwayne Devonish, Philmore Alleyne and Peter G. Alleyne [4] were there was no significance difference among the different age groups in the use of ICT

5. Conclusion

To help address this objective, the questionnaire was structured to cater for the different demographic groups in section A of the measuring instrument. Having examined the responses from the students, the researcher compared the responses of groups in relation to students' intention to use ICT for their studies and research and usage behaviour. Characteristics grouped include gender (male and female) and Age (young and old).

The analysis was conducted by using the independent-samples t-test in SPSS 16. Levene's test for equality of variance was applied to tests whether the variance (variation) of scores for the two groups compared is the same. The outcome of this test determines which of the t-values SPSS provide is correct for use. The choice is dependent on the Sig level of levene's test. If the Sig. value is above .05 then equal variances assumed, however if the significance level of Levene's test is at most .05 then variance of the two groups are not the same. Thus the data violate the assumption of equal variance. Depending upon the levene's test the appropriate Sig (2-tailed) was chosen. There exist significant difference in the mean scores on the dependent variable for the two groups when Sig. (2-tailed) is at most .05. However, if the value is greater than .05 then there exists no significant difference.

The findings from the analysis suggested that both gender and age groups showed significant difference in students' intention to use ICT for learning and research and use behaviour. The mean scores for males on the items which were significant exceeded that of female respondents. Thus, the findings suggested that male respondents use the ICTs provided by their institutions to communicate with their lecturers, search for information for research, contact peers and have forum discussions more than the female subjects. This can be attributed to female students' confidence level. They tend to have worries or nervousness or uncertainty about the responses when collaborating with their peers and lecturers. They also underestimate their skills in ICT usage. Another reason could be the attitude portray by peers and lecturers. Positive attitudes may encourage female students to use the ICTs for collaboration. The research finding also suggested that younger students' intention to use ICT provided by their institutions for learning materials and

enhance knowledge, exceeds that of the older students. The younger generation had ICT training at the senior high school, and most of them have enough time to explore, thus formulating intention to use ICTs for learning and research more than the older generation.

Promoters of ICT usage in higher education must institute measures that could bridge the gap between male and female ICT use behaviour. Self confidence building programs must be organized for the female students so that they can comfortably communicate with their peers and lecturers.

References

[1] Al-Zahrani, S., "An information management system model for the industrial incidents in Saudi Arabia: a conceptual framework based on SDLC methodology". *Journal of computer science* 2(5): 447-454, 2006.

[2] Bennett, S. J., Maton, K. A. & Kervin, L. K.., "The 'digital natives' debate: a critical review of the evidence", *British Journal of Educational Technology*, 39 (5), 775-786, 2008.

[3] Busari, A. O. "Identifying Difference in Perceptions of Academic Stress and Reaction to Stressors Based on Gender among First Year University Students" , *International Journal of Humanities and Social Science* Vol. 2 No. 14, 2012.

[4] Glenda G, Sonia M, Dwayne D, Philmore A. and Peter G. A., "Perceptions of information and communication technology among undergraduate management students in Barbados", *International Journal of Education and Development Using ICT*, Vol 2, No 4 ,2006

[5] Inoue, Y., University students' perceptions of computer technology experiences. *Paper presented at the AERA Annual Meeting*, April 9-13, 2007, Chicago

[6] Khalid Mahmood," Gender, subject and degree differences in university students' access, use and attitudes toward information and communication technology (ICT)", *International Journal of Education and Development using Information and Communication Technology(IJEDICT)*, , Vol. 5, Issue 3, pp. 206-216, 2009.

[7] Kripanont N. "Examining a Technology Acceptance Model of Internet Usage by Academics within Thai Business Schools", Tesis Ph.D, Victoria University Melbourne, Australia.2007.

[8] Kubiatko,M,, Halakova, Z., "Slovak high school students' attitudes to ICT using in biology lesson". *Computers in Human Behaviour*, 25(3), 743-748, 2009.

[9] Owusu-Ansah, S, "Application Of Information And Communication Technology (Ict): A Comparative Analysis Of Male And Female Academics In Africa", *Library Philosophy and Practice (journal).Paper* 108 ; http://digitalcommons.unl.edu/libphilprac/1087, 2013.

[10] Neil S. (2008), "An investigation of differences in undergraduates' academic use of the internet". In: *Active Learning in Higher Education*, 1, pp. 11-22, 9, 2008.

[11] Simin Z., Exploring the Gender Effect on EFL Learners' Learning Strategies, *Theory and Practice in Language Studies*, Vol. 2, No. 8, pp. 1614-1620, 2012

[12] Neuman, W. L, Social Research Methods: Qualitative and Quantitative Approaches, (4th ed). Boston: Allyn & Bacon, 2000

[13] Pallant, J., *SPSS survival manual: a step by step guide to data analysis using SPSS for windows* (Version 12). 2nd ed. Maidenhead: Open University Press, 2005.

[14] Venkatesh, V., & Morris, M. G. "Why don't men ever stop to ask for directions? Gender, social influence, and their role in technology acceptance and usage behavior", *MIS Quarterly*, 24 (1), 115-139, 2000.

22

Acceptance Process: The Missing Link between UTAUT and Diffusion of Innovation Theory

Achilles Kiwanuka[*]

International Medical and Technological University, Dar es Salaam, Tanzania
*Corresponding author: chllskiwanuka@yahoo.com

Abstract The Unified Theory of Acceptance and Use of Technology (UTAUT) has been widely used in research involving adoption and acceptance of technologies. The theory considers factors that influence behavioural intention and use behaviour of technology. The authors of UTAUT combined eight competing theories of technology acceptance including the Diffusion of Innovation theory. Despite the involvement of the characteristics that affect technology adoption from the Diffusion of Innovation theory, the authors of UTAUT did not include the process that technology progresses through to be adopted. This paper argues conceptually that technology adoption processes should be included in UTAUT to better predict technology acceptance and that future information systems research should endeavour to include the environment and process in which technologies are used.

Keywords: *UTAUT, Diffusion of Innovation, Innovation Decision Process, acceptance process*

1. Introduction

Information systems research concerning adoption and acceptance dates back many years ago. Some scholars have made a difference between adoption and acceptance whereas others have used the terms interchangeably. Reference [1] defined adoption as the use of a technology for the first time whereas acceptance as the continuous use of technology. Reference [2] viewed adoption as awareness, embracing and utilizing technology fully and acceptance as an attitude towards technology that is affected by many factors. The definitions given by the authors show that there is no universally accepted definition and usage of the terms despite the fact that they are continuously used in information technology research. For the purpose of this paper, we have taken on the definitions of [1] because they give a better picture of the progress towards full adoption of technologies. Reference [1] went ahead to suggest the process through which technology acceptance progresses to include three phases: attitude, adoption and acceptance.

Analysis has considered two main theories which are Unified Theory of Acceptance and Use of Technology (UTAUT) developed by [3] and Diffusion of Innovation Theory developed by [4]. The Innovation Decision Process of the Diffusion of Innovation theory considers five communication channels through which technologies have to go through in order to be adopted. The channels are knowledge, persuasion, decision, implementation and confirmation [4]. UTAUT considers performance expectancy, effort expectancy, social influence and facilitating conditions as the main constructs that affect usage intention and use behaviour [3]. Although [3] argued that they incorporated

Diffusion of Innovation theory in UTAUT, they did not consider the innovation decision process, that is, the stages through which an innovation progresses to be adopted. The communication channels or stages through which an innovation progresses are also termed as Innovation Decision Process [4].

2. Technology Adoption and Acceptance Theories

Theories and models are important in directing the research process [5] and scholars have reviewed the different theories of adoption and acceptance over the years. Many researchers have used Technology Acceptance Model (TAM) to explain adoption and acceptance of information technology and information systems. However, it is debatable whether it can be used to investigate all cases of information technology or information systems adoption and implementation [6]. Although TAM was one of the initial theories that were widely used in information systems research, it has some limitations. For instance, TAM does not consider social influence among the factors that influence technology acceptance [7]. Other scholars who have discussed the limitations of TAM include [8,9,10].

Reference [11] argued that it is essential to use at least two theories to attain a better understanding of multifaceted novel information technology adoption due to the limitations that one theory or model may have. Currently, there exists no universally accepted theory to explain information technology and information systems adoption. This situation leaves researchers in a "state of methodological vacuum and theoretical confusion" [9]. Thus, scholars have developed their own theories or extended the existing ones to cater for their research problems. This analysis has focussed on Diffusion of Innovation theory, UTAUT and the acceptance phases as put forward by [1]. Diffusion of Innovation theory has been chosen because [12] argued that the perceived characteristics of innovation diffusion account for between 47 and 87 percent of the differences in adoption of innovations. Likewise, UTAUT has been considered because it is argued by [3] that it predicts more than 70 percent of the likelihood to adopt technology.

2.1. Diffusion of Innovation Theory

Diffusion of Innovation theory has been used to study user adoption of innovation in many sectors including agriculture, sociology, information systems, and manufacturing, among others. According to [4], diffusion is "the process by which an innovation is communicated through certain channels over time among the members of a social system"; while an innovation is "an idea, practice, or object that is perceived as new by an individual or another unit of adoption" [[4], p.11]. Diffusion of Innovation theory considers five constructs that influence technology adoption. The constructs include complexity, observability, compatibility, triability and relative advantage [4]. The theory (as depicted in Figure 1) shows the process of innovation diffusion which includes five stages: knowledge, persuasion, decision, implementation and confirmation. The theory categorises the adopters of a technology into innovators, early adopters, early majority, late majority and laggards forming a bell shaped curve [12]. The theory further puts forward that prior conditions that may affect innovation adoption include innovativeness, norms of social systems, previous practice and felt needs.

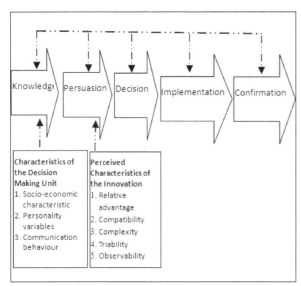

Figure 1. Innovation Decision Process (Adapted from [4])

Some researchers have revealed limitations of Diffusion of Innovation theory. References [13] and [14] noted that Diffusion of Innovation theory does not show the link between attitude and acceptance or rejection of an innovation. Furthermore, the connection between the innovation decision process and the characteristics of innovation is not clear. The theory only indicates that the technology passes through linear stages yet [15] observed that complex technologies do not disseminate in linear

stages. In addition, [16] argued that the constructs of Diffusion of Innovation are not likely to be strong predictors in situations where adoption of technologies is compulsory like in complex organisation settings.

2.2. Unified Theory of Acceptance and Use of Technology

UTAUT (as shown in Figure 2) was developed after considering eight competing theories and models of technology acceptance [3]. The competing theories that UTAUT put into consideration include the Theory of Reasoned Action (TRA), Technology Acceptance Model (TAM), Technology Acceptance Model 2 (TAM2), Diffusion of Innovation theory, Theory of Planned Behaviour (TPB), Model of PC Utilisation (MPCU), Social Cognitive Theory (SCT), and Combined Technology Acceptance Model and Theory of Planned Behaviour [3].

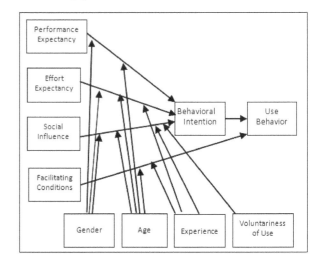

Figure 2. UTAUT Model (Adapted from [3])

According to [3], the four key components that affect technology acceptance are performance expectancy, effort expectancy, social influence, and facilitating conditions. Then, the moderating factors that lead to behaviour intention or use behaviour include age, voluntariness of use, experience and gender. Reference [3] defined performance expectancy as "a degree to which an individual believes that using the system will help him or her to attain gains in job performance". Further, they defined effort expectancy as "the degree of ease associated with the use of the system". Social influence was defined as "the degree to which an individual perceives that important others believe he or she should use the new system". Lastly, they defined facilitating conditions as "the degree to which an individual believes that organisational and technical infrastructure exist to support use of the system" [ibid].

Although using UTAUT is seen as best practice in measuring user acceptance [17], some limitations of the theory have been cited. UTAUT lacks the aspect of trust as one of the constructs in the theory [18,19]. Besides, it limits the mediating factors of technology acceptance to only four factors: age, gender, experience and voluntariness of use. UTAUT omits an important aspect of attitude of individuals towards the technology [2,20], yet adoption is strongly influenced by anticipated benefits [21]. In a meta-analytic review of findings from UTAUT studies, [17] found that there is only a strong correlation between performance expectancy and behaviour intention; although other relationships were significant, they were slightly weak.

The original authors of UTAUT expressed their results mathematically so as to validate them empirically. However, over the years, researchers have adopted the theory qualitatively to gain an in-depth understanding of the factors that affect user acceptance of technology. For instance, [22] utilised UTAUT qualitatively to assess factors and barriers that hinder the adoption of robotic-assisted surgery. In a study conducted by [2], the authors used a qualitative approach to UTAUT in the design of a modified model for the acceptance and adoption of mobile technology for the elderly. Reference [23] used a qualitative approach to UTAUT while investigating acceptance of e-health by health professionals in Africa and thus devised a revised model of it. UTAUT was also applied qualitatively by [19] to examine the merits of using motes in monitoring health.

3. Comparison between Diffusion of Innovation Theory and UTAUT

The authors of UTAUT created the model in order to lessen the burden of future researchers in combining constructs from different models [24]. UTAUT integrated

the perceived characteristics of innovation as follows: perceived advantage in performance expectancy, triability in performance expectancy, observability in performance expectancy, complexity in effort expectancy, and compatibility in social influence from the Diffusion of Innovation theory [3].

Whereas the constructs that affect acceptance of technology are important, the process through which they pass is equally vital for the success of information systems projects [25]. While [3] asserted to have used Diffusion of Innovation theory in UTAUT, the researchers did not consider Innovation Diffusion Process which involves the communication stages through which technology progresses through to be adopted. Figure 3 shows a diagrammatic representation of how communication stages of Diffusion of Innovation were not included when the authors of UTAUT combined eight competing theories of technology acceptance. Hence the necessity of combining Innovation Decision Process with UTAUT so as to come up with a better understanding of the acceptance process and constructs that affect the process of any innovation.

UTAUT is more applicable to users than organisations. Thus, it is more suitable to understanding studies that are mostly affected by human factors. Diffusion of Innovation theory is more suitable for organisational context and has been applied in a range of fields including agriculture, sociology and information systems [12]. Reference [12] mentioned that adoption in an organisation context is more complicated than at an individual level.

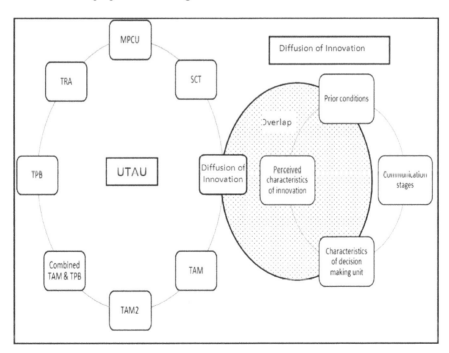

Figure 3. Overlap between UTAUT and Diffusion of Innovation Theory

Much as UTAUT is seen as the gold standard in understanding acceptance of information technology [17], it does not consider the phases that lead to adoption of technology that were considered by Diffusion of Innovation theory. In addition, cultural aspects that are crucial for successful adoption of technology are not considered in the UTAUT constructs that affect technology acceptance. Reference [26] added that

UTAUT fails to measure traits of individuals like innovativeness.

Researchers combine UTAUT with external theories and variables [24] in order to address weaknesses of the model. Reference [27] used UTAUT and the acceptance process by [1] to present a framework for the acceptance process of District Health Information System for vertical health programmes. Reference [28] used Diffusion of

Innovation and UTAUT in combination to test whether ICT (cellular phone) acceptability between countries was different. Reference [29] adopted both UTAUT and the five stages of Diffusion of Innovation theory in a qualitative nature to study user adoption of an online learning environment. Since technology adoption occurs in a complex environment and is affected by a multitude of factors, there is a need to study factors that affect the different stages through which technology adoption occurs.

4. Acceptance Process of Innovations

Reference [1] describes acceptance to include three phases i.e. attitude, adoption and acceptance. In the attitude phase, a consumer or user of a technology assess the technology and forms a mental picture of what he expects use and level of the technology. This stage is important before the adoption of any technology. Kollmann's phases are depicted in Figure 4. The process has nine elements which are fused into three phases. The assessment (attitude) phase involves raising awareness and interest and then forming expectations of the technology. Action (adoption) phase involves trying the technology, purchasing or adopting it and implementation. Use (acceptance) phase involves making a decision of whether to use the technology, using it and lastly terminating the use of it. In addition, the acceptance process of Kollmann shows that one might move from the attitude to the acceptance phase, skipping the adoption phase. However, in order to improve the chances of technology acceptance, the adoption phase is important and has to be monitored.

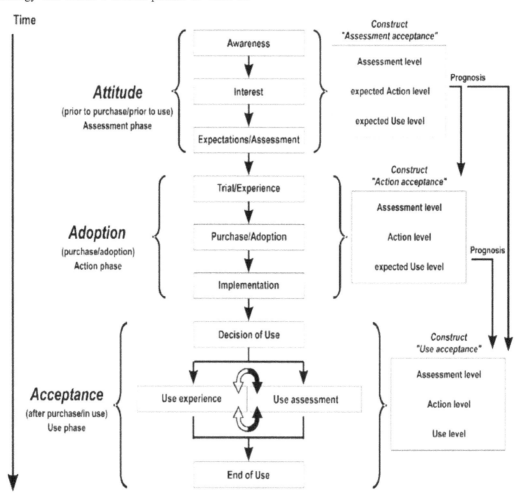

Figure 4. Scheme of Phases in the Acceptance Process [[1], p.140]

Much as some scholars have combined UTAUT with the Innovation Decision Process, the researcher proposes combining UTAUT with the acceptance process of [1]. Thus is because the latter combination addresses the weaknesses of Diffusion of Innovation theory cited by [13] and 14 that Diffusion of Innovation does not show a link between attitude and acceptance or rejection. Another reason why the acceptance phases are favoured over the Innovation Decision Process is that [4] showed innovation adoption to pass through linear stages yet in real life the situation does not occur that way. If someone feels compelled to return to a previous stage, they can do so to rectify any issues that might have occurred.

Combining constructs that affect technology acceptance with the stages through which technology acceptance progresses is important because it explains the environment in which technology adoption occurs. Additionally, the environment affects technology adoption more than the technical factors [30]. When combining UTAUT and the acceptance phases, the constructs of UTAUT can be assessed in the attitude phase to form a baseline, managed within the adoption phase and then evaluated within the acceptance phase to see whether expectations of stakeholders have been met [27].

5. Conclusion

Many scholars have derived models and theories from UTAUT and Diffusion of Innovation theory. Nevertheless, emphasis is mostly put on constructs and characteristics that affect technology acceptance. Researchers need to consider the phases through which technology acceptance progresses and put emphasis on important constructs in the different phases. Much as the terms diffusion, adoption, and acceptance have been used globally for information systems research, their definitions are yet to become clear. There is a need to show a clear-cut difference of their definitions to guide novel technology and innovation researchers. This paper shows the need to include the process of technology adoption and not just constructs of factors that affect technology adoption. Since many of the current theories lack the process aspect. Future research on information systems should endeavour to include the environment and process in which technologies are used.

References

[1] Kollmann, T. (2004). Attitude, adoption or acceptance? – measuring the market success of telecommunication and multimedia technology. *International Journal of Business Performance Management.* 6(2): 133-152.

[2] Biljon, J.V., and Renaud, K. (2008). Predicting technology acceptance and adoption by the elderly: a qualitative study. *SAICSIT 2008*, 6 - 8 October 2008, Wilderness Beach Hotel, Wilderness, South Africa.

[3] Venkatesh, V., Morris, M.G., Davis, G.B., and Davis, F.D. (2003). User acceptance of information technology: Toward a unified view. *MIS Quarterly.* 27(3): pp 425-478.

[4] Rogers, E.M. (1995). *Diffusion of Innovations.* 4th Edition. The Free Press. New York.

[5] Neuman, W.L. (2006). *Social research methods: qualitative and quantitative approaches (6th ed).* Pearson Education, Inc. Boston.

[6] Lee, Y.H., Hsieh, Y.C., and Hsu, C.N. (2011). Adding Innovation Diffusion Theory to the Technology Acceptance Model: Supporting Employees' Intentions to use E-Learning Systems. *Educational Technology & Society.* 14(4): 124 137.

[7] Davis, F.D., Bagozzi, R.P., Warshaw, P.R. (1989).User acceptance of computer technology: A comparison of two theoretical models. *Management Science.* 35(8): 982-1003.

[8] Bagozzi, R.P. (2007). The legacy of the technology acceptance model and a proposal for a paradigm shift. *Journal of the Association for Information Systems.* 8(4): 244-254.

[9] Benbasat, I. and Barki, H. (2007) Quo vadis TAM? *Journal of the Association for Information Systems.* 8(4): 211-218.

[10] Chuttur M.Y (2009). Overview of the Technology Acceptance Model: Origins, Developments and Future Directions, Indiana University, USA. *Sprouts: Working Papers on Information Systems.* 9(37).

[11] Oliveira, T. and Martins, M.F. (2011). Literature Review of Information Technology Adoption Models at Firm Level. *The Electronic Journal of Information Systems Evaluation.* 14(1): 110-121.

[12] Rogers, E.M. (2003). *Diffusion of Innovations.* 5th Edition. The Free Press. New York.

[13] Karahanna, E., Straub, D.W. and Chervany, N.L. (1999). Information technology adoption across time: a cross-sectional comparison of pre-adoption and post-adoption beliefs. *MIS Quarterly.* 23(2): 183-213.

[14] Chen, L., Gillenson, M., and Sherrrell, D. (2002). Enticing online consumers: An extended technology acceptance perspective. *Information and Management.* 39(8): 705-719.

[15] Lyytinen, K. and Damsgaard, J. (2001). What's wrong with the diffusion of innovation theory: The case of a complex and networked technology? *In Proceedings of the International Federation for Information Processing (IFIP).* Banff, Alberta, Canada.

[16] Prescott, M.B. and Conger, S.A. (1995). Information technology innovations: a classification by IT locus of impact and research approach. *Database for Advances in Information Systems.* 26(2-3): 20-41.

[17] Taiwo, A.A. and Downe A.G. (2013). The theory of user acceptance and use of technology (UTAUT): a meta-analytic review of empirical findings. *Journal of Theoretical and Applied Information Technology.* 49(1): 48-58.

[18] Alzahrani; M.E. and Goodwin, R.D. (2012). Towards a UTAUT-based Model for the study of E-Government Citizen Acceptance in Saudi Arabia. *World Academy of Science, Engineering and Technology.* 64: 8-14.

[19] Lubrin, E., Lawrence, E., Zmijewska, A., Navarro, K.F. and Culjak, G. (2006). Exploring the Benefits of Using Motes to Monitor Health: An Acceptance Survey. *Proceedings of the International Conference on Networking, International Conference on Systems and International Conference on Mobile Communications and Learning Technologies.* The Computer Society.

[20] Abukhzam, M. and Lee, A. (2010). Workforce Attitude on Technology Adoption and Diffusion. *The Built & Human Environment Review.* 3: 60-71.

[21] Kumar, V., Maheshwari, B., and Kumar, U. (2002). Enterprise resource planning systems adoption process: A survey of Canadian organizations. *International Journal of Production Research.* 40(3): 509-523.

[22] BenMessaoud, C., Kharrazi, H. and MacDorman K.F. (2011). Facilitators and Barriers to Adopting Robotic-Assisted Surgery: Contextualizing the Unified Theory of Acceptance and Use of Technology. *PLoS One.* 6(1).

[23] Ami-Narh, J.T. and Williams, P.A.H. (2012). A revised UTAUT model to investigate E-health acceptance of health professionals in Africa. *Journal of Emerging Trends in Computing and Information Sciences.* 3(10): 1383-1391.

[24] Williams, M.D., Rana, N.P., Dwivedi, Y. K. and Lal, B. (2011). Is UTAUT really used or just cited for the sake of it? A systematic review of citations of UTAUT's originating article. *19th European Conference on Information Systems*, Helsinki, Finland, 9-11 June 2011.

[25] Liao, C., Palvia, P., and Chen, J. (2009). Information technology adoption behaviour life cycle: Toward a Technology Continuance Theory (TCT). *International Journal of Information Management,* 29(4): 309-320.

[26] Rosen, P.A. (2005). The Effect of Personal Innovativeness on Technology Acceptance and Use. PhD Dissertation. Oklahoma State University.

[27] Kiwanuka, A., Kimaro, H., Senyoni, W., Thobias, J. (2015). A Framework for the Acceptance Process of District Health Information System for Vertical Health Programmes. IST-Africa 2015 Conference Proceedings Paul Cunningham and Miriam Cunningham (Eds). IIMC International Information Management Corporation, 2015.

[28] Yang, K.H., Lee, S.G. (2006). Comparison of the ICT Adoption Pattern: In the Case of Korea and the USA. La Crosse: Department of Management Information Systems, School of Business Administration, University of Wisconsin.

[29] Stigzelius, E. (2011). User adoption of an online learning environment. Aalto University School of Science. Master's thesis.

[30] Benbasat I, Goldstein D and Mead M (1987) "The Case Research Strategy in Studies of Information Systems 'MIS Quarterly.* 11: 369-386.

23

Estimating Plans along with Cost in Multiple Query Processing Environments by Applying Particle Swarm Optimization Technique

Sambit Kumar Mishra[1,*], Srikanta Pattnaik[2], Dulu patnaik[3]

[1]Deaprtment of Computer Sc.&Engg., Ajay Binay Institute of Technology, Cuttack
[2]S.O.A. University, Bhubaneswar
[3]Government College of Engineering, Bhawanipatna
*Corresponding author: sambit_pr@rediffmail.com

Abstract The Main idea of multiple query processing is to optimize a set of queries together and execute the common operations once. Major tasks in multiple query processing are common operation or expression identification and global execution plan construction. Query plans are generally derived from registered continuous queries. They are composed of operators, which perform the actual data processing, queries which buffer data as it moves between operators to hold state of operators. The complex part is to decompose queries and query plans and rearrange the sub queries and query plans on the network. The main functions to achieve an optimal query distribution are usually minimizing network usage and minimizing response time of queries. While dealing with query distribution problem, the challenges like modeling topology of the network, decomposing queries into some sub queries and sub query placement may be occurred. Operators are the basic data processing units in a query plan. An operator takes one or more streams as input and produces a stream as output. As in the traditional database management system, a plan for query connects a set of operators in a tree. The output of a child operator forms an input of its parent operator. In this paper it is aimed to retrieve the cost of query plans as well as cost of particles of swarm in multiple query processing environments by applying particle swarm optimization techniques.

Keywords: *query plan, swarm, NP hard, particle, SMT, personal best, global best*

1. Introduction

Complex queries being in common place usually have a lot of common sub-expressions, either within a single query, or across multiple such queries run as a batch.

Multi query processing aims at exploiting common sub-expressions to reduce evaluation cost. Multi query processing has been viewed as impractical, since earlier algorithms were exhaustive, and explore a doubly exponential search space.

Distributing on operators among a number of hosts is a NP hard problem. Particle swarm optimization and genetic algorithm may be used to compare them to each other. Encoding is a mapping from knowledge domain to the solution space where algorithm can process. Particle swarm optimization is a stochastic optimization technique. The algorithm is initialized with a population of random solutions. Each solution represents a particle. All particles move based on personal best and global best in the search space to find the best solution that ith particle has experienced so far. The algorithm repeats until a threshold is reached or it finds the optimal solution. In fact, after each iteration, the position of each particle updates with the velocity vector. Velocity vector is calculated based on personal best and global best. The basic particle swarm optimization is suitable to solving continuous problems. The particle swarm optimization algorithm first generates initial random particles and then assigns each particle to its personal best. After that it assigns the best personal best to the global best. The particle swarm optimization calculates the fitness value of each particle and then updates personal best and global best.

2. Review of Literature

Y.E. Ioannidis et.al [1] have suggested in their paper that most of the queries on relational databases require access to relations from multiple sites for their processing. The number of possible alternative query plans increases exponentially with increase in the number of relations required for processing the query.

M. Jarke et.al [2] have discussed in their paper that exploring all the query plans in this large search space, an exhaustive search, is not feasible. This problem in large databases is a combinatorial optimization problem and has been addressed by techniques like simulated annealing, iterative improvement, two-phase optimization, etc. The techniques, which reduce the search space, are based on plan transformation and have a cost model to assess the quality of query processing plans.

L. P. Mahalingam et.al [3] have discussed in their paper that the optimization strategy based on algebraic equivalences between similarity based operations that serve as rewrite rules is outlined in. Optimization rules based on similarity based algebraic framework properties and equivalence laws.

Ch. Li, Kevin et.al [4] have introduced a novel multi-criteria query optimization techniques for performing query optimization in databases, such as multimedia and web databases, which rely on imperfect access mechanisms and top-k predicates. They have also introduced cost model and optimization algorithms.

Stefan Riezler et.al [5] have implemented query processing using natural language, e.g. plain English, and for understanding English by the machine, statistical machine translation (SMT). This approach is to bridge the lexical gap between questions and answers. SMT-based query expansion is done by i) using a full-sentence para-phraser to introduce synonyms in context of the entire query, and ii) by translating query terms into answer terms using a full-sentence SMT model trained on question-answer pairs.

Raymond T. Ng et.al [6] have focused on logic programming in deductive databases. They have also extended deductive databases with probabilisties and given fixed point semantics to logic programs annotated with probabilities, but they have used absolute ignorance to combine event probabilities.

Norbert Fuhr et.al [7] have introduced a method for evaluating queries on probabilistic databases is to use complex events. They have also reviewed its limitations. Start by expressing q as a query plan, using the operators $\sigma, \pi, \times$. Then modify each operator to compute the event attribute E in each intermediate result: denote $\sigma i,\_ \pi i, \times i$ the modified operators. It is more convenient to introduce them in the functional representation, by defining the complex event ep(t) for each tuple t, inductively on the query plan p.

Praveen Seshadri et.al [8] have focused on decorrelation techniques. The use of the decorrelation techniques results in the query being transformed to a set of queries, with temporary relations being created. In this manner, the queries generated by decorrelation may have several subexpressions in common, and are therefore excellent candidates for multi-query optimization.

Subbu N. et.al [9] have implemented the correlated evaluation of queries because it may be more efficient on the query, and may not be possible to get an efficient decorrelated query using standard relational operations. In correlated evaluation, the nested query is repeatedly invoked with different values for correlation variables.

A. Pérez-Uribe et.al [10] have focused on optimization problems e.g. swarm intelligence, which is inspired by the social behavior of some insects such as ants and bees. Honey-bees mating optimization (HBMO) is a swarm intelligence optimization algorithm that models the behaviors of bees. Honeybees algorithms were used to model agent-base systems.

K. Bennett et.al [11] have experimented using PSO and genetic algorithm and found that PSO as well as genetic

algorithms could be elegantly useful to optimize database query plans.

We compared honey-bees, DPSO and genetic algorithm with each other and with centralized algorithm for each scenario. The centralized method reveals the effect of distribution.

M.J. Franklin et.al [12] have focused about high fan-in query plans. They have used low fan-in query plans. They have also focused on how the fitness value of each distribution algorithm changes over time and the honey-bees algorithm does not get trapped in local minima.

A. Sokolov et.al. [13] have Used the QPC values of the query plans in their experimental analysis, and found that fitter query plans are selected using the unbiased tournament selection technique. The selected query plans undergo crossover, with probability Pc, and mutation, with probability Pm, to generate the population for the next generation. This continues until the algorithm runs for a pre-specified number of generations GP. The top-query plans are then generated based on the QPC values.

T.V. VijayKumar et.al [14] have proposed an approach that uses Genetic Algorithm to generate 'close' query plans. The approach aims to generate query plans that are optimal with respect to the number of sites involved, and the concentration of relations in these sites, for answering the user query. This in turn would result in efficient query processing.

3. Algorithm

1. Initiate random particles and assign each particle to its personal best. Find the Initial global best.
2. While have enough time, calculate fitness of particles
3. For each particle, update personal best, global best
4. For each particle do these steps, e.g. update its position, return global best particle as solution

This algorithm may be simplified and elaborated as following.

1. Assign the size of swarm, for example in this case it is set to 10.
2. Allocate maximum query e.g. in this case 100.
3. Cognitive parameter, $c1=1$.
4. Social parameter, c2, is set to 4-c1.
5. Number of relations is set to 2.
6. Number of optimization variables, npar is set to 2.
7. Generate random population of continuous values and update the particle position
8. Evaluate random population of continuous variables from allocated queries & relations.
9. Generate random velocities by considering size of swarm and number of optimization variables.
10. Evaluate the cost of particle by considering CPU time, population of continuous values and velocities of the particles.
11. Evaluate the cost of swarm by considering the cost of particles along with CPU time.
12. Update the best local position for each particle.

4. Experimental Analysis

Consider two relations EMP and ASG where attributes to the relation EMP are ENo, EName, Title and attributes to the relation ASG are ENo, PNo, Resp, Dur.

If it is asked to find the names of employees who are managing a project, the query may be written as

SELECT EName
FROM EMP,ASG
WHERE EMP.ENo = ASG.ENo AND Dur > 37

Two possible transformations of the query may be represented in the following expressions.

Expression 1:

ΠEName(σDur>37$\cap$EMP.ENo=ASG.ENo(EMP × ASG))

Expression 2: ΠEName(EMP $\bowtie$ENO (σDur>37(ASG)))

Expression 2 avoids the expensive and large intermediate Cartesian product, and therefore typically is better.

Usually data may be horizontally) fragmented.

For example,

Site1: ASG1 = σENo$\leq$"E3"(ASG)
Site2: ASG2 = σENo>"E3"(ASG)
Site3: EMP1 = σENo$\leq$"E3"(EMP)
Site4: EMP2 = σENo>"E3"(EMP)
Site5: Result

Relations ASG and EMP may also be fragmented in the same way.

Relations ASG and EMP may also be locally clustered on attributes Resp and ENo, respectively.

Now consider the expression ΠEName(EMP $\bowtie$ENO (σDur>37(ASG)))

Tuples are uniformly distributed to the fragments; 20 tuples satisfy Dur>37

size(EMP) = 400, size(ASG) = 1000

tuple access cost = 1 unit; tuple transfer cost = 10 units

ASG and EMP have a local index on Dur and ENo

For example, Produce ASG's: (10+10) * tuple access cost =20

Transfer ASG's to the sites of EMPs: (10+10) * tuple transfer cost =200

Produce EMP's: (10+10) * tuple access cost * 2 =40

Transfer EMP's to result site: (10+10) * tuple transfer cost =200

Total cost= 460

Query processing is done in the following sequence: (1) query decomposition, (2) data localization, (3)global optimization, (4) local optimization.

Table 4.1. Cost of Particle and Swarm(Relation R1, Relation R2)

Sl.No.	Relation (R1)		Relation(R2)	
	Cost of particle	Cost of swarm	Cost of particle	Cost of swarm
1	60.817	121.52	60.164	120.87
2	61.387	122.09	61.414	122.12
3	61.543	122.25	60.288	120.99
4	60.992	121.69	61.291	121.99
5	60.83	121.53	61.77	122.47
6	61.066	121.77	61.66	122.26
7	61.529	122.23	60.304	121.01
8	59.764	120.47	61.139	121.84
9	60.554	121.26	61.835	122.54
10	61.18	121.88	60.86	121.56

Query optimization is a crucial and difficult part of the overall query processing. The objective of query optimization is to minimize the following cost function: I/O cost + CPU cost + communication cost.

Size of the swarm = 10;

No. of relations e.g. dimension of the problem,= 2;

Maximum number of iterations e.g. maximum no. of query = 100;

No. of optimization variables, npar=2;

Cognitive parameter, c_1 = 1;

Social parameter, c_2 = 4-c_1;

Constriction factor, C=1;

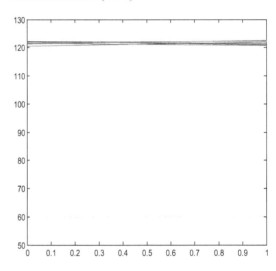

Figure 4.1. (Plan generation VS cost of swarm)

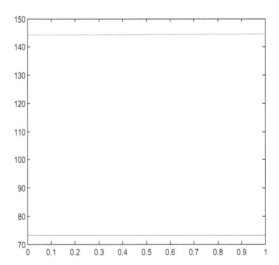

Figure 4.2. (Plan generation VS average cost of particle of swarm)

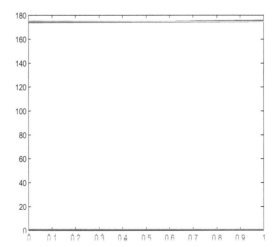

Figure 4.3. (Plan genetaion VS particle velocity)

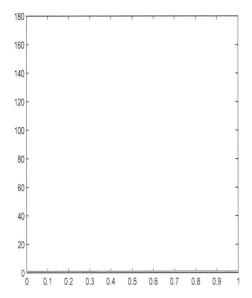

Figure 4.4. (Plan generation VS average cost of particle along with velocity)

5. Discussion & Future Direction

Usually data may be required to process the user query that may be spread over various locations with heterogeneity. So there may be a need to arrive at a query processing plan that entails an optimal cost for query processing. The query plans generated for the particular set of queries generally posed on databases distributed across various locations. The efficiency of query processing depends upon the closeness of the required data. Many query plans may be generated for a given query from multiple relations at various locations. So there may be a number of combinations of relations at various locations for query processing. As a result it may generate a quite large number of query plans. Among these query plans, optimal query plans may be identified having the required relations. It may be a complex problem if the number of relations accessed by the query is quite huge in number and each of the relations may have multiple copies across various locations. In the experimental evaluation it is seen that that the query plans generated are directly proportional to particles in the swarm as well as cost of swarm.

6. Conclusion

In this paper the query plans are generated to improve the response time of user queries. It is usually achieved by formulating the distributed query processing plan generation as a single-objective algorithm problem. It was also aimed to generate query plans with the desired data, for answering the user queries residing close to each other. It is found that the query plans generated are directly proportional to particles in the swarm as well as cost of swarm.

References

[1] Y.E. Ioannidis and Y.C. Kang, "Randomized algorithms for optimizing large join queries, ACM 1990.

[2] M. Jarke and J. Koch, "Query optimization in database systems," ACM Computing Surveys, volume 16, no. 2, pp. 111-152, June 1984.

[3] L. P. Mahalingam and K. S. Candan, Multi-Criteria Query Optimization in the Presence of Result Size and Quality Tradeoffs, Multimedia Tools and Applications Journal 23(3) (2004), 167-183.

[4] Ch. Li, Kevin Ch.-Ch. Chang, I. F. Ilyas, and S. Song, RankSQL: query algebra and optimization for relational top-k queries. In: F. Ozcan, editor, SIGMOD Conference. ACM, 2005, 131-142.

[5] Stefan Riezler, Statistical Machine Translation for Query Expansion in Answer Retrieval, Proceedings of the 45th Annual Meeting of the Association of Computational Linguistics, pages 464-471, Prague, Czech Republic, June 2007.

[6] Raymond T. Ng and V. S. Subrahmanian. Probabilistic logic programming. Information and Computation, 101(2):150-201, 1992.

[7] Norbert Fuhr and Thomas Rolleke. A probabilistic relational algebra for the integration of information retrieval and database systems. ACM Trans. Inf. Syst., 15(1):32-66, 1997.

[8] Praveen Seshadri, Hamid Pirahesh, and T. Y. Cliff Leung. Complex query decorrelation. In Intl. Conf. on Data Engineering, 1996.

[9] Subbu N. Subramanian and Shivakumar Venkataraman. Cost based optimization of decision support queries using transient views. In SIGMOD Intl. Conf. on Management of Data, Seattle, WA, 1998.

[10] A. Pérez-Uribe and B. Hirsbrunner,—Learning and foraging in robot-bees‖, in Meyer, Berthoz, Floreano, Roitblat andWilson (eds.)', SAB2000 Proceedings Supplement Book, Intermit. Soc. For Adaptive Behavior, Honolulu, Hawaii, pp. 185-194.

[11] K. Bennett, M.C. Ferris, and Y.E. Ioannidis, —A genetic algorithm for database query optimization‖, In Proc. of the 4th International Conference on Genetic Algorithms, 400-407, 1991.

[12] M.J. Franklin, S.R. Jeffery, S. Krishnamurthy, F. Reiss, S. Rizvi, et al., —Design considerations for high fan-in systems: the HiFi approach‖, In Proc. Of the CIDR Conf., Jan. 2005.

[13] A. Sokolov and D. Whitley, "Unbiased Tournament Selection," in proceedings of the 2005 conference on Genetic and Evolutionary Computation, pp. 1131-1138, 2005

[14] T.V. VijayKumar, Vikram Singh and Ajay Kumar Verma, "Generating Distributed Query Processing Plans using Genetic Algorithm", In the proceedings of the International Conference on Data Storage and Data Engineering (DSDE 2010), Bangalore, February 9-10, 2010, pp. 173-177, 2010.

24

Computer System Users are like Fish

Ralph M. DeFrangesco[*]

Drexel University, Philadelphia, PA
*Corresponding author: rd337@drexel.edu

Abstract This paper has looked at the habits of computer users when faced with a slow system and has drawn a direct correlation between how they react and fish population dynamics. A survey has been presented that supports the proposed theory.

Keywords: *systems, performance*

1. Introduction

This paper addresses the reactions of computer users when faced with a slow system. A correlation can be drawn between what a user does and fish population dynamics. In order to accomplish this, it is important to understand the connection between drivers and their impacts on fish populations [1]. This paper will prove useful to system stakeholders on how to improve their user's experience.

Slow systems

For many system users, slow systems are the norm. There are many components that go into making up a system: The server hardware, operating system, applications, the network and all of its components, the desktop, and the users operating system and applications. A slowdown in any one of these components could negatively affect the users response time.

Population dynamics

Population dynamics looks at entire populations and studies short and long-term changes to their composition. These changes could include size, age, make-up, or density. Additionally, population dynamics studies factors that affect the growth, stability, and decline of populations as well as the interactions of these factors.

Usefulness

System owners and readers who perform a system administration function will benefit the most from this paper. This paper attempts to explain how users might react when they log into a busy system.

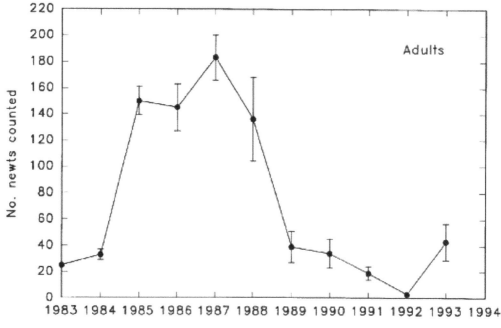

Figure 1.

2. Fish Population Dynamics

A given pond size can only sustain a certain amount of fish. If a pond only has a few fish in it, the fish will sense this and since there is no stress on them, they will begin to reproduce. As long as there continues to be little or no stress on them, they will continue to reproduce. Eventually, they will reproduce until they cannot move around comfortably, run low on food, or the oxygen drops to an unacceptable level. When the fish reach this point, several things can happen. The fish might stop reproducing, older fish may voluntary die off, or more mature fish might start eating younger fish in order to get to a level where there is less stress on them Eventually, the fish population will drop. The fish will detect this drop in population; the resultant drop in stress, start to reproduce again and the cycle will start over. According to [2], populations respond to environmental conditions.

Figure 1 shows the natural population dynamics of adult newts in their natural habitat for the years 1983 to 1994. As can be seen in the figure, the population grows until it hits a maximum number in 1987, then the population declines from 1987 to 1992 only to pick back up again starting in 1992 [3].

3. The Survey

The survey this paper used was conducted at a major university in Philadelphia, PA during the 2012 academic school year. A total of 32 students were surveyed. They ranged in age from 24 to 62 and were either in their junior or senior year. Four of the students were female.

Institutional Review Board approval was not required since this survey in no way impacted the student's grade or adversely affected the students in any psychological manner. This population was chosen as a matter of convenience and not tied to the fact that they were students.

4. The Survey Instrument

Each student was asked to fill out a survey. The survey tried to measure how they reacted in the past when they logged into a slow system. The instrument consisted of eight questions. The first two questions collected demographics asking age and gender. The survey in no way attempted to correlate age or gender to the results. The survey instrument is included in Appendix-A.

5. Survey Results

Questions #2 and #3 were the crux of the survey.
#2 When you were logged into a system, and it was busy, how did you react?
  a. I logged off and didn't try to login again.
  b. I logged off, but tried again later.
  c. I stayed logged in and waited it out.
#3 If you logged off, how long did you wait before trying again?
  a. Right away.
  b. One minute or less.
  c. Five minutes or less.
  d. One hour or less.
  e. More than one hour.
The following shows the responses from the survey:

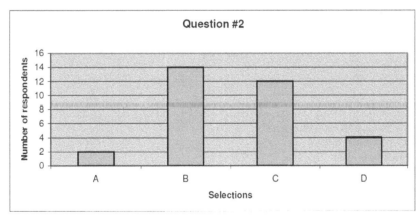

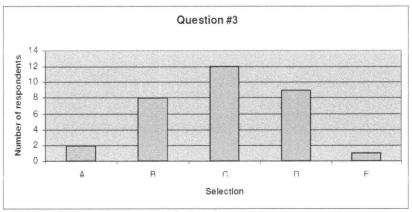

Users are like fish

Population structuring (growth and depopulation) is a behavioral response learned by fish early in their life [2]. Population dynamics are sensitive to changes in the environment [2]. The following is a model that can be used to calculate the population of a system after users start to logout:

Depopulation rate:

$$Dr = 100 \left[\frac{(N_0 - N_1)}{N_0} \right] \times 100$$

Where:

N_0= the initial population size
N_1= the ending population size
Let's use the following as an example:
$N_0 = 500$
$N_1 = 300$
Depopulation rate:

$$Dr = 100 \left[\frac{(500 - 200)}{500} \right] \times 100$$

Dr = 100 – (.4) x 100
Dr = 60%.

6. Application

The easy answer to fix a slow-down problem is to monitor resources and increase bandwidth and server processing capability as needed. However, this approach is rarely available today as budgets are shrinking. Monitoring is always a good practice and fairly inexpensive to do. If after monitoring, it is determined that there is a network congestion problem, traffic shaping is always an option. By applying Quality of Service (QoS)

rules to the network, priority can be given to specific traffic and improve response time. QoS is a cheap way to improve response time. Alternatively, the network can always be subnetted.

If the problem is on the server, then implementing a time-out policy for connections not being used will free-up connections and improve response time. This would stop users from "parking", a practice used by many users where they log into a system early in the morning and maintain the connection throughout the day, using it only when needed. This ties up connections and typically slows down a system.

7. Conclusion

This paper has connected fish population dynamics to how users react when logged into busy computer systems. A survey was conducted that supports this theory. The bottom line is that resources are not unlimited today. However, we if we understand users habits and reactions, it may help make informed decisions and improve the user experience.

References

[1] Eero, M., Lindegren, M. & Koster, F. (2011). The state and relative importance of drivers Of fish population dynamics: An indicator-based approach. *Ecological Indicators 15* (2012) 248-252.

[2] Kerr, L., Cadrin, S., & Secor, D. (2010). The role of spatial dynamics in the stability, Resilience, and productivity of an estuarine fish population. *Ecological Applications, 20*(2), 2010, pp. 497-507.

[3] Griffiths, R.A. (1997). Temporary ponds as amphibian habitats. *Aquatic Conservation: Marine and Freshwater Ecosystems, Vol. 7*, 119-126.

Survey

Age: _____
Gender: Male - Female

1. Have you ever logged into a system and it was extremely busy? (If no stop here. If yes, continue to #2)
2. When the system was busy, how did you react?
   a. I stayed logged in and waited it out.
   b. I logged off and tried again later.
   c. I logged off and didn't try again.
3. If you logged off, how long did you wait before trying again?
   a. Right away.
   b. One minute or less.
   c. Five minutes or less.
   d. One hour or less.
   e. More than one hour.
4. What would have helped your experience?
   a. A message stating it was "working"?
   b. A message telling you to log off and try later?
   c. A message telling you how busy the system is?
   d. No message, I knew what was happening?
5. Have you ever been told not to log into a system because it is busy processing data and you might impact the processing? Yes - No
6. Do you work fulltime? Yes - No

Note: Do not write in any answers. Only circle one answer.

25

Cloud Computing Adoption in the Higher Education (Sudan as a model): A SWOT Analysis

Mohmed Sirelkhtem Adrees[1,*], Majzoob K.Omer[2], Osama E. Sheta[1]

[1]Department of Information System, AL Baha University, AL Baha City, Saudi Arabia
[2]Department of Computer Science, AL Baha University, AL Baha City, Saudi Arabia
*Corresponding author: mkomer@bu.edu.sa

Abstract The use of cloud computing technology in higher education in the least developed countries represents a real opportunity for those countries. This study aims to perform SWOT analysis to determine the impact of the cloud computing implementation such as Strengths, Weaknesses, Opportunities and Threats (SWOT) in higher education institutions of the least developed countries, Republic of Sudan as model, and that from the perspective of Directors, Teachers and Students, to find the effect of strengths, weaknesses, opportunities and threats when using cloud computing technology in higher education. The study revealed positive results, because of the advantages offered by such as the flexibility and efficiency, and the ability to acquiring knowledge. There were drawbacks in the implementation of cloud computing such as privacy and security issues, and give this paper solutions to benefit from the opportunities, and to overcome the threats mentioned.

Keywords: cloud computing, SWOT, strengths, weaknesses, opportunities and threats

1. Introduction

At present, technological development affects all aspects of life. It affects the access to information, processing speed, and communications. Cloud computing is one of the forms of modern development. Which are used in developed countries to deliver innovative technology solutions to the problems faced by the users of the services in various sectors.

The Cloud computing is the development of applications that provide a solution for the development of infrastructure for higher education at a lower cost and fewer time requirements.

The Definition for Cloud computing is that "Cloud computing is a new way of delivering computing resources (network, services, servers, data storing), not a new technology" [1].

The least developed countries (LDCs) are a group of countries that have been classified by the UN as "least developed" in terms of their low gross national income (GNI), their weak human assets and their high degree of economic vulnerability [2].

SWOT is a basic, straightforward model that assesses what an organization can and cannot do as well as its potential opportunities and threats. The method of SWOT analysis is to take the information from an environmental analysis and separate it into internal (strengths and weaknesses) and external issues (opportunities and threats) [3].

SWOT Analysis or IE Matrix is a method of analysis to figure out strengths, weaknesses, opportunities, threats the company (whether they actually exist, or just an idea only), and put into the study and analysis, which relies on a simple idea, a look at the sources of power and opportunities for the company, It is then activated and supported and developed, and look at the weaknesses and threats to the company, and then eliminate or minimize the weaknesses or to get away from sources of threat if it is not possible to avoid them entirely.[10]

2. A Review of Literature

Mohmed S. Adrees, Majzoob K. Omer and Osama E. Sheta [4]. This paper aims to discuss and analyzing: concepts of cloud computing, cloud computing models, cloud computing services, cloud computing Architecture and the main objective of this paper is to how to use and applied cloud computing Architecture in higher education, in third world countries, the republic of Sudan as a model.

Ibe-Ariwa, K. C., & Ariwa, E.[8]. It is obvious that the effective application of cloud computing in developing economy will transform the traditional education model to computer based virtual applications with a focus on e-pedagogy. The knowledge domain and competencies required in the HEIs continues to act as draw backs in terms of skill acquisition and the development of sustainable innovative technological practices

Asiimwe, E. N., & Khan, S. Z [9]. Results show positive perceptions. Respondents revealed that ubiquitous computing and computer-mediated social interaction are important in their education due to advantages such as flexibility, efficiency in terms of cost and time, ability to acquire computer skills. Nevertheless disadvantages where also mentioned for example health effects, privacy and security issues, noise in the learning environment, to mention but a few. This paper gives suggestions on how to overcome threats mentioned.

3. Significance of the Study

Cloud computing is considered more threads interesting at the present time among the technological communities and educational, but its impact on higher education institutions Not scouted especially in Sudan one of the developing countries, this study will explore the impact of cloud computing in higher education institutions, through the use of SWOT analysis .

3.1. Research Objectives

1. To explore the strengths and benefits of using cloud computing in higher education in Sudan
2. To explore weaknesses, and challenges facing the application of cloud computing in higher education in Sudan.
3. To assess the opportunities in the application of cloud computing in higher education in Sudan.
4. To assess the threats that prevent the implementation of cloud computing in higher education in Sudan.

3.2. Proposed Contribution

This research aims to show the way that use cloud computing in higher education in Sudan, identifying the benefits, and the current usage scenarios and suggest the style of the successful implementation of cloud computing in higher education institutions in Sudan.

3.3. Method

This study takes a deductive approach. It has been chosen method of interviews to collect data. The sample was grouped into three categories: (senior management, teachers and students). It included senior management group (36) members. The group included 47 teachers from Sudanese universities. The group included 320 students.

3.4. Survey

The study examined the following areas:
Strengths: What are the top five things that must be preserved and strengthened?
Weaknesses: What are the top five things that must be improved?
Opportunities: What opportunities can benefit from them?
Threats: What are the variables that can negatively affect the use of cloud computing?

Table 1. Highlights Result by categories

Category	Strengths	Weaknesses	Opportunities	Threats
Directors	Instruction quality , The possibility of application, value, Ease of administration, The possibility of execution, Solving technical problems	Digital literacy is required, Privacy, Data security, Training requirement, A new item in the budget	Increase knowledge, User can use latest technology, Distance Learning, The expansion of educational programs	Competition from other higher education institutions, US sanctions on Sudan, Budget cuts, Security concerns
Teachers	Student support services, value, Technology, Instruction quality, teachers support,	Process improvement, Tackling poor infrastructure, Collaboration between students and teachers, High speed internet connection requirement	Increase (students, knowledge, programs, technological literacy), New technology, Adaptive to future requirements	Affordability, Budget shortfalls, The culture of traditional education, There is no planning and strategies, Loss of connectivity, Data security
Students	Student support services, value, Technology, Increase their technical skills	Instruction quality, Lack of interest by students, Technological illiteracy	Technological literacy, Enhance knowledge, Easy access to resources,	Student issues, internet costs, Internet Services, lack of tools, Addiction to technology

4. SWOT Analysis of Cloud Computing with View of Institutions of Higher Education

The SWOT analysis of cloud computing with View of institutions of higher education result divided into four Categories:

4.1. Strengths

The strengths of cloud computing in the Sudanese higher education institutions include: the quality of education, value, solving technical problems, reduce costs, improve control over time and space.

The most important strengths to use cloud computing is reducing the cost in terms of educational institutions suffer in the least developed countries and Sudan as one of these countries, a significant lack of education budgets. Shown in Figure 1.

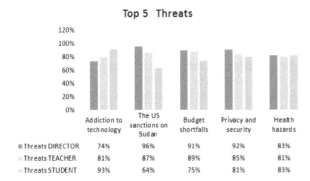

Figure 1. Top Five Strength Evaluation

Easy access to educational resources through cloud computing at any time and in any place leads to increased cooperation between students and teachers, leading to an increase in knowledge and achieve make the most of available resources.

Facing higher education institutions lack adequate resources and expenses. Cloud computing has the ability to provide all of them.

The strengths of cloud computing in the Sudanese higher education institutions include: the quality of education, value, solving technical problems, reduce Cost, improve control over time and space.

The most important strengths to use cloud computing is reducing the cost in terms of educational institutions suffer in the least developed countries and Sudan as one of these countries, a significant lack of education budgets.

Easy access to educational resources through cloud computing at any time and in any place leads to increased cooperation between students and teachers, leading to an increase in knowledge and achieve make the most of available resources.

Facing higher education institutions lack adequate resources and expenses. Cloud computing has the ability to provide all of them.

4.2. Weaknesses

Weaknesses of cloud computing in higher education institutions include: training requirements, technical erase illiteracy, lack of internet access, integration with local programs is difficult, lack of physical control of the data, the lack of commitment to service quality and availability.

While the main weakness of cloud computing in higher education institutions as follows:

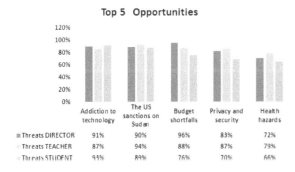

Figure 2. Top Five Weakness Evaluation

Implementation of cloud computing in higher education is not an easy task because they are many factors with the adoption and implementation more dependent on cloud service provider. Many universities and colleges do not have an Internet connection to connect to the cloud, in this case, it is difficult to implement cloud computing. Communication is a prerequisite to the Internet. Shown in Figure 2.

4.3. Opportunities

Opportunities in cloud computing in higher education institutions include: increasing knowledge, increasing the number of beneficiaries of university education, distance education, the expansion of the educational programs, ease of access to resources, data storage capacity, reducing the digital divide.

Two main and important opportunities of using of cloud computing in higher education institutions as follows:

With the use of cloud computing in the Sudanese institutions of higher education, access to opportunities to learn new technology.

In the event of any problems, the cloud provider to provide a quick fix without service interruption. Shown in Figure 3.

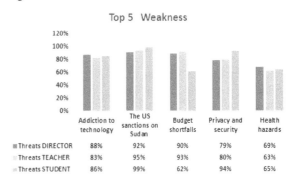

Figure 3. Top Five Opportunities Evaluation

4.4. Threats

Threats of Cloud Computing in Higher Education Institutions include: security concerns, data security, and the loss of contact, addiction to technology, US sanctions on Sudan, and the budget deficit.

The main threats in the adoption of cloud computing in the Sudanese institutions of higher education are security concerns relating to the security of student data because the data value and must be preserved, security is very important in the cloud, the main barrier to adopt cloud computing in education. Shown in Figure 4.

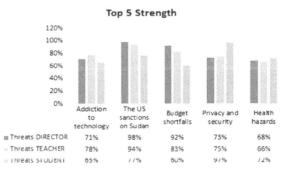

Figure 4. Top Five Threats Evaluation

Table 2. study result for strength and weaknesses

Top 3 Strengths	Top 3 Weaknesses
Better control of the resources	Data transfer bottlenecks
Environmental protection	lack of physical control of data
Cost effective	post training required

Table 3. study result for Opportunities and Threats

Top 3 Opportunities	Top 3 Threats
Adaptive to future needs	Data security
Quick solution of the problem	Hidden Cost
Standardized process	Compatibility reduction

Table 4. SWOT analysis Result

Top 5 Strengths	Top 5 Weaknesses
Accessibility: 24/7	poor infrastructure
Help in getting knowledge quickly	technology/equipment breakdowns
Mobility: Anywhere	Digital Divide
Easily communicate	Data security
Cooperative	Technological illiteracy
Top 5 Opportunities	**Top 5 Threats**
Increase knowledge	Addiction to technology
data storage capacity	US sanctions on Sudan
Reduce the digital divide	Budget shortfalls
Digital literacy	Privacy and security
Advantages of distance education	Health hazards

5. Discussion and Conclusion

To Support for this technology must develop a strategic plan aimed at supporting better use of cloud computing and the creation of uniform rules for the use of, and develop appropriate calibrated for optimal use.

Cloud Computing in higher education can generate multiple features that will enable the Sudanese higher education institutions to compete with each other and compete with global institutions, also contribute to the creation of a knowledge generation contributes to the development of his country.

In order to increase the acceptance of cloud computing, it is necessary to take measures are:

- Clear rules in dealing with the serviceprovider.

- secure data, applicability.
- Contact more reliable Internet.

We suggest, multi solutions to overcome the threats and take advantage of opportunities:

- enforce privacy and security policies.
- impose control and prevention of cheating in exams and assessments methods

Invest in technology cloud computing.

- reduce the digital divide through the use of cloud computing technology.
- erase technical illiteracy.
- encourage research, which aims to provide education accessible to everyone using computers.

References

[1]   ENISA, Cloud computing: benefits, risks and recommendations for information security, 2009.

[2]   http://www.nationsonline.org/oneworld/least_developed_countries.htm.

[3]   http://www.investopedia.com/terms/s/swot.asp.

[4]   Mohmed, s ,Adrees & Majzoob, K, Omer & Osama E. Sheta (2015) Cloud Computing Architecture for Higher Education in the Third World Countries (Republic of The Sudan as Model) (IJDMS) Vol.7, No.3, June 2015

[5]   Ghaffari, K., Delgosha, M. S., & Abdolvand, N. (2014). Towards Cloud Computing: A SWOT Analysis on its Adoption in SMEs. arXiv preprint arXiv:1405.1932.

[6]   Masrom, M., & Rahimli, A. (2015). Cloud Computing Adoption in the Healthcare Sector: A SWOT Analysis. Asian Social Science, 11(10), p12.

[7]   Valkanos, E., Anastasiou, A., & Androutsou, D. (2009). The importance of SWOT Analysis for educational units that belong to the field of Vocational Education and Training: The case of the State Institute (IEK) of Epanomi in Thessaloniki, Greece1.

[8]   Ibe-Ariwa, K. C., & Ariwa, E. Green Technology Sustainability and Deployment of Cloud Computing in Higher Education.

[9]   Asiimwe, E. N., & Khan, S. Z. (2013). Ubiquitous Computing in Education: A SWOT Analysis by Students and Teachers. In 12th World Conference on Mobile and Contextual Learning (mLearn 2013), 18.

[10]   Omer, M. K. A., Adrees, M. S., & Sheta, O. E. Alternative Central Mobile Application Strategy to Deaf and Dumb Education in Third World Countries.

Can Blind People Use Social Media Effectively? A Qualitative Field Study of Facebook Usability

Rakesh Babu*

School of Information Studies, University of Wisconsin-Milwaukee Milwaukee, United States
*Corresponding author: babu@uwm.edu

Abstract Social media allow people to communicate, collaborate and socialize for personal and professional matters. However, their sight-centered design can present access and usability problems for the blind. Existing quantitative approaches to usability testing do not provide in-depth assessment of the problem. This paper presents a qualitative approach to test social media usability, and illustrates its application to evaluate Facebook for the blind. Think-aloud observation of six blind participants generated verbal evidence of their Facebook interaction experiences. Verbal protocol analysis explained the nature of interaction challenges in performing common Facebook functions. Design standards analysis explained design errors in Facebook interface. It helped identify remedial measures to potentially improve Facebook usability. Findings demonstrate the utility of the qualitative approach to feasibly evaluate social media usability for blind users. It shows how blind users think, act and perceive in performing common social media functions non-visually. This has implications for the design of non-visual user interfaces to access social media through 'Internet of Things' and in multi-tasking situations.

Keywords: *Social media, usability, blind user, verbal protocol analysis, Web Content Accessibility Guidelines, Non-Visual Interaction*

1. Introduction

Social networking sites (SNS)such as Facebook and Twitter offer a conducive platform to communicate, collaborate and socialize – personally and professionally [1]. There are 2.3 billion registered users of the ten most popular SNS [2]. SNS is used all over the world, by all types of users for numerous reasons. Government agencies such as the Central Intelligence Agency and the Environmental Protection Agency use SNS as a productivity tool [3]. Merchants such as McDonalds, Whole Foods, Best Buy and Zappos use SNS to sell their merchandise [4]. It is reasonable to expect that SNS will remain a mainstay of the future information society. However, the myriad benefits of social media that the sighted world continues to enjoy are not available to people who are blind. This is primarily because Web 2.0 technologies are sight-centered by design and lack the needed accessibility and usability. Accessibility allows blind users access to all features and functionality of a website [5]. Usability is how well a website fits with a blind user's conceptualization of completing online tasks it supports [5]. Both accessibility and usability are necessary to derive the intended utility of a website. [6] This research is concerned with blind people's ability to derive SNS utility.

The blind are a significant user group comprising 39 million totally blind and 246 million partially blind. [7] They access SNS and other web sites primarily by listening to content read aloud by screen reader (SR) software. They conceptualize Web interactions differently than sighted users. Extant literature recognizes that SR-mediated SNS interaction is inherently problematic. [1,8] These problems may result from poor design choices that necessitate visual interaction with content and controls. [8] However, it is unclear as to how these interaction problems hamper goal accomplishment for blind SNS users. Existing approaches to usability evaluation such as automated testing, heuristics evaluation and user testing fail to provide an in-depth assessment of the problem. [9] Critical questions that remain unanswered include: What is the nature of blind users' SNS interaction challenges?; and What can we do about these challenges?

This paper presents a qualitative approach to SNS evaluation for blind users and demonstrates its application to understanding the nature of their accessibility and usability problems in performing common SNS functions. We conducted an exploratory field study with six blind Facebook users. Think-aloud observations generated rich verbal evidence of their thoughts, perceptions and actions in performing three common SNS functions. Verbal protocol analysis [10,11] and an integrated problem-solving framework [11] generated in-depth, contextually-situated, experiential knowledge of their interaction challenges in searching for people, communicating with others, and planning social events. Design standard analysis [12] identified design errors responsible and potential remedial measures.

What follows is a description of our methods, participants, material and procedure. Subsequently, results and discussion is presented. Finally, we discuss contribution, implications and future work.

2. Materials and Methods

2.1. Methodology

We used concurrent verbal protocol analysis (VPA) to collect and analyze context-rich evidence of blind users' SNS interaction experiences. In this technique, participants work on tasks and concurrently verbalize their thinking. [5] This technique is suitable for in-depth examination of user-system interaction [13] and evaluates systems usability effectively. [14] Think-aloud verbalizations of participants are captured in audio recordings, which are transcribed and decomposed into segments. Each segment is categorized using a coding scheme. [5] Babu, Singh and Ganesh [15] adapted VPA for a closer examination of blind users' actions in completing online tasks. Babu [11] developed a coding scheme to capture the nuances of blind users' interaction challenges. Babu and Singh [12] employed design standards analysis to determine the accessibility and usability character of an interaction challenge. We use a combination of the adapted VPA, the Babu [11] coding scheme, and design standards analysis for an in-depth, contextually-situated, experiential understanding of blind users' SNS interaction challenges.

2.2. Participants and Site

We recruited six participants, mean age 19 years, with one to two years of familiarity with SNS. Three participants were students at the Texas School for the Blind and Visually Impaired (TSBVI) and three at the Michigan Commission for the Blind Training Center (MCB/TC) at the time of the study. These institutions have technology instructors to train students in the use of screen readers, computers and the Web. They facilitated recruitment of participants for our study. Given it was a field study, TSBVI and MCB/TC campuses were the research sites.

2.3. Tasks and Material

We designed three Facebook tasks as the context for investigating participants' SNS interactions. Task choice was guided by the researchers' knowledge and experience in working with blind and sighted SNS users. The tasks were:
1. Searching for people;
2. Communicating with others;and
3. Planning social events.

2.4. Searching for People

A first and basic task every social media user undertakes is searching for friends and choosing a subset from the search results. This task requires a search query on Facebook where users locate the SNS search field; type

appropriate search term(s); and activate the search button. The SNS search field is one of two search fields on the account home page along with the "Web Search" field. Appropriate terms to search for Facebook users include full name and email. The search button immediately precedes the search fields. Successfully executing the search query generates a list of results with links to profile pages of users with matching names, followed by an "Add Friend" button.

2.5. Communicating with Others

Social media is used to communicate with friends and family by exchanging messages. This task on Facebook requires: navigating to a user profile page; navigating to her Timeline; locating the message text box; typing a message; and activating the Post button. Successfully posting a message displays the message text on the Timeline along with other posted messages.

2.6. Planning Social Events

Social media allow subscribers to plan adhoc events. Facebook allows users to accomplish this task by: navigating to the Events page; activating the Create Event; filling in each field in the Create Event form with relevant information; and activating the Create button. Successfully creating an event generates a notification for all invitees regarding the name, location, timing and guest list for the event.

Material included an SNS platform, an observation study protocol, and computers equipped with an SR and Internet connection. The SNS platform comprised multiple Facebook pages supporting the three tasks described above. The observation study protocol included a Word document describing the research objective and think-aloud technique. It included a think-aloud practice exercise for an online task. It also included instruction to complete the three Facebook tasks. This document was available on the home screen of the study computer.

2.7. Procedure

2.7.1. Data Collection

After receiving IRB approval, we emailed a flier seeking research participants for the field study to US institutions serving the blind. TSBVI and MCB/TC agreed to help by facilitating recruitment and providing lab space. Students who agreed to participate completed a questionnaire seeking demographic and background information. They scheduled study sessions during summer 2012 at the site closest to them during after-school hours. Each session commenced with a familiarization of the research, and the think-aloud technique. They reviewed the observation study protocol and practiced thinking aloud while performing the practice task. They logged on to their Facebook accounts, visited each task environment and completed the tasks while thinking aloud. Each participant took roughly two hours to complete the three tasks. We audio recorded each participant's verbal protocols and transcribed verbal protocols including participant verbalizations, participant-investigator conversation and screen reader audio.

2.7.2. Data Analysis

We employed two analytic techniques—verbal protocol analysis and design standard analysis.

We performed verbal protocol analysis on the rich verbal evidence to examine participant thoughts, perceptions and actions in Facebook interactions. We decomposed each transcript into segments representing single units of thought. Three independent coders coded nearly 21,000 segments using categories of an integrated problem-solving framework. [11] Coded segments accounted for roughly 13 hours' worth of data. Coders were free to assign multiple codes to a segment if necessary. We used Cohen's kappa to assess inter-rater reliability, which yielded a reliability measure of 0.8 (N = 16,748). We identified segments representing interaction problems that manifest as dissonance or failure. [11] Problems where the situation was not comprehensible to the participant due to inadequate system feedback were labeled as Dissonance. Problems corresponding to situations where participants' action did not yield expected outcome were labeled as Failure. We analyzed only codes that all three coders agreed upon and identified segments representing interaction problems that hampered participants' ability to perform tasks effectively.

We performed design standard analysis on the VPA results to determine the accessibility and usability character of dissonance or a failure. Design standards include Web Content Accessibility Guidelines success criteria and usability heuristics. [16] This analysis provided a basis to compare our results with the WCAG guidelines – the de facto standards on Web accessibility and usability for users with disabilities. We retraced participants' interaction paths and identified associated design elements and mapped problematic design elements and the accessibility and usability criteria violated. Together, VPA and design standard analysis provides our research the needed user-centered understanding of SNS accessibility and usability problems in social learning tasks.

I am on my facebook page. I want to search for you. I go to the top of the page by pressing Control Home.
<Facebook>

I am going to the edit field by pressing E.
<Editable text, search>

I am going to try searching you by your name. I type in your name.
<John Doe >

Press Tab
<Search Button>

It takes me to Search Button. Press Enter.
<Search. Editable text. Blank. Search>

It says "Search Editable Text Blank". That means it took me back to the Edit Field. I am going to the top of the page by pressing Control Home.
<Facebook search. Start of page>

That indicates that we are on the facebook search results. Now I am going to try pressing n to go to next text. Hopefully it takes me to the results.

<Doe John. Department of information systems. Office. phone. Email. Web directory.....>

I don't think that's the one. So I'm going to press Down Arrow to see another result.

<Heading level 2, Microsoft academic search. Badwa John Doe. CVIIT international Institute of information technology...... Pin 500032. Link academic research, Microsoft. Heading level 2. link microsoft academic search. John Doe Baba. the rank of the paper is calculated by considering the author published conference channel>

Pressing Down Arrow to see if I can find matching names.

<Link academic research. microsoft link see more results by Bing. Bing results like this>
Ok, it's not coming up

<Link all results. link people. link pages. link roots. Link applications. Link Web. Link Web results. Link post by evidence. Link create an add. link 4 to 5 start to build your own>

It suggests some kind of weird ad I guess. Let's approach this differently. What I am going to do is

I am going to click one other link that I see here that would possibly help. I am going to press Up Arrow till I get "Show All Results".

<Link people. link pages. link roots. link applications. link web. link web results. link people. link All Results>

"All Results". I press Enter on it.
[Silence]

I press Control Home to go to the top of the page.
<Facebook Search>

I press N to see if I can find something here.
<All results. Link pages>

Press Down Arrow
<Link roots. Link applications. Link web links. Web results. Post links. Created links. Recover links. Join your friends and million. Link recover.

Your recover magic link. Export this. Add links. Link Face book. Copyright Facebook>

Hmm tricky facebook. I think I may have typed in the name incorrectly. Or, I may have searched in the wrong search box. I am going back to my home.
<Facebook>

The name that I entered did not come up. So I am going to try pressing E.
<Search button search>

But we tried that already, and it didn't work. I am going to press E one more time. Hopefully, that will take me to another edit box where I can enter information into.

<Enter email or name. Editable text>

I think this is where I enter stuff. I don't know.

Figure 1. Verbal evidence of confusion about relevant search field for people search

3. Results

Our analysis showed that basic SNS functions that typical sighted users take for granted proved problematic for participants and were perceived as vexing. Multiple interface elements (content and controls) that make up the task environment for an SNS function created dissonance or hampered goal accomplishment for participants. Since these interface elements failed to meet their objectives for blind users, they were in 'error'. Hence, we refer to such problematic controls and content presentation as 'design errors'. Each design error represents a violation of extant accessibility and usability principles based on the W3C Web Content Accessibility Guidelines. Based on normative design principles, we suggest design improvements to the task to alleviate blind users' interaction challenges, and facilitate their effective participation in online social networking. In the following, we describe and discuss these problems grouped by task.

3.1. Difficulties in Searching for People

Analysis showed that participants faced multiple problems searching for people on Facebook. These problems included confusion about relevant search fields, ambiguity about appropriate search terms, and inability to understand reasons for failure. We present evidence of these problems using verbal reports comprising participant utterances and screen reader announcements (in angular brackets). To help the reader better appreciate the problem,

we indicate participant pauses (reflecting additional information processing and cognitive effort) and screen reader silences (representing lack of system feedback).

We first present evidence of the confusion about the relevant search field. The participant logged on to her Facebook account and intended to search for one of the authors.

Figure 1 shows the participant's confusion about which search field to use to search for a friend on Facebook. It indicates that the home page contained at least two search fields - one for a regular Web search and another for specific SNS search. As the participant browsed down this page from the top left corner, she first came across the Web search field and could not "see" that there was another search field, due to the sequential nature of non-visual interaction. The Web search field lacked a descriptive caption to communicate its purpose. Consequently, the participant assumed that Web search was the relevant search field and was baffled by the failure to obtain relevant search results.

Figure 2 presents evidence of ambiguity about appropriate search terms. The participant located the relevant search field, and typed in the search terms to find the author.

<Enter email or name. Editable text>
This edit box is where I think I can enter the name of the result. It read "Enter name or email". This is a different edit box. I am going to type the name again.
<John Doe> Press Enter
<Doe> [Silence] <Editable text. Button, search> [Beep]

And it took me back to "Editable Text". So I am going to see if this works. Hopefully it will work. I am going to press control home again to go to the top of the page.

<Facebook search. Start of page>
I am going to press N again to see if I am at the right place

<Can't find what you are looking for? Search for people by email. Editable text>
Okay that's not it. So I keep pressing down arrow

<Link all results. link people. link pages. link roots. link applications. Link web links. web results. link post by evidence, created by links. Link like. Link report this ad. Want to rule the world? Link report. Link like. More apps. Facebook copyright >

And once you enter facebook copyright thing it indicates that there is no result. I don't know how there is no results. I have to see why. I will go back because I don't think I entered the information correctly. I am going to press Alt Left Arrow again.
[Silence]

Ok, now it should be already on my home page.
<Facebook. Start of page>
And I am going to my next heading to see what it says by pressing H.

< Home. Heading level one link.>
It says "Home". I am going to press h again.
<application. Zero. Heading level 4 link>
And it says "Application". But don't think I want that. Press H again.

<Friend's online, Heading level 4>
"Friends online". I don't want that either.
<suggestions, Heading level 4>
And "Suggestions". Again.

<welcome to Facebook Heading level 2>
And it says welcome to Facebook. That's an indication that I am already on face book page. So I am going to press Down Arrow from here and see what happens.
<link upload a photo>

And that's not what I want. Keep pressing Down Arrow.

<Heading level 3. Heading level 3. fill the profile with information. Help your friends by profile information. link edit profile. Heading level 3. Heading level 3. Heading level 3. activate your local phone>

I know that I need to search but just don't know how. I keep searching and nothing's coming up. I am going to press Control Home to go to the top of the page.

<Facebook. Start of page>
Now I am going to press E again.

<Search editable text>
And it takes me to the search box. I am going to the other search box by pressing E again.

Figure 2. Verbal evidence of ambiguity about appropriate search terms for people search

The participant could not determine an appropriate term to search. The label indicated that a user could be searched by name or email. She tried searching for the author first using name and then using email. However, the query did not yield any result for either term; she consistently got the message "no results found ..." The participant suspected she may have made a typo and tried to rectify this unknown error. She could not tell what search terms could possibly generate the desired result.

Figure 3 presents evidence of inability to understand the reason for a failed search. The scenario is the participant tried to search the author by name and by email without luck; the search query did not yield any result. She decided to give it one more try.

> *I am back to my home log on page. I do not know why I am not getting it for some reason.*
>
> *<enter name or email editable text.>*
> *I type*
> *<john0208 at gmail dot com>*
>
> *Press Enter.*
> *<No results found for john0208>*
>
> *It says that no results found for you.*
>
> *<Heading, check your spelling or try another turn. Try searching by email. Editable text. button search. editable text. Blank.>*
> *Ok, this is little weird. Hmm. I wonder why.*

Figure 3. Verbal evidence of inability to understand reason for failed people search

The evidence in Figure 3 shows the search query using email did not yield any result. Importantly, the participant did not receive any explanation as to why the query failed - she just heard "Check your spelling or try another term." However, the participant had spelled the name and email correctly and was appropriately baffled by the failure.

Participants faced problems searching for people on Facebook. Problems include confusion about which search field to use, ambiguity about what search term is appropriate and an inability to tell why a search query failed. These problems correspond to three design errors: improper labeling of the Web search, lack of clarity about appropriate search terms, and incomprehensible explanations for a failed search query. According to the Web Content Accessibility Guidelines (WCAG), these design errors represent accessibility and usability problems. Improper labeling of the Web search field is a violation of WCAG Success Criterion (SC) 1.1.1 that requires a descriptive label conveying the utility of the field. Ambiguity about appropriate search term violates SC 3.3.2 and 3.3.5. SC 3.3.2 requires supplementing SNS search field with clear instruction on appropriate search terms and avoiding common mistakes in searching for people. SC 3.3.5 requires provision of "Context-Sensitive Help" that guides users in executing an effective SNS search without getting distracted from the search task. Random explanation for failed search query violates Success Criteria 3.3.1 and 3.3.3. SC 3.3.1 requires displaying a text message following the activation of Search button clearly explaining the reasons for the failed search query (e.g. incorrect search term used). SC 3.3.3 requires this text message to include suggestion on how to fix the faulty SNS search. Random explanation for failed search query also violates Norman's [17] Feedback Principle that requires full and continuous feedback about SNS response to an SNS search attempt.

3.2. Problems in Communicating with Others

Analysis showed that participants faced problems in communicating with others on Facebook. This is due to the problems in locating the Timeline—Facebook's message board. Problems included in ability to identify the Timeline section and difficulty perceiving the Timeline input area. We present evidence of these problems using verbal reports that include participant utterances and screen reader announcements. The participant navigated to her friend's Facebook profile with the intention to say "Hello." She browsed the friend's profile page looking for the Timeline.

> *<Broadcasting location. Heading Level 5. One friend likes this>*
> *I am arrowing to find "Send person a message".*
> *< link heading level 4. link heading level 4. see all. link report. link chat. link like. clickable link. photo clickable. link discussion. clickable link video. End of list. link create an ad. link report>*
> *Still arrowing down. Now I am looking for some kind of a link that tells me "Write on his wall". I am just exploring. Since I have never written on someone's Wall, I am not sure if I'm going to see "write on his wall".*
> *< link home. link chat>*
> *I wonder if I go back by pressing Shift H, will it give some information?*
> *<home. link heading level 1. link alt+ shift + messages>*
> *Ok I am going down now.*
> *< link alt. button search. clickable link account. out of list. link suggest a friend. welcome to new channel>*
> *I was pressing shift H to go back. It said "Home", which I am on. Probably my page with his information. Ok, now I am pressing Down Arrow.*
> *<broadcasting location. heading level 5>*
> *I wonder if I click on his name, will it probably say that? Because I am seeing his messages and everything from his friends. But I couldn't verify that I am on my friend's Wall. The system is not very accessible.*

Figure 4. Verbal evidence of problems locating the Timeline to communicate with others

As Figure 4 reveals, the participant could not locate her friend's "Timeline" after scanning her profile page multiple times. She came across a section of the page with messages from other people. She supposed this possibly to be the friend's Timeline. However, she could not tell this with certainty as there was no descriptive label to identify the message board. Moreover, she could not find the input area to type a message.

Participants faced problems communicating with others on Facebook. Their real problem was locating the Timeline. This problem arises due to the absence of any descriptive label identifying the Timeline section, and the obscurity of the input area to type a Timeline post. WCAG explains that the difficulty communicating with other SNS users represents accessibility and usability problems in Facebook design. The absence of a descriptive label for the Timeline violates Success Criterion 2.4.10. This requires the message board content to be organized under a separate section identifiable through its descriptive title. Obscurity of the Timeline's input area violates WCAG Success Criterion 1.1.1. This requires a descriptive caption for the input field clearly communicating its purpose.

3.3. Problems in Planning Social Event

Analysis showed that participants faced problems planning an event on Facebook. Specifically, they could not schedule the event effectively. This is due to the problem choosing a desired date. We present evidence of this problem using verbal reports that comprises participant utterances, SR announcements (enclosed in angular brackets), and system-generated non-verbal sounds (enclosed in square brackets). The participant navigated to the "Create Event" page on Facebook. She wanted to plan for a get-together with selected friends on Memorial Day.

Ok, I am going to create a Memorial Day event.
<Creat an Event, heading level 2>
It says create an event. I am going to press down arrow.
<Entering table. When. Entering table. Editable text, today. Drop down list, time 9:30pm. Link add end time. Leaving table. what are you planning? Editable text. Blank. Where? Editable text. Blank. Link add street address. More info? Editable text. Blank. Who is invited? Link Select guests. Check box. Anyone can view and RSVP. Check box. Show the guest list. Button create event. Entering table>
Ok, I pretty much have an idea what I have to do. I am going to press Shift H. I have to enter all the information to the search boxes, like when I am going to invite. I am going to enter this information into the edit field where there is a drop down box. I am going to enter "Select". Press Shift H to go back to heading.
<Create an event, heading level>
Press Down Arrow.
<Entering table. When. Entering table. Editable text, today>
And it says "When". We want this to be a "Memorial Day". So, thirty first.
<Entering table. Button. Drop down list. Entering table. 9:30 pm. Editable text, today>
Ok.
<End of Line. Y. End of. Y Y Y Y Y Y. End of line. Leaving table. When. Entering table>
I am going to press Home.
<End of. Y Y Y Y Y>
I am trying to see
<Selected all>
if I can clear the text in this edit box. And, it took me back for some reason. Back to another page, the previous page I have been.
<Your home page displays interesting content>
And that's not good.
<No more headings. Events. Heading level. You have no up. Create an event>
Create an event again.
<Home. [beep]. zero. [beep]. zero. editable text. button create an event, heading level. entering table. When. entering table. editable text, today>
Ok, I am going to try typing in.
<5 43.28. Y. End of line. Entering table. Button. drop down list. time 9:30 pm. editable text, today. Y. Edit time button. Drop. link add a time. drop down list. editable text, today. Leaving table. Blank. Leaving table. heading level 2. create an event. entering table. editable text, today. End of Y Y Y Y Y. End of line. Y. End of line>
I do not know what is going on here. I am trying to enter some text into it.
<editable text>
It is not allowing me to type in anything. it keeps saying "Today".
<End of line. Y>
I am trying to delete that "Today". And it still keeps saying "Today". I am trying to press Delete key, and it did not do anything.
<End of. why>
So, I don't know what to do.
<End of... Leaving table. editable text. today. Entering table, Button. Drop down list. time 9:30 pm. Zero>

Figure 5. Verbal evidence of problem in scheduling event

As the evidence in Figure 5 reveals, the participant could not edit the date field in the "Create an Event" form. The default value for this field was "Today". The participant tried to delete this default value in order to input the desired date. However, she could neither delete "Today" nor insert the desired date - May 31. Her action to delete the default value with the use of Backspace resulted in backward page navigation. By the time she realized, she had navigated multiple pages back. A closer examination of the evidence shows that the Backspace occasionally behaved like the browser's back button. So, the first few Backspace key presses did not do anything. But subsequent key presses triggered backward page navigation. And all this while, the participant had no clue what was going on.

Participants could not plan an event effectively on Facebook. They faced difficulty editing the Date field of the Create Event form to schedule the event. In addition, they dealt with the nuisance of backward page navigation when trying to delete a default field entry. These problems correspond to two design errors— date field not operable through keyboard and backward page navigation triggered by Backspace without explicit user request. WCAG explains these design errors represent accessibility and usability problems in Facebook design. Specifically, the lack of keyboard operability of the date field is a violation of Success Criterion 2.1.3. This requires the field to be editable through key commands. The backward page navigation triggered by Backspace is a violation of Success Criterion 3.2.5. This requires that only an explicit user request should trigger a page change.

4. Discussion

The qualitative evaluation of Facebook usability provided an in-depth, contextually situated and experiential knowledge of participants' interaction challenges in performing basic SNS functions and identified the responsible design elements. Each of the three SNS functions examined was problematic. Participants faced multiple types of problems performing these functions. Problems included challenges that require greater time and effort, and roadblocks that necessitated sighted assistance to continue. These problems were linked to poorly designed controls and content presentation used to design these basic SNS functions on Facebook. In fact, these design errors that created roadblocks and challenges for participants represent violation of multiple accessibility and/or usability criteria as defined by WCAG and other design standards.

Searching for people on Facebook was problematic. Participants could not tell which search field to use, what search terms would be appropriate, and why a search query failed. These problems resulted from design errors such as improper labeling of the Web search field, ambiguity about appropriate search terms, and random explanation of failed search queries. Communicating with other Facebook users was problematic. Participants could not locate the Timeline to post their messages. The problem resulted from design errors such as lack of organization and descriptive section header for the Timeline, and lack of descriptive caption for the input field. Planning an event was also problematic. Participants

could not use the Create Event form effectively. Specifically they were unable to set the schedule of the event. This resulted from two design errors--date field not operable through keyboard and backward page navigation triggered by Backspace without explicit user request.

A secondary yet valuable outcome of our qualitative evaluation was a set of design improvements to potentially improve the accessibility and usability of these three SNS functions of Facebook. For example problems in searching for people can be reduced by providing (1) a descriptive label for the Web search field communicating its purpose unequivocally; (2) instruction accompanying SNS search field describing appropriate search terms and common errors; (3) context-sensitive help that describes the process of effective SNS search; (4) complete, accurate and continuous feedback about SNS response to a search query; and (5) descriptive error message suggesting how to rectify it following a failed search query. Problems in communicating with other Facebook users can be reduced by providing (1) Timeline as a distinct section having a descriptive section header; (2) instruction on how to access the Timeline's input area; and (3) descriptive label for the Timeline's input area. Problems in planning social events on Facebook can potentially reduce by providing: (1) keyboard support for operating the date field; (2) instruction about performing edit functions in date field using key commands; and (3) page navigation only when the user requests. Our ongoing research examines the feasibility of these proposed design improvements through interviews with web developers first and then the development of a prototype system to validate this claim. Examination of multiple instances of failures and development of interventions to remediate them is the focus of our on-going work, based on the research presented here.

5. Conclusions

The central premise of the research reported here is that millions of blind people cannot utilize social media effectively due to significant accessibility and usability barriers. To resolve this issue, we need answers to two critical questions: What is the nature of blind users' SNS interaction challenges? And, what can research do to reduce or eliminate these challenges? To answer these questions, we need to carefully examine blind users' thoughts, perceptions and actions in SNS interaction tasks, and analyze their challenges vis-à-vis extant design standards on Web accessibility and usability. The qualitative approach forwarded in this paper helps bring closure to this research problem.

The approach evaluates SNS accessibility and usability in a more comprehensive manner. Its hallmark is a combination user-centered and task-based approach, [15] with verbal protocol analysis, [5] an integrated problem-solving framework [11] and design standards analysis [12] for an in-depth, contextually-situated and experiential understanding of the problem. The paper demonstrated the feasibility and utility of this technique through an exploratory field study that examines the Facebook interaction experiences of 6 blind users. Three basic SNS functions—searching for people, communicating with others, and planning social events were studied. Results illustrate the nature of users' interaction problems, why these challenges arise and what can be possibly done about these challenges. It shows that blind users cannot effectively search for people, communicate with others or plan events on Facebook. They experienced dissonance and often failed to achieve their goals due to poor design choices. It explained what they go through in dealing with these dissonant conditions or failures. Additionally, it identified potential design modifications to reduce or eliminate these challenges. Such understanding is needed to develop design principles on SNS accessibility and usability for non-visual interaction.

Researchers in Information Systems, Cognitive Science, and Human-Computer Interaction could utilize our qualitative approach to investigate accessibility and usability of other Facebook functions (e.g., inviting friends to a network, joining interest groups, sharing multimedia content), other SNS (e.g., Twitter, MySpace, Orkut), and other social media genre (e.g. weblogs, wikis, social bookmarking sites). They could use this approach to better understand how blind users conceptualize a problem situation, and how they deal with it. Such understanding is necessary to develop (a) blind-minded help mechanisms to guide the blind in effective SNS interactions; and (b) design principles on systems accessibility and usability for non-visual interaction. Nonvisual interaction assumes significance for the use of Internet of Things and in multi-tasking situation where one task demands constant visual attention.

Understanding blind users' SNS interaction experiences represents the first step in creating a user group profile for the blind. User group profiles are an essential component of user-centered design that define the unique characteristics of a specific user type. [18] User profiles of under-studied user groups such as the blind aid in design decision-making for universally usable systems. [19] A blind user profile that explicates the unique accessibility and usability needs of this atypical user population is helpful to design more accessible and usable websites. [20] Our findings provide important clues to the accessibility and usability requirements to make SNS functions blind-friendly. This can form the basis for developing a blind user profile for social media. Developers and designers can use such a blind user profile to significantly enhance SNS utility for the blind.

Our future research will further investigate the problems identified in this study to develop a more robust and in-depth understanding of the nature of blind users' SNS accessibility and usability problems. Specifically, our ongoing and future research will create a more comprehensive understanding of these problems by replicating this study with a larger set of participants with varying skill levels and age ranges. In addition, we will conduct future research using other common SNS functions and other SNS platforms to create a knowledge base of blind users' accessibility and usability needs and challenges. Findings from these ongoing and future studies will allow greater generalizability of our results.

6. List of Abbreviations

MCB/TC: Michigan Commission for the Blind Training Center.

SC: Success Criterion.
SNS: Social Networking Site.
SR: Screen Reader.
TSBVI: Texas School for the Blind and Visually Impaired.
VPA: Verbal Protocol Analysis.
W3C: World Wide Web Consortium.
WCAG: Web Content Accessibility Guidelines.

References

[1] Wentz B., and Lazar J., "Are separate interfaces inherently unequal? An evaluation with blind users of the usability of two interfaces for a social networking platform," in Proceedings of the Conference 2011, ACM, 91-97.

[2] Qualman, E., "Social network user statistics," Socialnomics, August 16, 2011. [Online]. Available: http://www.socialnomics.net/2011/08/16/social-network-users-statistics/. [Accessed September 18, 2013].

[3] Herman, J., "Social networks and government," How To. gov, April 19, 2013. [Online]. Available: http://www.howto.gov/social-media/social-networks. [Accessed July 21, 2013].

[4] Jewell, M., "American Express, Twitter team up on retail deal," Huffington Post, March 6, 2012. [Online]. Available: http://www.huffingtonpost.com/2012/03/07/american-express-twitter_n_1326342.html. [Accessed July 21, 2013].

[5] Babu, R., Developing an understanding of the accessibility and usability problems blind students face in web-enhanced instruction environments. [Doctoral Dissertation]. Pro Quest Dissertations and Theses. (Accession Order No. AAT 3473492), 2011.

[6] Babu, R., "Understanding challenges in non-visual interaction with travel sites: An exploratory field study with blind users," First Monday, 18 (12), December 2013. Available: http://firstmonday.org/ojs/index.php/fm/article/view/4808. [Accessed February 2, 2014].

[7] World Health Organization, "Visual impairment and blindness," WHO. int, October 2013. [Online]. Available: http://www.who.int/mediacentre/factsheets/fs282/en/. [Accessed December 19, 2013].

[8] Buzzi, M.C., Buzzi, M., Leporini, B., and Akhter, F., "Is Facebook really 'open' to all?" in IEEE International Symposium on Technology and Society (ISTAS), NSW, 327-36.

[9] Mankoff, J., Fait, H., and Tran, T., "Is your Web page accessible? A comparative study of methods for assessing Web page accessibility for the blind," in Proceedings from the CHI 2005, ACM, 41-50.

[10] Isenberg, D.J., "Thinking and managing: A verbal protocol analysis of managerial problem solving," Academy of Management Journal, 29 (4), 775-788, August 1986.

[11] Ericsson, K.A., and Simon, H.A., Protocol analysis: Verbal reports as data, MIT Press, Cambridge, MA, 1984.

[12] Babu, R., and Singh, R., "Enhancing learning management systems utility for blind students: A task-oriented, user-centered, multimethod evaluation technique," Journal of Information Technology and Education-Research, 12, 1-32, 2013. [Online]. Available: http://www.jite.org/documents/Vol12/JITEv12ResearchBabu001-032.pdf. [Accessed August 7, 2013].

[13] Todd P., and Benbasat, I., "Process tracing methods in decision support systems: Exploring the black box," Management Information Systems Quarterly, 11 (4), 493-512, December 1987.

[14] Cotton, D., and Gresty, K., "Reflecting on the think-aloud method for evaluating E-learning," British Journal of Educational Technology, 37 (1), 45-54, January 2006.

[15] Babu, R., Singh, R., and Ganesh, J., "Understanding blind users' Web accessibility and usability problems," AIS Transactions on Human Computer Interaction, 2 (3), 73-94, July 2010.

[16] World Wide Web Consortium, "Web Content Accessibility Guidelines (WCAG) 2.0," W3. Org, December 11, 2008. [Online]. Available: http://www.w3.org/TR/WCAG20. [Accessed January 9, 2014].

[17] Norman, D.A., The design of everyday things, Basic Books, New York, 2002.

[18] Nielsen, J. and Landauer, T.K., "A mathematical model of the finding of usability problems," in Proceedings of the INTERACT' 93 and CHI' 93 conference on human factors in computing systems, ACM, 206-213.

[19] Obrenovic, Z., Abascal, J., and Starcevic, D. "Universal accessibility as a multimodal design issue," Communications of the ACM, 50 (5), 83-88, May 2007.

[20] Henry, S.L., Martinson, M.L. and Barnicle, K. "Beyond video: accessibility profiles, personas, and scenarios up close and personal," in Proceedings of UPA, 2003.

Permissions

All chapters in this book were first published in AJIS, by Science and Education Publishing; hereby published with permission under the Creative Commons Attribution License or equivalent. Every chapter published in this book has been scrutinized by our experts. Their significance has been extensively debated. The topics covered herein carry significant findings which will fuel the growth of the discipline. They may even be implemented as practical applications or may be referred to as a beginning point for another development.

The contributors of this book come from diverse backgrounds, making this book a truly international effort. This book will bring forth new frontiers with its revolutionizing research information and detailed analysis of the nascent developments around the world.

We would like to thank all the contributing authors for lending their expertise to make the book truly unique. They have played a crucial role in the development of this book. Without their invaluable contributions this book wouldn't have been possible. They have made vital efforts to compile up to date information on the varied aspects of this subject to make this book a valuable addition to the collection of many professionals and students.

This book was conceptualized with the vision of imparting up-to-date information and advanced data in this field. To ensure the same, a matchless editorial board was set up. Every individual on the board went through rigorous rounds of assessment to prove their worth. After which they invested a large part of their time researching and compiling the most relevant data for our readers.

The editorial board has been involved in producing this book since its inception. They have spent rigorous hours researching and exploring the diverse topics which have resulted in the successful publishing of this book. They have passed on their knowledge of decades through this book. To expedite this challenging task, the publisher supported the team at every step. A small team of assistant editors was also appointed to further simplify the editing procedure and attain best results for the readers.

Apart from the editorial board, the designing team has also invested a significant amount of their time in understanding the subject and creating the most relevant covers. They scrutinized every image to scout for the most suitable representation of the subject and create an appropriate cover for the book.

The publishing team has been an ardent support to the editorial, designing and production team. Their endless efforts to recruit the best for this project, has resulted in the accomplishment of this book. They are a veteran in the field of academics and their pool of knowledge is as vast as their experience in printing. Their expertise and guidance has proved useful at every step. Their uncompromising quality standards have made this book an exceptional effort. Their encouragement from time to time has been an inspiration for everyone.

The publisher and the editorial board hope that this book will prove to be a valuable piece of knowledge for researchers, students, practitioners and scholars across the globe.

List of Contributors

Omisore O. M and Samuel O. W
Department of Computer Science, Federal University of Technology, Akure, Nigeria

Boumedyen Shannaq
Computer science and Information Technology Department, Mazoon College, "University College", Muscat, Sultanate of Oman

Fabeha Waqar Shmas and Ahmad Waqas
Department of Computer Science, Sukkur Institute of Business Administration, Sukkur, Pakistan

Zeeshan Bhatti, Dil Nawaz Hakro and Aamir Ali Jarwar
Institute of Information and communication Technology, University of Sindh, Jamshoro

Nahla Aljojo
Faculty of Computing and Information Technology, Information Systems Department, King AbdulAziz University, Jeddah, KSA

Carl Adams
School of Computing, University of Portsmouth, Portsmouth, UK, Buckingham Building, Lion Terrace, Portsmouth PO1

Abeer Alkhouli
HE 3Faculty of Sciences, Department of Statistics, King AbdulAziz University, Jeddah, KSA

Huda Saifuddin
Arts and Humanities College, Cognitive Psychology Department, King AbdulAziz University, Makkah, KSA

Iqbal Alsaleh
Faculty of Economics and Administration, Information Systems Department, King AbdulAziz University, Jeddah, KSA

Grace Leah AKINYI and Christopher A. MOTURI
School of Computing and Informatics, University of Nairobi, Nairobi, Kenya

Gul Muhammad, Jamaludin Ibrahim, Zeeshan Bhatti and Ahmad Waqas
Kulliyyah of Information and Communication Technology, International Islamic University Malaysia

Alexander Kharchenko
Department of Computer Informational Technologies, National Aviation University, Kyiv, Ukraine

Ihor Bodnarchuk
Department of Computer Science, Ternopil Ivan Pul'uj National Technical University, Ternopil, Ukraine

Vasyl Yatcyshyn
Department of Computer Engineering, Ternopil Ivan Pul'uj National Technical University, Ternopil, Ukraine

Cheporov Valeriy
Economic Faculty, V.I. Vernadsky Crimean Federal University, Simferopol, Republic of Crimea

Omolaye P. O
Department of Electrical and Electronic Engineering, University of Agriculture, Makurdi, Benue State, Nigeria

Pius Daniel
Department of Public Administration, Federal Polytechnic, Nasarawa, Nigeria

Orifa A. O
Department of Business Education, Adeyemi College of Education, Ondo, Nigeria

Vladislav ZAALISHVILI
Laboratory of Engineering Seismology, Center of Geophysical Investigations of VSC RAS and RNO-A, Vladikavkaz, Russia

Alexandr KANUKOV and Dmitry MELKOV
Laboratory of Instrumental Monitoring of Hazardous Natural-Technogenic Processes, Center of Geophysical Investigations of VSC RAS and RNO-A, Vladikavkaz, Russia

Jean Bosco Nk. Ndushabandi and Agnes N. Wausi
School of Computing and Informatics University of Nairobi, Kenya

Shyam Nandan Kumar
M.Tech-Computer Science and Engineering, Lakshmi Narain College of Technology-Indore (RGPV, Bhopal), MP, India

Amit Vajpayee
Department of Computer Science and Engineering, Lakshmi Narain College of Technology-Indore (RGPV, Bhopal), MP, India

Pastor Meshack Akhusama and Christopher Moturi
School of Computing and Informatics University of Nairobi, Kenya

Selamawit Molla Mekonnen and Zegaye Seifu Wubishet
Department of Informatics, University of Oslo, Oslo, Norway

Manish Gubhaju and Ali Al-Sherbaz
The University of Northampton, Northampton, United Kingdom

Martin Aruldoss and V. Prasanna Venkatesan
Department of Banking Technology, Pondicherry University, Puducherry, India

T. Miranda Lakshmi
Department of Computer Science, Research and Development Centre, Bharathiyar University, Coimbatore, India

Jin Huan Zhang, Khin War War Htike, Ammar Oad and Hao Zhang
School of Information Science and Engineering, Central South University, Changsha, Hunan, P.R. China

Li Chao
Math and Computer Science, University of Houston-Victoria, Victoria, United States

Anwar Mohd. Mansuri
Department of Computer Science and Engineering, MIT Mandsaur, Mandsaur, India

Prithviraj Singh Rathore
Department Master of Computer Application, MIT Mandsaur, Mandsaur, India

Samuel NiiBoi Attuquayefio
Information Technology Department, Methodist University College, Accra Ghana

Hillar Addo
Information Technology Department, University of Professional Studies Accra, Ghana

Achilles Kiwanuka
International Medical and Technological University, Dar es Salaam, Tanzania

Sambit Kumar Mishra
Deaprtment of Computer Sc.&Engg., Ajay Binay Institute of Technology, Cuttack

Srikanta Pattnaik
S.O.A. University, Bhubaneswar

Dulu patnaik
Government College of Engineering, Bhawanipatna

Ralph M. DeFrangesco
Drexel University, Philadelphia, PA

Mohmed Sirelkhtem Adrees and Osama E. Sheta
Department of Information System, AL Baha University, AL Baha City, Saudi Arabia

Majzoob K.Omer
Department of Computer Science, AL Baha University, AL Baha City, Saudi Arabia

Rakesh Babu
School of Information Studies, University of Wisconsin-Milwaukee Milwaukee, United States

Index